Law and Philosophy Library

Volume 113

The Law and Philosophy Library, which has been in existence since 1985, aims to publish cutting edge works in the philosophy of law, and has a special history of publishing books that focus on legal reasoning and argumentation, including those that may involve somewhat formal methodologies. The series has published numerous important books on law and logic, law and artificial intelligence, law and language, and law and rhetoric. While continuing to stress these areas, the series has more recently expanded to include books on the intersection between law and the Continental philosophical tradition, consistent with the traditional openness of the series to books in the Continental jurisprudential tradition. The series is proud of the geographic diversity of its authors, and many have come from Latin America, Spain, Italy, the Netherlands, Germany, and Eastern Europe, as well, more obviously for an English-language series, from the United Kingdom, the United States, Australia, and Canada.

More information about this series at http://www.springer.com/series/6210

Thomas Bustamante
Bernardo Gonçalves Fernandes
Editors

Democratizing Constitutional Law

Perspectives on Legal Theory and the Legitimacy of Constitutionalism

Springer

Editors
Thomas Bustamante
Universidade Federal de Minas Gerais
Belo Horizonte, Minas Gerais, Brazil

Bernardo Gonçalves Fernandes
Universidade Federal de Minas Gerais
Belo Horizonte, Minas Gerais, Brazil

ISSN 1572-4395 ISSN 2215-0315 (electronic)
Law and Philosophy Library
ISBN 978-3-319-28369-2 ISBN 978-3-319-28371-5 (eBook)
DOI 10.1007/978-3-319-28371-5

Library of Congress Control Number: 2016937647

Printed on acid-free paper

This Springer imprint is published by Springer Nature
The registered company is Springer International Publishing AG Switzerland

Contents

About the Authors

Contributors

Luís Roberto Barroso Supremo Tribunal Federal, Brasília, DF, Brazil

Thomas Bustamante Universidade Federal de Minas Gerais, Belo Horizonte, Minas Gerais, Brazil

Vera Karam de Chueiri Faculdade de Direito, Universidade Federal do Paraná, Curitiba, PR, Brazil

Stephen Gardbaum MacArthur Foundation Professor of International Justice & Human Rights, UCLA School of Law, Los Angeles, CA, USA

Roberto Gargarella Facultad de Derecho, Universidad Torcuato di Tella, CABA, Argentina

Eric Ghosh School of Law, University of New England, Armidale, NSW, Australia

Bernardo Gonçalves Fernandes Universidade Federal de Minas Gerais, Belo Horizonte, Minas Gerais, Brazil

Ronaldo Porto Macedo Jr. Faculdade de Direito, Universidade de São Paulo, São Paulo, SP, USA

Fundação Getúlio Vargas – Escola de Direito, São Paulo, SP, Brazil

Andrei Marmor Cornell Law School, Cornell University, Ithaca, NY, USA

Gonzalo Andres Ramírez Cleves Universidad Externado de Colombia, Bogotá, Colômbia

Katharina Stevens Department of Philosophy, McMaster University, Hamilton, ON, Canada

Mark Tushnet Harvard Law School, Cambridge, MA, USA

Wil J. Waluchow Department of Philosophy, McMaster University, Hamilton, ON, Canada

Christopher F. Zurn Philosophy Department, University of Massachusetts Boston, Boston, MA, USA

Biographies

Luís Roberto Barroso is a justice of the Brazilian Federal Supreme Court and a full professor of constitutional law of the State University of Rio de Janeiro (Universidade do Estado do Rio de Janeiro, UERJ). He is currently a visiting professor of the University of Brasília (UnB). Barroso has a doctorate from UERJ and a master of laws from Yale Law School. He has a postdoctoral fellowship from Harvard University Law School. He has been a visiting professor at the University of Poitiers (France) and from the University of Wroclaw (Poland).

Thomas Bustamante graduated from the Federal University of Juiz de Fora, Brazil, and has a master's degree from the State University of Rio de Janeiro (UERJ) and a doctorate in law from the Pontifical Catholic University of Rio de Janeiro, with a period of research at the University of Edinburgh, in the UK, with a CAPES scholarship. He is currently associate professor at the Federal University of Minas Gerais (UFMG), where he is a permanent member of the Centre of Graduate Research Studies in Law. He has been a lecturer at the University of Aberdeen, in the UK, from 2008 to 2010, and an adjunct professor at the Federal University of Juiz de Fora (from 2004 to 2008), where he has been head of the Department of Public Law. He has been a postdoctoral fellow at the University of São Paulo in the year of 2015. He undertakes financed research with grants from the CNPQ and the National Council of Justice. Among his publications featured are the books *Argumentação Contra Legem* (2003) and *Teoria do Precedente* (2012) and the edited books *On the Philosophy of Precedent* (2012), with Carlos Bernal Pulido; *Argument Types and Fallacies in Legal Argumentation* (2015), with Christian Dahlman; and *Human Rights, Rule of Law and the Contemporary Social Challenges in Complex Societies* (2012), with Oche Onazi.

Vera Karam de Chueiri has a law degree from the Universidade Federal do Paraná, a master's degree from the Universidade Federal de Santa Catarina, a master's in philosophy from the New School for Social Research, and a doctorate in philosophy from the New School for Social Research. She is currently a professor of constitutional law from the Law School of the Federal University of Paraná (UFPR). Her publications include the books *Fundamentos de Direito Constitucional* (2008) and *Before the Law: Philosophy and Literature* (2006).

Stephen Gardbaum is the MacArthur Foundation professor of international justice and human rights at the University of California in Los Angeles. He was a Guggenheim fellow in 2011–2012 and a Straus fellow at New York University in 2012–2013. An internationally recognized constitutional scholar, Gardbaum received a B.A. with first class honors from Oxford University, an M.Sc. from London University, a Ph.D. in political theory from Columbia, and a J.D. from Yale Law School. He is a solicitor of the Supreme Court of England and Wales and teaches constitutional law, comparative constitutional law, international human rights, European Union law, and comparative law. Professor Gardbaum's scholarship focuses on comparative constitutional law, constitutional theory, and federalism. One of his recent publications is the book *The New Commonwealth Model of Constitutionalism* (Cambridge University Press, 2013).

Roberto Gargarella is a doctor in law (UBA 1991, Univ. Chicago 1993). He has been a postdoctoral scholar at Balliol College, Oxford (1994). He was visiting professor at Pompeu Fabra (Barcelona), Columbia University (NY) and Bergen and Oslo (Norway), among others, and visiting researcher at NYU, Harvard, and ITAM (Mexico). His last books are *The Legal Foundations of Inequality* (Cambridge UP 2010) and *Latin American Constitutionalism* (OUP, 2013).

Eric Ghosh is a senior lecturer in the Law School at the University of New England, NSW, Australia, where he teaches jurisprudence and administrative law. His research interests include the republican political tradition, deliberative democracy, and constitutional theory. His articles have been published in journals including *Oxford Journal of Legal Studies* and *History of Political Thought*.

Bernardo Gonçalves Fernandes graduated in law from the Federal University of Minas Gerais. He has a master's degree in constitutional law from the Federal University of Minas Gerais and a doctorate from the same university. He is currently associate professor of constitutional theory and constitutional law of the Federal University of Minas Gerias and adjunct professor of the Pontifical Catholic University of Minas Gerais. He has taught at the Federal University of Ouro Preto. He has experience in public law, with emphasis in legal hermeneutics, constitutional theory, and constitutional law. He is author of Brazil's best-selling textbook on constitutional law, with an average edition of 20,000 copies per year (*Curso de Direito Constitucional*, 7th edition, 2015).

Ronaldo Porto Macedo Jr. has a law degree, a degree in social sciences, a master's in philosophy, and a doctorate in law, all from the University of São Paulo. He is full professor of legal philosophy at the University of São Paulo and professor of political philosophy, ethics, and legal theory at the Law School of Getúlio Vargas Foundation. He has been a visiting scholar at Harvard Law School (1994–1996) and a visiting researcher at Yale Law School (2002). He has also done a postdoctoral sabbatical year at King's College of London. Among his publications are the books

Do Xadrez à Cortesia (2013), which has been translated into Spanish, *Carl Schmitt e a Fundamentação do Direito* (2nd edn, 2011), and *Direito e Interpretação* (2011).

Andrei Marmor is the Jacob Gould Schurman professor of philosophy and law, at the University of Cornell. Prior to joining Cornell in 2015, he was professor of philosophy and Maurice Jones Jr professor of law at the University of Southern California. Having obtained his first law and philosophy degrees at the Tel Aviv University in Israel and a D.Phil. at Oxford University, UK, he returned to Tel Aviv University, where he taught as professor of law for ten years, before moving to the USA. His most recent books include *Social Conventions: From Language to Law* (Princeton, 2009), *Philosophy of Law* (Princeton, 2011), and *The Language of Law* (Oxford, 2014). His books and articles also appeared in numerous translations, including Chinese, Spanish, Portuguese, Hebrew, and Italian. Marmor is the founding editor of the *Journal of Ethics and Social Philosophy* and the editor of several important volumes in legal philosophy, including, most recently, *The Philosophical Foundations of Language in the Law* (with Scott Soames, Oxford 2011) and *The Routlege Companion to Philosophy of Law.*

Gonzalo Andres Ramírez-Cleves is juris doctor from the Universidad Complutense de Madrid (2003) and has a specialization degree in constitutional law and politics from the Centro de Estudios Constitucionales y Políticos de Madrid (2000) and a law degree from the Universidad Externado de Colombia (1997). Among his publications the following books are featured: *Los límites a la reforma constitucional y las garantías – límites del poder constituyente: los derechos fundamentales como paradigma* (Universidad Externado de Colombia, 2003); *Límites de la reforma constitucional en Colombia: El concepto de constitución como fundamento de la restricción* (Universidad Externado de Colombia, 2005), and *Pobreza, globalización y derecho: ámbitos global, internacional y regional de regulación* (Universidad Externado de Colombia, 2009).

Katharina Stevens is a doctoral candidate in the Philosophy Department at McMaster University, Hamilton, Canada. Her publications include: *The Virtuous Arguer: One Person, Four Roles* (*TOPOI*, 2015) and *Arguments for Rhetorical Arguments: A Response to Aikin* (together with Christopher Tindale in: Cogency, 4:1, 2012).

Mark Tushnet is William Nelson Cromwell professor of law at Harvard Law School. He is the coauthor of four casebooks, including the most widely used casebook on constitutional law; has written numerous books, including a two-volume work on the life of Justice Thurgood Marshall and, most recently, *Advanced Introduction to Comparative Constitutional Law, In the Balance: The Roberts Court and the Future of Constitutional Law, Why the Constitution Matters*, and *Weak Courts, Strong Rights: Judicial Review and Social Welfare Rights in Comparative Perspective*; and has edited several others. He was president of the Association of

American Law Schools in 2003. In 2002 he was elected a fellow of the American Academy of Arts and Sciences.

Wil J. Waluchow is a professor of philosophy and Senator William McMaster chair in constitutional studies at McMaster University, Hamilton, Canada. His publications include: *Inclusive Legal Positivism* (Oxford: Clarendon Press, 1994) and *A Common Law Theory of Judicial Review: The Living Tree* (Cambridge: Cambridge University Press, 2007).

Christopher F. Zurn is professor of philosophy at the University of Massachusetts Boston. Along with journal articles, he has authored *Deliberative Democracy and the Institutions of Judicial Review* (Cambridge UP, 2007) and *Axel Honneth: A Critical Theory of the Social* (Polity, 2015) and coedited *New Waves in Political Philosophy* with Boudewijn de Bruin (Palgrave Macmillan, 2009) and *The Philosophy of Recognition: Historical and Contemporary Perspectives* with Hans-Christoph Schmidt am Busch (Roman & Littlefield, 2009).

Chapter 1
Introduction

Thomas Bustamante and Bernardo Gonçalves Fernandes

The problem of constitutionalism and the legitimacy of its core institutions, in particular the judicial review of democratically-enacted legislation, is probably as old as the invention of the idea of a constitutional democracy in the beginning on the nineteenth century. The debate about the democratic legitimacy of constitutional courts and the authority to interpret the constitution has been going on for quite a while, and the emblematic decision of *Marbury v. Madision* merely settled and gave juristic form to an institutional design that was under discussion for a long time. More than 20 years before Marshall's admission of the power to pronounce as null and void an enactment contrary to the U.S. Constitution, his arguments in support of judicial review of parliamentary legislation had already been raised by Alexander Hamilton in a sophisticated way, as we can read in one of the Federalist Papers:

> The judiciary … has no influence over either the sword or the purse; no direction either on the strength or the wealth of the society, and can take no active resolution whatever. It may truly be said to have neither *force* nor *will* but merely judgment; and must ultimately depend upon the aid of the executive arm even for the efficacy of its judgments […].
>
> The complete independence of the courts of justice is peculiarly essential in a limited Constitution. By a limited Constitution, I understand one which contains specified exceptions to the legislative authority; such, for instance, as that it shall pass no bills of attainder, no *ex post facto* laws, and the like. Limitations of this kind can be preserved in practice no other way than through the medium of courts of justice, whose duty it must be to declare all acts contrary to the manifest tenor of the Constitution void. Without this, all the reservations of particular rights and privileges would amount to nothing (Madison et al. 1787, Paper 78, 437–438).

As we can learn from the fragment above, since the beginnings of constitutionalism one of the central arguments to justify the authority of the courts to adjudicate on the validity of an act of parliament was its immunization from ordinary politics

T. Bustamante (✉) • B.G. Fernandes
Universidade Federal de Minas Gerais, Avenida João Pinheiro, 100,
Belo Horizonte, Minas Gerais 30.130-180, Brazil
e-mail: tbustamante@ufmg.br; bernardogaf@yahoo.com.br

T. Bustamante, B.G. Fernandes (eds.), *Democratizing Constitutional Law*,
Law and Philosophy Library 113, DOI 10.1007/978-3-319-28371-5_1

and the special kind of impartial and uninterested *judgment* that they exercise. Legalistic reasoning, in itself, could assure the kind of objectivity required for reviewing the constitutionality of legislation and providing a measure of stability and mutual control among the three branches of political power.

Yet it did not take long for the critics of judicial review to realize that Hamilton's assumption about the court's isolation from ordinary politics is problematic from the empirical point of view, since it does not take into consideration the reasonable and good-faith disagreement that is pervasive among both the participants of the law-making procedures and the judges who sit in the court to review the decisions of the legislature.

In the face of disagreement, Hamilton's contention that the court is protected from the contingencies of political debate and exercises a technical and unbiased judgment about the violations of the constitution, which are expected to be clear from the text of the Constitution itself, looses much of the grip that it had when the U.S. Constitution was drafted. If, in spite of our mutual effort to that effect, we cannot agree on the meaning of the Constitution, or the scope of the abstract principles and values comprised in its wording, then the judgment of the court lacks any specific feature that makes it qualitatively different from that of the people or their representatives in a legislative assembly. Though this argument is presented, even today, as one of the strongest reasons for suspicion about the legitimacy of constitutional review, in the pages of Jeremy Waldron, Mark Tushnet, Larry Kramer and many others, it was already present in Abraham Lincoln's "First Inaugural Address" delivered on 1861, as one can read in the following fragment, which was recently quoted by one of the most radical critics of judicial review in contemporary legal philosophy:

> No foresight can anticipate, nor any document of reasonable length contain, express provisions for all possible questions. Shall fugitives from labor be surrendered by national or State authority? The Constitution does not expressly say. *May* Congress prohibit slavery in the territories? The Constitution does not expressly say.
>
> From questions of this class spring all our constitutional controversies, and we divide upon them into majorities and minorities. If the minority will not acquiesce, the majority must, or the government must cease. There is no other alternative; for continuing the government, its acquiescence on one side or the other… Unanimity is impossible; the rule of a minority, as a permanent arrangement, is wholly inadmissible; so that, rejecting the majority principle, anarchy, or despotism in some form, is all that is left (Lincoln 1989, 221, quoted on Waldron 2000, 62).

Many of the arguments that Waldron (1999) nowadays directs against constitutional review, on the basis of a more modern notion of "reasonable disagreement" borrowed from Ralws' political liberalism (Ralws 1999), were already available in the beginning of the nineteenth century, even if we concede that they lacked the philosophical refinement that they do today.

The contribution that legal philosophy and legal theory provided to this debate, however, has risen in a significant way. Legal and philosophical debates about the nature of law and legal institutions are no longer limited to the disjunctive alternative between, on the one hand, a Platonic form of natural law theory that fails to account for the social and institutional nature of law and, on the other hand, a primitive form of legal positivism that ignores the functions and the moral values of the legal system, failing to understand the sources of the normativity of law and the legitimate authority that the law claims for itself.

On the camp of legal positivism, for instance, Joseph Raz's theory of authority offers not only a conceptual account of legal validity and of the pre-emptive character of authoritative legal pronouncements, but also a normative theory of legitimate authority and of the moral obligation to obey the law. The problem of the normativity of law, for instance, is no longer reduced to a sociological inquiry of the empirical factors that establish the social efficacy of a legal ruling. On the contrary, it is studied as a philosophical account of the normative role played by the law in the practical reasoning of its addressees.

A theory of law, for Raz, is also a part of a more abstract philosophical theory of authority and political legitimacy in a liberal society, the task of which is not only to expound the necessary features of legal systems. Tough it is also an account of the validity conditions for a given legal system, a jurisprudential theory of law is a normative conception to explain why legal authorities are practically important and how they can provide content-independent directives that bind citizens in a political community. As Raz has put it in his seminal work *The Morality of Freedom*, the famous "service conception of authority", with the three thesis that define it (the dependence thesis, the pre-emptive thesis and the normal justification thesis), has both an "explanation of the concept of authority", insofar as it purports to "advance our understanding of the concept by showing how authoritative action plays a special role in people's practical reasoning", and a normative aspect, to the extent that its three thesis "instruct people how to take binding directive, and when to acknowledge that they are binding" (Raz 1986, 63).

A theory of the legitimacy of legal institutions like courts and legislatures, for instance, is in a significant part a theory of legal authority and the legitimacy conditions for the institutions that claim the right to govern the populace in our political societies.

On the camp of non positivism, on the other hand, Ronald Dworkin develops an interpretivist theory of law that is significant, among other things, because it reconnects legal philosophy and legal practice, moral argumentation and legal reasoning, and legal and political philosophy.

In one of Dworkin's most cited fragments, Dworkin upholds that jurisprudence is the "silent prologue to adjudication" (Dworkin 1986, 90). To offer any response to a legal problem, one must assume, or presuppose, even if unaware of this implicit assumption, a conception of legality which establishes what is to count as a "ground of law" for the interpretation that one defends. No "empirical" proposition about the content of the law, for Dworkin, can be true or false without some more general proposition about when legal propositions are grounded and what kind of reason may be accepted as a "legal" reason. As Guest explains, what Dworkin is doing with this thesis is to get rid of a "mystique" that surrounds the word "philosophy", that assumes that it is distinct or superior from the argumentative practices that we engage in. "Dworkin says we can't fully engage in practice without some idea – an ideally good idea – of a theoretical account of what we should or should not be doing; it wouldn't make sense to be engaged in a practice unless we had at least some notion of what were right or wrong ways of going about it" (Guest 2013, 3).

By the same token, Dworkin sees the law as a "branch" of morality, though it is an institutionalized branch where normative propositions are true or false in a more specific context. Dworkin rejects the idea of law and morality as separate systems, and replace it for what we might call an "integrated view" where law is a department of morality that concerns what we ought to do to each others in the political community to which we belong (Dworkin 2013). This account has an important bearing on the character of legal and political philosophy, as we can read in the following fragment:

> General political philosophy treats, among many other issues, legislative rights. A theory of law treats legal rights, but it is nevertheless a political theory because it seeks a normative answer to a normative political question: Under what conditions do people acquire genuine rights and duties that are enforceable on demand in the way described? (Dworkin 2013, 406).

Dworkin would hold, contrary to an intuition that is widely accepted among legal philosophers, that there is no such thing as a meta-ethics, in the sense that arguments about the nature of morality, law, justice, liberty, democracy and a cluster of "interpretive" or "political" concepts, as he calls it, are not value-free descriptions of the concepts they purport to explain, but rather moral arguments for a conception about what these ideas should be (Dworkin 2004).

But the idea that legal philosophy is, at least in some ways, a branch of political philosophy need not be regarded as unique to the defendants of non-positivism. It may well be the case, as Waldron has recently argued, that legal philosophy is understood as political philosophy or a special case therein (Waldron 2002), even if, in the end, this philosophical inquiry gives us moral and political arguments to uphold a *normative* type of positivism, where the separability between law and morality and the Razian social sources thesis are defended because they are more consistent with the point or the moral values behind the law (Waldron 2001).

All these arguments, on both sides of the positivism and non-positivism divide, are invitations to expand the boundaries of jurisprudential inquiry into the direction of interdisciplinary works with legal dogmatics, political theory, political science, and many other possible subjects. They allow for a newer and richer account of moral and political disagreement, which has important implications for several topics that have to do with democracy and the authority of constitutional courts, such as: the philosophical and political question of the legitimacy of constitutional courts, which will be addressed in the first part of this book, the construction of theories of institutional dialogues and proposals of new models of constitutional deliberation, that will be the focus of part two, the development of new models of constitution-making and constitutional reform, which are the subject of part three, the definition of strategies for fulfilling constitutional promises and increasing democratic participation, that are discussed in part four, and, finally, the debates about the appropriate interpretive theory for constitutional law, which is the theme of the last part of the book.

As mentioned in the previous paragraph, the book is divided in five parts. The first part, entitled "Challenging and Defending Judicial Review", has three essays that address the ongoing debate on the moral legitimacy of constitutional courts.

Marmor's "Randomized Judicial Review" (Chap. 2) is a follow-up from some of his critical works on the legitimacy of constitutional review (Marmor 2007a, b), but based on different argument. He basically proposes a thought-experiment, which would consist in substituting the current U.S.-style systems of judicial review for a randomized system in which the constitutional court would be replaced by a computer that would deliver constitutional decisions on a random basis, with no fixed criterion other than a lottery. Implausible as that hypothesis may seem at first sight, Marmor puts forward a clever philosophical argument to suggest that from the moral point of view there is little that could be said in favour of the current system of judicial review, when contrasted with the hypothetical random model. As he says, "the current system of constitutional judicial review is fraught with many arbitrary elements, to an extent that makes the system only marginally better, if at all, compared with an overtly and blatantly randomized system" (Chap. 2).

In Chap. 3, Bustamante also takes a critical stand on the moral justification of the authority of constitutional courts. His paper is divided in two parts. The first part analyses the nature of the authority of the decisions of constitutional courts, with a view to showing that the derogatory effect of the court's decisions which annul a legislative enactment on constitutional grounds provides exclusionary reasons in the sense of the legal philosophy of Joseph Raz. The author argues, however, that this exclusionary effect is not a feature of the "law in general" or the "central" cases of law application, for in most cases, including statutory interpretation when the validity of the statute is not contested, a Dworkinian account that understands the law as always dependent upon interpretation, even when previous interpretations have already been offered, provides a better account of the practice of law. The second part, in turn, assesses two possible justifications for the authority of constitutional courts: Raz's Normal Justification Thesis, which provides an instrumental account of the justification of legal authority, and a form of democratic justification offered by Waldron and Christiano, among others, that grounds the authority of law on the intrinsic value of democracy as a form of law-making procedure that protects the people's own judgments about controversial issues of politics and public morality. He argues that this Democratic Justification of legal authority is more robust than the Normal Justification Thesis, but that only the latter is available to justify the authority of constitutional courts. We would have, therefore, an imbalance between the authority of constitutional courts and legislatures. While the legislature's enactments lack the exclusionary character that Raz assigns to them and can only be justified in an instrumental way, the court's derogatory decisions have such pre-emptive power to create exclusionary reasons for action, but the only justification that is available for such power is the instrumental justification provided by the Normal Justification Thesis. This provides an argument, for the author, against the models of strong constitutional review.

In Chap. 4, in turn, Justice Barroso provides an argument for the opposite conclusion. The analysis, however, is less abstract than that of the previous two chapters. He begins with a historical overview of the global ascent of judicial review after the end of World War II and of the role that constitutional courts have been playing in the establishment of many democracies throughout the world. By the same token, Barroso takes up the problem of the deficit of representative legitimacy of parliaments and the insufficiency of electoral mechanisms to establish a link between representatives and ordinary citizens in contemporary democratic states. The basic argument is that under appropriate circumstances courts can help legislatures overcome this democratic deficit by establishing a practice of constitutional dialogue between the courts and the legislature itself. Furthermore, courts are in a better position to represent the people in an indirect way, by their deliberative and argumentative capacity in the protection of fundamental rights that are underprotected by the legislature. As the author claims in the opening section of the chapter, "it may be the case, under certain circumstances, that it will be up to the Supreme Court to be responsive to unattended social demands presented as legal claims of rights".

The second part is concerned with institutional dialogues and constitutional deliberation, and is also composed of three chapters.

In Chap. 5, Gardbaum expands the analysis of the New Commonwealth Constitutionalism that he made in an important and successful book about the attempt to institutionalize, in common law legal systems such as the United Kingdom, Canada, New Zealand and some provinces of Australia, a model of judicial review without judicial supremacy (Gardbaum 2013). As Gardbaum has stated in previous writings, he thinks that the models of "constitutional dialogues", as they sometimes appear in the texts of constitutional lawyers committed to a strong system of judicial review, is not always sufficient to respond to the democratic objections raised against the models of judicial supremacy. Even if the dialogue model may establish some kind of communication between courts and legislatures in the long run, or a wholesale deliberation between courts and legislatures, it is still compatible with a system in which the judiciary retains the final word for the specific matters under discussion in the case at hand (Gardbaum 2013, 27–28). In the chapter, the author presses some of his previous arguments forward, and explores the "relevant meaning of judicial supremacy (that the model rejects) in light of certain potential misunderstandings and alternative senses that could be given to the term" (Chap. 5). The normative point of the inquiry is to provide further arguments to defend his claim that judicial review without judicial supremacy is easier to defend on moral grounds than the strong systems of judicial review that are predominant in most Western countries.

Gargarella, in Chap. 6, undertakes a philosophical and historical analysis of the debate that is going on in political philosophy about "dialogic constitutionalism, dialogic justice and dialogic judicial review". Though he is sympathetic to this idea of a collaborative effort of legislatures and courts in the interpretation of the constitution and in the protection of rights, he is not entirely optimistic about the application of theses models as they stand, especially in the context of Latin American constitutions. There are "reasons for concern", as he concludes, "particularly if we are not willing to modify the basic structure of the system of checks and balances on which it is usually based", that is less open to dialogue and equal political standing on constitutional matters than some defendants of the dialogue model might assume.

In Chap. 7, in turn, Fernandes offers an account that is more sympathetic to dialogues theory and less optimistic about Waldron's normative arguments against judicial review. The basic contention of the chapter is that even though Waldron's battle against judicial review has some interesting insights about the shortcomings of judicial supremacy, it is based on an unrealistically charitable, if not naïve, picture of legislatures, which assumes in an uncritical way the legitimacy of parliaments. Furthermore, Waldron himself has recognized in some of his recent papers (Waldron 2006, 2010) that the majoritatian principle cannot be accepted unconditionally, and that the core case against judicial review is based on a set of legitimacy conditions for the legislative political process. Nonetheless, even if Waldron is wrong about the illegitimacy of strong judicial review, his arguments provide a robust case for a model of institutional dialogues.

The Third part is also composed of three chapters, which are commonly concerned with the institutional alternatives for constitutional change in contemporary democracies.

Chapter 8, by Tushnet, aims to analyse two new models of constitutional change that have been recently tested in Iceland, where an attempt to make a new constitution by crowd-sourcing has been made, and Brazil, where the Supreme Court adopted a practice of public hearings about controversial issues about rights and constitutional morality before they are settled by a binding decision. In the case of Iceland, Tushnet attempts to explain the reasons for the failure of the promise to achieve "higher levels of public participation than in the traditional methods of constitution-making" (Constitutional Assemblies or, in a more timid way, ordinary constitutional amendments). The failure of Iceland's attempt, according to his argument, can teach us important lessons about public participation in constitution making. Brazil's experience, on the other hand, is still in its early days, but is based on a sound principle that purports to be a blending of "political constitutionalism", which "gives legislatures and executive officials a large and honoured place in constitutional interpretation", and the traditional forms of judicial constitutionalism. Both strategies for constitutional making, however, are presented as methods for constitutional making of interest for comparative constitutional law.

Zurn offers, in turn, in Chap. 9, a philosophical normative model for assessing institutional possibilities for democratic modes of constitutional change, in particular to recent forms of constitutional experimentation. According to Zurn's normative account, six ideals should play a decisive role to ground the legitimacy of new constitutional projects: "operationalizability, structural independence, democratic co-authorship, political equality, inclusive sensitivity, and reasons-responsiveness". These ideals, for the author, can be used to "gauge the normative worth of different mechanisms for carrying out such change. The framework is developed with reference to recent constitutional developments (e.g., in Venezuela, South Africa, Colombia, Bolivia, and Iceland) highlighting distinct criteria and showing how they appear to capture the general direction of institutional innovation".

In Chap. 10, Ramíres Cleves turns to a more concrete development of protection against unlawful constitutional change in Colombia, based on the so-called "constitutional replacement doctrine", which evolved by judicial construction in spite of the absence of any specific constitutional provision granting such power to the court. The core idea is that the court is entitled to protect a set of principles considered part of the constitutional essence of a democratic system of government, such as the prohibition of a second re-election of the President of the Republic, in order to protect the goal of political pluralism. After introducing the doctrine of the Colombian constitutional court, which has been developed in five cases where it has been applied over the last few years, Ramírez Cleves presents some of the main objections that the doctrine has met and offers a reply to these criticisms, in order to uphold the view that the court's doctrine constitutes a legitimate model of constitutional dialogues between the court and the other branches of political power.

The penultimate section, in turn, concerns the right to participation as the core of the justification for political legitimacy, and addresses the possibility of clashes between the claim to self-government, by the people, and the dominant tradition of constitutional law.

Chueiri's Chap. 11 deals with the promise of a radical constitution, with a more ambitious conception of self-government and democratic constitutionalism. The argument is divided in three parts: the first starts with Post's assumption that democratic constitutionalism "implies a collective intervention by the people (a shared voice), which assumes the ineradicable tension between collective self-governance and the rule of law in order to establish the ongoing structure of democratic states". In the second part, she discusses the link between constituent power, sovereignty and the Constitution, and in the third part, the relation between constitutionalism and democracy. Furthermore, the chapter constitutes and effort to deal with a diachronic form of constitutionalism that requires an empowerment of active citizens in a constitutional democracy to redeem the promises made by the constitution, which can only be done by radicalization of popular participation in the making of the constitutional democracy.

In Chap. 12, which closes the 4th session, Ghosh presses forward some of his earlier arguments in defence of judicial review by constitutional juries (Ghosh 2010). The theoretical framework from which he argues is Waluchow's conception of "community's constitutional morality" (CCM), which consists of those "true moral commitments that are tied to its constitutional law and practices" (Waluchow 2008, 77). A promising candidate for justifying the authority of the settlement of constitutional controversies in a policy, whether or not such settlement is the product of the action of a constitutional court, is a deliberative model in which these community-related constitutional values are tested and specified. One of the core assumptions of the chapter, as the author himself clarifies in the introduction to his paper, is to show that the claim to combine a commitment to CCM and a deliberative model of democracy can be redeemed by the institutionalization of a model of constitutional juries.

The fifth and final part, in turn, takes up the serious problem of the relations between legal theory and interpretation in democratic states, with emphasis on constitutional interpretation.

Waluchow and Stevens, in Chap. 13, offer a defence of Waluchow's approach to constitutional interpretation widely known as "common law constitutionalism" (Waluchow 2007). The challenge of the chapter is to respond to the objection that the resource to common law principles in the interpretation of the written constitution empowers the judges to determine the meaning of the constitution on the basis of their own subjective moral views. To counter this objection, the authors apply Strauss' view that "any interpretation should be compatible with the current meaning of the words of which a constitutional text is composed" (Chap. 13). While referring to the constitution's normative concepts, judges may use the common law approach to constitutional interpretation in order to interpret the abstract principles referred to in the constitution on the basis of the community's own constitutional morality.

Finally, in Chap. 14, Macedo Júnior offers a powerful defence of Dworkin's interpretivism against the conventionalist view advocated by the mainstream positivist accounts of the nature of law. The chapter carefully explains the methodological disagreement between Dworkin and authors such as Hart or Marmor, who use the analogy with chess to explain the character of the rules of law. On the basis of Dworkin's analogy between law and courtesy, Macedo Júnior attempts to show how the chess analogy is problematic because the law should be understood as an interpretive or "political" concept in the sense of Dworkin (1986, 2004).

The common point of all the chapters of the book is a concern with the political legitimacy of institutions in constitutional democracies. They should be of great interest not only for legal and political philosophers, but, in the same measure, to political scientists, practicing lawyers (both in constitutional law and in other more specific areas), comparative lawyers and institutional designers. The general principle on which all authors agree, with regards to the future of constitutionalism, is that the legitimacy of constitutional institutions is predicated on democracy, although they might disagree about conceptions of democracy and their adequacy to any particular legal system.

References

Dworkin, Ronald. 1986. *Law's empire*. Cambridge, MA: Belknap.

Dworkin, Ronald. 2004. Hart's postscript and the character of political philosophy. *Oxford Journal of Legal Studies* 22: 1–37.

Dworkin, Ronald. 2013. *Justice for hedgehogs*. Cambridge, MA: Belknap.

Gardbaum, Stephen. 2013. *The new commonwealth model of constitutionalism: Theory and practice*. Cambridge: Cambridge University Press.

Ghosh, Eric. 2010. Deliberative democracy and the countermajoritarian difficulty: Considering constitutional juries. *Oxford Journal of Legal Studies* 30: 327–359.

Guest, Stephen. 2013. *Ronald Dworkin*, 3rd ed. Stanford: Stanford University Press.

Lincoln, Abraham. 1989. First innaugural address. In *Speeches and writings 1859–1965*, 215. New York: Library of America.

Madison, James, Alexander Hamilton, and John Jay. 1787. *The federalist papers*, ed. Isaac Kramnick. Reprinted in 1987. New York: Penguin Books.

Marmor, Andrei. 2007a. Are constitutions legitimate? In *Law in the age of pluralism*, 89–123. Oxford: Oxford University Press.

Marmor, Andrei. 2007b. Authority, equality and democracy. In *Law in the age of pluralism*, 57–88. Oxford: Oxford University Press.

Rawls, John. 1999. *Political liberalism,* expanded edition. New York: Columbia University Press.

Raz, Joseph. 1986. *The morality of freedom*. Oxford: Oxford University Press.

Waldron, Jeremy. 1999. *Law and disagreement*. Oxford: Oxford University Press.

Waldron, Jeremy. 2000. "Despositism in Some Form": Marbury v. Madison. In *Great cases in constitutional law*, ed. R.P. George, 55–63. Princeton: Princeton University Press.

Waldron, Jeremy. 2001. Normative positivism. In *Hart's postscript: Essays on the postscript to the concept of law*, ed. Jules Coleman, 410–433. Oxford: Oxford University Press.

Waldron, Jeremy. 2002. Legal and political philosophy. In *The Oxford handbook of jurisprudence & philosophy of law*, ed. Jules Coleman and Scott Shapiro, 352–381. Oxford: Oxford University Press.

Waldron, Jeremy. 2006. The core of the case against judicial review. *Yale Law Journal* 115: 1346–1406.

Waldron, Jeremy. 2010. A majority in the lifeboat. *Boston University Law Review* 90: 1043–1057.

Waluchow, W.J. 2007. *A common law theory of judicial review: The living tree*. Cambridge: Cambridge University Press.

Waluchow, W.J. 2008. Constitutional morality and bills of rights. In *Expounding the constitution: Essays in constitutional theory*, ed. Grant Huscroft, 65–92. Cambridge: Cambridge University Press.

Part I
Challenging and Defending Judicial Review

Chapter 2
Randomized Judicial Review

Andrei Marmor

Abstract One of the main arguments in support of constitutional judicial review points to the need to curtail the legal and political power of majority rule instantiated by democratic legislative institutions. This article aims to challenge the counter majoritarian argument for judicial review by showing that there is very little difference, at least morally speaking, between the current structure of constitutional judicial review in the US, and a system that would impose limits on majoritarian decisions procedures by an entirely randomized mechanism. The argument is based on a hypothetical model of a randomized system of judicial review, and proceeds to show that between the actual practices of judicial review in the US, and the hypothetical randomized model, there is not much to recommend the former. The current system of constitutional judicial review is fraught with many arbitrary elements, to an extent that makes the system only marginally better, if at all, compared with an overtly and blatantly randomized system.

2.1 Introduction

Any reasonably informed observer of U.S. constitutional cases would have to admit that most of the important constitutional decisions of the Supreme Court are reached on (so-called) ideological grounds.[1] The justices' moral, political, sometimes even religious, convictions tend to influence, not to say determine, the outcome of their decisions on constitutional matters, though, of course, rarely the public reasons given for them. The reasons are always cast in legal terms and phrased as legalistically as possible. But when we hear the outcome of constitutional cases, we are very rarely surprised. To the extent that an upcoming decision is not entirely predictable,

[1] I use the word "ideology" here only in deference to common usage in American legal and political discourse. The word is not meant to have any relation to the original, Marxist notion of ideology; it should be regarded as no more than a shortcut for what, following Rawls, we can call "comprehensive morality," encompassing moral and ethical convictions, religious world views, political views and affiliations, etc.

A. Marmor (✉)
Cornell Law School, Cornell University,
226 Goodwin Smith Hall, Ithaca, NY, USA
e-mail: am2773@cornell.edu

T. Bustamante, B.G. Fernandes (eds.), *Democratizing Constitutional Law*,
Law and Philosophy Library 113, DOI 10.1007/978-3-319-28371-5_2

the uncertainty is due to one swing vote – at most two – on the Court. I am not suggesting that this is always the case. Some decisions on constitutional matters are not fraught with overt moral, political or religious issues, and sometimes it is difficult to trace the justices' reasons to any particular ideological convictions. But most of them are. And in most constitutional cases, decisions depend on the individual makeup of the Court. In some periods, liberal justices dominate and we get, by and large, liberal outcomes; in others, as nowadays, conservative justices form the majority and we get, by and large, conservative decisions. Either way, surprises are very rare and even if they occur, in retrospect they are often explicable on grounds of political maneuvering in or by the Court.[2]

None of this is news, of course. On the contrary, the general perception of constitutional cases in the U.S. as ideologically determined is widely known, publically debated and, generally speaking, entirely on the surface of public consciousness. But this begs an obvious question: Why do we go for it? What moral-political reasons can support a constitutional structure that gives an essentially nondemocratic institution, composed of a handful of people appointed for life and not (professionally or politically) accountable to anyone, the power to prevail over the decisions of the democratically elected Congress and state legislatures? Considering the enormous resources we spend on maintaining the democratic process, it seems utterly puzzling that we are willing to put the outcome of this process at the mercy of an unelected institution that is not democratically accountable.

Most supporters of constitutionalism in the U.S. tell us that it is precisely the nondemocratic nature of the Court – its detachment from representative democratic procedures – that warrants the current constitutional structure. What we need, we are told by supporters of constitutionalism, is precisely this counter-majoritarian element in the system, in order to curtail, at least to some extent, the political and legal power of the majoritarian decision procedures that are instantiated by the democratic legislative institutions. In other words, and simply put, the idea is that constitutional judicial review is needed as a countermeasure to ordinary democratic procedures, as a limit on majority rule. I am not suggesting that this is the only rationale on offer justifying the current U.S. system of constitutional judicial review. But it is the one that I will consider in this paper.

There are, of course, various ways to push back on the counter-majoritarian rationale of constitutionalism. Some political philosophers have argued that no such curtailment is needed. They say that majority rule, adequately structured, is fair and good, and that there is no need for judicial review[3]; others have argued that, even if there is such a need, the current system of judicial review is fraught with too many difficulties and raises more problems than it solves. In this essay, however, I want

---

[2] A nice example is the recent decision on the constitutionality of the Affordable Care Act ("Obamacare") (National Federation of Independent Business v. Sebelius, 567 U.S. [2012], 132, S. Ct 2566). Chief Justice Roberts' decision to side with the liberal branch of the Court surprised many, but I think it is clear enough that Roberts's decision was politically motivated, partly, though, by internal Court politics.

[3] See, for example, Waldron (1999) and Tushnet (1999).

to suggest a different line of response to the counter-majoritarian rationale of judicial review. I will argue that there is very little difference between the current structure of constitutional review in the U.S. and a system that would impose limits on majoritarian decision procedures by an entirely randomized mechanism. Showing that may not amount to a conclusive argument against judicial review, far from it, but I hope it will give us some pause.

2.2 The Randomized Hypothetical

Imagine that we could construct the following system: Instead of a constitutional court or supreme court with constitutional judicial review, we design a randomized system of judicial review. Here is how it might work (hypothetically, of course): Every new law enacted by the legislature is automatically submitted to the "judicial review computer." Similarly, every constitutional challenge to a governmental policy or practice is filed with the same computer system (instead of the courts). Let us assume that a panel of lawyers feeds the computer with the set of possible legal outcomes of each challenge. Normally the set would be either pass or fail constitutional muster, but sometimes it could be a bit more complex, perhaps dividing the challenge to several options. As a simplifying assumption for now, we will postulate that the set of outcome options is both very limited in scope and fairly technical.[4] Then, at the end of the year, the computer runs a program that yields a totally random selection of "cases" that it strikes down as "unconstitutional" and therefore legally invalid. How many of them? Well, we can easily determine some formula in advance, say, a certain number of cases based on factual parameters gleaned from the history of judicial review in the last century or so[5] – or any such mechanical, but essentially randomized, method. Let me call this the Randomized Judicial Review process, or RJR, in contrast with the actual Constitutional Judicial Review system we have, which I will henceforth label as CJR.

Obviously, the RJR system would have to be a bit more sophisticated and complex for it to be plausible, even as a hypothetical. For one thing, we would need some initial screening procedures. For another, we would need some process, judicial or other, to determine some basic factual findings that would be needed to ground the constitutional challenges. Both of these issues can be resolved, however, without insurmountable difficulties. We can imagine a system whereby lower courts

[4] I realize that this is a very simplified assumption and that it ignores familiar problems of agenda settings and framing effects. However, there is no need to worry about it too much in the present context, as we will see in the sequel, a modified version of the hypothetical (that will be called RJR*) avoids these problems.

[5] We would not want the formula to pick out a certain percentage of challenges because there may not be a check on the number of such challenges filed. A fixed number of decisions on "unconstitutionality" would be more sensible.

would have to certify constitutional challenges, and determine their factual groundings, before they can be filed with the randomizing computer.

So here is the question I would like to pursue in this essay: How would RJR differ, in significant moral-political ways, from CJR? I will try to show that between the hypothetical RJR and the actual CJR the differences are rather insignificant, morally speaking, and, in any case, provide no good reasons to prefer the actual to the hypothetical. At this point you might think that the issue is moot because there is absolutely nothing to support a randomized process of judicial review; it is just too crazy. Well, crazy it might be, but two considerations lend it some support: First, just like the current CJR, it puts a limit on majority rule. It curtails, to the same extent, at least quantitatively (ex hypothesis), the majority's ability to enact laws or implement policies by a regular majority vote. Second, a consideration of fairness may count in favor of a purely randomized system. When you have a winner and a loser in a legal battle, and neither side is obviously right or wrong (more on this later), a randomized decision procedure gives each side an equal chance of success or failure. In any case, it is not my argument to recommend RJR. The argument is to show that compared with RJR, CJR is not really superior – not by much, anyway.

Before we proceed, an obvious objection needs to be answered. Surely, people would think, it matters what the constitution *says*. After all, there is a written constitution, with some determinate legal content, and it is the constitutional text and its legal content that judges need to implement by their decisions. Cases ought to be determined by the legal content of the constitutional text (and perhaps well-entrenched constitutional doctrines and precedents). Therefore, the argument would go, the main difference between RJR and CJR consists in the fact that RJR is totally insensitive to the legal prescriptions embodied in the Constitution, whereas CJR is guided by the constitutional text, even if imperfectly so. Let me call this the obvious objection.

It is difficult to answer the obvious objection in the abstract. The extent to which the content of constitutional documents actually guides constitutional decisions of courts varies a great deal between different jurisdictions. I will confine myself here to the U.S. model, and to the realities of constitutional judicial review in the United States.[6] So, here is the answer to the obvious objection: It is true that the constitutional text matters; the legal content expressed in the U.S. Constitution is not without significant legal ramifications. But the difference the constitutional text makes is rarely in play in the kind of cases that the U.S. Supreme Court decides on constitutional matters, for two main reasons: First, when the constitutional text evidently determines a given outcome, litigation is very unlikely to ensue. Parties have no money to waste on, and courts no patience and resources to deal with, cases in

[6] By this I do not want to suggest that the constitutional systems prevalent in most countries are just slight variations on the U.S. model, far from it. The U.S. model of constitutionalism is unique in many respects, and probably more problematic than most. Some of these differences I highlighted elsewhere and I will not reiterate them here. See Marmor (2007). In any case, for whatever it is worth, my analysis in this essay is confined to the U.S. example.

which a legal outcome simply follows from the public meaning of the relevant legislative text, be it constitutional or ordinary legislation. To put matters simply: Easy cases do not make it to the Supreme Court. If litigation makes it to the Supreme Court as a constitutional case, it is almost invariably because the text is not clear enough to dictate a particular result. I am talking about "the text" here, but we can easily extend the argument to include not only the text of the written Constitution but also deeply entrenched constitutional doctrines or precedents as well.[7] The point holds true even if we allow for a much broader sense of what constitutes "the constitutional text."

Second, and this may be more unique to the U.S. model, the Supreme Court itself gets a huge amount of discretion in determining the cases it is willing to hear. Only a small fraction of constitutional challenges filed get certified by the Court itself for hearing.[8] So the Court sets its own agenda, year by year, choosing from a wide variety of options. How does it make the choice? Obviously, the Court tends to choose the kind of cases in which it can make a difference. Naturally, those are the kind of cases in which reading the text and understanding what it says is just not going to suffice for a clear inference to the outcome. The Court would tend to grant cert in cases in which some reasonable argument can be made that the Constitution prescribes X rather than Y, or Y rather than X. In short, again, the Court would hardly ever grant cert to hear an "easy case," one in which every competent lawyer would reach the same legal conclusion. That just does not happen.[9]

To recap, briefly: The first assumption I make here, and one that I think is hardly controversial, is that if a constitutional case makes it to the Supreme Court it is not going to be the kind of case in which the constitutional text and deeply entrenched precedents, if you will, are simply going to determine a legal outcome. Constitutional cases at the Supreme Court level, at least, tend to be those in which plausible arguments can be made to interpret the Constitution one way or another, whereby none of the plausible readings is obviously dictated by the text. So there is that. And then, as we mentioned at the beginning, the result of the case is typically a function of the individual composition of the Court. Different justices would reach different conclusions, depending on their comprehensive moral, political and religious convictions. I am sure that one could give some exceptions and counterexamples. But I think we are entitled to assume here that, by and large, very few constitutional cases

[7] True, it sometimes happens that a long-held precedent is overturned by the Court, but that hardly ever happens without prior warning; it normally comes after years of uncertainty, following signals that the current Court is not happy with the doctrine or precedent in question and might be willing to change it.

[8] It is difficult to separate the data on constitutional certiorari; overall, the U.S. Supreme Court gets about 9000–10,000 petitions a year and grants cert to about 100 cases.

[9] It may be worth keeping in mind that differences in decisions between Circuit Courts of Appeal constitute one of the main reasons for the Supreme Court to grant cert; thus, many of the constitutional cases heard before the Supreme Court have a history of split decisions in lower-level appellate federal courts.

are actually determined, legally speaking, by the meaning of the text, by what the U.S. Constitution simply says.[10]

The obvious objection may have a point, however, when you think about the legal impact of the constitutional text in those cases that do not make it to appellate courts, because the legal content of the Constitution is just clear enough to determine particular outcomes. In other words, supporters of CJR could claim that, even if my previous argument is correct, and easy constitutional cases do not make it to the Supreme Court, countless legal issues are determined by the Constitution simply because it is clear enough what the Constitution mandates or requires. That, of course, is quite true. The constitutional text, and probably even more so, the well-entrenched constitutional doctrines and precedents, make a significant legal difference in countless cases in which the legal content of the constitutional law is not in any serious doubt.

However, we can easily accommodate this concern by revising the hypothetical structure of RJR. Instead of assuming that all constitutional challenges are automatically submitted to the randomizing computer, we can confine the randomization mechanism to those cases that do make it to appellate courts, under the current CJR system, and fail to muster unanimous decision at the appellate level.[11] The idea here involves a great simplification. It would take the unanimity of the decision by the appellate court as a proxy for cases in which the constitutional text, and perhaps deeply entrenched constitutional doctrines, are clear enough to determine particular results. And then, failure of unanimous consent on a constitutional case would be taken as an indication of some plausible controversy. Randomization would kick in, according to this revised system, only in cases of some actual legal controversy at the appellate courts level. Let us call the revised system RJR*. As I said, the use of unanimity at the appellate courts or the Supreme Court level should not be taken to be more than a simplifying assumption. It should be seen as a proxy for drawing the line between cases in which no serious legal doubt about the constitutional legal content can be raised, and those in which some plausible legal argument can be made to decide the case one way rather than another. It is not a perfect proxy, for sure, but good enough to make the argument here. Therefore, if you take the obvious objection to have a point, just think about RJR* instead of the original scheme; assume that randomization kicks in only in those cases in which there is some actual doubt about constitutional requirements. That would still cover the vast majority of cases that make it to the Supreme Court under the current CJR.

[10] I should not protest too much if all this sounds like a superficial recount of ideas floated almost a century ago by the American Legal Realists. I am not endorsing their view wholesale, far from it. My comments above are confined to constitutional cases that make it to the U.S. Supreme Court. For reasons I have explained elsewhere in detail (Marmor 2014), the reality in ordinary cases of statutory interpretation is very different. But that is not our concern here.

[11] And perhaps when there is a split in the decisions of circuit courts on the same constitutional matter.

2.3 Objections to RJR

Having answered the obvious objection only takes us so far. We need to consider more serious objections to RJR. In what follows, I will consider four main arguments purporting to show the superiority of CJR: the argument from public perception, the argument based on the rule of law, the argument from incentives and the social consensus argument. I will try to show that none of these arguments provides a compelling reason to prefer CJR over RJR.

Let me begin with the problem of public perception: I would not deny the allegation that RJR is not going to be popular with the general public. People would find it very difficult to accept, as a matter of political legitimacy, any system of constitutional review that is so overtly random and, thus, arbitrary. We would like to think that the boundaries of political legitimacy are not set by a computer program that strikes down, randomly, some democratic decisions as legally invalid. In short, it is difficult to imagine that anything like an RJR system would be socially and politically acceptable. And, of course, I am not claiming that it is a realistic, feasible scheme that can be implemented. But the question is whether this is a serious worry in the dialectical context of the argument, and I do not quite see how it would be, for two main reasons: First and foremost, because the point of the thought experiment I suggest here is not to convince us that we could actually replace our constitutional law with something like RJR. Since the argument is not based on the actual feasibility of RJR, the fact that it would be unlikely to be accepted by the public is neither here nor there. The second problem is that the public-perception argument does not go very deep. It does not give us any substantive reasons to prefer CJR over RJR, apart from the fact that CJR looks better, so to speak. Looking morally better does not make something morally better; it just makes it easier to live with it. And the fact that something is generally accepted by the public, as U.S. constitutionalism undeniably is, is not really an argument in its favor. One should always keep in mind that many things that are widely accepted by the public, even for a very long time, can turn out to be wrong and morally misguided. To conclude: The fact that RJR cannot be publically accepted is not going to tell us why CJR is preferable to RJR.

Perhaps a more serious objection to RJR can be drawn from the ideal of the rule of law. *The rule of law* means a lot of different things to different people, but at least we all share the view that it purports to capture the idea that it is good to be governed by law. I would not want to deny that this is a commendable ideal and that governance should always be subject to law and constrained by it.[12] The question is why would RJR violate the rule of law? Surely RJR does not violate it simply on grounds of employing a randomized mechanism for yielding some legal results. Various randomized mechanisms for allocating burdens or entitlements are often employed by legal systems in ways that are largely deemed fair and proper. Lotteries, of various kinds, are legal in many jurisdictions, and even if we have all

[12] In fact, I defended this position in Marmor (2010).

sorts of reservations about some of them, violation of the rule of law is not one of those qualms. More to the point, licenses for various scarce resources, for example, are sometimes allocated on the basis of a lottery system, and often that is precisely the fair and equitable way of reaching the relevant outcome. For example, a municipality that allocates, say, some building permits, or taxicab licenses, on the basis of a fair lottery would clearly not violate the rule of law. So it is not the randomization element, per se, that would seem to violate the rule of law in RJR.

Perhaps the problem is not randomization, per se, but the sense that randomizing legal outcomes in such a way amounts to a form of *arbitrary* decision-making; the thought might be that RJR is overtly not responsive to reasons, legal or other, whereas CJR, even if random to some extent, and not quite constrained by law, is at least responsive to reasons. Remember, however, that if legal norms actually determine a constitutional result, it is very unlikely to be litigated at the Supreme Court level. So we are initially not considering here cases in which the relevant legal reasons fully determine a particular result. Nevertheless, I can see why a process that is clearly not even purporting to be responsive to reasons might seem very suspect from the perspective of the rule of law virtues. But it should not be, at least not without further premises.[13] Here is an example: My teenage daughter likes to buy clothes, lots of them. Normally, I am happy to oblige (with my credit card). Forget the cost, and assume it is not the issue. The main worry I have is that it is not good for her, in the long run, to be able to buy just about any fashionable clothes she fancies. It is not good for her to have no limits. Now suppose that I give my daughter an option: I can either tell her that I get to impose a limit, once in a while, based on my own judgment of what she really needs – notice, a judgment that purports to be responsive to reasons – or else I can randomize the system. I tell her that we will input all her requests into a computer program (call it the veto-machine) that will randomly select, once in a while, some items that she cannot buy. And let us assume that we can guarantee that my own decisions and the veto-machine's limits would be comparable in the quantity of the limits it sets. I can assure you that, given this choice, my daughter would prefer the randomized system. Though clearly not responsive to reasons, the veto-machine is at least more respectful of her own choices. It does not convey the message that she has made a bad choice; it makes no claim to replace her own judgments, only to impose some quantitative limit, as it were. So between my decisions and the veto-machine's arbitrary choices, my daughter would be quite right to choose the one that is less judgmental and more respectful of her own choices, even if, ex hypothesis, the quantitative results are going to be the same. Some of her choices will be vetoed randomly, but respectfully.

But now you might think that another worry comes to the surface: what my daughter loses with the veto-machine is her right to be heard, that is, her right to

[13] Another concern in the vicinity here might be the concern that RJR violates the principle that like cases should be treated alike. But it is far from clear what this principle really is, and what violates it. These are complicated issues that would take us too far from our present concerns. See Marmor (2005a).

present her arguments and make her case for her choices and preferences. And this sounds like a serious concern. Many people regard the right to have one's day in court, or the right to judicial hearing, as one of the central principles of the rule of law. And perhaps it is. So now the question becomes whether RJR violates the rule of law because it denies the relevant parties, that is, the parties to a potential constitutional litigation, the right to hearing, that is, the right to present their case and make reasoned arguments in a court of law.[14] The answer is tricky: of course that in an obvious technical sense, RJR denies this right; you don't get your day in court, the randomizing computer is doing the work for you. But the real question is whether the relevant parties to constitutional litigation have the kind of right that is claimed to be violated here. I would not want to deny that in countless types of cases, generally speaking, the right to have one's day in court is a very important one. Surely we could not imagine a fair and sensible system of criminal and private law without due process and full implementation of the right to hearing. It is not the general justification of such a right that I would like to call in question. The pertinent question here is whether denying parties a right to *constitutional* litigation is denying people a right that they have. There cannot be a simple answer to this question. To begin with, we wouldn't want to say that in a country like the United Kingdom, where there is no written constitution, and where constitutional litigation, though gradually developing perhaps, is still very limited, people's right to constitutional litigation is violated; if there is no judicial or quasi-judicial decision to be made, you don't have a right to present your case in court. My point is that the right to litigate and have one's day in court in a constitutional matter is entirely parasitic on the desirability of CJR. Since it is the rationale of CJR that I am calling into question here, simply assuming that without it the right to have one's day in court is denied, is assuming the very point that needs to be proved.

In other words, there is a serious moral-political question about the right to constitutional litigation. Remember that a constitutional challenge is a legal challenge to a democratic process; what parties litigate in constitutional cases are decisions that resulted from democratic procedures. Of course people should have the right to challenge any public decision, whether democratically made or not. The question is why should they have such a right outside the ordinary democratic processes and institutions? Why should one have a right to challenge a decision that has been reached by democratic means in ways that are essentially non-democratic? Of course this is precisely the question that goes to the heart of the justification of constitutional judicial review. So once again, just assuming that CJR is preferable to RJR on grounds of the right to hearing, is putting the cart in front of the horse in the dialectics of this argument. If and to the extent that CJR is preferable to RJR, then people's right to have their day in court is one that should be respected. I don't see how one can justify the rationale of having a judicial, as opposed to a democratic decision, on the grounds that one has the right to present one's arguments. Arguments can be presented in a democratic process just as well. What calls for justification here is the exception to democratic procedures, namely, the removal of a decision

[14] I am grateful to Leticia Morales for pushing this point.

from it and handing it to the courts, and I fail to see how we can justify this removal by appealing to a right to hearing. First we need to show that there is a justification for removing a certain decision from the ordinary democratic processes by handing them to a court, and then we can talk about the right to hearing and its proper implementation.

Perhaps the most plausible concern about the rule of law with RJR is the concern about fair warning: Presumably the idea is that, under a system of RJR, legislatures and the law's subjects would have no way of knowing in advance which laws and regulations might be struck down as unconstitutional and thus legally invalid. The question is, how is that different from the same problem we have with CJR? Constitutional uncertainty is something we have lived with for a long time. In countless cases, legislatures have enacted laws and government agencies have implemented policies that have later been found unconstitutional, sometimes much later, by the Court. If there is a problem of fair warning here, and there probably is, the difference between CJR and RJR is only quantitative, if that. Perhaps somewhat greater uncertainty is to be expected under RJR compared with CJR. But even so, remember that the numbers here are very small. Only a very small number of laws and regulations get struck down as unconstitutional every year; it amounts to a tiny fraction of legislative and administrative output. Furthermore, even if the level of uncertainly with RJR is somewhat higher, we gain something in terms of fairness. Thus, overall, it is not clear that RJR fares much worse compared with CJR on the overall metrics of the rule of law. Perhaps to the contrary: If some random element in a system allocates legal rights and entitlements, ideals of the rule of law would counsel us to make those elements overt and fair, rather than conceal them under high-minded judicial practices.

2.4 Constitutional Principles and Incentives

Let me turn to the third main problem with the hypothetical system of RJR, namely, that it does not guarantee any form of compliance with constitutional principles, whatever we take them to be. It is, after all, random. In contrast, one can say, in favor of CJR, that it operates as an inducement to compliance. Even if, say, Congress cannot be sure that a proposed piece of legislation would be deemed unconstitutional by the Supreme Court, Congress is at least aware of the possibility that it might be. In other words, CJR operates like a threat looming large over the legislature and other governmental agencies, constantly reminding them, as it were, that whatever they do might come under review, and, if found unconstitutional, would be struck down. One can make an argument, therefore, that, even if the threat is often underspecified, it is an incentive that, generally speaking, in the long run, induces compliance and enhances good constitutional behavior, as it were. It makes other branches of government at least *try* to remain within their legitimate boundaries.

One obvious question here is: compliance with what? We have already noted that, if the constitutional text (broadly construed) is clear and determinate, cases do not tend to make it to the Supreme Court. And we saw that by employing something like RJR*, we can handle the issue of compliance in cases of clear and determinate constitutional prescriptions, where no reasonable argument can be made to understand the constitutional requirements one way rather than another. Now, of course, many constitutional scholars have argued that courts ought to apply or be able to figure out some underlying constitutional principles, even if they are not explicitly prescribed in the constitutional text.[15] I will not try to put pressure on this assumption here (I have done that elsewhere[16]). Even if you think there are some determinable answers to what counts as legitimate constitutional practices, CJR is not going to provide the incentive to comply with such principles. I other words, I do not believe that we have an answer to the question of "compliance with what?" but this is not the issue I am going to press here.

The main problem with the argument under consideration consists in its underlying assumption that legislators necessarily want to avoid constitutional challenges to their legislative acts. The assumption is that, if legislators know in advance that a piece of legislation they seek to enact is likely to be struck down as unconstitutional, they would refrain from trying to enact it. But that is just not necessarily, or even typically, the case; scholars have long pointed out that legislators often go ahead with an act they expect to be struck down as unconstitutional because it gives them the populist political benefit vis-à-vis their constituents without actually bearing the responsibility for the unwanted consequences of the proposed legislation.[17] Here is a schematic scenario: Suppose that there is strong popular support for a legal measure, say X, to be enacted. Suppose that X is a questionable measure from a constitutional perspective, one that might be struck down by the Supreme Court. If the legislators believe that voting for X is going to be popular with their constituents, even if they share the qualms about the desirability of X and/or its constitutionality, they would act rationally if they go ahead and enact X. If X is struck down by the Supreme Court, the legislators gain the popularity benefit from their constituency supporting X, while shifting responsibility for the measure's failure to the Court. If the Court upholds X, the legislators get both the popularity benefit and the legal-moral support of the Court, a kind of vindication that X is not unconstitutional after all. Either way, voting for X is a win-win situation from the legislators' perspective.

The general lesson from this is simple: Unconstitutionality does not necessarily operate as a sanction; it does not necessarily deter legislatures from enacting questionable measures. It is often to the contrary: Without CJR, legislatures would have to bear full responsibility for the ramifications of the legal measures they enact. With the constitutional guardianship of the Court, legislatures can behave irresponsibly by shifting the responsibility to the Court. Therefore, CJR does not typically induce constitutionally responsible behavior; often it does the exact opposite.

---

[15] See, for example, Waluchw (2007).

[16] See Marmor (2007).

[17] See, for example, Garrett and Vermeule (2001) and references there.

Of course, supporters of CJR may claim that such distorted incentives are the exception, not the rule. Most of the time, they would say, CJR provides the right incentives; it only fails to do so under some specific set of circumstances that are rather exceptional. But I seriously doubt that this optimistic view is also realistic. Remember that we could easily shift the argument from RJR to RJR*: If the unconstitutionality of a proposed piece of legislation is entirely on the surface, in no plausible legal doubt, legislatures would not have the political incentive to go ahead with the legislation. It is difficult to gain political traction with measures that are obviously and transparently unconstitutional. Populist pressure tends to build up around measures that seem constitutional to some, though not to others. Legislators tend to push for enactments that they can present as passing constitutional muster with some, even if strained, plausibility. Having the guardianship of the Supreme Court in the background in such cases only gives politicians the incentive to forge ahead, not to back down, for the reasons mentioned above.

In other words, perhaps unconstitutionality provides incentives to refrain from legislation in the clearest and most transparent cases. But RJR* would not apply there anyway. To make the argument for the preference of CJR to RJR*, proponents would have to show that, even when the constitutionality of a proposed legal measure is in some plausible doubt, the looming threat of the Court rendering the law unconstitutional – even if this threat is vague and uncertain – is likely to keep the legislature in check. I do not quite see what presumed incentive structure completes the argument here. A threat is a threat only if its materialization constitutes a setback for the relevant agents. It is difficult to see what setback to politicians' interests is in play here. If the constitutionality of the measure they seek to enact is in some doubt, why would they refrain from forging ahead?

There might be one type of case in which even a vague and uncertain threat of unconstitutionality provides some incentive to back down, namely, when the relevant measure forms part of a policy change the executive branches of the government seek to implement, and its obstruction by the Court would constitute a serious impediment to the implementation of the policy. In such cases, the looming threat of unconstitutionality should provide the government with an incentive to avoid the threat and modify its proposed policy accordingly. One should think that this would be the case particularly with policy changes that involve heavy costs. But, even then, it turns out to be difficult to generalize. The executive branches of government are not free of populist temptations. They may also have an incentive to take the risk of obstruction or even failure of the policy they wish to implement if they can blame it on the courts, particularly when the policy in question is very popular with the administration's constituency.[18]

[18]A good recent example is the enactment of the Affordable Care Act. No doubt legislators were fully aware of the fact that various aspects of the law are going to be constitutionally challenged in courts, as they are, yet it did not stop the legislature from enacting it. In fact, a crucial aspect of the law, where constitutional challenge could have been easily avoided by labeling the mandate to purchase insurance as a federal tax, the legislature opted for a much more problematic formulation and only for political reasons.

To sum up the argument from incentives, the main problem with the argument in favor of CJR is that unconstitutionality does not necessarily operate like the threat of a sanction that could deter political actors from succumbing to populist temptations. On the contrary, the more populist the temptation for a legislative act, the less likely that CJR's presumed deterrent effect would have any real impact. In terms of incentive structures, there is no advantage to CJR over RJR*.

2.5 Counter Majoritarianism

The intuitive appeal of the argument I try to articulate here crucially depends on the premise that a very significant random element is already present in the current system of CJR. Constitutional decisions of the Supreme Court reflect a certain distribution of ideologies espoused by justices on the Court at any given point in time; furthermore, given the appointment procedures and especially the justices' unlimited tenure on the Court, the particular distribution of moral, political and religious views on the Court is not necessarily representative of the views held by the general population.[19] Now, of course, supporters of CJR would claim that this is as it should be. After all, if the whole point of CJR is to act as a counterbalance to majority rule, curtailing the populist temptations of such procedures, the fact that the Court is not a representative institution is probably a good thing. But presumably it is a good thing only if it is not essentially random. If there is something both non-representative in the Court's constitution, and yet the likely outcomes of its decisions are random relative to the views and preferences of the majority, then we might as well have RJR, which at least satisfies a certain criterion of fairness. In short, my point is that the non-representative or non-majoritarian nature of the Court is not, by itself, a reason to prefer it over any other randomized non-majoritarian system; it has to be *non-majoritarian in the right way*.

So what makes the Court non-majoritarian in the right way? Some people might find it strange to think of the U.S. Supreme Court as a non-majoritarian institution when its decisions are reached by a regular majority vote. But we can bracket this concern for a while. Let us look at the kind of considerations invoked in support of the idea that decisions of the U.S. Supreme Court are likely to impose limits on majority rule in some sense that is preferable to a random decision procedure. Some of the familiar points we can dismiss quickly. One consideration often mentioned points to the legal expertise of the justices. Even if we do not doubt that the justices are ideologically divided and often follow partisan political views, they are, after all, great legal minds, endowed with a huge amount of expertise in the law. That is true, of course; I would be silly to deny that the justices are among the greatest legal experts in the country. But the problem is that most constitutional cases, certainly most that really matter, are not about technical legal issues. They pose moral-

[19] As a striking reminder, consider the fact that all the current justices on the U.S. Supreme Court are either Catholics or Jews. There is not a single Protestant justice on the Court.

political problems, and the dilemmas the Court faces are moral and political dilemmas, not legal ones. Expertise in the law does not make anyone an expert in morality, even if there is such a thing, which I doubt.[20]

Similar considerations apply to the deliberation process in the Court. One might think that the adversarial and intellectual nature of Court deliberations are conducive to reasoned decisions that are likely to result in sound decision. After all, justices are presented with a wide range of arguments from both sides, they get an opportunity to question the attorneys in oral hearings, they have to explain their decisions in a detailed and argumentative manner, and so on and so forth. There is a lot to be said in favor of the relatively intellectual nature of this process. But the truth is that the process makes very little difference. At the end of the day, there is a vote, and the vote, as we noted, almost invariably reflects the moral, political and religious convictions that the justices started with. I am sure that the process helps the justices and their clerks formulate their legal opinions in more reasoned and argumentative manner; it does not help them to see the world differently from what they are used to. If I am wrong about this, we should have seen many more cases in which constitutional decisions of individual justices surprise informed observers. But the fact is that surprises are very rare, and almost always relate to the decision of a swing voter on the Court, the justice who tends to be the ideological independent, so to speak. That does not seem to be anti-majoritarian in the right way; it is anti-majoritarian in a random way, depending on historical circumstances, such as which justice was appointed by whom, when and how long the justice hangs on to his or her job on the Court.

If we want to find some serious considerations that support the idea that the Court's nondemocratic character constitutes some anti-majoritarian limit on democratic procedures in the right way, we need to look at deeper structural factors. We need to look at the kind of constraints that the Supreme Court, as an institution, is likely to impose on majority rule regardless of its momentary, accidental, personal composition. Some rough and vague generalizations are possible; it is generally true that courts tend to be relatively conservative institutions. They tend to reflect elitist world views. Courts typically avoid extreme positions on most social and moral issues and, crucially, they tend not to fall too far out of line with the views and dispositions of the median voters in the country. Courts tend to remain within fairly secure boundaries of social consensus, not statistically and accurately so, for sure, but roughly and generally.[21] That is so mostly because their power base is social acquiescence, not brute force. Courts gain all the power they have from the perception of the population that the power they exercise is legitimate. They cannot act, at least for the long run, in ways that would antagonize their power base, which

[20] I have elaborated on this and similar arguments in greater detail in Marmor (2005b), ch 9.

[21] The very high likelihood that the US Supreme Court, conservative as it is, is expected to uphold a constitutional right to same-sex marriages later this year is a striking example of the point I make in the text. It shows how justices are willing to sacrifice even deeply held religious and moral conviction in the service of the court's long term social legitimacy.

is, essentially, popular acquiescence to their legitimacy.[22] This is evident in cases of national emergencies, when courts tend to rally to the flag as quickly and as unreflectively as everybody else in the country.

So where does all this lead? Well, it leads to the idea, a kind of reassurance, that, even if there is something random and arbitrary in the outcomes of constitutional cases of the Supreme Court, at least the boundaries are relatively secure. The chits are unlikely to fall far out of line with the national-cultural consensus. Let us suppose that this piece of armchair political science is true. The problem is that it would not support a good argument. If what makes CJR non-majoritarian in the right way is based on the premise that CJR is likely to reflect social-cultural consensus, at least generally and in the long run, as it were, then why do we need it to begin with? It would seem that we lost the underlying rationale of CJR, which is to put some limits on majority rule. Surely the ordinary democratic processes reflect social consensus with greater accuracy than the courts. In short, if the main justification for preferring CJR over RJR rests on the assumption that constitutional decisions are likely to reflect social consensus, the need for any form of constitutional judicial review is cast in serious doubt. Democratic legislative processes tend to do a much better job in that; they tend to be much more attuned to social and cultural trends in society than the courts.

2.6 Conclusion

Attentive readers may have noticed that I have said nothing so far about the role of CJR in protecting individual rights – in particular, the rights of vulnerable minorities. Surely if a serious consideration counts in favor of CJR, the protection of rights is one of them, perhaps the most important one. The question of whether CJR is more or less likely to protect the rights and interests of vulnerable minorities in society is a serious and difficult one and I will not deal with it here. Elsewhere, I raised some doubts about it, in some detail, and I will not repeat the argument here. Besides, as some philosophers have pointed out, the issue is, largely, an empirical one. It needs to be examined, on the basis of historical evidence, whether CJR has done a good job of protecting the rights of vulnerable minorities in society, or not. And history does not seem to side with the supporters of constitutionalism in this respect, at least not evidently so.[23] But, again, I will not go into this here. My argument in this paper is not meant to provide an overall assessment of the arguments for and against constitutional judicial review. It is only meant to suggest that the

[22] You might think that the infamous Lochner era is a counter-example. To some extent it is, of course, but not entirely. First, keep in mind that the Court's rulings in this period represented the deeply entrenched ideology of the capitalist elite in the U.S.; it was not out of touch with social realities. Secondly, bear in mind that the Lochner era lasted only a couple of decades, eventually succumbing to the progressive movements that came to dominate U.S. political reality.

[23] See Waldron (1999) and Marmor (2005b).

counter-majoritarian rationale of CJR is seriously wanting. The current system of CJR is fraught with arbitrary elements, to an extent that makes the system only marginally better, if at all, compared with an overtly and blatantly randomized system. As I warned from the start, this is not a conclusive argument against CJR, but it should give us some pause.

Acknowledgment I am grateful to Leticia Morales, Alex Sarch, and the participants of the Legal Theory Workshop McGill University for helpful comments on earlier drafts.

References

Garret, Elizabeth, and Adrian Vermeule. 2001. Institutional design of a thayerian congress. *Duke Law Review* 50: 1277–1333.

Marmor, Andrei. 2005a. Should like cases be treated alike? *Legal Theory* 11: 27–38.

Marmor, Andrei. 2005b. *Interpretation and legal theory*, 2nd ed. Oxford: Hart Publishing.

Marmor, Andrei. 2007. Are constitutions legitimate? In *Law in the age of pluralism*, 89–123. Oxford: Oxford University Press.

Marmor, Andrei. 2010. The ideal of the rule of law. In *A companion to philosophy of law and legal theory*, 2nd ed, ed. Dennis Patterson, 666–674. Malden: Blackwell.

Marmor, Andrei. 2014. *The language of law*. Oxford: Oxford University Press.

Tushnet, Mark. 1999. *Taking the constitution away from courts*. Princeton: Princeton University Press.

Waldron, Jeremy. 1999. *Law and disagreement*. Oxford: Oxford University Press.

Waluchow, W.J. 2007. *A common law theory of judicial review: The living tree*. Cambridge: Cambridge University Press.

Chapter 3
On the Difficulty to Ground the Authority of Constitutional Courts: Can Strong Judicial Review Be Morally Justified?

Thomas Bustamante

Abstract A theory of authority has important implications for justifying the institutions of judicial review. In this paper, I attempt to take part in the current debates about the authority of constitutional courts, with a view to showing some of the difficulties of systems of strong judicial review in constitutional democracies. On the one hand, I discuss two theses put forward by Joseph Raz, the Pre-Emptive Thesis and the Normal Justification Thesis. On the other hand, I try to explain how the authority of a constitutional court's decision looks like in the contexts provided by Raz's two theses, as well as how a theoretical account of legal authority might provide the basis for a normative critique of the systems of strong judicial review. In short, I hold that the Pre-Emptive Thesis does not offer a clear picture of the authority of law in general, since it does not provide a complete explanation of the argumentative character of law and the interpretive dimension of legal reasoning. Nonetheless, I think that it is able to explain the authority of constitutional courts in systems of strong judicial review, since at least some of their decisions cut off further deliberation about the validity of certain statutes and have the pre-emptive status that Raz assigns to the law in general. This is not the case, as I intend to show, in systems of weak judicial review, where the decisions of the court lack pre-emptive force and the legal issues are open to further interpretive activity by citizens and institutions. This distinction has a practical import, since even if the instrumental justification for legal authority provided by Raz's 'Normal Justification Thesis' is too weak to justify the pre-emptive authority of strong judicial review, it might turn out to be enough to provide a moral justification for a system of weak judicial review.

T. Bustamante (✉)
Universidade Federal de Minas Gerais, Avenida João Pinheiro, 100,
Belo Horizonte, Minas Gerais 30.130-180, Brazil
e-mail: tbustamante@ufmg.br

T. Bustamante, B.G. Fernandes (eds.), *Democratizing Constitutional Law*,
Law and Philosophy Library 113, DOI 10.1007/978-3-319-28371-5_3

3.1 Introduction

A theory of authority has important implications for justifying the institutions of judicial review. In this paper, I attempt to take part in the current debates about the authority of constitutional courts, with a view to showing some of the difficulties of systems of strong judicial review in constitutional democracies.

On the one hand, I discuss two theses put forward by Joseph Raz, the Pre-Emptive Thesis and the Normal Justification Thesis. On the other hand, I try to explain how the authority of a constitutional court's decision looks like in the contexts provided by Raz's two theses, as well as how a theoretical account of legal authority might provide the basis for a normative critique of the systems of strong judicial review.

In short, I hold that the Pre-Emptive Thesis does not offer a clear picture of the authority of law in general, since it does not provide a complete explanation of the argumentative character of law and the interpretive dimension of legal reasoning. Nonetheless, I think that it is able to explain the authority of constitutional courts in systems of strong judicial review, since at least some of their decisions cut off further deliberation about the validity of certain statutes and have the pre-emptive status that Raz assigns to the law in general. This is not the case, as I intend to show, in systems of weak judicial review, where the decisions of the court lack pre-emptive force and the legal issues are open to further interpretive activity by citizens and institutions. This distinction has a practical import, since even if the instrumental justification for legal authority provided by Raz's 'Normal Justification Thesis' is too weak to justify the pre-emptive authority of strong judicial review, it might turn out to be enough to provide a moral justification for a system of weak judicial review.

I expect to be able to demonstrate, in the final section, that the authority of a constitutional court only can be justified in an instrumental way, and that this justification fails to provide a solid basis for strong judicial review.

My argument will take the following steps. In the second part of the essay, I consider the 'nature' of the authority of constitutional courts. I begin with an analysis, in Sect. 3.2.1, of Raz's understanding of legal authority. This analysis is followed, in Sect. 3.2.2, by an appreciation of Greenberg's criticism against the 'Standard Picture' of jurisprudence, of which Raz is probably the most important exponent, and a short overview of Dworkin's interpretive theory of law. Section 3.2.3 explores, in the same direction as the previous one, the relations between legal argumentation and the character of law, with a view to providing general guidelines for choosing between the conceptions of legal authority presented in Sects. 3.2.1 and 3.2.2. Section 3.2.4, at last, considers the authority of constitutional courts and the varieties of explanations available to understand the decisions that strike down a particular statute on the basis of its unconstitutionality. These explanations are important here because I will hold that any explanation available for the nature of the authority of constitutional courts has significant implications for the legitimacy of these institutions. In the third part, on the other hand, I focus on the justification of legal authority and on the important task of providing the grounds for the legitimacy of judicial review. While the first section of this part (3.3.1) assesses Raz's Normal Justification Thesis, the second section (3.3.2) comments on the procedural theories that criticize this thesis and attempts to provide an egalitarian justification of 'democratic authority'. The third section (3.3.3), in turn, deals with the difficulties that arise when one takes up the task of constructing a moral justification for the authority of constitutional courts. This is followed by Sect. 3.3.4, which deals with the specific moral burdens that fall upon the strong systems of judicial review. The last section (3.3.5), finally, provides the only ground that I believe to be helpful to justify the practice of judicial review, which can be found in one of the arguments presented by Dworkin in his defense of judicial review. Along with Waldron, I argue that Dworkin has a good argument, but that it is at pains to vindicate a system of strong judicial review. The authority of judicial review, as I maintain in the concluding section, is much easier to justify in a system of weak courts that lack final authority to decide about the validity of a legislative provision.

3.2 The Nature of the Authority of Constitutional Courts

3.2.1 The Mainstream Understanding of the Nature of Legal Authority

According to the mainstream jurisprudential position about the nature of law, one of the necessary and distinctive features of a legal system is that it both possesses *de facto* or effective authority and either claims or is believed to have *de iure* or legitimate authority.

The kind of authority that we are considering here is of the practical, rather than theoretical, type. Practical authorities do not merely affect one's judgment by giving him or her a reason to believe in something, as theoretical authorities do, but provide instead a reason to *act* in a certain way (Raz 1994a, 211).

The basic idea is that judgments of legal authorities provide reasons for action of a special type, which are regarded as 'content-independent'. As Hebert Hart has put it, a reason is 'content-independent' when it purports to 'function as a reason independently of the nature or character of the actions to be done' (Hart 1990, 101). If an authority commands me to act in a certain way, I need not to assess whether her judgment is correct or whether she is acting on the right reasons, since the directive of the authority replaces the first-order reasons that I might have to determine the action to be performed. When a policeman signals for me to stop at a crossroad, it is irrelevant whether I believe that the way is clear and I could safely cross the road at a given time. The fact that he commands me to stop provides a reason for me to do it. Content-independent reasons, therefore, are supposed to be reasons 'simply because they have been issued and not because they direct subjects to perform actions that are independently justifiable' (Shapiro 2002, 389).

Hence, 'authoritative directives are unlike ordinary reasons in that they are not only reasons to act in accordance with their content, but also reasons to pre-empt other reasons for action' (Shapiro 2002, 404). The classical example to explain this pre-emptive character of an authoritative directive is the case of two people who refer a certain dispute to an arbitrator. By accepting the authority of the arbitrator, the disputants agree to abide by her decision, investing her with the right to settle the dispute and replace the balancing of reasons that they would otherwise need to perform in order to determine the course of action to be followed in the case at hand.

According to Raz, there are two important features in this arbitration example. First, though the arbitrator's decision is a reason for action, it is related to 'other reasons which apply to the case'. It is not merely a reason to be added to these other reasons, but rather based on them, 'to sum them up and to reflect their outcome' (Raz 1986, 42). Because the arbitrator's decision depends on these other reasons that apply to the disputants, Raz call these latter reasons 'dependent reasons'. The connection between the authoritative directives and the reasons in which they are grounded is explained by the Dependence Thesis, which says that 'all authoritative directives should be based on reasons which already independently apply to the subjects of the directives and are relevant to their action in the circumstances covered by the directive'. (Raz 1986, 47).

This brings us to the Pre-Emptive Thesis, which is Raz's second and most distinctive contention about authoritative pronouncements. 'The arbitrator's decision', for Raz, 'is also meant to replace the reasons on which it depends'. In agreeing to obey her decision, the disputants 'agreed to follow her judgment of the balance of reasons rather than their own'(Raz 1986, 42). The arbitrator's decision is a protected or pre-emptive reason because it will 'settle for them what to do' and displace the dependant reasons on which it is based (Raz 1986, 42). To say that the law has authority means that its existence is a protected reason for performing an action, i.e. 'a reason for conforming action and for excluding conflicting considerations' (Raz 2009b, 29).

The law enjoys effective authority, thus, 'if its subjects or some of them regard its existence as a protected reason for conformity' (Raz 2009b, 29). Though this feature presupposes a positivistic account of law, insofar as the content of a legal norm must be ascertained without resource to a moral argument, it also establishes an important connection between the concepts of *de facto* or effective authority and *de jure* or legitimate authority. To have effective authority the law must both 'claim that it possesses legitimate authority' and be 'capable of possessing legitimate authority' (Raz 1994a, 215). The explanation of effective authority requires that of legitimate authority, since a person has effective authority 'only if the people over whom he has that authority regard him as a legitimate authority' (Raz 2009b, 28).

One can notice here an important connection between law and morality, given that the effective authority of the law depends at least in part on its ability to ground the claim to authority that it raises or to convince the people subject to its authority that its normative power to enact content-independent directives is morally justified.

Furthermore, Raz is convinced that the law facilitates social coordination and 'conformity with reason', inasmuch as it has a *moral task* that, put abstractly, 'is to secure a situation whereby moral goals which, given the current social situation in the country whose law it is, would be unlikely to be achieved without it, and whose achievement by the law is not counter-productive, are realized' (Raz 2009a, 178).

Nevertheless, this necessary connection between law and morality does not affect the Separability Thesis, which is the core commitment of legal positivism. In spite of the fact that Raz acknowledges that legal systems have a moral point, and that sometimes these systems may 'include moral language in constitutional norms' and allow judges to engage in moral argumentation while making validity decisions, the Pre-Emptive Thesis entails a strong version of the positivistic Social Sources Thesis, which argues that law 'consists only of authoritative positivist considerations', identifiable 'without resort to further moral argument' (Raz 1994b, 205–6).

One of the distinctive functions of the law, therefore, would be its 'settlement function', which is considered essential to the important coordination function assigned to the legal system. In this perspective, the law 'provides the benefits of authoritative settlement, as well as the related but still content-independent benefits of inducing socially beneficial cooperative behavior and providing solutions to Prisoner's Dilemmas and other problems of coordination' (Alexander and Schauer 1997, 1371).[1]

3.2.2 *Off the Mainstream: Greenberg and Dworkin on the Authority of Law*

Of the many comments made on Raz's Pre-Emptive Thesis, there is at least one objection that requires our attention now, which is posed by Gerald Postema. Postema thinks that the Pre-Emptive Thesis is appealing while we consider the application of a statute, but is in trouble to square with the sort of reasoning that is required by a typical common lawyer. Common law decisions 'establish law in the course of adjudicating particular decisions', in such a way that the content of the *ratio decidendi* 'must be extracted from the recorded opinion of the precedent', in a reasoning process that 'depends heavily upon the interpreter's grasp of general

[1]The main argument from these authors, with regard to the law's coordination function, is borrowed from Gerald Postema, who believes that 'it is a defining feature of the law that it channels social behavior not by altering the social or natural environment of action or by manipulating the (nonrational) psychological determinants of action; rather, it relies on rules which guide actions and structure social interaction, thereby providing rational agents with reasons by which they can direct their own behavior' (Postema 1982, 187).

principles of common law and a shared sense of reasonableness and fairness' that inevitably rests on 'evaluative' or 'moral' argument (Postema 1996, 95–6).[2]

If this picture is correct, then the theory of authority under consideration might be at odds with the typical reasoning of common law. How could a defendant of Raz's Pre-Emptive Thesis respond to this? The typical reply would be to argue that in such cases the court's *rationale* is unsettled, so that a subsequent court is 'creating', instead of 'applying', an authoritative legal statement. In cases where the law is unsettled the judge would have to base her decision on moral or extra-legal considerations.[3] Legal authorities, in hard cases, would be under a 'legal obligation to apply extra-legal standards', just like a lawyer is legally bound to apply foreign rules in a case involving parties from different jurisdictions (Shapiro 2011, 272).

As a consequence, Raz believes that legal reasoning implies more than simply 'applying' the law. When the law is underdetermined, the task of legal officials is to reason 'in accordance with the law', which involves more than merely 'establishing the law' (Raz 1994c, 332–3). Legal reasoning, in this sense, 'is not simply reasoning about what legal norms already apply to the case', but also a reasoning that has 'valid legal norms among its major or operative premises', and 'combines them nonredundantly in the same argument with moral or other merit-based premises' (Gardner 2001, 215–6).

Thus, the Razian theory of authority entails a model of *adjudication* that is not always at odds with other theories of adjudication that adopt a very different view on the character of authoritative legal statements. Perhaps an example will illustrate this point. We can consider here one of the cases that Ronald Dworkin offered to respond to Hart's Postscript to *The Concept of Law*, which concerns marked-shared liability of the producers of a drug, the consumption of which has caused someone to acquire a serious medical condition unknown at the time in which it was commercialized (Dworkin 2006, 143).[4]

How would Raz and Dworkin suggest that this case should be handled by a court of justice? In the light of the theoretical gap between these two authors, one could expect significant differences between the reasoning processes of the defendants of these two different points of view. Let me verify, however, the possibility of a connection between those different conceptions of legality. According to Dworkin, judges 'should try to identify general principles that underlie and justify the settled

[2] I will leave open for the moment whether this point can be extended beyond common law reasoning, as MacCormick purports to do when he ascribes an arguable character to the law and sustains that the political ideal of the Rule of Law implies, contrary to the idea of authoritative settlement, that the legal domain is the 'locus of argumentation'. See MacCormick (2005).

[3] By accepting the Pre-Emptive Thesis, one has to accept that the law is 'settled' only when legal authorities provide its solution. In such cases, for Raz, 'judges are typically said to apply the law, and since it is source-based, its application involves technical, legal skills in reasoning from the sources and do not call for moral acumen' (Raz 2009b, 49–50). But if a legal question, on the other hand, is 'not answered by standards deriving from legal sources', then it 'lacks a legal answer' and the judge's decision 'rely at least partly on moral and other extra-legal considerations' (Raz 2009b, 50).

[4] For a real case, see Sindell v. Abott Labs., 607 p. 2d 924, 935–38 (1980).

law of product liability, and then apply those principles to this case' (Dworkin 2006, 143).[5] The arguments that should be binding upon the judges, therefore, are those that stem from the principles of political morality that provide the best possible justification for the legal system, i.e. which provide an arrangement that shows this system in its best light and makes it the best it can be (Dworkin 1986). Would a Razian judge attempt to do anything different?

In spite of Raz's strict account of authoritative legal statements, I do not believe that a Razian judge would do an entirely different job. She would almost certainly not hold that in a case of market-shared liability the law was 'settled', and would probably resort to extra-legal (moral) considerations in order to determine the right principle to be adopted in the case at hand. The judge would be no longer applying, but rather *interpreting* the law. And once we consider Raz's general account on interpretation it becomes clear that the interpretive attitude will not deviate very much from Dworkin's perspective. An interpretation, for Raz, should not always be understood as a 'retrieval' of an original meaning. It can instead be seen as 'an explanation of the work interpreted which explains why it is important, to the extent that it is' (Raz 1995, 170–171).[6] Though the process of *legal* interpretation is informed by the ideas of authority and continuity, there is also a room for equity considerations and for innovation in the interpretation of legal sources. Legal interpretation should be both backward-looking, aiming to secure fidelity to the law and continuity, and forward-looking, giving weight to other moral considerations: 'courts whose decisions determine the fortunes of many people must base them on morally sound considerations' (Raz 2009a, 354–5).

Though there may be some specific differences in these approaches to adjudication and interpretation, it is not implausible to say that in both cases moral considerations determine the content of the decision and the formation of the precedent that will be referred to by other courts in the future. One could wonder, thus, why Raz and Dworkin diverge so intensely about legal authority, if they both advocate theories of adjudication that have so much in common. Why is that so?

---

[5] Dworkin continues: 'They might find, as the drug companies insisted, that the principle that no one is liable for harm that neither he nor anyone for whom he is responsible can be shown to have caused is so firmly embedded in precedent that (the Plaintiff) must therefore be turned away with no remedy. Or they might find, on the contrary, considerable support for a rival principle – that those who have profited from some enterprise must bear the costs of that enterprise as well, for example – that would justify the novel market-share remedy. (...) *Everything depends on the best answer to the difficult question of which set or principles provides the best justification for the law in this area as a whole*' (Dworkin 2006, 144).

[6] The general picture of Raz's views on interpretation can be explained thus: 'An interpretation is an explanation of the work interpreted which highlights some of its elements and points to connections and inter-relations among its parts, and between them and other aspects of the world, so that (1) it covers adequately the significant aspects of the work interpreted, ... and is not inconsistent with any aspect of the work; (2) it explains the aspects of the work it focuses on; and (3) in doing the above it elucidates what is important in the work, and accounts – to the extent that it is possible – for whatever reasons there are for paying attention to the work as a work of art of its kind. *The more successful it is in meeting these criteria, and the more important the meaning it justifiably attributes to the work, the better the interpretation*' (Raz 1995, 171).

I believe that Mark Greenberg has a persuasive answer for this question, and that such answer helps us devise an alternative account to understand both the authority of *law*, in general, and the authority of *constitutional courts*, in particular. Greenberg believes that Raz and the mainstream approaches to jurisprudence are implicitly committed to a widely accepted, yet often unarticulated, view that the law is some kind of 'ordinary linguistic meaning or mental content', which can be ascertained by a model that might be called the *'command paradigm'*. This conception, as Greenberg puts it, holds that 'what is authoritatively pronounced becomes a legal norm – or, equivalently, becomes legally valid – simply because it was authoritatively pronounced' (Greenberg 2011, 44).

What explains the popularity of the Standard Picture, for Greenberg, is the fact that most of the scholars in contemporary jurisprudence share what he designates as the Explanatory Directness Thesis, which holds that the authoritativeness of the pronouncement is (1) '*prior* in the order of explanation of the obtaining of the legal norm' and (2) '*independent* of the pronouncement's (specific) content and consequences', in a way that (3) there are no explanatory intermediates between the authoritative pronouncement's being made and the norm's obtaining' (Greenberg 2011, 46).

The critics of the Standard Picture, in turn, think that it is wrong to say that the validity of a norm is established in a single moment by a single authoritative enactment, in the form of the Explanatory Directness Thesis. Greenberg offers two examples of general conceptions of legality which depart in a significant way from the Standard Picture of legal authority.

The first conception is Dworkin's model of 'Law as Integrity'. This theory is based on a normative model of community that sees the polity as a 'community of principles', i.e. a political community in which people share the assumption that their lives are 'governed by common principles, not just rules hammered out in political compromise' (Dworkin 1986, 211). The law of such community must 'be both made and seen, so far as it is possible, to express a single, coherent scheme of justice and fairness in the right relation' (Dworkin 1986, 219). While establishing the content of the law, legislators and adjudicators must adopt the best constructive interpretation of such principles of political morality that justify the legal system as a whole. As Greenberg summarizes, the content of the law 'bears a less straightforward relation to the content of legal texts than it does on the Standard Picture' (Greenberg 2011, 56), since it must coincide with 'the best constructive interpretation of past legal decisions' (Dworkin 1986, 262). The content of the law, therefore, is itself *dependant on interpretation*.[7]

The second conception is Greenberg's own view that the content of law 'consists of a certain general and enduring part of the *moral profile*' of a given community. A society's moral profile, on this account, consists of 'all of the moral obligations, powers, permissions, privileges and so on that obtain in that society' (Greenberg

[7] At this point, Greenberg stresses that on Dworkin's account 'there is necessarily some vagueness in the initial specification of the legal practices because which practices are relevant one is ultimately itself the outcome of interpretation' (Greenberg 2011, 56, note 18).

2011, 56–7). Greenberg calls his view the Dependence View. He claims that 'the relevant part of the moral profile is that which comes to obtain in certain characteristic ways', and that 'the relation between the content of the law and the content of legal utterances is, roughly speaking, that the content of the law is a certain aspect of the impact of legal utterances (and other actions) on obligations, powers, and so on' (Greenberg 2011, 57).

Both Dworkin and Greenberg depart from the Standard Picture because neither of them is convinced that the law's authority comes to be with a content-independent enactment. The identification of authoritative enactments, for Dworkin, is merely the 'pre-interpretive' stage of legal reasoning (Dworkin 1986, 65–6). When a legislative enactment adds something to the content of law, it does not do that by simply issuing a content-independent directive that displaces the moral reasons that one may have to act in a certain way. On the contrary, it supplements the legal practice by altering the set of principles that 'constitutes the best total justification' of this practice (Greenberg 2011, 59). By the same token, on Greenberg's Dependence View the legislative enactment of a statute may also add something to the law, but even when it does so 'the explanation will be that the enactment changes the relevant circumstances (described in the moral profile), thus changing what people are morally required or permitted to do' (Greenberg 2011, 59).

There are, however, relevant differences between Dworkin's model of Law as Integrity and Greenberg's Moral Impact Theory of Law. Whereas Dworkin upholds that the law is constituted by the set of principles that best justifies legal practices and legal institutions, Greenberg thinks that the law is the 'moral *impact* or *effect*' of the actions of these institutions, i.e., 'the moral obligations that obtain in light of those actions' (Greenberg 2014, 1301). The content of the law, for him, is not equivalent to the principles that bind legal institutions, but is rather the set of moral obligations that result from the action of legal officials. The important question, for Greenberg, is not what morally justifies the statute, but rather 'what is morally required as a consequence of the lawmaking actions' (Greenberg 2014, 1303). Authoritative pronouncements, therefore, change a society's moral profile only in an indirect way. They do not create obligations directly, but rather 'change our moral obligations by changing the relevant circumstances' (Greenberg 2014, 1310).

For the argument developed in this paper, however, Greenberg's criticism on the Standard Picture is more important than his own view about the nature of law and its implications for legal interpretation, insofar as my worry about Raz's position is motivated not only by the fact that it provides an unattractive explanation for how the law comes to be or how the content of the law is ascertained, but also by its failure to account for the distinctively argumentative character of law.

Raz's method for asserting the validity of law is in trouble to provide a general account of how the legal system works, since it focuses exclusively on how individual enactments arise and assumes that the linguistic content of a legal provision is instantly created by a single utterance of its author. According to Raz, 'to establish the content of the statute, all one need to do is to establish that the enactment took place, and what is says. To do that one needs little more than knowledge of

English (including technical legal English), and of the events which took place in Parliament on a few occasions' (Raz 1994a, 221).

This general view on legal authority, according to Dworkin, would be an 'eccentric conception' of authority, which is guilty of a 'heroic artificiality' and contradictory with common sense (Dworkin 2006, 209). For Dworkin, Raz does not take seriously both (1) the *theoretical disagreements* about the *grounds of law* – i.e., the disagreements about the law's foundations or the meta-propositions that make a legal proposition true or false – and (2) the law's dependency upon interpretation. The problem of Raz's account is not merely that the content of the law is equated with the content of an authoritative utterance, but that Raz believes that the law can be ascertained in a non-argumentative way.

I fear, however, that this is not the main concern of Greenberg's objection to the Standard Picture. Whereas Dworkin appeals to a normative ideal of 'integrity' that requires judges to engage in a constructive interpretation with a view to making the law the best it can be, in the light of the institutional history and the basic principles of political morality underlying the legal system, Greenberg's conception of law is not committed to legal constructivism. The content of the law can be ascertained in a different way. To determine how a legislator alters the content of the moral profile, the Moral Impact Theory 'makes no appeal to Dworkinian interpretation' (Greenberg 2014, 1301). On the contrary, it assumes that 'working out the content of the law is *not* a genuinely hermeneutic enterprise', and involves instead a 'straightforward moral reasoning about the moral consequences of various facts and circumstances' (Greenberg 2014, 1302).[8]

I will assume, therefore, that Dworkin's position is a more promising candidate for replacing the Standard Picture of legal authority and offering a powerful challenge to Raz's account of the authority of law.

3.2.3 The Argumentative Character of the Law

In the debate between Raz, Greenberg and Dworkin, I am more likely to agree with the latter. Dworkin's view that legal authority does not antecede, but rather is established by, interpretation offers a sound explanation for legal authority because it draws a broad picture that is not at odds with the legal practice and, most importantly, because it provides a plausible explanation for the distinctively argumentative character of law. This feature was well captured by Neil MacCormick's institutional approach to the practice of law (MacCormick 2005, 13). According to MacCormick, as a normative order, 'and as a practical one', the law is 'in continuous need of adaptation to current practical problems' (MacCormick 2005, 6). The

[8] I thank Mark Greenberg for pointing out to me in oral conversation that, because of these differences with Dworkin, the Moral Impact Theory cannot be used to support the point that I am trying to make in Sect. 3.2.4 bellow.

recognition of the Rule of Law as a political ideal implies the recognition of law's domain as the '*locus* of argumentation' (MacCormick 2005, 13).

In this interpretation, the relative indeterminacy of law is not something to be regretted. It has to do with the ideal of the Rule of Law and with the procedural rules of argumentation that are presupposed in the institutional structure that it provides. The Rule of Law itself implies a certain degree of indeterminacy in the legal system (MacCormick 2005, 26).

If this interpretation of the political ideal of the Rule of Law is correct, legal argumentation 'carry implications for the concept of law' that can no longer be reconciled with most forms of legal positivism (Bertea 2008).[9]

The idea of an argumentative character of law, however, needs to be further specified. The core point is not only that law consists in a social practice that is sensitive to reasons, or that legal rulings depend on a critical appraisal of arguments pro and against a solution to a legal problem. This feature alone is plainly consistent with a positivistic understanding of the sources of law. A Hartian positivist, for instance, will necessarily hold that the internal point of view requires from legal officials a 'critical reflective attitude' towards the rule of recognition. But no legal positivist denies that this commitment to the rule of recognition is consistent with a lot of disagreement about whether the requirements of the rule of recognition are satisfied in a given case, and many (if not most) legal positivists claim that their accounts of legality can explain even the kind of disagreement that Dworkin classified as 'theoretical', in the sense that it is a disagreement about the 'grounds' or the foundations of law. One of the positivistic replies to Dworkin could be, for instance, that the rule of recognition remains a plausible explanation both for the identification of legal rules and for law's capacity to guide social action even if there are some exceptional and specific cases in which legal officials disagree over the criteria of legality allegedly laid down in the rule of recognition, or over how such criteria should be interpreted.[10]

---

[9] One of the implications of this rapport between legal argumentation and the very idea of law, for Bertea, is that MacCormick moves toward 'the same legal paradigm' as Dworkin's jurisprudence (Bertea 2008, 13ff).

[10] This strategy is pursued, for instance, by Matthew Kramer and Jules Coleman. In his defense of Hartian legal positivism, Kramer argues that there is no reason to think that the presence of theoretical disagreements about the meaning of the conventional rule of recognition undermines the possibility of that law-identifying resource: 'Legal conventions provide the opportunities for disputations concerning possible modifications to the conventions themselves. They render legitimate the questioning of their own bearings, and provide *fora* where such questioning can be carried on' (Kramer 1999, 149). In a similar way, Coleman thinks that positivism is immune from the Dworkinian challenge of theoretical disagreements: 'Dworkin cuts no ice against the conventionality thesis: there is no reason to think that a social rule cannot also be controversial in some of its applications' (Coleman 2001, 117). By the same token, Marmor argues that Dworkinian disagreements about criteria of legality among judges are always in the margins, and almost never go all the way down to the core of the rule of recognition. According to his position, 'there is an inherent limit to how much disagreement about criteria of legality it makes sense to attribute to judges, because the judges' own role as institutional players is constituted by those same rules that they allegedly disagree about' (Marmor 2009, 162–3). A slightly different point is made by Scott

The idea that the law is argumentative becomes more important when one considers the *way* in which the law must be an argumentative practice. For Dworkin, the basic idea is that the social practice of law is *distinctively* argumentative, in the sense that participants of legal discourses must take up an 'interpretive' attitude towards the law – recognizing that it has a *point* or purpose that makes it *valuable* as such, and constructing it in the way that makes it the best it can be, on the basis of a critical appraisal of this point. To understand the law it is not enough to identify its sources; on the contrary, one must engage in a constructive interpretation of this practice. For Dworkin, therefore, the intentionality of law – or its *point* – is grounded on political-philosophical values, or, in other words, on a certain conception of justice. As Ronaldo Macedo explains, Dworkin thinks that 'legal practices only achieve the sense that they actually have in the society that we live insofar as they satisfy a requirement of legitimacy' (Macedo Júnior 2013).

I am assuming, therefore, that the distinctively argumentative character of law entails the kind of interpretive attitude that Dworkin is arguing for. If this is true, the fact that the law is the outcome of an interpretation is *not* the only consequence of the argumentative character of law. Further from being dependent on a constructive interpretation, legal propositions, for Dworkin, remain *open to further interpretive activity* in the so-called 'post-interpretive' stage of legal reasoning. Hence, legal propositions must be open to new interpretive circles.

For this reason, I think that Raz is wrong to suppose that the law is to be 'found' in a previously determinate set of social sources. The validity of a law cannot be merely a question of fact, but rather needs to be at least in a significant part a matter of argument. The law is hardly ever 'settled' and its rules are ordinarily defeasible, for they are inevitably subjected to a constructive interpretation that might lead to revisions and even to exceptions in their operative conditions (MacCormick 2005, 241).

Like the late MacCormick, I am convinced that Dworkin's perspective of Law as Integrity is at least generally correct because it explains not only how the law becomes binding in practice, but also because it provides a better account of the argumentative character of law. On Dworkin's theory of law, the very idea of community depends on an interpretive understanding of law and legal practices. Instead of a social fact that can be ascertained by a neutral observer, the law 'is not exhausted by a catalogue of rules and principles'. It is more specifically 'an interpretive, self-reflective attitude that makes *each citizen* (who is also an interpreter) responsible for imagining what his society's public commitments to principle are, and what these commitments require in new circumstances' (Dworkin 1986, 413).

Nonetheless, in spite of the attractiveness of this interpretive and argumentative understanding of law, I am convinced that it is not fully capable of acknowledging

---

Shapiro, who thinks that Dworkinian theoretical disagreements need not to be seen as concerning the 'grounds' of law or the fundamental criteria of legal validity, since one can easily translate them into disagreements about the interpretive methodology to be adopted in the case at hand (Shapiro 2011, 282–306). I have disputed Shapiro's attempt to reconfigure all theoretical disagreements as meta-interpretive disagreements in Bustamante (2012, 506–7).

the 'essence' of the law and providing, as Finnis has said, *'the one feature* used to characterize and to explain descriptively the whole subject-matter' (Finnis 2011, 6). Dworkin's explanation of legal authority will probably leave out a relevant set of 'peripheral cases' (Finnis 2011, 11). Yet, in spite of the incapacity to establish an 'univocal meaning' of theoretical terms, it is interesting because it is fit to explain the law's practical purpose and offers an account of the 'central cases' – or, as Aristotle has put it, the 'focal meaning' – of the institutions of law and legal reasoning (Finnis 2011, 9–11).

What is it, then, that Dworkin's approach to legal authority is missing?

As I will argue in the following section, it does provide reasonable explanations about how the 'law in general' operates, or at least how it is supposed to operate, but it fails to explain in a fully comprehensive way the authority of constitutional courts.

3.2.4 On the Authority of Constitutional Courts

I have been arguing that the distinctively argumentative character of law poses a serious challenge to Raz and the mainstream account of legal authority. As a rule, Dworkin's interpretivism is probably a better explanation of how legal systems operate than Raz's Pre-Emptive model of authoritative legal enactments.

I intend to argue, in this session, that there is one exception to this partial conclusion. This exception is constituted by the cases where a constitutional court holds that a formally correct legal enactment is unconstitutional and refuses to enforce it in the situation at hand. In systems of strong judicial review, where courts have formal authority to strike down a particular legal statute, this power is regarded as part of the ordinary process of application of law (Waldron 2006, 1354).[11]

My point is that Dworkin is probably right about the way in which the law is built and applied in the central cases, but perhaps not in a peripheral case where a constitutional court annuls an act of parliament that was duly enacted and followed the legislative procedure established in the Constitution. In these cases, the Razian conception of authority provides a clearer explanation of how the court's authoritative legal pronouncement operates in the case at hand.

In these cases, the court's decision does not limit itself to offering a 'constructive interpretation' of the law, as Dworkin believes. On the contrary, its pronouncement is *deconstructive* in the sense that it does not merely specify a principle or add up a new norm to be considered in the future cases, but rather invalidates by a single authoritative pronouncement the majority decision reached by a legislative enactment. Constitutional courts in such cases provide, indeed, *exclusionary reasons* in Raz's sense, pre-empting the dependent reasons that one might have to comply with the enactment of the legislature. The court's ruling acts as an exclusionary reason

[11] In a system of 'weak' judicial review, on the other hand, 'courts may scrutinize legislation for its conformity to individual rights but they may not decline to apply it (or moderate its application) simply because rights would otherwise be violated' (Waldron 2006, 1355).

because it provides a reason to 'refrain from acting' on the balancing of reasons undertaken by the legislature.[12] After the court pronounces the unconstitutionality of an act, the general normative issue is no longer 'arguable' or open to new arguments and interpretations.[13]

This assertion may appear to some as inconsistent with the reservations that I had against the Razian picture of common law reasoning while I was discussing Postema's objections to this account.[14] Common law reasoning, as I argued above, is a typical form of interpretive legal reasoning. Though the practice of *stare decisis* implies that the case law creates a legal obligation to abide by a previous decision, common law courts 'do not treat the formulations of law in earlier cases as exhaustive formulations, but as formulations which were *sufficiently* exhaustive *in the context in which they were made*' (Simpson 1961, 165). Such formulations, as A W Simpson argues, are such that the case law is 'always open to latter courts to introduce exceptions' which are based, at least in part, on a *moral* justification for distinguishing the case at hand (Simpson 1961, 165).[15] Instead of appealing to pre-emptive reasons, 'arguments (in common law reasoning) to the effect that this or that is the law are commonly supported by reference to ideas which are not specifically legal' (Simpson 1973, 87).

The similarities between common law and constitutional adjudication may lead, therefore, to an objection to the point that I am trying to argue for. How, you may ask, can I hold that in constitutional adjudication the court's pronouncement is pre-emptive in the same way as Raz thinks that the law as a whole is? What is so special

---

[12] An exclusionary reason, for Raz, is a type of second-order reason that one has to exclude other reasons that may be applicable to a certain case. A second-order reason is any reason to act for a reason or to refrain from acting for a reason. An exclusionary reason is a second-order reason to refrain from acting for some reason' (Raz 1999, 39).

[13] I will leave open here whether this point can be extended beyond the central cases of judicial review. It is possible to argue, for instance, that my reasoning would imply that Raz's model of laws as 'exclusionary reasons' applies whenever a court has the power to resolve conflicts of laws, such as a conflict between a federal law and a state law in a Federation. I do not think, however, that this possibility affects the argument that I am about to put forward in Part II of this paper, since the justification of the power to resolve normative conflicts in a Federation is not as intrusive in the will of the people as the ordinary powers of judicial review are. What is at stake in conflicts between federal and state laws is not the political judgment of the states or the federal government, as compared to the court's judgment, but rather the different claims of authority raised by the states and the federal government. In conflicts between federal and state laws, there is an unavoidable necessity of *determining who is competent* to decide, and the issue is not what answer to a moral controversy is best, but merely which sphere of government has authority to decide it. In spite of the initial appearance, this situation is not identical to the core cases of judicial review. In federal conflicts of laws, a court does not solve a reasonable disagreement about a rights issue and lacks final authority to settle in a final way the solution to the disagreement at stake. I would like to thank Seana Shiffrin for attracting my attention to this point.

[14] See supra, section 1.2.

[15] In Simpson's view, 'distinguishing does not simply involve pointing out a factual distinction between two cases; it involves further the use of this factual distinction as a *justification* for refusal to follow the earlier case' (Simpson 1961, 175).

about constitutional reasoning that makes the general model that I used to explain both the legislation and the common law unfit to account for its authority?

To be coherent with what I argued earlier in this essay, I must demonstrate that there is an important difference between common law cases and cases of strong judicial review. Nonetheless, this distinction does not appear to reside in the reasoning process of the court. In the hard cases decided by a constitutional court, Dworkin's view that constitutional adjudication is a sort of 'moral reading' of the constitution is descriptively more accurate than Raz's view that when the judges resort to moral argument or other extra-legal considerations, they are no longer using their 'legal skills' or 'applying the law'.[16] On Dworkin's description, the reasoning of constitutional courts is neither strictly legal nor purely moral. One of its distinctive features is that moral and political concepts are embedded in the sources of law, so that many legal concepts can only make sense if they are illuminated by moral considerations (Dworkin 2006, 51). But these moral concepts do not necessarily retain their original senses once they have been incorporated into legal documents. As Waldron persuasively explains, 'what we have here is a mélange of reasoning – across the board – which, in its richness and texture, differs considerably from pure moral reasoning as well as from the pure version of black-letter legal reasoning that certain naïve positivists might imagine' (Waldron 2009, 12). This hybrid or intertwined type of reasoning stems from the interpretive attitude that one is supposed to adopt while constructing the meaning of the legal sources, and is not different from the interpretive attitude of common lawyers in hard cases. Dworkin appears to be correct, therefore, about the nature of judicial reasoning, even when we are considering the reasoning of constitutional courts. Hence, the distinction between a decision of the constitutional court and a common law form of judicial decision-making lies less on the reasoning process than on the *effects* of the decision.

I do not think, however, that this poses an insurmountable difficulty for the point that I am trying to raise about the pre-emptive authority of constitutional courts. To say that the *reasoning process* followed by a constitutional court, when it declares that a given statute is void or no longer valid, is not qualitatively different from that of a common lawyer, when she follows a precedent, *does not* amount to saying that the *nature the authoritative settlement* of these decisions is necessarily the same.

Even though some would argue that the 'settlement function' of constitutional courts is the same as that of the 'rule of precedent', I believe that this may or may not be true, depending on the case at hand.[17]

In order to illustrate this point, let us compare two abortion cases that have been decided by different constitutional courts. In *Roe v. Wade*, on the one hand, the Supreme Court of the United States decided that the right to privacy, under the 'due

[16] See Dworkin (1996, 1–31) and Raz (2009b, 49).

[17] In defense of the settlement function of constitutional courts, Alexander and Schauer have argued that 'just as a rule of precedent recognizes the value of settlement for settlement's sake, so too does a constitution exist partly because the value of uniform decisions on issues as to which people have divergent substantive views and personal agendas' (Alexander and Schauer 1997, 1376).

process clause' of the 14th Amendment, should be extended to protect a woman's decision to have an abortion. The court held that in regard to abortions performed during the first trimester of pregnancy, the decision must be left to the woman and to the judgment of her doctor. States lack authority to limit this right, even if it is to protect the potentiality of human life. By implication, thus, all statutes enacted to prevent women from making an abortion before the third trimester lack legal validity and should be regarded as deprived of legal effects.[18] On the other hand, in a recent case of the Brazilian Federal Supreme Court, the court did not address the issue whether the federal statute which considers abortion a criminal offence is incompatible with the constitution, but decided that women have the right to have an abortion when there is a medical diagnostic that she is carrying an anencephalic fetus, and that no legislation that considers the abortion a criminal offence shall be applicable to these cases.[19]

By considering these cases, I am not interested in the answer to the question whether abortion is morally or legally accepted. On the contrary, I want to focus on the level of generality of the decision and on whether it leaves open a post-interpretive revision of its contents by future constitutional judges. My intention is merely to show that in the former decision the court provides to the officials and the people in general an exclusionary reason for acting in a certain way and quashes the statutes that counter the authoritative pronouncement issued in the holding of the judicial decision, whereas in the latter decision the court merely solves an 'application problem', with a view to determining the appropriate application of a constitutional norm to a situation whose features are unspecified in the literal wording of the legislative enactment (Günther 1993, 38). What the court aimed to do in this case is merely to determine whether X has a right to abortion *all things considered*. The court no longer solves a 'problem of justification' and is not concerned with the justification of 'only the norm itself', but rather engages in an 'application discourse' where the real issue is not whether a norm is generally valid, but if it ought to be followed 'in a particular situation in the view of all the particular circumstances' of the case (Günther 1993, 36–38). One can see, therefore, that in the latter case the court proceeds nearly in the same manner as a common lawyer. Constitutional adjudication, in such types of decision, coincides with the 'common law conception' of constitutionalism supported by Wil Waluchow. One of the nuclear points of a Charter of Rights, for Waluchow, is precisely to compensate for our lack of knowledge, in advance, about 'what our rights and freedoms are' in every dispute. By investing the judges with the power to interpret the constitution or the Bill of Rights, the legal system handles the 'epistemic limitations in respect to the effects of the government action on moral rights' (Waluchow 2007, 11).[20]

[18] *Roe v. Wade*, 410 U.S. 113, 93 S. Ct. 705, 35 L. Ed. 2d 147 (1973).

[19] Brazil. STF, ADPF n. 54/DF, Pleno, Rel. Min. Marco Aurélio, j. 12.04.2012.

[20] According to Waluchow, 'these are moral rights about whose exact nature we are often undecided or cannot agree on in advance but whose importance has been recognized in the decision to include them within a Charter of Rights and Freedoms. Once we see Charters and judicial review in this different light, we can not only see our way clear to a better understanding of the disputes between

I believe that these examples show that the idea of 'constitutional adjudication' can comprise more than the strong variant of judicial review. The two examples of constitutional decision that I offered in the previous paragraph are thus two alternative classes of constitutional cases. While the former is a typical case of a strong form of judicial review, in which a court drafts an authoritative decision that annuls a legislative enactment and solves a general problem of legal validity, the latter merely interprets the law in a way that avoids a statute to come into conflict with a constitutional right. Thought the court fixes how the law shall be interpreted for the time being, the legislative text remains intact and is still open to new understandings at a future interpretive round. In other words, the text of the legislative provision still counts as a valid *source of meaning* in post-interpretive debates. Though the court adds new specific meanings to the decision of the legislature, it does not even purport to replace its general political judgment in a pre-emptive way.

Even the so called systems of 'weak judicial review' – such as the case of the United Kingdom, New Zealand and the Australian State of Victoria – admit the 'interpretive mandate' to read down the statutes that appear to violate the Charter of Rights whenever it is possible to do so.[21] This interpretive mandate, as Mark Tushnet explains, directs the courts to 'engage in two acts of interpretation: they must interpret the substantive rights protections, and then determine whether the statutory provision at issue can be interpreted in a manner consistent with their interpretation of the rights protections' (Tushnet 2009, 26).

To be sure, even a legal system that does not allow any sort of judicial review of the legislation – and lack even a statutory authorization to 'read down' a legislative provision in order to make it coherent with a set of rights, as it was the case of France and the United Kindgom a few years ago – might accept the kind of 'constructive interpretation' that nowadays is typical in systems of weak review. In the 1930s English decision *R. v Bourne*, for instance, a surgeon who performed an abortion on a 15 year old girl impregnated by violent rape was acquitted on the ground that the Crown was not entitled to prosecute him unless there was no reasonable doubt that he had not acted in good faith 'with a view to protecting the life,

---

their critics and their advocates, but we can also see why they can be very good things to have – even in a society fully committed to the ideals of democracy and subject to the endless disputes caused by our epistemic limitations' (Waluchow 2007, 11).

[21]The interpretive power to 'read down' statutes which conflict with statutory bills of rights is expressly stated in the United Kingdom's *Human Rights Act 1998*, c 42, s 3 (1), in the New Zealand *Bill of Rights Act 1990*, s 6, and in the Australian State of Victoria's Charter of Rights (s 32(1)). Not all commentators, however, would agree with my reconstruction of this interpretive power. James Allan, for instance, argues that 'the hoped-for middle ground desired by some bill of rights proponents is elusive', and that these Bills of Rights are not compatible with parliamentary sovereignty 'in any substantive sense' (Allan 2011, 110). Contrary to Allan, I think that these powers are not fully incompatible with parliamentary sovereignty and do provide an interesting middle ground as compared to the systems of strong judicial review. I am particularly convinced on this matter by Goldworthy's and Gardbaum's views that this interpretive power is a viable option and is not inconsistent with the essential postulate of parliamentary sovereignty. See Goldworthy (2010, 299–304) and Gardbaum (2013, 44).

understood as the continuing sane and healthy existence, of the girl in question'.[22] As MacCormick reports, 'the law's express prohibition on performing or procuring abortion was (considered) subject to an implied exception', in an interpretive move that remain accepted for three decades, until the Abortion Act was passed by Parliament in 1967 (MacCormick 2007, 248).

The decision of English courts in a case like *R. v. Bourne* does not differ in a significant way from that of a constitutional court in a case like the Brazilian decision which introduced an exception to a generally accepted anti-abortion rule. They both lack the pre-emptive character that Raz is attributing to the legal system. These decisions resemble a law-making process '*by aggregation*', which is typical not only of Roman jurists and contemporary common lawyers,[23] but also of the medieval courts in Western Europe.[24] The core point of this method of legal development is that the judge does not accept the assumption that there is always only *one* individual rule of law that determines the content of a legal obligation. Instead of endorsing the 'atomistic' assumption that legal obligations stem from a direct application of a previously constructed legal norm,[25] the judge seeks to construct the law in a way that allows the *harmonization* of any given rule with the previous set of norms of the legal system to which it belongs (Hespanha 2006, 115). The exceptions on the prohibition of abortion in these decisions are *not* supposed to 'replace' or 'repeal' the statute that they purport to qualify. On the contrary, they claim to cohere with it. The whole point of this form of judicial reasoning is to add or aggregate something to the current meaning of the previous set of laws, rather than replace the wording of the text by a new rule that is as general and comprehensive as the previous one.[26]

We can see, therefore, that there are two ways in which the decision of a constitutional court can acquire its authority: first, by quashing a particular legislative

[22] *R. v Bourne* [1939] 1 KB 687; [1938] 3 All ER 615, quoted in MacCormick (2007, 248).

[23] See Buckland and McNair (1939).

[24] See, for instance, Hespanha (1978, 78), where the distinction between legal development 'by aggregation' and by 'substitution' is explained.

[25] On a critique of Raz's atomism, see Greenberg (2011, 49–50).

[26] The law-making activity by 'aggregation' can be contrasted with the law-making activity of legislatures. As Hespanha explains, legislatures tend to develop the law by *replacing* previous rules with new ones that stem from the novel legislative enactments (Hespanha 2005, 118). The clearest picture to understand the similarities between constitutional courts and legislatures is Kelsen's image of the constitutional court as a 'negative legislator'. The key to distinguish legislation from adjudication, for Kelsen, is that legislators tend to create general norms, whereas judges and officials that are said to 'apply' the law create individual norms that are valid only for the case at stake. A formal declaration of unconstitutionality, therefore, has the same effect as the creation of a new norm to derogate the previous enactment regarded as incompatible with the constitution. 'Since the annulment of a law has the same general character as its enactment', we can say that the former is no different in meaning from the statute itself, albeit with a 'negative signal'. Even though the court cannot create positive laws, it certainly acts as a 'negative legislator' (Kelsen 1928, 224–5).

provision and blocking any further deliberation about its merits, as it happens only in legal systems that adopt the strong form of judicial review; and second, by giving the appropriate interpretation of a basic right in concrete situations not envisaged when the Charter was originally issued. While the former purports to settle the law and determine its final interpretation, the latter holds that the content of the law is never final and is open to new interpretations. Whereas the former is better explained by the Razian conception of legal authority, the latter is at odds with such description of how the legal system operates and is more compatible with Dworkin's conception of the way authoritative enactments operate in legal practice.

One may wonder, at this point, what is the relevance of this distinction for the purposes of my inquiry in this essay. My answer will be as straightforward as possible: the Razian view implies a conception of the authority of the courts that attributes to them a legal power much harder to justify than that of the Dworkinian view or any other account of legal authority that falls outside of the mainstream understanding, which regards legal enactments as pre-emptive and content-independent. It might turn out to be possible that one can provide a moral justification for the latter even when such justification is not available to the former. But there is no reciprocity in this statement, since it is never the case that one can offer a justification to the former that would not work also as a justification to the latter.

I advocate, in the second part of this essay, two theses about the authority of constitutional courts: first, that there is no available moral justification to attribute to a constitutional court the kind of authority that Raz envisages, and second, that although the arguments that Raz deploys to justify the authority of law are incapable of providing a justification for these decisions, they might be able to justify the authority of a system of weak judicial review.

3.3 The Justification of Authority and the Burdens of Constitutional Courts

I have left aside until now one of the main problems that I wish to address in this essay, which is the moral justification of the authority of constitutional courts. It is now time to take up this issue. I will analyze in this second part of the essay two alternative views about the legitimacy of authority in general, which are the most popular candidates for a reasonable justification of the authority of constitutional courts. The first is provided, again, by Raz, who argues that an authority is legitimate when she is in a better position, as compared to her subjects, to pass judgment on the balancing of the first-order reasons that apply to them. The second, in turn, is provided by those who reject his instrumental justification for such authority and believe that it can be justified by a procedural perspective that is based on the idea of fairness, in the same way as democracy is.

3.3.1 The Normal Justification Thesis

According to Raz, the main argument to provide a moral justification for an authority is to show that by following the directives of the authority a person is more likely to comply with the dependent reasons which apply to her than if she refused to follow the commands of the authority and decided to figure out by herself on which reason she should act (Raz 1986, 71). Authorities, therefore, exercise a 'mediating role' between their subjects and the independent reasons that they have to act in a certain way. One has legitimate authority over a person when such person is likely to be better-off by following the reasoning of the authority than her own reasoning on the matter at stake.

Raz calls this conception the 'service conception' of authority, for he thinks that the authority acts *in service of her subjects* by helping them to act on the *right reasons*. Under the Service Conception, 'authorities have the power to tell us what to do because we benefit, in some sense, from their having such power' (Shapiro 2002, 431). When subjects are in a bad position to balance the dependent reasons that they have to act in a certain case, they should rely on the authority to mediate between themselves and these reasons (Raz 1986, 56). The heart of the normative account that Raz offers to justify legal authority lies on the Normal Justification Thesis (NJT), which claims that 'the normal way to establish that a person has authority over another person involves showing that the alleged subject is likely better to comply with reasons which apply to him (other than the alleged authoritative directives) if he accepts the directives of the alleged authority as authoritatively binding and tries to follow them, rather than by trying to follow the reasons which apply to him directly' (Raz 1986, 53).

This mediating role of authoritative directives explains, for Raz, why they are a special type of 'second-order' reasons for action. Though they pre-empt most of the reasons on which they are based, 'directives and rules derive their force from the considerations which justify them' (Raz 1986, 59). In other words, 'it is the truth or the soundness of the decisions which counts ultimately. Truth and soundness provide the argument for the legitimacy of authority' (Raz 1989, 778).[27] Authorities are legitimate only to the extent that they facilitate the subjects to comply with the right reasons that are already available to them. On the NJT, the power arrangements and institutions in a given society are justified only instrumentally, in such a way that 'one structure of government is more legitimate than another when one is more likely to track the balance of dependent reasons than another' (Shapiro 2002, 432). Even democracy, for Raz, is justified only in instrumental terms, i.e. 'if it leads, by and large, to good government' (Marmor 2005, 317).

It is this purely instrumental character of the NJT, as Raz's critics correctly point out, that makes it a problematic justification of the authority of law. The main problem of NJT is that it is a *purely substantive theory of legitimacy*, which is satisfied with a demonstration that an authoritative directive conforms with right reasons,

[27] I borrowed this quote from Marmor (2005, 317).

and makes no assessment on how this directive is reached (Hershovitz 2003, 212). The NJT is considered implausible as a general explanation for the legitimacy of the law because it misses the intrinsic value of *democratic procedures* for justifying legal authority. There is nothing in NJT that makes an authoritative pronouncement valuable in itself. It entails that an authority is legitimate, 'never because there is anything inherent in the authority that confers this status, but merely to the extent that obeying it brings about better compliance with the reasons that are independent of the authority' (Christiano 2004, 278). The legitimacy of the authority is established by an 'indirect justification' that is entirely based on the *outcomes* of the exercise of authority, which are deemed to be valuable 'however they are brought about' (Christiano 2004, 278).

By advocating this indirect justification of authority, Raz ends up assuming a heavy burden for his theory of the moral legitimacy of the state and the legal institutions. The legitimacy of an authority becomes entirely dependent upon the existence of a larger set of values and conditions, which must be properly specified if they are to acquire any binding status in a given society. As Leslie Green has argued, this indirect justification requires a 'specification of why a particular indirect strategy is the optimal one'. Hence, 'whether or not authority can be justified morally is thus a complex matter which cannot be decided in advance without considering the precise sort of indirect argument offered' (Green 1988, 58).

Green's point about the conditional character of these indirect justifications helps me reinforce my view that the NJT attracts for itself a heavy burden which makes it at best insufficient for justifying the authority of 'the state' or 'the law in general'. As Waldron points out, the NJT is based entirely on outcome-related reasons – which usually operate in a very general level and cut on both sides –, completely neglecting the process-related reasons that might be available for that task. When it comes to establishing why a legal authority should be accepted, for instance, outcome-related reasons are, on Waldron's interpretation, 'at best inconclusive' (Waldron 2006, 1375).

The idea that we can base the legitimacy of the state or the legal system 'on the prospect that individual's compliance with morally important reasons would be improved as a result of their acceptance of authority', as Raz seems to believe, is problematic because it ignores the 'moral significance of disagreement among citizens about the proper organization of their political communities' (Christiano 2004, 279). Part of the point of politics, as Christiano explains, is precisely to create organizations to 'make decisions when there are *serious disagreements* regarding the matters to be decided' (Christiano 2004, 280). The NJT seems to be unaware of this fact and attracts for itself not only the duty to specify the *values* that justify an authoritative legal pronouncement, but also the charge of describing *the whole set of circumstances* in which the authority is justified by these values.

A much easier task can be done, on the other hand, by the theories that intend to justify the authority of the law on the authority of democracy, as I intend to show in the next section.

While Raz's theory of legitimacy presupposes a 'division between rulers and subjects – a division between the duty-bound and the binders -', the ideal of a democratic government is grounded on a view of political action as a form of 'collective action', i.e. as 'the action of the community through various procedures and decision functions that operate on the preferences or views of its members' (Hershovitz 2003, 210). Democracy does not see an authority as having a 'right to rule' upon the others; on the contrary, the main source of political legitimacy are the procedures by means of which 'we are binding ourselves through acts of legislation' (Hershovitz 2003, 210).

3.3.2 The Democratic Justification Thesis

I will consider from now on an alternative to NJT, which attempts to justify the authority of law on 'process-related reasons'. Such reasons are reasons for decisions that should stand 'independently of considerations about the appropriate outcome' of the decision-process (Waldron 2006, 1372). By appealing to these reasons, one can associate the authority of law with the authority of democracy, as well as with the claim that the directive of an authority is justified because it is the product of a process which is accepted as *fair* and shows *respect* for the different values, interests and opinions of the citizens that participate in the making of the decision.

This perspective assumes that *democratic* decisions can acquire a binding status and morally obligate independently of their contents. The authority of the law is justified because it is the product of a democratic settlement. Democratic procedures legitimate an authority 'because they represent power-arrangements that are fair' and empower citizens to have 'an equal ability to exert control over their life and the life of the community' (Shapiro 2002, 432). The value of democratic authority, contrary to NJT, is no longer based on its instrumental features, but rather on its intrinsic value that stems from its respect for the autonomy and the political equality of the participants in the decision-process. 'Rather than violating one's autonomy, heeding rules that one believes to be mistaken can be an affirmation of the value of autonomy in general. It shows respect for the rational faculties of others, recognizes the fairness of accepting burdens in cooperative ventures, and supports the equality in distribution of power through society' (Shapiro 2002, 432).

One of the most successful attempts to provide, contrary to the NJT, a procedural and democratic justification of the authority of law is offered by Jeremy Waldron, who claims that legislation has a special dignity, which is grounded in the special *achievement* that it represents for permitting 'concerted, co-operative, co-ordinated, or collective action in the circumstances of modern life' (Waldron 1999, 101). In order to explain this special importance of the legislation, Waldron introduces the idea of 'circumstances of politics', which obtain when our widespread disagreement about some of the fundamental issues of our political community co-exists with a shared conviction of the special importance of having a common framework or decision-process to handle this disagreement in a fair and respectful way. 'The felt need among the members of a certain group for a common framework or decision or course of action on some matter, even in the face of disagreement about what that framework, decision or action should be, are the *circumstances of politics*' (Waldron 1999, 102).

Democratic legislation passed under the circumstances of politics is worthy of respect because of the 'achievement' that it represents, which enables 'action-in-concert in the face of disagreement.' It claims authority as law 'because it is a *respectful* achievement – because it is achieved in a way that is respectful of the persons whose action-in-concert it represents' (Waldron 1999, 108–9). Under the circumstances of politics, on Waldron's view, the principle of majority-decision acquires a special importance insofar as it shows equal consideration for the individuals who participate in the voting and decision-processes to overcome their disagreements about the key controversial matters in a constitutional democracy. This is done in two particular ways: (1) by respecting their 'differences of opinion about justice and the common good', and (2) by embodying the principle of 'respect for each person in the process by which we settle on a view to be adopted as *ours* even in the face of disagreement' (Waldron 1999, 109).

The method of majority-decision, moreover, 'gives *equal* weight to each person's view' in the process by which one view is settled as the group's. It embodies the principle of equality and establishes thereby a *fair* method of decision-making (Waldron 1999, 114).

This justification of the authority of legislation is thus grounded in the fact that procedural fairness is intrinsically valuable, rather than merely instrumental. In the realm of political actions the requirement of fairness deserves a special status because it is a requirement of the idea of 'respect for people's right to personal autonomy', according to which 'people should create, as far as possible, their own lives through successive decisions and choices of their own' (Marmor 2005, 319). The value of respect for people's autonomy, as Marmor suggests, 'requires a political structure in which everybody has a fair chance to participate, and this is what democratic decision procedure aims to achieve' (Marmor 2005, 319). The point, in short, is that democratic authority is intrinsically valuable because respect for people's autonomy entails a right to 'an equal participation in the political decision process', which can only be observed by processes of public deliberation followed by majority decisions among citizens with equal status in the political community.[28]

In the context of *disagreement* or *different interests* and *different judgment* about our political alternatives, with regard to social justice and moral rights, democratic decisions are open and publicly discussed, in the deliberative stage, and fairly obtained by majority-voting, in the decision stage. They acquire an *intrinsic moral value* that is lacking in any instrumental justification of the authority of legal enactments. As Christiano has argued, 'the facts of diversity, fallibility, disagreement, cognitive bias and the interests that we have in publicity provide the key to the final stretch of the argument for democracy', which can be summarized thus:

---

[28] I will take this connection between autonomy and democratic participation for granted. For a more developed account of the reasoning required to establish this necessary connection between autonomy and this right to equal participation, see Marmor (2005) and Christiano (2004).

> When there is disagreement about justice and the common good, the uniquely best way to take everyone's judgment seriously, so that equality is publicly embodied, is to give each person an equal say in how the society ought to be organized. And this in turn is the way publicly to realize equal advancement of interests. Therefore the principle of the public realization of equality supports democracy as the uniquely best realization of equality under the circumstances of disagreement and fallibility (Christiano 2004, 276).

Democracy, under this perspective, is the *only* way to overcome our disagreement with equal respect and consideration, the 'uniquely just solution' to political conflict, and the only decision-process that may legitimate the outcomes 'even when they are unjust in the eyes of some' (Christiano 2004, 277).

This provides a justification of legal authority more robust as compared to the Normal Justification Thesis. Let us call it the Democratic Justification Thesis (DJT). This thesis can be asserted thus: *an institution has intrinsically legitimate authority over a person, independently of the existence of any instrumental reason to that effect, when the directives of this institution are the outcome of a public and fair decision-process in which such person has a right to an equal participation.* The Democratic Justification Thesis provides, thus, the most powerful justification available for the authority of a legal institution.[29]

[29] The point of DJT, as it is understood here, is to provide an *alternative* to NJT in the justification of political authority. But this is not the only possible way to read the relation between DJT and NJT. One can argue, for instance, that committing to the result of a given decision-procedure is morally justified precisely because a subject is more likely to *better comply with the reasons that apply to herself* by following the directive resultant from this procedure than by making a first-order judgment about the proper course of action to take. According to this argument, 'where I have reason to comply with the results of a particular decision procedure, doing so will help me to conform better than I might otherwise do to the reason I have" (Hershovitz 2003, 219). Yet this reconstruction comes with a price. As Hershovitz correctly argued, this reconstruction 'makes the normal justification thesis empty' (Hershovitz 2003, 219), since what is doing the work here is no longer NJT, but the process-related reasons for having the hypothetical decision-procedure. Let us consider, in the following lines, an example that illustrates the deficiency of the proposed reconstruction, which is Jeremy Waldron's attempt to apply NJT in order to explain the authority relations between officials that face the risk of issuing conflictive directives to the same subjects. In the case of relations between courts and legislatures, which is the standard example of these relations, Waldron sees the court as an agent who has a *prima facie* duty 'not to disrupt' the relation of an authority (A) and a subject (C). If the relation between A and C can be justified by NJT, the duty of another official (B) to respect the settlement of the legislature (A) arises because of the *public* character of A's authority enactments, which purport to resolve issues of 'common concern', and the special value of social coordination according to an 'established procedure' that allows subjects to 'identify answers as salient, even when there are disagreements as to what that answers should be' (Waldron 2003, 68). In this hypothesis, B should refrain from issuing contradictory directives once she acknowledges the importance of social coordination and the value of the procedures established for the settlement of moral and political disagreements in the community. As we can see, Waldron's argument in this paper seems to lead to the conclusion that the value of social coordination can also be justified by NJT, although the latter is applied no longer to the relation between A and C, but instead to the relations between or among officials like A, B and all other institutions who claim authority over C. Unlike Waldron, however, I tend to see the process-related reasons for social coordination that Waldron gives in the example as an *independent moral argument* that supplements NJT in order to show the value of the right procedures for public settlement of issues of common concern. Perhaps this independent moral argument could be something like the version

3.3.3 *On the Difficulty to Ground the Authority of Constitutional Courts*

I have described in this essay two different views about the nature of authority and two alternative views about the moral justification of authoritative directives.

With regard to the *nature* of authority, the first view that I summarized above was the mainstream position elaborated by Raz, which can be labelled 'Pre-Emptive' because it claims that the judgment of an authority is both *content-independent* and *exclusionary*, in the sense that the reasons that the authority provides are not simply added to the dependent reasons that a person may have, but rather replace these dependent reasons because they are assumed to reflect the outcome of their appropriate balancing.

The second view, in turn, acknowledges MacCormick's argumentative or 'arguable' character of law. This view is defended by legal philosophers that, on the one hand, move apart the 'Standard Picture' of legal authority (as Greenberg defines it) and, on the other hand, acknowledge the interpretive and argumentative character of law.

This distinction is important for me because I am convinced that the second view is more attractive as a general description of how the legal system operates both in common law reasoning and in statutory interpretation, whereas the first view is a better description of how constitutional courts act when they strike down a statute enacted by the legislature. If we think of the 'central cases' of legal practice, where the 'law in general' is at stake, it is sensible to argue that when the *law* creates a legal obligation, Dworkin's account is more appropriate. Nonetheless, as I argued in Sect. 3.2.4, this jurisprudential account misses some important 'peripheral cases' that appear in constitutional adjudication, in which the decision of the constitutional court annuls a statute by pronouncing its unconstitutionality. In this particular type of authoritative legal pronouncements, the court's decision is deconstructive and blocks further deliberation about the validity of a law pronounced by the representatives of the people. Raz's pre-emptive account of legal authority provides a more accurate explanation for this particular legal setting.

I think that this poses a legitimacy problem for the authority of constitutional courts. Why is that so? The basic idea is that the pre-emptive character of legal authorities makes an authoritative pronouncement valid merely because the authority has pronounced it. While in the central cases (including statutory interpretation and common law cases) the law is argumentative and the subjects have a non-negligible room for constructive interpretation and for incorporating moral arguments as valid reasons for determining the contents of a legal provision, even after the issuance of the authoritative enactment, in the peripheral case of a pronouncement

of DJT that I am defending here. But if this is the case, then I think that we may use DJT to justify not only the duty of B not to disrupt the relation between A and C, but also the relation between A and C in the first place. DJT will apply directly to justify the enactments of the legislature, and this will provide a justification for the legislature more robust than NJT. I should thank Rafael Bezerra Nunes for helping me clarify my position on this point.

of unconstitutionality the court is simply cutting down any further deliberation. It quashes a law and leaves no room for further interpretive activity in adjudication. Hence, the very nature of the authoritative pronouncements of constitutional courts in a system of strong judicial review, where the courts are empowered to strike down a procedurally correct enactment of the legislator, imposes a heavy burden on these pronouncements, which is not at stake when we consider the central cases, where the authority of law can be explained without the peremptory force that the Pre-Emptive Thesis usually entails.

Things get even worse for judicial review when we consider no longer the nature of the authoritative pronouncements of constitutional courts, but the *moral justification* that is available for this kind of authority. When the law is established by an act of a democratic legislature, the Democratic Justification Thesis provides an intrinsic justification for the statutory provisions enacted through the legislative process. One needs not to consider, at least in the majority of the cases, the instrumental efficacy of a piece of legislation in order to establish the legitimacy of its enactment. The very fact that a statute presents itself as the outcome of a decision-process that is publicly conducted and respectful of the citizen's right to an 'equal participation' is enough to provide a moral justification for the authority of democracy. But when we focus on constitutional courts the picture is very different. Constitutional courts, in spite of their relevance for assessing the reasonableness of the *outcomes* of the democratic procedures, are under a very heavy burden of proof. Even those who believe that it is possible to justify the powers of a constitutional court on the basis of the 'very principles that underpin democracy' (including the need to protect publicity, equality and participation in the advancement of one's interests) sometimes recognize that constitutional courts have a 'nondemocratic character' which makes them vulnerable, at least in part, to the critic of the skeptics of judicial supremacy, who believe that there is no *a priori* moral justification for disenfranchising the majority of the people in the cases where there is a widespread disagreement about the rights that we have (Christiano 2008, 288).

Constitutional courts are nondemocratic institutions, according to Waldron, because they are based on the aristocratic claim that the most controversial political disagreements about rights and principles in a political community should not be resolved according to the citizens' *own* judgment. Politics, for Waldron, is *'always* a matter of judgment', and the core of the democratic claim 'has always been that the people are entitled to govern themselves by their own judgments' (Waldron 1999, 264).

Even if there is 'no general principled reason' for rejecting a constitutional court with the power of judicial review of the legislation, neither there is any principled reason for accepting it as it is (Christiano 2008, 281). On balancing, any argument for a constitutional court with the powers of strong judicial review is 'an *essentially instrumental* one', as Christiano has argued in the following excerpt:

> Other things being equal, the loss to public equality that results from bad court decisions is greater than the gain to public equality when the court makes a good decision. This is because the loss that arises from a court making a bad decision (say striking down democratic legislation that accords with public equality) is a double loss while the gain from the

> court striking down bad democratic legislation is not as great. But this implies that a constitutional court can be justified only if the good decisions significantly outnumber or outweigh in importance the bad decisions (Christiano 2008, 280).

Though the courts may serve legitimate purposes while interpreting and specifying the rights that are abstractly stated in the constitution or equivalent legal document, their lack of democratic justification places a heavy burden on them when they strike down a particular legal statute.

This helps us understand what makes Waldron so suspicious about the idea of replacing a majority decision of the representatives of the people by a simple majority decision of the judges in a constitutional court. The claim that the court might stake to participate in the political process, with a view to dictating the solution to a moral disagreement in a hard case, is merely *instrumental* – and not a matter of 'entitlement' – because the court is not deciding its own faith, but rather making moral judgments in the name of the whole society.

When I argue, following Waldron and Christiano, that such claim is 'instrumental', I mean that in a constitutional democracy one can justify the authority of the constitutional court not because it represents the members of the political community and is naturally entitled to decide on their behalf, but merely because under certain conditions its rulings may trigger a public reasoning about the fundamentals of the community and help to protect the basic rights enshrined in the Bill of Rigths.

As a rule, the authority of the constitutional court is justified under the assumption – not always empirically verifiable – that the court somehow serves democracy by facilitating compliance with the 'democratic conditions' that, in a liberal society, entail that the government must have a 'concern for the equal status of citizens' (Dworkin 1996, 17).

In order to establish the legitimacy of a constitutional court we need a cost-benefit analysis that is to be measured in purely instrumental terms. If we are to accept a justification for the overriding powers that constitutional courts have over democratic legislation, then we cannot rely on intrinsic justifications such as the Democratic Justification Thesis. We are only left with instrumentalist accounts such as Raz's Normal Justification Thesis, which makes the legitimacy of the institution of judicial review entirely dependent upon the fulfillment of a detailed set of conditions that the defendant of judicial review must be able to specify. I will call these conditions the 'Circumstances of Judicial Review'.

3.3.4 On the Principles Underlying Democracy and the Legitimacy of Strong Judicial Review

Before we move on to specifying some of the 'circumstances of judicial review' (or at least *one* of such circumstances), I would like to consider whether it is possible to justify the judicial review of a democratically enacted law on the basis of the 'principles that underpin democracy', as Christiano suggested in an excerpt quoted earlier in this essay. On the basis of Marmor's views stated above, I assume that the authority of democracy stems from the value of 'equal respect for people's autonomy', which 'needs to be implemented by acknowledging a *right to an equal participation in the decision process*' (Marmor 2005, 330).

Does the practice of judicial review help protect this right? I think that we need at least some theoretical reflection about the general features of the right to equality in the political decision-process before we can offer a plausible answer to this question, and I will try to provide this theoretical background by focusing on Marmor's explanation of the right under consideration. For Marmor, a political process that leads to an authoritative settlement comprises 'two main stages: *deliberation* and *decision*' (Marmor 2005, 331). We can assess the political power of a citizen by determining her capacity to participate in these two stages of the political process. Nevertheless, the value of political equality manifests itself in a different way in each stage of the political decision-process, as Marmor explains with the help of Dworkin's distinction between 'impact' and 'influence' in political decisions (Dworkin 2000, 191).[30]

At the deliberative stage, political equality is a matter of equality of influence, which is satisfied by the principle of 'equality of opportunity of political influence' in the public deliberations that precede the actual decision by majority voting (Marmor 2005, 333). People's autonomy is fostered when a democracy provides an equal opportunity of influence through a wide range of principles and institutions that are regarded as 'essential to the proper functioning of a democracy' (Marmor 2005, 333). At the stage of authoritative decision, on the other hand, political equality cannot be satisfied with the idea of equality of influence, but requires instead the concept of equality of impact. Though there may be many different institutional arrangements that equally satisfy this requirement, it is not very difficult to conclude that, at least in the final stage of actual decision-making, the practice of judicial review faces a serious difficulty to ground its normative power to quash a democratically enacted law. The idea of 'political equality', in the stage of actual decision-making (the second stage), points only to *process-related reasons* about the right to *participate* in the decision-processes of the political community, and this class of reasons are not available for justifying the authority of a constitutional court.

It is this *procedural* aspect that is missing in the optimistic accounts that recognize in the courts a representative character in the sense of Robert Alexy. Contrary to the position defended in this essay, Alexy thinks that constitutional courts can be legitimized by a wide conception of representation, which comprises not only votes and elections, but also arguments and reasons. Alexy thinks that a 'deliberative' conception of democracy embodies two kinds of representation: 'volitional' and 'argumentative'. Legislators are linked to their constituents by volitional and

[30]According to Dworkin (2000, 191), 'someone's impact in politics is the difference he can make, just on his own, by voting for or choosing one decision rather than another. Someone's influence, on the other hand, is the difference he can make not just on his own but also leading or inducing other to believe or vote or choose as he does'.

argumentative representation, whereas Constitutional Courts are accountable to the citizens exclusively by their capacity to disclose sound and correct arguments in support of their authoritative decisions, which must be effectively understood and endorsed by their audiences on the basis of the ideal of a 'discursive constitutionalism' (Alexy 2005, 578–9). Alexy thinks that this is enough to conclude that the courts have an 'argumentative representation' to issue authoritative interpretations of constitutional rights.

The problem with this position, in my opinion, is that it underestimates the importance of the 'decision' stage in the political process. For a political decision to be legitimate, it is not sufficient that it is allegedly in the interest of the people, but it must also respect the people's autonomous judgments about these reasons. In order to defend his position, Alexy would have to deny that the people, at the decision stage, have the *right* that we have been discussing in this section, which is the right to a 'fair distribution of the *actual power* to *make* the decision' (Marmor 2005, 333). Marmor's distinction between the 'deliberation' and the 'decision' stages of the political process of reaching an authoritative settlement of our major disagreements about our rights helps us see that the current attempts to offer a moral justification for the judicial review of the legislation are based *only* on the contribution that it can offer to increase public participation in the *stage of deliberation* about a particular rights issue. If constitutional courts are to be justified, it is *not* because they have a 'representative' character, but only because there might be some instrumental justification for their existence.

Constitutional courts, in systems of strong judicial review, do not enhance the participation of citizens in the 'decision stage'. On the contrary, they normally *disenfranchise* these citizens at this stage and claim to provide 'exclusionary reasons' for not acting on the democratically-enacted laws. It becomes, therefore, very difficult to ground the powers of strong judicial review on the same principles that justify the authority of democracy.

3.3.5 Dworkin's Instrumental Defense of Judicial Review and the Authority of Weak Constitutional Courts

The most paradigmatic defense of judicial review, nowadays, is Dworkin's attempt to reconcile the ideas of democracy and constitutionalism. Constitutionalism, both in the United States and in all of the places where it has found a root, is linked to the conception of government and politics that Bruce Ackerman has described as 'dualist democracy', which distinguishes two levels of decisions that may be made in a political community. On the first level one finds the genuine 'direct' decisions of the people concerning their fundamental laws, which are described as a 'higher lawmaking,' whereas on the second level one finds the 'normal lawmaking' of ordinary legislation (Ackerman 1993, 6–7). This distinction between 'normal' and 'constitutional' politics captures the core assumption of constitutionalism. It is on the basis of this distinction that Dworkin proposes his 'constitutional conception of democracy', which understands democracy as not necessarily linked to the principle of majority decision. The 'constitutional' conception of democracy, as he writes, 'denies that it is a defining goal of democracy that collective decisions always or normally be those that a majority or plurality of citizens would favor if fully informed and rational', and claims instead that the defining point of democracy is 'that collective decisions (should) be made by political institutions whose structure, composition, and practices treat all members of the community, as individuals, with equal concern and respect' (Dworkin 1996, 17). It is this key constitutional decision that supports the moral rights entrenched in a Bill of Rights, which are understood to express the 'democratic conditions' under which Government may be exercised in that political community (Dworkin 1996, 17).

One can notice here an important similarity between Dworkin and Raz. The heart of Dworkin's argument for judicial review lies on the *instrumental* capacity of the institutions of judicial review to protect the *democratic conditions*. His advocacy of judicial review is based on the following claims: (1) the majoritarian process – the political process that leads to a legislative decision – 'encourages compromises that may subordinate important issues of principle' (Dworkin 1996, 30); (2) judicial review is a 'pervasive feature' of our political life, 'because it forces political debate to include argument over principle, not only when a case comes to the Court but long before and long after' (Dworkin 1985, 70); and (3) 'individual citizens can in fact exercise moral responsibilities of citizenship better when final decisions involving constitutional values are removed from ordinary politics and assigned to courts, whose decisions are meant to turn on principle, not on the weight of numbers or the balance of political influence' (Dworkin 1996, 344).

I am not entirely convinced, however, of the plausibility of the assumptions (1) and (3) in Dworkin's general argument in defense of judicial review. Contrary to Dworkin, I believe that a special value should be attributed to the compromises that a political community may reach about the contents of the rights that we have and the positions that they entail.

Dworkin argues that compromises about moral rights may represent a threat for the appropriate enforcement of these rights, since political majorities may subordinate important issues of principle by means of 'checkerboard laws', which are intrinsically flawed because they do not make sense under any coherent scheme of moral values (Dworkin 1986).[31] Yet there might be good reasons to think that this conclusion is too strong. One might argue, contra Dworkin, that these views on compromise are based on bias and that he fails to recognize the moral worth of political compromises achieved under the scenario of a *public reasoning* to overcome our reasonable disagreements.

The danger of checkerboard compromises, which subordinate issues of principle, is nearly non-existent when the procedural requirements of public deliberation

[31] An example of such checkerboard compromises, for Dworkin, would be a law granting the right to make an abortion for women born in even days, while denying such right to those born in odd days.

are satisfied. Under the context of reasonable disagreements, which includes 'conflicting' and 'incommensurable' positions, Richard Bellamy correctly advocates that compromises need not to be seen as 'shoddy' or unprincipled. On the contrary, they are often products of 'the mutual recognition by citizens of the reasonableness of their often divergent points of view by seeking to accommodate these various perspectives within a coherent program of government' (Bellamy 2007, 192–3). Compromises about rights are valuable because they strengthen the idea of 'non-domination' of any citizens and reinforce the value of the 'rule of law' (Bellamy 2007, 194).[32] Rather than an illegitimate negotiation about matters of principle, compromises are more often than not a mutual agreement among autonomous citizens who are willing to respect each other as equally important individuals in spite of their deep disagreement about a particular moral or political issue.

Instead of attributing a moral stigma to compromises achieved under Waldron's 'circumstances of politics', Bellamy thinks that compromises can be fair because the parties show 'equal concern' with regard to the opponent's substantive views and observe the procedural requirement of hearing all sides before a particular position is reached. This account of political compromise shows that there is special value in compromises reached through a process of fair and decent deliberation under the context of a public reasoning. Nonetheless, it shows also that a moral decision in the name of the whole society only can be 'principled' if this 'public reasoning' is both accessible to all citizens and undertaken by the citizens themselves, or at least by someone entitled to make a compromise in their name.[33]

As long as a compromise about rights matters is reached under the conditions of procedural fairness and equal opportunities to influence the deliberation and to participate in the actual decision-making, there is nothing wrong in letting the people themselves discuss the terms of the agreement that is to be constructed about the contents of a given principle and the individual rights that this principle entails.

This point becomes even more important if we realize that in the ordinary business of constitutional courts *the judges themselves resort to compromises* in the same way as legislators and the interested parties do. The ability to reach compromises in court about a particular rights issue is normally described by lawyers and political scientists not as a vice, but, on the contrary, as an important *judicial virtue* that is widely known among the defendants of judicial review as the virtue of 'collegiality'. As we can read in a nice recent book about the deliberative role of the courts in a constitutional democracy, 'collegiality pushes deliberators to find *principled compromise* where spontaneous agreement proves unviable'. A collegial constitutional court, therefore, is marked by 'a spirit of accommodation, a default preference for compromising instead of concurring or dissenting, a willingness to locate points of conflict and dissolve them'. It implies 'a pressure to deflect "in

[32] In other words, 'compromises are a natural part of a process that "hears the other side" and seeks to avoid dominating citizens by failing to treat the reasons that they offer equally' (Bellamy 2007, 193).

[33] I am referring here, to two of the seven senses that Bellamy thinks that 'public reasoning' can assume. See Bellamy (2007, 179).

deference to one's colleagues'" (Hübner Mendes 2013, 131). Collegiality, to use a familiar image among the defendants of the principle of judicial supremacy, is the 'intimacy beyond affection' that reigns among the judges in their internal deliberations about the solution to a given case (Coffin 1980, quoted in Hübner Mendes 2013, 129).

There is no aprioristic reason, therefore, to prefer a compromise reached by a bunch of *judges* over a compromise reached by *We, the People*, about the contents and the interpretation of the rights that we have settled for ourselves in the Bill of Rights.[34] Dworkin's assumption regarding the deleterious effects of political compromises about individual rights is not only empirically undemonstrated, but also instrumentally inefficient for granting the powers of judicial review, since the compromises reached by the courts in constitutional adjudication are at least as worrying as any other compromise between majorities and minorities in the political assemblies.

Dworkin, therefore, is left with only *one* argument to defend his claim that judicial review may be justified in constitutional democracies. The only sound moral reason that he is able to provide in favor of the institution of judicial review is that judicial review is important because it forces the political community to deliberate about matters of right and principle that can be neglected in the political judgments of the majorities in a constitutional democracy. Judicial review becomes important precisely because it can 'force political debate to include argument over principle' and break the inertia that sometimes arises when the interested groups cannot reach a compromise by the ordinary means. More importantly, it also incites a public deliberation about a rights-claim and creates an authentic 'forum of principle' where citizens can expect a reasonable justification for the authoritative settlement of the fundamental controversies that they have about the contents of their rights.[35]

As we can see, this is an argument that follows a structure similar to Raz's Normal Justification Thesis. The constitutional court, under this view, acts *in service* of the general citizens, since it is in a better position to balance all the reasons of principle that are applicable to these citizens even though such reasons were not visible in the ordinary political debates. The court's decision is relevant because it facilitates the people to comply with the reasons of principle that they have to act in

[34] As I argued in a review of Hübner Mendes' book, 'a court that resorts to an internal compromise to settle issues of political morality pays a high price in order to achieve the benefits of a unanimous decision. By hiding the internal disagreements and resorting to a compromise, a judge assumes the risk of establishing a priority of the views of her colleagues over the opinions of the representatives of the people, insofar as deference to the judgment of the other judges often implies, when the validity of an act is at stake, defiance to the judgment of the legislature' (Bustamante 2015).

[35] Dworkin is not the only one to follow this strategy for justifying the authority of constitutional courts. Rawls, for instance, holds that constitutional courts are the most important *locus* of public reasoning, and Kumm describes them as a forum of 'Socratic contestation' that is essential for democracy. I believe, however, that these accounts share the most important features of Dworkin's model. They justify the court's power in a similar way and are exposed to the same objections that one may rise against Dworkin. See Rawls (1999, 231–41) and Kumm (2007).

a certain way. As it happens in Raz's Normal Justification Thesis, the directives of the constitutional court 'derive their force from the considerations which justify them'. It is *because* the court's decision is based on principles that are not always considered in the political deliberations that we should accept the authority of the courts.

Even Jeremy Waldron, one of the toughest critics of judicial review, concedes that this may be a good argument for us to have a constitutional court. The court can be justified as 'a mechanism that allows citizens to bring these issues to everyone's attention as they arise' (Waldron 2006, 1370). Nonetheless, as Waldron explains, this is *not* an argument for strong judicial review. Important as this alerting role of a constitutional court might be, it is 'an argument for weak judicial review only', and not for a 'strong form of the practice in which the abstract question of right that has been identified is settled in the way that a court deems appropriate' (Waldron 2006, 1370). In effect, in systems of weak judicial review, where courts lack final authority to settle the matters of a controversy about the rights that we have in the political community,[36] courts can act as a 'checking point' in the system, having an 'interpretative, alerting and informing function with respect to rights issues' (Gardbaum 2013, 64).

The main virtue of these weak-form systems of judicial review, in my opinion, is that they neither withdraw from the people or their representatives the *moral responsibility* for the interpretation of the rights that they possess, nor impinge upon the people's right to have their fair share of the power to participate in the *making* of the decision. Given that the decisions of the courts in a weak-system of judicial review are not final and stand only to the extent that they place a burden of argument on the officials that intend to exert their power to override them, the responsibility for rights is dispersed among 'all three branches of government' rather than centralized in the courts (Gardbaum 2013, 68). It may foster, as the legal systems that belong to the New Commonwealth Model of Constitutionalism intend to do, 'a stronger and deeper rights consciousness in all institutions exercising public power' (Gardbaum 2013, 69).

When we focus on the decision stage of the political process, it is harder to find a moral justification for the power of the courts to quash a legislative decision in a constitutional democracy. Neither intrinsic reasons stemming from the values that underlie democracy nor instrumental justifications such as Dworkin's argument that

[36] In the characterization of 'weak' judicial review adopted in this paper I am offering however, an approach that might appear to be slightly broader than Waldron's. It might be possible to include, under this category, also the legal systems which allow the courts to engage in judicial review to protect the *procedural* aspects of constitutional democracy with a view to reinforcing representation and promoting participation of excluded minorities, but *not* to promote a direct application of the *substantive* values upheld by the judges of the court or replace a 'reasonable' judgment of the representatives of the people by a 'reasonable' judgment of the court. The argument of this essay is target, primarily, to models of judicial review that endorse the idea of judicial supremacy and allows judges to give a final judgment about the most abstract and controversial judgments of political morality. On the possibility of judicial review to promote representation and procedural democracy, see Ely (1980).

the court may facilitate public reasoning are capable of justifying such power under the circumstance of deep disagreement about a rights issue. While the systems of weak judicial review are premised on the principle that 'democracy requires a reasonable legislative judgment to trump a reasonable judicial one,' (Gardbaum 2013, 65) in legal systems with strong judicial review it is the other way round.[37]

The legitimacy problem of strong judicial review becomes visible when we consider the fact of disagreement in the contemporary democracies of the Western world. As Waldron has shown in his famous criticism against judicial review, there are sound process-related reasons for accepting as fair a legislative decision made in the light of a profound and persisting disagreement about the rights that we have in a given society, and there seems to be no analogous moral reasons to justify its invalidation by an equally divided court.

On the one hand, an advocate of a majority decision by a legislature, when questioned by a citizen defeated in a deliberation about rights, may ground her position in the theory of 'fair elections', in which all citizens have equal opportunities to participate in the decisions about the composition of the legislature. Furthermore, the principle of 'majority decision' (MD), 'better than any other rule', must be accepted because it is 'neutral as between the contested outcomes, treats participants equally, and gives each expressed opinion the greatest weight possible compatible with giving equal weight to all opinions' (Waldron 2006, 1388). That is to say: while adopting MD, we commit ourselves with the principle of political equality, which provides a reasonable justification for legislative supremacy at least in the 'core cases' that make judicial review morally unjustified.[38]

On the other hand, this kind of justification is *not* available when the power to resolve our good faith disagreements is assigned to a majority decision among a small number of judges in a constitutional court. 'MD is appropriate for persons who have a moral claim to insist on being regarded as equals in some decision-process', whereas constitutional judges lack any moral basis for their claim to participate because their claim is 'functional', rather than a matter of 'entitlement' (Waldron 2006, 1392). According to Waldron, the attempt to vindicate the judicial supremacy and reconstruct democracy as suspicious about the MD is described as

[37] In the U.S. legal system, for instance, many people think this is the actual way in which constitutional decisions operate. The holding of *Cooper v. Aaron*, 358 U.S. 1 (1958) is considered a paradigmatic statement of this principle, for the court argued that it follows from the principle of judicial supremacy (as stated in Marbury v. Madison) that the interpretation settled by the Supreme Court is also part of the 'supreme law of the land'. For a critical discussion of this principle, see Tushnet (2000).

[38] The 'core cases', for Waldron, are those in which the following four assumptions are satisfied: one can find '(i) democratic institutions in reasonably good working order, including a representative legislature elected on the basis of universal adult suffrage; (ii) a set of judicial institutions, again in reasonably good order, set up on a non-representative basis to hear individual lawsuits, settle disputes, and uphold the rule of law; (iii) a commitment on the part of most members of the society and most of its officials to the idea of individual and minority rights; and (iv) persisting, substantial, and good faith disagreement about rights (i.e., about what the commitment to rights actually amounts to and what its implications are) among the members of the society who are committed to the idea of rights'. See Waldron (2006, 1360).

an 'insult', particularly when we consider the fact that 'judges disagree among themselves along exactly the same lines as the citizens and representatives do, and that the judges make their decisions, too, in the court-room by majority voting' (Waldron 1999, 15).

Waldron has good arguments, therefore, to support his claim to decouple the ideas of 'rights' and 'judicial supremacy'. Though there is no incoherence between democracy and constitutionalism, insofar as democracy itself presupposes and instantiates some fundamental rights, the contents of democratic rights must be determined by *democratic means* if they are to comply with democracy's requirements of fairness and equal respect for the different views upheld by the members of the political community. The critics of judicial review need not to be seen as criticizing the idea of rights in general. On the contrary, they are based on the people's right to participate in the deliberation about the rights that they have in the political community.[39]

3.4 Conclusion: On the Circumstances of Judicial Review and the Strong Systems of Judicial Review

If correct, my argument in the second part allows me to hold, amongst other things, the following theses about the authority of constitutional courts.

1) There are no intrinsic moral reasons for the authority of constitutional courts. On the contrary, these courts face a much heavier moral burden of justification than ordinary legislators and common law courts do, inasmuch as they do not decide in an intrinsically democratic way and none of the principles underlying democracy provide a special justification for a decision-process which attributes to the courts the final authority to decide a controversial issue about the rights that people have in the political community.
2) The claim to legitimate authority that constitutional courts stake is instrumental in the same way as Raz's Normal Justification Thesis is. This requires a supporter of the authority of the constitutional courts to specify all the *relevant set of conditions* that provide the kind of indirect justification for the authority of constitutional courts.
3) The instrumental justification available to justify the legitimacy of judicial review, as we have seen in Dworkin's argument of the 'forum of principle', is too weak to provide a justification of the systems of strong judicial review – where the court has final authority to quash a legislative provision – but might be potent enough to offer a sound argument in support of a weak system of judicial review.

[39] Waldron's own words are particularly illuminating in this point: 'I am tired of hearing opponents of judicial review denigrated as being rights-skeptics. The best response is to erect the case against judicial review on the ground of a strong and pervasive commitment to rights' (Waldron 2006, 1366).

I would like to discuss, in this concluding section, some of the consequences of the second and the third theses above.

With regard to thesis 2, if the argument for constitutional courts is conditional, as I believe it to be, then 'institutional rules' that regulate the process of deliberation in the court and the 'efficacy' of the court's decisions must be adjusted to fit the conditions which define the adequate circumstances of judicial review.

One of the most important challenges for a theory of the authority of the institutions of judicial review, therefore, is to specify the conditions that make the circumstances of judicial review. Nonetheless, I do not intend to do this in the remaining paragraphs of this conclusion. My ambition in this final section is more humble, for I merely want to show that in a well-working democracy, which takes both rights and democracy seriously, *one of the conditions* that make the 'circumstances of judicial review' is that the institutional environment of the state provides room for a legislative *override* of the court's final decisions about not only the contents of our rights, but in particular about the *validity of the enactments of the legislature*.[40]

There should be little room, in a community of citizens committed to a respectful protection of human rights, for an *exclusionary power* of a constitutional court to strike down a statute on the ground that it violates a particular provision of the Bill of Rights. By giving the courts final authority to annul a legislative enactment, the traditional systems of strong judicial review do not take disagreement seriously and show little respect for political equality and the autonomy of the people.

The traditional argument that justifies the powers of constitutional courts on the assumption that they are privileged 'forums of public reasoning' seems insufficient for granting to the courts a power to settle with final authority the controversies about our rights. Even though this instrumental justification may be good enough to

---

[40] I will leave open the question of how the legal system can satisfy this requirement, since there are many different institutional arrangements that equally comply with this moral exigency. Even without an express provision attributing an overriding power to the legislators, a legal system that has an amendment rule that does not require more than an ordinary majority vote would still be compatible with this requirement (Gardbaum 2013, 40, note 65). I believe that this can be the case even for a legal system with a stronger decision rule, which requires more than an ordinary majority while not imposing too difficult a burden on the legislature. Brazil's constitution, for instance, can be amended by a *supermajority* of 3/5 of the members of the Senate and the Chamber of Deputies, which needs to be confirmed in two sessions in each house. Given the frequency of amendments in the last 25 years (almost 90 amendments) this does not prove to be a very heavy burden. It is much probable, therefore, that the argument against strong judicial review places a much more serious challenge to the U.S. Supreme Court than to the Brazilian *Supremo Tribunal Federal*. Nonetheless, there is one point that seems to distance Brazil from the 'pure form' of 'weak judicial review'. The Brazilian Federal Supreme Court is also empowered to strike down constitutional amendments whenever its members believe that such amendment has the 'tendency to abolish' the principles stated in article 60 § 4th of the Constitution. These principles include the protection of all of the 'Fundamental Legal Rights' and the general clauses of the 'Republican Government', the 'Federation' and the 'Separation of Powers'. The vagueness of these clauses and the extent of this normative power make the judicial review of constitutional amendments a threat to the mechanism of institutional dialogue that the 'weak' forms of judicial review intend to promote.

support the conclusion that constitutional courts can play an important role in deliberative democracies, it does not suffice to ground the view that the courts should have authority to settle matters with the final authority that they currently have in the vast majority of the states that embraced the practice of judicial review.

Political decisions about the contents of rights take place, as a rule, in the context of reasonable disagreement among the decision participants, in which more often than not there are different and mutually exclusively decisions that are equally acceptable from the point of view of the general principles embodied in the Bill of Rights. There are no grounds for replacing, as traditional systems of strong judicial review do, a reasonable decision of the legislature by a reasonable decision of a non-representative constitutional court.

Whatever might be the circumstances that justify judicial review in a particular legal system, I am convinced that one of these circumstances will be that under normal circumstances *no constitutional court should have the power to quash, in an irreversible way, the validity of a law that is formally enacted by the legislative assemblies*.

This brings us to the thesis 3 in the scheme that I presented in the beginning of this concluding section. If we consider the systems of weak judicial review, where the courts lack pre-emptive authority to settle the disagreements that we have over a rights issue, then the instrumental justification available for the authority of constitutional courts might be successful. Without its power to pronounce exclusionary directives that replace the rules enacted by the legislature, constitutional courts would look like the 'central cases' of legal authority, which can be explained according to the pictures developed by Dworkin in his model of Law as Integrity.

The decisions of constitutional courts, when they issue a Declaration of Incompatibility with a Bill of Rights, as the U.K. courts may do, would engender a post-interpretive deliberation about the matter at stake, and no longer could be described as peremptory or pre-emptive in Raz's sense.

Under these conditions, the people's right to their share of power to *decide* by themselves the controversies over their rights is entirely preserved, and the instrumentalist justification of the authority of constitutional courts offered by Ronald Dworkin becomes an attractive way to support the authority of constitutional courts.

These considerations call out for a new type of normative justification for the very existence of constitutional courts, which does *not* include the principle of *judicial supremacy*. I think that Stephen Gardbaum's commentaries on the general features of the New Commonwealth Model of Constitutionalism is in line with the kind of justification that I am arguing for:

> The commonwealth model does not only (...) provide a new form of judicial review. It also provides a new justification of judicial review. For once shorn of judicial supremacy, the task of defending a judicial role in rights protection is a different – and easier – one. A model of constitutionalism that provides for judicial rights review of legislation but gives the legal power of the final word to ordinary majority vote in the legislature is normatively, and not only practically, different from one that does not. Indeed, even if it turns out (as certain critiques maintain) that there is little or no practical difference between the power of

> courts under certain instantiations of the new model and judicial supremacy, there is still a normative difference between them. Despite the current fairly strong political presumption against use of the legislative override in Canada, there is still a straightforward sense in which exercises of judicial review are more democratically legitimate than in the United States because of the existence of the override power (Gardbaum 2013, 36).

It makes a big difference, even if Parliament decides not to use the power of override, whether the courts lack a final authority on a particular matter about fundamental legal rights. The efficacy of the court's pronouncements would no longer depend merely on authoritative settlement, but also on the soundness of the reasons that the court is able to provide. Once a court is deprived of the final authority to settle a rights issue in a definitive way, the other powers of the state are also involved as participants in the interpretation of the Bill of Rights. The eventual tension between democracy and constitutionalism is nuanced, and citizens regain control of their own moral code.

One of the most important challenges for constitutional theorists (and legislators) of this Century is thus to provide the philosophical arguments required to support (and to design institutions needed to enhance) the principles that underlie the new systems of weak judicial review, whether these systems are located in the common law world or not. Even in the legal cultures where judicial review is deeply entrenched, there should be important institutional mechanisms for increasing the democratic legitimacy of the constitutional courts and empowering the people and the other spheres of government to *participate* in the deliberations and the democratic decisions about the rights that they have.

Acknowledgments This chapter has benefited from critical inputs from several contributors, with whom I am deeply indebted for the helpful criticisms and suggestions. I am grateful to Stephen Gardbaum, Mark Greenberg, Seana Shiffrin, Georgios Pavlakos and the participants of the UCLA Legal Theory Workshop, where its first draft was presented in the Fall of 2014; to Enrique Cáceres, Imer Flores, Verónica Rodriguez-Blanco, Carlos Montemayor, Jorge L. Fabra and the participants of the III Jornadas Internacionales de Filosofía del Derecho of the Autonomous University of México in 2014; to Ronaldo Porto Macedo Júnior, who kindly hosted and supervised me on a 1-year postdoctoral fellowship at the University of São Paulo in 2015, where I had a chance to improve this chapter in many aspects; to Rafael Bezerra and the wonderful undergraduate students who participated in my reading group on Legal Philosophy at the University of São Paulo in 2015; to my colleagues Bernardo Fernandes, Fabrício Polido, Mariah Brochado, Marcelo Cattoni, Leandro Zanitelli and Andityas Moura at the Law School of the Federal University of Minas Gerais; and, last but not least, to my research students Igor Enríquez, Ana Luísa de Navarro Moreira, João Vítor Martins, Christina Brina, Lucas Paulino, Adriano Borges and Franklin Marques Dutra, at the UFMG, who have always been my most important interlocutors. The annual postdoctoral fellowship at the University of São Paulo, where part of the research that led to this paper was undertaken, was generously funded by FAPESP (São Paulo Research Foundation, Grant 2014-9810-4), but the research received funding also from FAPEMIG (Minas Gerais Research Foundation, Grant PPM-00178-14) and from the CNPq (Brazilian Council of Scientific and Technological Development, Grant 484975/2013-7). To these agencies, which are among the most important entities that support science and philosophy in my home country, I am deeply grateful.

References

Ackerman, Bruce. 1993. *We the people, volume 1: Foundations*. Cambride, MA: Belknap.

Alexander, Larry, and Frederick Schauer. 1997. On extrajudicial constitutional interpretation. *Harvard Law Review* 110: 1359–1387.

Alexy, Robert. 2005. Balancing, constitutional review and representation. *International Journal of Constitutional Law (I-CON)* 3: 527–581.

Allan, James. 2011. Statutory bill of rights: You read words in, you read words out, you take parliament's clear intention and you shake it all about – Doin' the Sankey Hanky Panky. In *The legal protection of human rights: Sceptical essays*, ed. T. Campbell, K.D. Ewing, and A. Tomkins, 108–126. Oxford: Oxford University Press.

Bellamy, Richard. 2007. *Political constitutionalism: A republican defence of the constitutionality of democracy*. Cambridge: Cambridge University Press.

Bertea, Stefano. 2008. Law and legal reasoning. *Northern Ireland Legal Quarterly* 58: 5–20.

Buckland, W.W., and Arnold D. McNair. 1939. *Roman law and common law: A comparison in outline*. Cambridge: Cambridge University Press.

Bustamante, Thomas. 2012. Book review: Legality, by Scott Shapiro. *Legal Studies: The Journal of the Society of Legal Scholars* 32: 499–507.

Bustamante, Thomas. 2015. Review article: The ongoing search for legitimacy: Can a 'Pragmatic yet Principled' deliberative model justify the authority of constitutional courts? *Modern Law Review* 78: 372–393.

Christiano, Thomas. 2004. The authority of democracy. *The Journal of Political Philosophy* 12: 266–290.

Christiano, Thomas. 2008. *The constitution of equality: Democratic authority and its limits*. Oxford: Oxford University Press.

Coffin, Frank Morey. 1980. *The ways of a judge: Reflections from federal appelate bench*. Boston: Houghton Mifflin.

Coleman, Jules. 2001. *The practice of principle: In defence of a pragmatist approach to legal theory*. Oxford: Oxford University Press.

Dworkin, Ronald. 1985. *A matter of principle*. Cambridge, MA: Belknap.

Dworkin, Ronald. 1986. *Law's empire*. Cambridge, MA: Belknap.

Dworkin, Ronald. 1996. *Freedom's law: The moral reading of the American constitution*. Cambridge, MA: Belknap.

Dworkin, Ronald. 2000. *Sovereign virtue: The theory and practice of equality*. Cambridge, MA: Belknap.

Dworkin, Ronald. 2006. *Justice in robes*. Cambridge, MA: Belknap.

Ely, John Hart. 1980. *Democracy and distrust: A theory of judicial review*. Cambridge, MA: Harvard University Press.

Finnis, John. 2011. *Natural law and natural rigths*, 2nd ed. Oxford: Oxford University Press.

Gardbaum, Stephen. 2013. *The new commonwealth model of constitutionalism: Theory and practice*. Cambridge: Cambridge University Press.

Gardner, John. 2001. Legal positivism: 5 1/2 myths. *American Journal of Jurisprudence* 46: 199–227.

Goldsworthy, Jeffrey. 2010. *Parliamentary sovereignty: Contemporary debates*. Cambridge: Cambridge University Press.

Green, Leslie. 1988. *The authority of the state*. Oxford: Oxford University Press.

Greenberg, Mark. 2011. The standard picture and its discontents. In *Oxford studies in philosophy of law, Vol. 1*, ed. Leslie Green and Brian Leiter, 39–106. Oxford: Oxford University Press.

Greenberg, Mark. 2014. The moral impact theory of law. *Yale Law Journal* 123: 1288–1342.

Günther, Klaus. 1993. *The sense of appropriateness: Application discourses in morality and in law*. Trans. J. Farrel. Albany: State University of New York Press.

Hart, H. L. A. 1990. Commands and authoritative legal reasons. In *Authority*, ed. J. Raz. New York: New York University Press. 92–114.

Hershovitz, Scott. 2003. Legitimacy, democracy and razian authority. *Legal Theory* 9: 201–220.
Hespanha, António Manuel. 1978. Sobre a prática dogmática dos juristas oitocentistas. In *A história do direito na história social*, 70–149. Lisbon: Livros Horizonte.
Hespanha, António Manuel. 2005. *Direito luso-brasileiro no Antigo Regime*. Florianópolis: Fundação Boiteux.
Hespanha, António Manuel. 2006. Direito Comum e Direito Colonial: porque existe e em que consiste um direito colonial brasileiro. *Panóptica* 3: 95–116, Available at: http://www.panoptica.org.
Hübner Mendes, Conrado. 2013. *Constitutional courts and deliberative democracy*. Oxford: Oxford University Press.
Kelsen, Hans. 1928. La garantie juridictionnelle de la Constitution (La Justice constitutionnelle). *Revue du droit public et de la science politique* 35: 197–257.
Kramer, Matthew. 1999. Also among the prophets: Some rejoinders to Ronald Dworkin's attacks on legal positivism. In *In defense of legal positivism: Law without trimmings*, 128–192. Oxford: Oxford University Press.
Kumm, Mathias. 2007. Institutionalizing Socratic contestation. *European Journal of Legal Studies* 1: 1–32.
MacCormick, Neil. 2005. *Rhetoric and the rule of law*. Oxford: Oxford University Press.
MacCormick, Neil. 2007. *Institutions of law*. Oxford: Oxford University Press.
Macedo Júnior, Ronaldo Porto. 2013. *O direito em desacordo: o debate entre o interpretativismo e o convencionalismo jurídico*. São Paulo: University of São Paulo, Law School, Dissertation presented as a requirement in a public competition for a Chair in Legal Theory and Philosophy of Law, 2013 (multiple copies on file at the University Library).
Marmor, Andrei. 2005. Authority, equality and democracy. *Ratio Juris* 18: 315–345.
Marmor, Andrei. 2009. *Social conventions – From language to law*. Princeton: Princeton University Press.
Postema, Gerald J. 1982. Coordination and convention at the foundation of law. *The Journal of Legal Studies* 11: 165–203.
Postema, Gerald J. 1996. Law's autonomy and public practical reason. In *The autonomy of law: Essays on legal positivism*, ed. R. George, 79–118. Oxford: Clarendon Press.
Rawls, John. 1999. *Political liberalism*, expanded edition. New York: Columbia University Press.
Raz, Joseph. 1986. *The morality of freedom*. Oxford: Oxford University Press.
Raz, Joseph. 1989. Liberalism, skepticism and democracy. *Iowa Law Review* 74: 761–786.
Raz, Joseph. 1994a. Authority, law and morality. In *Ethics in the public domain – Essays in the morality of law and politics*, 210–237. Oxford: Oxford University Press.
Raz, Joseph. 1994b. The problem about the nature of law. In *Ethics in the public domain – Essays in the morality of law and politics*, 195–209. Oxford: Oxford University Press.
Raz, Joseph. 1994c. On the autonomy of legal reasoning. In *Ethics in the public domain – Essays in the morality of law and politics*, 326–340. Oxford: Oxford University Press.
Raz, Joseph. 1995. Interpretation without retrieval. In *Law and interpretation: Essays in legal philosophy*, ed. Andrei Marmor, 155–175. Oxford: Oxford University Press.
Raz, Joseph. 1999. *Practical reason and norms*, 2nd ed. Oxford: Oxford University Press.
Raz, Joseph. 2009a. *Between authority and interpretation: On the theory of law and practical reason*. Oxford: Oxford University Press.
Raz, Joseph. 2009b. *The authority of law*, 2nd ed. Oxford: Oxford University Press.
Shapiro, Scott. 2002. Authority. In *The Oxford handbook of jurisprudence & philosophy of law*, ed. Jules Coleman and Scott Shapiro, 382–439. Oxford: Oxford University Press.
Shapiro, Scott. 2011. *Legality*. Cambridge, MA: Belknap.
Simpson, A.W.B. 1961. The ratio decidendi of a case and the doctrine of binding precedent. In *Oxford essays in jurisprudence – First series*, ed. A.G. Guest, 148–175. Oxford: Oxford University Press.
Simpson, A.W.B. 1973. The common law and legal theory. In *Oxford essays in jurisprudence – Second series*, ed. A.W.B. Simpson, 77–99. Oxford: Oxford University Press.

Tushnet, Mark. 2000. Marbury v. Madison and the theory of judicial supremacy. In *Great cases in constitutional law*, ed. R.P. George, 17–54. Princeton: Princeton University Press.

Tushnet, Mark. 2009. *Weak courts, strong rights: Judicial review and social welfare rights in comparative constitutional law*. Princeton: Princeton University Press.

Waldron, Jeremy. 1999. *Law and disagreement*. Oxford: Oxford University Press.

Waldron, Jeremy. 2003. Authority for officials. In *Rights, culture and the law – Themes from the legal and political philosophy of Joseph Raz*, ed. Lukas H. Meyer, Stanley L. Paulson, and Thomas W. Pogge, 45–69. Oxford: Oxford University Press.

Waldron, Jeremy. 2006. The core of the case against judicial review. *Yale Law Journal* 115: 1346–1406.

Waldron, Jeremy. 2009. Judges as moral reasoners. *International Journal of Constitutional Law (I-CON)* 7: 2–24.

Waluchow, W.J. 2007. *A common law theory of judicial review: The living tree*. Cambridge: Cambridge University Press.

Chapter 4
Reason Without Vote: The Representative and Majoritarian Function of Constitutional Courts

Luís Roberto Barroso

Abstract This essay starts with a brief overview of some of the changes and new developments in constitutional law in the past decades. It also provides a brief account of the ascent of the Judiciary in most democracies, as well as the expansion of constitutional jurisdiction throughout the world. The main topic of the essay, however, are the two roles played by constitutional courts in our days: the counter-majoritarian role, which is widely studied by constitutional theory, and the representative role of such courts, a subject that has been neglected by constitutional scholars in general, with few exceptions. The argument is developed in a cosmopolitan fashion, drawing from authors and experiences from different parts of the world; however, it uses the court of a new democracy – the Supreme Court of Brazil – as a case study. In polities in which the legislature struggles with a major democratic deficit – and until it can be properly overcome –, it may be the case, under certain circumstances, that it will be up to the Supreme Court to be responsive to unattended social demands presented as legal claims of rights. Furthermore, in some exceptional situations, the Court may need to play the part of an enlightened vanguard, pushing history forward. At the conclusion, though, the essay emphasizes the idea of institutional dialogues as the best path between legislative omission and judicial supremacy.

4.1 Introduction

In the exchange excerpted below, two professors in one of the most prestigious universities in the world discuss the role of the Judiciary branch and Supreme Court in democracies. Both are progressive and committed to social development. The first interlocutor believes that only the Legislature should be able to bestow rights and to activate social progress. The second thinks that the Legislature should have

L.R. Barroso (✉)
Supremo Tribunal Federal, Praça dos Três Poderes, Brasília, DF 70175-900, Brazil
e-mail: gabmlrb@stf.jus.br

T. Bustamante, B.G. Fernandes (eds.), *Democratizing Constitutional Law*, Law and Philosophy Library 113, DOI 10.1007/978-3-319-28371-5_4

the first duty to act; however, if it fails to do so, that the power to act should then shift to the Judiciary.

- Professor 1: "In the long run, through the Legislature, people will make the right choices, thus guaranteeing the fundamental rights of all, including the right of a woman to terminate a pregnancy she does not want or of homosexual couples to freely express their love. It's just a matter of waiting for the right time".
- Professor 2: "And until then, what should we say to same-sex partners who wish to live out their affection and a shared life project now? Or to the woman who wants to interrupt a non-viable pregnancy which causes her great suffering? Or to a black father who wants his child to have access to an education that he, himself, never had? [Should we say–] 'Sorry, History is running a bit behind; come back in one or two generations'?".[1]

This work deals precisely with this duality of perspectives. It explores the subject of the representative role of supreme courts, their enlightening function, and the situations in which they can legitimately drive History forward. Written for a seminar presented in Belo Horizonte, Brazil, this study makes use of some aspects of the Brazilian experience and case law. The argument put forth, however, is based on international literature and aspires to universal legitimacy, being valid in a good number of contemporary democratic constitutional states.

The conclusion reached is quite simple and easily demonstrated, although, to some extent, contrary to conventional wisdom. In some scenarios, because of the multiple conditions that affect or paralyze the majoritarian political process, it is up to the Supreme Court or the constitutional court to guarantee the majority rule and the same dignity to all citizens. Majoritarian politics, led by elected representatives, is a vital component of democracy. But democracy is much more than the mere numerical expression of a greater number of votes. Beyond this purely formal aspect, democracy has a substantive dimension, which entails the guarantee of values and fundamental rights. Alongside these formal and substantive dimensions, there is, still, a deliberative one, made up of public debate, arguments, and persuasion. Contemporary democracy therefore requires votes, rights, *and* reason. This is the subject of this essay.

4.2 The New Constitutional Law and the Ascent of the Judiciary

At the end of World War II, countries in continental Europe underwent a major institutional redesign, with repercussions of short, medium, and long term on the Roman-Germanic world at large. Constitutional law came out of the conflict entirely

[1]This debate took place at Harvard University, between Professor Mark Tushnet and this author, in November 7th, 2011. Entitled *Politics and the Judiciary*, a video recording is available at https://www.youtube.com/watch?v=giC_vOBn-bc. Accessed 26 August 2015. Also on this subject, see Tushnet (1999) and (2009), and Barroso (2012, 237–283).

reconfigured, both as to its object (new constitutions were enacted), and as to its role (centrality of the Constitution over the law). As well, the ways and means of interpreting and applying its standards were also altered (emergence of new constitutional hermeneutics). These dogmatic changes were also accompanied by a remarkable institutional change, denoted by the creation of constitutional courts and the steady rise of the Judiciary. In lieu of the legislative rule of law prevalent in the nineteenth century, arose the constitutional rule of law, with its many implications.[2] This new model has been identified as Postwar Constitutionalism, New Constitutional Law or Neoconstitutionalism.[3]

This new constitutional law evolved in an environment of profound transformation within legal culture, which included: (i) the attenuation of legal formalism, (ii) the development of a post-positivistic philosophical view and (iii) the transition of the Constitution to the center of the legal system. Constitutional texts became more analytical, with the provision of an extensive catalog of fundamental rights. Furthermore, societies grew more complex and plural. As a consequence, there was a reduction in the ability to address a large number of questions through express normative provisions, increasing the experience of uncertainty in the law. In this environment, both the Constitution and infra-constitutional laws transferred decision-making power to the interpreters of the legal system, through the use of principles and open-texture clauses. Judicial interpretation, in turn, started to resort more frequently to concepts and techniques such as balancing, proportionality, and reasonableness.

At the same time as these philosophical, theoretical, and practical developments, there was a significant institutional rise of the Judiciary Branch. The phenomenon is worldwide and is also, temporally and historically, associated with the end of World War II. Since that time, the world has realized that the existence of a strong and independent Judiciary is an important component in the preservation of democratic institutions and fundamental rights. This is accompanied by a kind of disillusionment with majoritarian politics and the inability of parliaments to generate consensus on certain controversial issues. The reference to New Constitutionalism is, ultimately, *descriptive* of this new reality, marked by the expansion of the role of the Constitution, the ascent of the Judiciary, and a less formalistic and positivistic legal interpretation. But the idea of new constitutionalism, in endorsing these transformations, also has a *normative* dimension. It is therefore not only a way of describing contemporary constitutional law, but also of wishing it so. A legal system that leaves its traditional comfort zone, which is one of conserving relevant political achievements, and begins to embody a promotional function, thus becomes an instrument of social progress.

---

[2] On the topic, see Ferrajoli (2003).

[3] For two important collections on the topic, in Spanish, see Carbonell (2003) and (2007). For a valuable collection of texts in Portuguese, see Quaresma et al. (2009). The ideas developed in the following two paragraphs were originally systematized in Barroso (2005).

4.3 The Expansion of the Constitutional Jurisdiction and Its Various Roles

Throughout the second half of the twentieth century, countries in continental Europe and those that followed the Roman-Germanic tradition, in general, witnessed a major paradigm shift with respect to constitutional design and theory: the transition from a legislative rule of law to a constitutional rule of law.[4] In the old model, the Constitution was understood primarily as a political document, containing rules that could not be directly applied and that therefore depended upon further expansion by the Legislature or the Executive Branch. Nor was there judicial review by the Judiciary – or, where there was, it was timid and mostly irrelevant. In this environment, the centrality of the law and the supremacy of parliament prevailed. Within a constitutional rule of law, the Constitution becomes legal norm. From there, it not only regulates the procedure for enactment of legislation and other normative acts, but it also sets limits as to its content, and imposes duties of performance on the State. This new model was governed by the centrality of the Constitution and judicial supremacy, defined as the primacy of a constitutional court or Supreme Court in setting the final and binding interpretation of constitutional norms.

The expression *constitutional jurisdiction* refers to the interpretation and application of the Constitution by judicial bodies. In the United States and countries that adopt its model of judicial review – such as Brazil – that power is exercised by all judges and courts, with the Supreme Court at the top of the system. The constitutional jurisdiction comprises two distinct components. In the first one, the Constitution is directly applied to the situations contemplated within it. For example, the recognition that a particular power belongs to the federal government instead of the states, or the right to freedom of expression without prior censorship. Also under this component falls the role, more complex and politically sensitive, of remedying unconstitutional omissions, in instances in which the absence of a regulatory provision frustrates the exercise of a fundamental right. The second component involves the indirect application of the Constitution, which occurs when the interpreter uses the Constitution as a parameter to assess the validity of other normative questions (judicial review) or to determine their best meaning, among different possibilities (interpretation according to the Constitution). In sum: the constitutional jurisdiction includes the power employed by judges and courts in the direct application of the Constitution. It also includes the indirect application of the Constitution through the exercise of judicial review of laws and of acts of the government in general, as well as through the interpretation of the legal system according to the Constitution.

From a political and institutional standpoint, the exercise of constitutional jurisdiction by supreme courts or constitutional courts around the world involves two types of components: one counter-majoritarian, and the other representative. On one hand, the counter-majoritarian component is one of the most studied themes in

[4] On the topic, see Ferrajoli (2003, 14–17) and Zagrebelsky (2005, 21–41).

constitutional theory, and for many decades has deliberated the democratic legitimacy of judicial invalidation of acts from the Legislative and Executive Branches. On the other hand, legal scholarship and opinion leaders in general have ignored the representative function. Nonetheless, in some parts of the world, notably in Brazil, this second role has become not only more visible, but, circumstantially, more important. This essay attempts to shed light on this phenomenon, which has, oddly, gone unnoticed, despite being possibly the most important institutional transformation of the last decade.

4.3.1 The Counter-Majoritarian Role of the Supreme Courts

Supreme courts and constitutional courts in general – comprising the Federal Supreme Court in Brazil – conduct judicial review of normative measures, including those arising from the Legislative Branch and the head of the Executive Branch. In carrying out this assignment, these courts can invalidate acts of Congress or Parliament – comprising representatives elected by the people – and the President of the Republic, elected with more than fifty million votes. That is to say: in Brazil, eleven Justices of the Supreme Court (actually six, since the absolute majority is enough), who never received a single popular vote in their elevation to their position, may superimpose their interpretation of the Constitution over the one conceived of by elected officials vested with representative mandates and democratic legitimacy. To this circumstance, which generates apparent incongruity within a democratic state, constitutional theory gave the nickname "the counter-majority difficulty".[5]

Despite occasional theoretical contention,[6] this counter-majoritarian role of judicial review is almost universally accepted. The democratic legitimacy of the constitutional jurisdiction settled on the basis of two main grounds: (a) the protection of fundamental rights, that corresponds to the ethical and justicial minimums of a political community[7] and are not susceptible to being trampled on by majoritarian political deliberation; and (b) the protection of the rules of democracy and of channels of political participation for all.[8] Most countries in the world give the Judiciary, and in particular its supreme or constitutional court, a sentinel status against the risk of a tyranny of the majority.[9] This prevents the oppression of minorities and the distortion of the democratic process. Today, there is reasonable con-

[5] The term is a classic from the work of Alexander Bickel (1986, 16 ff).

[6] E.g., Waldron (2006), Tushnet (1999), and Kramer (2004).

[7] The equivalence between human rights and minimum reserve of justice is used by Robert Alexy in several of his works. See, *e.g.*, Alexy (2005a, 76).

[8] For this proceduralist view of the role of constitutional jurisdiction, see Ely (1980).

[9] The term was used by John Stuart Mill (2002, first edition: 1874), where he wrote: "the tyranny of the majority is now generally included among the evils against which society requires to be on its guard".

sensus that the concept of democracy goes beyond the notion of a majority rule, requiring the assimilation of other fundamental values.

One of these core values is the right of every individual to equal concern and respect,[10] that is, to be treated with the same dignity of others – which includes having their interests and opinions taken into account. Democracy, therefore, beyond the procedural dimension of embodying a majority rule, enjoys a substantive dimension, including values of equality, freedom and justice. This is what truly transforms it into a collective project of self-government in which no one is deliberately left behind. More than the right to equal participation, democracy means that those defeated in the political process, as well as minority segments in general, are not abandoned and left to fend for themselves. Just the opposite, they retain their position as equally worthy members of the political community.[11] In most of the world, the guardian of these promises (Garapon 1999) is the Supreme Court or constitutional court, because of its ability to be a forum of principles (Dworkin 1981) – constitutional values, not politics – and public reason – that is, arguments that are acceptable by everyone who is part of the debate (Rawls 2005). This is due at least in part to the independence of its members from the electoral process and to the fact that its decisions have to provide normative and rational arguments in their support.

It should be mentioned that, in Brazil, the counter-majoritarian role of the Supreme Court has been exercised, as it is proper, with self-restraint. In fact, in situations in which neither fundamental rights nor preconditions of democracy are at stake, the Court has been deferential to the reasonable discretion of the Legislative and Executive branches. For this very reason, the number of federal law provisions effectively declared unconstitutional under the 1988 Constitution is relatively low.[12] Admittedly, in what amounts to a Brazilian singularity, there are some precedents in which constitutional amendment provisions were declared invalid by the Supreme Court.[13] But, again, there is nothing of special significance, in quantity or quality. In some emblematic cases of adjudication of political decisions – such as the legitimacy or not of embryonic stem cell research, the validity or not of federal law providing affirmative action measures destined to improve the access of Afro-Brazilians to universities, and the constitutionality of the Presidential Decree which demarcated a large area of the state of Roraima as indigenous reservation – the Court's

[10] Dworkin (1977), 181.

[11] See Mendonça (2014, 84).

[12] Based on a survey prepared by the Secretariat of Strategic Management of the Federal Supreme Court of Brazil, it was possible to identify 93 provisions of federal law declared unconstitutional since the enactment of the Constitution of 1988 – a less than significant number, especially when you consider that no less than 5379 federal ordinary laws, and 88 complementary laws, have been edited in the same period.

[13] See STF, published on 13.09.1994, ADI 939, per Justice Sydney Sanches; STF, ADI 1.946, published on 16.05.2003, per Justice Sydney Sanches; STF, published on 02.18.2005, ADI 3.128, per Justice Cezar Peluso; STF, published on 05.19.2011, MC in ADI 2.356, per Justice Ayres Britto; STF, published on 12.19.2013, ADI 4.357 and ADI 4.425, per Justice Luiz Fux.

opinions, in each, favored self-restraint and worked to preserve decisions already made by Congress or by the President.

So far, this work has focused on justifying the democratic legitimacy of the counter-majoritarian role carried out by the constitutional jurisdiction, and demonstrating that there is no equivalence between the concept of democracy and the majoritarian principle. Before examining the issue of the representative function of the supreme courts and presenting its conclusion, this essay shall confront a world-widely complex and sensitive issue, embodied in the following question: to what extent can it be said, without clinging to a fiction or a disconnected idealization of facts, that legislative acts correspond effectively to the will of the majority?

4.3.2 The Crisis of Political Representation

For many decades, throughout the democratic world, the discourse about the crises of parliaments and the difficulties of political representation has been recurrent. From Scandinavia to Latin America, a mixture of skepticism, indifference, and dissatisfaction marks the relationship between civil society and politicians. In countries where voting is not compulsory, abstention rates reveal a general disinterest in participation in the political process. In countries with compulsory voting, such as Brazil, a very low percentage of voters are able to remember whom they voted for in the last parliamentary elections. Dysfunctionality, corruption, and over-influence of private interests are issues globally associated with political activity. And, despite this, in any democratic state, politics are an essential. Nevertheless, the current shortcomings of representative democracy are too obvious to ignore.

The inevitable consequence of a representative system is the risk of an inadequate expression of the majoritarian will of the people. As stated, the phenomenon is universal to some extent. In the United States, whose domestic politics have global visibility, excesses in political campaign financing, infiltration of religion into the public arena, and the radicalization of some partisan discourses have degenerated the public debate and pushed ordinary citizens away. A similar fate has befallen countries in Latin America and Europe, with left-wing populism in one, and the right-wing kind in the other. Brazil, likewise, is in a delicate situation in which political activity has become detached from civil society, which in turn has begun to look at it with indifference, suspicion, or contempt. Over the years, the wide exposure of the dysfunctions in political campaign financing, the oblique relationship between the Government and members of Congress, and the use of public office for personal gain, have revealed the wounds of a system that generates much indignation and few results. In short: legal scholarship, which in the past had been solely interested in issues related to the counter-majoritarian difficulty of constitutional courts, begins to turn its attention to the democratic deficit of political representation (Graber 2008).[14]

---

[14] See, *e.g.*, Graber (2008). See also Barroso (2005).

This crisis of legitimacy, representativeness, and functionality of Parliaments generated as a first consequence, in different parts of the world, an invigoration of the Executive branch. In recent years, however, and especially in Brazil, there has been an expansion of the Judiciary and, notably, the Federal Supreme Court. In a curious paradox, the fact is that in many situations judges and courts have become more representative of aspirations and social demands than traditional political institutions. It is strange, but we live in an era in which society relates more with its judges than with its parliamentarians. Take the following illustration: when the Brazilian National Congress sanctioned research with embryonic stem cells, the issue went unnoticed. When the law was challenged in the Brazilian Supreme Court, it led to a national debate. It is imperative to seek a better understanding of this phenomenon, explore any positive potential it may have, and remedy the distortion it represents. Constitutional theory has not yet analytically elaborated the subject, despite the inevitable conclusion that democracy no longer flows exclusively through its traditionally legitimized vectors.

4.3.3 The Representative Role of the Brazilian Federal Supreme Court

Le grand art en politique, ce n'est pas d'entendre ceux qui parlent, c'est d'entendre ceux qui se taisent.[15] Etienne Lamy

To this point, this essay seeks to emphasize the substantiation of the concept of democracy, which, in addition to not fully corresponding with the majority principle, has searched for new mechanisms of expression. One of these has been the transfer of political power – including some degree of judicial lawmaking – to bodies such as the Brazilian Federal Supreme Court. This section explores this phenomenon, both in its internal dynamics and in its causes and consequences. In the contemporary institutional arrangement, which presents a confluence between representative democracy and deliberative democracy,[16] the exercise of power and authority is legitimized by votes and arguments. There is no doubt that the traditional model of separation of powers, designed in the nineteenth century and which survived the twentieth century, no longer has breadth to justify, to the fullest extent, the structure and functioning of contemporary constitutionalism. To use a cliché,

---

[15] *"The great art in politics is not to listen to those who speak, it is to listen to those who stay silent"*. Etienne Lamy.

[16] For a discussion of the precursors of the idea of deliberative democracy, the reader is encouraged to consult such authors as John Rawls, with his emphasis on reason, and Jürgen Habermas, with his emphasis on communication. On deliberative democracy, see, among others, Gutmann and Thompson (2004) and Souza Neto (2006).

parodying Antonio Gramsci, we live in a time in which the old is dead and the new is yet to be born.[17]

A brief clarification is called for at this point. Many advocates of the idea of deliberative democracy defend a modest role for constitutional jurisdiction,[18] urging constitutional courts to adopt an attitude of self-restraint in cases involving substantive matters. Some of them emphasize that the role of constitutional jurisdiction is justified only when it is directed to ensuring equal conditions for a democratic deliberation.[19] However, one cannot detach the contours of deliberative democracy and of the role of supreme courts from the specific social and political contexts where they will be playing their parts. In Brazil, for example, a persistent crisis involving the legitimacy, representativeness and effectiveness of legislatures and majoritarian politics has elevated the Supreme Court to the center stage of public debate concerning certain sensitive matters. Of course, there are problems and difficulties associated with this phenomenon, but they will not be addressed in this essay. The point that I will be making here is that the Brazilian Supreme Court, combining moments of self-restraint with others of more expansive constitutional intervention, coupled with an intense and continuous interaction with civil society, has acted in favor, and not to the detriment of, the idea and practice of deliberative democracy.

The doctrine of the counter-majoritarian difficulty, previously studied, is based on the premise that the decisions of elected bodies such as the Brazilian National Congress would always express the will of the majority. As well, conversely, a judgment given by a Supreme Court, whose members are not elected, would never do so. Any empirical study discredits these two propositions. For numerous reasons, the Legislature does not always express the sentiment of the majority.[20] Besides the already mentioned democratic deficit resulting from the failures in the electoral and political party systems, it is possible to point out some others. Firstly, parliamentary minorities can act as veto players,[21] blocking the adoption of the will of the parliamentary majority. In other cases, the self-interest of the legislative body pulls it towards decisions that frustrate the popular sentiment. In addition, legislatures around the world are subject to possible capture by special interests – a euphe-

[17]The original quote by Antonio Gramsci, in its most common English translation, reads: "The crisis consists precisely in the fact that the old is dying and the new cannot be born; in this interregnum a great variety of morbid symptoms appear" (Gramsci 1971, 276). See also interview by sociologist Zigmunt Bauman, available in Portuguese at http://www.ihu.unisinos.br/noticias/24025-%60%60o-velho-mundo-esta-morrendo-mas-o-novo-ainda-nao-nasceu%60%60-entrevista-com-zigmunt-bauman. Accessed 27 May 2015.

[18]The idea of deliberative democracy varies among influential thinkers. I am utilizing here the most widespread concept, based on Elster (1998, 8) and Gutmann and Thompson (2004, 3–7).

[19]See, with some variation between them, Nino (1996, 199), Ely (1980) and Habermas (1996, 238 ff).

[20]About this topic, see Lain (2012). See also Klarman (1997).

[21]*Veto players* are individual or collective agents with the ability to interrupt or stop the advancement of an agenda. On the topic, see Abramovay (2012, 44 ff).

mistic term that identifies the accommodation of the interests of certain influential political or economic agents, even when in conflict with the collective interest.[22]

For many reasons, it is not unusual or surprising that the Judiciary, in certain contexts, is the best interpreter of the majority sentiment. I will start with one that is less explored by legal scholarship in general, but particularly significant in Brazil. In Brazil, judges are recruited in the first instance by official public entrance exams. This means that people from all social backgrounds, provided they have attended a law school and have devoted themselves to systematic and diligent study, can join the Judiciary. This state of affairs has led, over the years, to a drastic democratization of the Judiciary. However, access to a seat in Congress still involves high financial costs, which often requires a candidate to seek funding and partnerships with different economic and business players. This fact produces an inevitable alliance with specific interests. For this reason, in some circumstances, judges are able to represent better – or at least more independently – the will of society. One could counter that this argument is not valid for the members of the Brazilian Federal Supreme Court. However, virtually all the members of the Court have come from legal professions in which entrance occurs by competitive official public exams.[23]

There are several other reasons in addition to this one. First, judges have the guarantee of lifelong tenure. As a consequence, they are not subject to the short-term tribulations of electoral politics, nor, at least in principle, to populist temptations. A second reason is that the courts can only act on the initiative of the parties: lawsuits cannot be brought *ex officio*, that is, from the bench. Moreover, judges and courts cannot judge beyond what has been asked, and have a duty to hear all concerned parties. In the case of the Federal Supreme Court, in Brazil, in addition to the mandatory participation of the Head of the Prosecutor's Office and the Solicitor General in several lawsuits, it is possible to convene public hearings and accept *amici curiae* briefs. Last but not least, judicial decisions must be motivated. This means that, to be valid, these decisions can never be an act of pure discretionary will: the legal system imposes on judges of all levels the duty to present reasons, that is, the grounds and arguments of his reasoning and persuasion.

This last point warrants a closer look. In a traditional and purely majoritarian view, democracy would correspond to an *electoral legitimation* of power. According

---

[22] This subject has been studied through public choice theory, which aims at desmistifying the association between law and the will of the majority. For an overview of the arguments, see Brandão (2012, 205).

[23] In the Court composition as of July, 2014: Celso de Mello was a member of the São Paulo Public Prosecutor's Office. Gilmar Mendes and Joaquim Barbosa came from the Federal Prosecutor's Office. Carmen Lúcia and Luís Roberto Barroso were State Attorneys. Luiz Fux and Teori Zavascky came, respectively, from the state and federal judiciary. Rosa Weber, from labor court. The other three Justices, even though not admitted through public official entrance exam (but by appointment) to the institutions that they were part of, came from victorious careers: Marco Aurélio Mello (Labor Prosecutor's Office and later Justice at the Labor Superior Court), Ricardo Lewandowski (Appellate Judge at the São Paulo State Tribunal, having been admitted into the Judiciary through the "*quinto constitucional*", that is, the fifth of the court seats devoted to members of the Bar) and Dias Toffoli (Solicitor General's Office).

to this criterion, fascism in Italy and Nazism in Germany could be seen as democratic, at least at the time they were installed into power and the period in which they had support of the majority of the people. In fact, according to this last criterion, even the Medici administration, at the height of the military regime in Brazil, would pass the test. This is a problematic thesis. In addition to being sworn into office, power is legitimized, too, by actions and intended purposes.[24] Returning to the idea of deliberative democracy, which is, precisely, based on a *discursive legitimacy*: political decisions should be preceded by free, ample and open public debate, after which the *reasons* for the choices then made should be provided. That is why it has been said earlier that contemporary democracy is made of votes and arguments. An important insight in this area is provided by the German legal philosopher Robert Alexy, who referred to constitutional courts as an *argumentative representative of society*. According to his view, the only way to reconcile the constitutional jurisdiction to democracy is to conceive it, too, as popular representation. Rational people are able to accept solid and correct arguments. Democratic constitutionalism has a discursive legitimacy, which is the process of the institutionalization of reason and righteousness (2005b, 278 ff).

A few additional comments are in order. The first one is of a terminological character. If the thesis that representative bodies may not reflect the majority will is to be accepted, a judicial order that invalidates an act of Congress may not be counter-majoritarian. What it will invariably be is *counter-representative,*[25] seeing that the parliament is the body par excellence of popular representation. However, the assertion made above that judges are less susceptible to populist temptations does deserve a counterpoint. It must not be taken for granted that judges are immune to this dysfunction. Especially in an era of televised trials,[26] with intensive press coverage and repercussions in public opinion, an impulse to please the audience is a risk that cannot be discarded. But I think that any impartial observer can bear witness that this is not the rule. Another risk is that judges in Brazil pass arduous and competitive official entrance exams that require long preparation, only after this process becoming qualified public servants. This may bring about the pretense temptation to superimpose a certain judicial rationality to the circumstances of the other Powers, governed by logics often more complex and less Cartesian. Even so, judicial arrogance is as bad as any other, and it is to be avoided.

The fact that judges are not subject to certain vicissitudes that affect the two political branches is not, of course, a guarantee that the supreme courts will lean in favor of a society's majority view. The truth, however, is that a careful observation of reality reveals that this is exactly what happens. In the United States, decades of

[24] See Moreira Neto (1992, 228–231). This author discusses original, current and purposive legitimacy of political power.

[25] This specificity has been well addressed. See Mendonça (2014, 213 ff).

[26] In Brazil, the sessions of the Federal Supreme Court, including the deliberation phase, are transmitted by broadcast television.

empirical studies demonstrate this point.[27] The same is true in Brazil. In two relevant decisions, the Brazilian Federal Supreme Court upheld a ban on nepotism in the three branches of government,[28] in clear alignment with the demands of society regarding administrative morality. The thesis then defeated was that only the Legislature could impose such restrictions.[29] The Brazilian Federal Supreme Court also answered to the social desire for judicial reform, despite resistance from other sectors of the Judiciary,[30] when examining the legitimacy of the creation of the National Council of Justice (CNJ) as a body devoted to judicial oversight, and when affirming the concurrent jurisdiction of the Council to initiate disciplinary proceedings against judges.

With regard to political partisan loyalty, the position of the Brazilian Federal Supreme Court was even bolder, establishing the loss of mandate by any member of Congress that changes parties.[31] Although it suffered criticism for excessive activism, it is beyond doubt that the decision fulfilled a social demand that had remained unanswered by Congress. Another example: in an ongoing lawsuit, in which the legitimacy or not of political campaign contributions from corporations is being examined, the Brazilian Federal Supreme Court, clearly reflecting the majority sentiment, has signaled for a reduction in the influence of money in the electoral process.[32] The Court is performing, in slices, incompletely, and without the possibility of systematization, the political reform that society calls for.

In addition to the purely representative role, supreme courts occasionally play the role of an enlightened vanguard, in charge of pushing History forward when it stalls. This is a dangerous power, to be exercised with great parsimony, because of the democratic risk it represents, and so that the constitutional courts do not become hegemonic. But, once in a while, the court can indeed play that indispensable role. In the United States, it was through a pivotal move by the Supreme Court that the illegitimacy of racial segregation in public schools was declared, in *Brown v. Board of Education*.[33] In South Africa, it fell to the Constitutional Court to abolish the

[27] See Lain (2012) See also Dahl (1957, 285), as well as Rosen (2006). This last author wrote: "Far from protecting minorities against the tyranny of the majority or thwarting the will of the people, courts for most of American history, have tended to reflect the constitutional views of majorities" (Rosen 2006, xii). Along the same lines, as already mentioned, see Tushnet (1999, 153).

[28] That is what happened in the Direct Action of Constitutionality/ADC 13, per Justice Carlos Ayres Britto, and in the edition of the Binding Precedent/Súmula Vinculante 13, which prohibits the appointment of relatives up to third degree to commissioned positions or gratified functions.

[29] In support of the view that the National Council of Justice (CNJ) should not have this power, *see* Lenio Streck, Ingo Wolfgang Sarlet e Clèmerson Merlin Clève, Os Limites Constitucionais das Resoluções do Conselho Nacional de Justiça (CNJ) e do Conselho Nacional do Ministério Público (CNMP). Available at http://www.egov.ufsc.br/portal/sites/default/files/anexos/15653-15654-1-PB.pdf. Accessed 26 August 2015.

[30] ADI n° 3367, per Justice Cezar Peluso, e ADI n° 4.638, per Justice Marco Aurélio.

[31] MS n° 26.604, per Justice Cármen Lúcia.

[32] ADI n° 4.650, per Justice Luiz Fux.

[33] 347 U.S. 483 (1954).

death penalty.[34] In Germany, the Federal Constitutional Court had the final word on the validity of the criminalization of Holocaust denial.[35] The Israeli Supreme Court reaffirmed the absolute prohibition of torture, even in the interrogation of suspected terrorists, in a war-torn social environment that had become lenient with this practice.[36]

In Brazil, the Federal Supreme Court granted equal status between same-sex unions and conventional common-law unions, paving the way for marriage between same-sex couples.[37] It was perhaps not a majority position in society, but the protection of a fundamental right to equality granted legitimacy to the decision. The same happened to the decision permitting the termination of pregnancies involving anencephalic fetuses.[38] These are emblematic examples of the enlightened role of the constitutional jurisdiction. In these two specific cases, a phenomenon drew special attention. Due to the controversial nature of the two subjects, a significant number of scholars stood against the decisions – "not because they were against its substance, absolutely not…" – but because they believed the matter fell within the power of the Legislature, not the Supreme Court. However, as there were fundamental rights at stake, this was a problematic position. It contrasts the formal principle of democracy – the political majorities are entitled to decide – to the material principles of equality and human dignity, favoring the former in both cases.[39] It put procedure above outcomes, which does not seem the best prioritization.[40]

Sometimes, there occurs a reaction to the type or mode of progress proposed by the Supreme Court – a backlash. A paradigmatic legislative backlash occurred in response to the *Furman v. Georgia*[41] case in 1972, in which the United States Supreme Court declared the death penalty unconstitutional as then applied in 39 States. The underlying principle of the decision was that juries in criminal trials lacked uniformity in the application of the death penalty, and that it was disproportionately applied against minorities. By 1976, however, most states had adopted new death penalty laws, bypassing the decision of the Court. In *Gregg v. Georgia,*[42] the United States Supreme Court upheld the validity of the new version of that

[34] *S v. Makwanyane and Another* (CCT3/94) [1995] ZACC 3. Available at http://www.saflii.org/za/cases/ZACC/1995/3.html

[35] 90 *BVerfGe* 241 (1994). See Brugger (2002).

[36] *Public Committee Against Torture in Israel v. The State of Israel & The General Security Service*. HCJ 5100/94 (1999). Available at http://elyon1.court.gov.il/files_eng/94/000/051/a09/94051000.a09.pdf. Accessed 26 August 2015.

[37] ADPF n° 132 and ADI n° 142, per Justice Carlos Ayres Britto.

[38] ADPF n° 54, per Justice Marco Aurélio.

[39] On formal and material principles, and criteria for balacing them, see Alexy (2014) On page 20, Alexy wrote: "To admit a competency of the legislator democratically legitimated to interfere with a fundamental right simply because he is democratically legitimated would destroy the priority of the Constitution over ordinary parliamentary law".

[40] Many scholars take a different view of the matter. See, for example, Habermas (1996, 463 ff).

[41] 408 U.S. 238 (1972).

[42] 428 U.S. 153 (1976).

State's criminal law. Also, in *Roe v. Wade,*[43] the famous decision that decriminalized abortion, the reaction was enormous, radically dividing public opinion.[44] In Brazil, there are few cases of normative reaction to decisions of the Federal Supreme Court. Some examples are the decisions regarding the privileged forum for cases involving certain authorities,[45] municipal taxes for street lighting,[46] progressive rates for property taxes in urban areas,[47] collection of contributions from beneficiaries of social security,[48] and the definition of the number of municipal councilors.[49]

There are several decisions from the Brazilian Federal Supreme Court that contribute to social progress in Brazil, and that can be presented in support of the thesis advocated for throughout this work, especially in regards to the importance of the democratic role of the constitutional jurisdiction. They all fall within the realm of constitutional law, but also have an impact on other branches of law, as outlined below:

Civil law: ban on imprisonment due to the breach of duty of a depository, recognizing the effectiveness and prevalence of the Pact of San Jose, Costa Rica over national law.

Criminal Law: declaration of unconstitutionality on the ban on the downgrading to the most favorable incarceration conditions in prison sentences involving cases of drug trafficking and other offenses considered heinous.

Administrative law: proscription of nepotism in the three Powers.

Right to health: imposition on the public healthcare system a duty to offer free medication for the treatment of HIV-positive patients in financial need.

Right to education: recognition of the governmental duty to effectively realize the right to early childhood education, therein including access to day care and preschool opportunities.

Political rights: ban on unimpeded change of political party after election, under penalty of disqualification from office for violation of the democratic principle.

---

[43] 410 U.S. 113 (1973).

[44] On the topic, see Post and Siegel (2007).

[45] The Brazilian National Congress passed a law reinstating the Brazilian Federal Supreme Court's competency to judge public authorities after they had already left office. The law sought to overcome precedent set by the Court itself. However, in a singular case of judicial reaction to the legislative reaction, the Brazilian Federal Supreme Court declared the law unconstitutional, saying that it was not within the Congress' power to review the interpretation of the Constitution given by the Court through ordinary law. See STF, ADI 2.797, published on 12.19.2006, per Justice Sepúlveda Pertence.

[46] The Constitutional Amendment 39/02 reversed the opinion set by the Brazilian Federal Supreme Court's decision in the Extraordinary Appeal/RE 233.332/RJ, per Justice Ilmar Galvão.

[47] The Constitutional Amendment 29 (2000) overcame the understanding of the Court and expressly conceded the progressiveness.

[48] Constitution Amendment 41 (2003) reversed the understanding reached in ADI 2010/DF, per Justice Celso de Mello.

[49] Constitution Amendment 58 (2009) overcame the precedent set in RE 197.917/SP, per Justice Maurício Corrêa.

Rights of public servants: regulation, through the decision on a writ of injunction, of the right to strike of public servants and employees.

Rights of people with disabilities: recognition of a right to free use of the interstate public transportation system by people with disabilities, proven in need.

Protection of social and religious minorities:

(i) *Religious minorities*: recognition that freedom of expression does not protect manifestations of racism, which also comprises anti-Semitism.
(ii) *Racial minorities:* assertion of the constitutionality of affirmative action measures in favor of blacks, mixed-race and indigenous people.
(iii) *Same-sex couples:* equalization of the rights of same-sex partners in stable unions to those of conventional common law unions and right to civil marriage.
(iv) *Indigenous communities:* demarcation of the Raposa Serra do Sol indigenous reservation as a contiguous area.

Freedom of scientific research: declaration of the constitutionality of embryonic stem cells.

Women's rights: recognition of the right to the therapeutic anticipation of delivery in case of anencephalic fetuses; declaration of the constitutionality of the Maria da Penha Law, which provides for severe punishment of domestic violence against women.

Three comments before concluding. First, the constitutional jurisdiction, as this essay has tried to demonstrate, has served the country well. As well, the concern about abuse by judges and courts is not without merit, and one must be prepared to prevent its occurrence.[50] However, in the real world, only a very limited number of decisions by the Brazilian Federal Supreme Court can be said to have arguably gone beyond what is acceptable. And in the few cases in which this occurred, the Court itself undertook to rectify the situation.[51] Therefore, the democratic and civilizing potential of a constitutional court should not be overlooked on the basis of imaginary fear. Criticism of Brazilian Federal Supreme Court decisions, both desirable and legitimate in a pluralistic and open society, usually comes from either those dissatisfied with specific results or from a certain niche minority within academia, which operates on different theoretical assumptions from those stated herein. Moreover, it is befitting to propose a crucial question[52]: Why is the argument that constitutional jurisdiction acts in undemocratic patterns not accompanied by a popular dissatisfaction with the role played by the Supreme Court? How to reconcile that the very opposite is indeed the case: in Brazil and abroad, the approval ratings

[50] For a reflection on the topic, using as theoretical framework Niklas Luhmann's systems theory, see Campilongo (2001, 63).

[51] In the decision involving the demarcation of the Indigenous Reservation Raposa Serra do Sol, in requests for clarification, the scope of the so-called "condicionantes" therein established was limited, to explain that it did not prospectively bind new demarcations. See Pet. 3388 – ED, per Justice Luís Roberto Barroso.

[52] See Mendonça (2014, 19–20).

of the constitutional courts are often well above those enjoyed by the legislatures.[53] Most certainly, this should not lead to hasty or overly broad conclusions. However, a criticism that is anchored on a formal vision of democracy, but without a people, should not impress.

The second comment is intuitive. As stated several times already, as a rule, political decisions should be taken by those who indeed receive votes. Therefore, the Legislature and the head of the Executive branch have a *prima facie* general preference in dealing with all matters of interest for the Government and society. And, when they have acted, the courts must be deferential toward the legislative or administrative choices made by public officials legitimated by popular vote. The constitutional jurisdiction should only be imposed in such cases if the opposition to the Constitution is clear, or if an offense to fundamental rights or to the rule of law has taken place. However, as the reader will have intuited so far, the constitutional jurisdiction plays a greater role when the Legislature has remained silent. It is in the normative gaps or unconstitutional omissions that the Supreme Court assumes an incidental leading role. As a result, in the end, it is the Congress itself that holds the final decision, including on the appropriate level of judicialization of life.

In a third note before concluding this essay, it is worth incidentally pointing out a phenomenon known by legal scholarship as *constitutional dialogue,* or *institutional dialogue.*[54] Even though the constitutional court or supreme court is the final interpreter of the Constitution in each case, three noteworthy concepts can subvert or mitigate this condition, namely: (a) the interpretation of the Court can be overcome by an act of the Parliament or Congress, usually by constitutional amendment; (b) the Court may return the matter to the Legislature, setting a deadline for resolution; or (c) the Court may urge the Legislature to act, resorting to the so-called "appeal to the legislator." In the Brazilian experience there are many precedents that fall under the first hypothesis, as is the case of the wage cap for public servants,[55] and the calculation basis for social security contributions,[56] in addition to the others already mentioned earlier in this section.

In regards to the second concept for such dialogue, a court-set deadline for Congress to legislate, there are already precedents in Brazil in regards to the creation of Municipalities[57] and the reformulation of the criteria adopted in the system of distribution of funds to the States (the State Participation Fund or *Fundo de*

[53]According to a survey by IBOPE, an independent polling organization, held in 2012, the Brazilians index of confidence in the Brazilian Federal Supreme Court is 54 points (on a scale from 0 to 100). The Congress achieved 39 points. See http://www.conjur.com.br/2012-dez-24/populacao-confia-stf-congresso-nacional-ibope. Accessed 27 August 2015.

[54]The term has its roots in Canadian legal scholarship. See Hogg and Allison (1997).

[55]ADI 14, per Justice Celio Borja, decision on 09.13.1989. Right after the Constitution of 1988 went into force, the Supreme Court held that the compensation ceiling referred in art. 37, XI, did not apply to "personal benefits", frustrating *de facto* the restraint of abuses in this area. Two constitutional amendments were necessary to overcome this understanding: Amendment 19 (1998) and Amendment 41 (2003).

[56]RE 166.772, per Justice Marco Aurélio, published on 12/16/1994.

[57]ADI 2240, per Justice Eros Grau.

Participações dos Estados).[58] However, compliance within the period determined by the court is not always achieved. Finally, with respect to the third concept in constitutional dialogue, already this was the understanding for many years in the Brazilian Federal Supreme Court case law on the writ of injunction.[59] A very significant case of informal institutional dialogue took place with respect to art. 7, I, of the Constitution, which provides for the enactment of a supplementary law regulating the discipline of compensatory damages against dismissal without cause or arbitrary dismissal of a worker. In deciding the injunction, the plenary of the Brazilian Federal Supreme Court ruled that the court itself would set the indemnity criteria, in view of the more than two decades of failure by the Brazilian Congress to do so.[60] Given this new provocation, the Congress passed in record time Law 12.506 (2011), regulating the matter.

More recently, two instances of institutional dialogue took place. When deciding a criminal case against a Senator of the Republic, the Federal Supreme Court, by a tight majority vote, interpreted a specific provision of the Constitution (art. 55, VI, §2) so as to confer to the Legislature – not to the Court – the power to strip the mandate of a member of the Congress declared guilty of a crime.[61] The Justices that withheld the majority opinion stressed their severe criticism of the scheme imposed by the Constitution, urging Congress to revisit the topic.[62] Shortly after the decision, the Federal Senate approved a Constitutional Amendment Bill overcoming the unsatisfactory treatment of the matter. In late 2015, the bill was still pending before the House. In another case, a federal deputy was sentenced to more than 13 years in prison, to be served initially in closed facilities (which means the prisoner is not allowed to work outside the prison system).[63] Once the issue of his loss of mandate was submitted to the House of Representatives, the majority decided not to revoke it. In writ of mandamus filed against this decision, an injunction was granted by the Justice presiding over the case, on the grounds that in cases of incarceration in closed conditions, the loss of mandate should occur by declaration of the House's leadership, and not by a political decision of the Plenary.[64] Before the judgment on the merit of the writ of mandamus, the House of Representatives abolished the provision of a secret ballot on the matter, and decided in favor of the loss of mandate.

[58] ADI 3682, per Justice Gilmar Mendes. In this case, the Brazilian Federal Supreme Court set a deadline of 18 months for the Brazilian National Congress to remedy the omission regarding the enactment of the supplementary law required by art. 18, § 4 of the Constitution, regarded as essential for the creation of municipalities by state law.

[59] The writ of injunction is a constitutional law suit provided by the Brazilian Constitution aimed at remedying unconstitutional legislative omissions. For a long period, the Supreme Court held that the only possible decision on writ of injunctions was to communicate to Congress its delay and neglect. Subsequently, the Court went on to create the missing norm on its own, usually by analogy with any existing law.

[60] MI 943/DF, per Justice Gilmar Mendes.

[61] AP 565, per Justice Carmen Lúcia (Ivo Cassol case).

[62] See opinion per Justice Luís Roberto Barroso in the MS 32.326.

[63] AP 396, per Justice Carmen Lúcia (Natan Donadon case).

[64] MS 32326, per Justice Luís Roberto Barroso.

What can be drawn from that final note is that the current model cannot be characterized as judicial supremacy. The Brazilian Federal Supreme Court has the prerogative to be the ultimate interpreter of the law, in cases that are submitted to its examination, but it does not own the Constitution. Much to the contrary, the meaning and scope of constitutional norms are set in interaction with society, with the other Powers and with institutions in general. A loss of dialogue with society, the potential inability to justify its decisions or to be understood, would undercut compliance with and legitimacy by the Court. Moreover, any claim of hegemony over the other branches would subject the Court to a change in its institutional design, or to the overruling of precedent by constitutional amendment, powers which belong to the Brazilian National Congress. Therefore, the power of the Brazilian Federal Supreme Court has clear limits. In institutional life, as in life in general, no one is too good and, above all, no one is good alone.

4.4 Conclusion

The decades that followed the end of World War II witnessed a vertiginous institutional rise of the Judiciary and constitutional jurisdiction. It would not be an exaggeration to state that the American model of constitutionalism prevailed in many parts of the world, with its features of centrality of the Constitution, judicial review, and judicialization of disputes involving fundamental rights. In this essay, I have tried to show that supreme courts – as the Brazilian Supreme Court, for example – have come to play, along with their traditional counter-majoritarian role, a representative function, by which they satisfy social demands not met by the majoritarian political process. Evidently, in the execution of such an assignment, the constitutional court is not authorized to impose its own convictions. Guided by the relevant legal sources (norms, legal scholarship, case law), constitutional principles and civilizing values, the court shall interpret the social sentiment, the spirit of its time, and the course of History with the right balance of prudence and audacity.

As can be clearly seen, I am an advocate of constitutional jurisdiction. To my credit, I held this position long before I became a constitutional judge. I think it plays a very important role even in mature democracies such as the United States, Germany, or Canada. But I consider it even more important in countries that have experienced recent re-democratization, or of late democratization. In these countries, as is common, the majoritarian political process cannot fully meet the social demands, due to historical distortions in the distribution of power and wealth. Certainly, one should not live under the illusion that the Judiciary is immune to these distortions. However, circumstances associated with the way by which judges enter into their judgeships, their institutional guarantees, and the type of relationship they have with society (which is not linked to votes or short-term goals) enhances their suitability for the use of reason and the protection of fundamental rights. For sure, the essential condition is that they can escape ordinary politics – as has been, fortunately, the case in Brazil.

References

Abramovay, Pedro. 2012. *Separação de poderes e medidas provisórias*. São Paulo: Campus, at 44 et seq.

Alexy, Robert. 2005a. *La institucionalización de la justicia*. Granada: Editorial Comares.

Alexy, Robert. 2005b. Balancing, constitutional review, and representation. *International Journal of Constitutional Law* 3: 572–581.

Alexy, Robert. 2014. Princípios formais. In Robert Alexy. *Princípios formais e outros aspectos da teoria discursiva*, ed. Trivisonno, Alexandre Travessoni Gomes, Aziz Tuffi Saliba and Mônica Sette Lopes, 3–36, Rio de Janeiro: Forense.

Barroso, Luís Roberto. 2005. Neoconstitucionalismo e constitucionalização do Direito. *Revista de Direito Administrativo* 240: 1–42.

Barroso, Luís Roberto. 2012. *O novo direito constitucional brasileiro: contribuições para a construção teórica e prática da jurisdição constitucional no Brasil*. Belo Horizonte: Editora Fórum.

Bickel, Alexander. 1986. *The least dangerous branch:* The supreme court at the bar of politics. New Haven: Yale University Press.

Brandão, Rodrigo. 2012. *Supremacia judicial versus diálogos institucionais: a quem cabe a última palavra sobre o sentido da constituição*. Rio de Janeiro: Lumen Juris, at 205.

Brugger, Winfried. 2002. Ban on or protection of hate speech? Some observations based on German and American law. *Tulane European & Civil Law Forum* 17: 1–22.

Campilongo, Celso Fernandes. 2001. *Política, sistema jurídico e decisão judicial*. São Paulo: Max Limonad.

Carbonell, Miguel. 2003. *Neoconstitucionalismo(s)*. Madrid: Trotta.

Carbonell, Miguel. 2007. *Teoría del neoconstitucionalismo: ensayos escogidos*. Madrid: Trotta.

Dahl, Robert A. 1957. Decision-making in a democracy: The supreme court as a national policy-maker. *Journal of Public Law* 6: 279–295.

Dworkin, Ronald. 1977. *Taking rights seriously*. Cambridge, MA: Harvard University Press, at 181.

Dworkin, Ronald. 1981. The forum of principle. *New York University Law Review* 56: 469–518.

Elster, Jon. 1998. Introduction. In *Deliberative democracy*, ed. J. Elster. Cambridge: Cambridge University Press.

Ely, John Hart. 1980. *Democracy and distrust: A theory of judicial review*. Cambridge, MA: Harvard University Press.

Ferrajoli, Luigi. 2003. Pasado y futuro del Estado de derecho. In *Neoconstitucionalismo(s)*, ed. Miguel Carbonell. Madrid: Trotta.

Garapon, Antoine. 1999. *O juiz e a democracia: o guardião das promessas*, 2nd ed. Rio de Janeiro: Revan.

Graber, Mark A. 2008. The countermajoritarian difficulty: From courts to congress to constitutional order. *Annual Review of Law and Social Science* 4: 361–362.

Gramsci, Antonio. 1971. *Selections from the prison notebooks,* (ed. and Trans. Q Hoare, and G. N. Smith). New York: International Publishers.

Gutmann, Amy, and Dennis Thompson. 2004. *Why deliberative democracy?* Princeton: Princeton University Press.

Habermas, Jürgen. 1996. *Between facts and norms: Contributions to discourse theory of law and democracy*. Cambridge: The MIT Press.

Hogg, Peter, and Allison A. Bushell. 1997. The charter dialogue between courts and legislatures (or perhaps the chart isn't such a bad thing after all). *Osgoode Hall Law Journal* 35: 75–124.

Klarman, Michael J. 1997. The majoritarian judicial review: The entrenchment problem. *The Georgetown Law Journal* 85: 491–554.

Kramer, Larry. 2004. *The people themselves: Popular constitutionalism and judicial review*. New York: Oxford University Press.

Lain, Corinna Barrett. 2012. Upside-down judicial review. 2012. *The Georgetown Law Review* 101: 113–184.

Mendonça, Eduardo. 2014. *A democracia das massas e a democracia das pessoas: uma reflexão sobre a dificuldade contramajoritária*. Manuscript.

Mill, John Stuart. 2002. *On liberty*. Mineola: Dover Publications, at 14. (first edition: 1874).

Moreira Neto, Diogo de. Figueiredo. 1992. *Teoria do poder, Parte I*. São Paulo: Revista dos Tribunais.

Nino, Carlos Santiago. 1996. *The constitution of deliberative democracy*. New Haven: Yale University Press.

Post, Robert, and Reva Siegel. 2007. Roe rage: Democratic constitutionalism and backlash. *Harvard Civil Rights-Civil Liberties Law Review* 42: 373–434.

Quaresma, Regina Quaresma, Maria Lúcia de Paula Oliveira, and Farlei Martins Riccio de Oliveira. 2009. *Neoconstitucionalismo*.

Rawls, John. 2005. *Political liberalism*. New York: Columbia University Press, at 231 et seq. (first edition: 1993).

Rosen, Jeffrey. 2006. *The most democratic branch: How the courts serve America*. New York: Oxford University Pres.

Souza Neto, Cláudio Pereira. 2006. *Teoria constitucional e democracia deliberativa*. Rio de Janeiro: Renovar.

Streck, Lenio, Sarlet, Ingo Wolfgang, and Clève, Clèmerson Merlin. Os Limites Constitucionais das Resoluções do Conselho Nacional de Justiça (CNJ) e do Conselho Nacional do Ministério Público (CNMP). Available at http://www.egov.ufsc.br/portal/sites/default/files/anexos/15653-15654-1-PB.pdf. Accessed 26 August 2015.

Tushnet, Mark. 1999. *Taking the constitution away from courts*. Princeton: Princeton University Press.

Tushnet, Mark. 2009. *Weak courts, strong rights: Judicial review and social welfare rights in comparative constitutional law*. Princeton: Princeton University Press.

Waldron, Jeremy. 2006. The core of the case against judicial review. *Yale Law Journal* 115: 1346–1406.

Zagrebelsky, Gustavo. 2005. *El derecho dúctil: ley, derechos, justicia* (Spanish trans: Marina Gascón). Madrid. Trotta.

Part II
Constitutional Dialogues and Constitutional Deliberation

Chapter 5
Decoupling Judicial Review from Judicial Supremacy

Stephen Gardbaum

Abstract In previous work, I have characterized one of the two constitutive features of the new general model of constitutionalism adopted over the last 30 years in Canada, New Zealand, the United Kingdom, and two sub-national units in Australia as decoupling judicial review from judicial supremacy. In this chapter, I aim firstly to clarify this feature by exploring the relevant meaning of judicial supremacy (that the model rejects) in light of certain potential misunderstandings and alternative senses that could be given to the term. Then, in the belief that judicial review shorn of judicial supremacy is easier to defend than the standard version in which they are combined, I present the case for this part of the general model.

5.1 Introduction

The general model of constitutionalism adopted over the last 30 years in Canada, New Zealand, the United Kingdom, and two sub-national units in Australia has two constitutive features. These are: (1) a formalized process of pre-enactment political rights review of legislation involving the executive and legislative branches of government and (2) weak-form or "penultimate" judicial review (Gardbaum 2013).[1] In previous work, I have characterized this second feature as decoupling judicial review from judicial supremacy.[2] In this chapter, I aim firstly to clarify this characterization by exploring the relevant meaning of judicial supremacy (that the model rejects) in light of certain potential misunderstandings and alternative senses that could be given to the term. Then, in the belief that judicial review shorn of judicial supremacy is easier to defend than the standard version in which they are combined, I present the case for this part of the general model.

[1] The term "penultimate judicial review" was coined by Michael Perry (2003).

[2] Starting with Gardbaum (2001), although I did not at that time use the term "weak-form judicial review" to describe the phenomenon. This was introduced by Tushnet (2003).

S. Gardbaum (✉)
MacArthur Foundation Professor of International Justice & Human Rights, UCLA School of Law, 385 Charles E. Young Dr. East, Los Angeles, CA 90095, USA
e-mail: gardbaum@law.ucla.edu

T. Bustamante, B.G. Fernandes (eds.), *Democratizing Constitutional Law*, Law and Philosophy Library 113, DOI 10.1007/978-3-319-28371-5_5

5.2 What Judicial Review Without Judicial Supremacy Means (and Does Not Mean)

In earlier work, I argued that the decoupling of judicial review from judicial supremacy means that although courts have powers of constitutional review of legislation, their decisions are not necessarily or automatically authoritative on what the law of the land is. Unlike the case under judicial supremacy, judicial decisions on constitutional issues are *not* unreviewable by ordinary legislative majority. Accordingly, judicial supremacy concerns the allocation of power between courts and legislatures on the resolution of constitutional issues, including of course contested rights issues.

Some recent critiques of the model have implicitly or explicitly called into question its treatment of judicial supremacy by claiming that it (a) relies on an overstated or caricatured conception of judicial power under traditional (i.e., strong-form) judicial review and/or (b) focuses only on "formal" or legal powers and ignores the practical dimension of how they interact with various real world factors, whether political, cultural or institutional. Thus, it is suggested that judicial supremacy is mistakenly conceived as granting essentially unlimited authority to courts, whereas in most systems even within the realm of formal powers there are counterweights. These include the possibility of legislative jurisdiction-stripping, constitutional amendments to overrule judicial decisions, and the non-binding nature of their rulings on future executive and legislative conduct. On the power versus practice distinction, it is argued that strong-form judicial review does not in fact always or necessarily result in judicial supremacy, where, for example, courts defer to legislatures. By the same token, weak-form judicial review may in practice result in judicial supremacy, where legislatures tend to defer to the judicial view. The emphasis on – indeed obsession with – the "final say" overstates the practical consequences of a court decision; indeed, in the real world there is no such thing as the final word on constitutional issues (Kavanagh 2009; Carolan 2013).

To begin a clarification of what exactly judicial supremacy – and hence judicial review without it – means for the purposes of the general model, it may be useful to compare it with other concepts of supremacy commonly used in legal and political discourse: constitutional, legislative and federal supremacy. The comparison makes clear that "supremacy" per se is about normative hierarchy, and very often about which law/position prevails where two conflict with each other. Thus, "constitutional supremacy" means that the constitution is the highest type or source of law in a legal system, higher on the normative scale than legislation, and it prevails over all other types of law in cases of conflict. Similarly, "federal supremacy" means the same thing with respect to conflicts between federal and state/provincial law: all federal law, of any type, trumps all state, including state constitutional law. "Legislative supremacy" means that legislation is the highest type of law in a legal system, and prevails over other types of law – such as common law, regulations or secondary legislation – where they conflict. It follows that there can be no substantive judicial review of legislation for conflict with a higher legal source because there are none, although there will be rules for the resolution of conflicts between two statutes. For the same reason, the legislative power is legally unlimited.

So, too, the concept of judicial supremacy concerns a hierarchy of norms, but it operates not in the context of what happens when two laws conflict with each other but rather of *whether there is a conflict*. In other words, it resolves a second-order conflict between parties/institutions rather than a first-order one between laws. Its essential meaning is that a judicial decision made in the proper exercise of its jurisdiction is legally authoritative on whether there is a conflict between the higher law constitution and a statute, and prevails over the opinions of all other relevant parties and institutions presented in that proceeding. In particular, judicial decisions on constitutional matters stand higher in the normative hierarchy than those of executives and legislatures made in the context of defending a challenged statute. In the rights context, such judicial decisions typically involve several sub-issues, including (1) the interpretation of the statute, (2) the interpretation of relevant constitutional provisions, and (3) whether any limits on rights are justified, with respect to each of which there may be disagreements not only between the parties but ultimately between the court and the legislature. Accordingly, judicial supremacy includes, but is not limited to, supremacy in interpreting the constitution in this context. Part of the legally authoritative or "supreme" nature of such judicial decisions is that in execution of the first-order principle of constitutional supremacy, having determined that there is a conflict, the court will treat or declare the unconstitutional law as invalid. If this occurs within a "concrete judicial review" or case or controversy procedure, the court will refuse to apply the statute.[3]

Let me illustrate judicial supremacy and its consequences with the familiar example of same-sex marriage in the United States. When the Supreme Court recently pronounced, by five votes to four, in the context of an appeal against a lower court ruling and as part of its decision in the case that there is a constitutional right to same-sex marriage,[4] this amounted to a legally authoritative resolution of a highly contested – and litigated – rights issue. Its view prevails over the conflicting view of the defending states and all/any other institutions. In other words, the Supreme Court's decision has higher legal status than that of all of the other participants in the debate. It provides an authoritative interpretation of the (existing) constitution – yes, it includes this right – which binds all other courts in the country. Henceforth, any state or federal entity that enacts or enforces a ban on same-sex marriage – perhaps because it disagrees with the Supreme Court's interpretation of the Constitution – may be sued by a party with standing and the ban will be invalidated on the authority of the Supreme Court's decision,[5] *whether or not* the Supreme Court decision itself legally binds the state or federal entity in the first

[3] It should be noted that constitutional supremacy does not necessarily entail such judicial execution: it is possible to have a supreme law constitution without either granting courts the power of judicial review (of legislation) or providing for judicial supremacy. For example, the constitution of the Netherlands expressly denies courts the power to review legislation, and the Canadian constitution grants legislatures the power to reinstate statutes invalidated by the courts.

[4] Obergefell v. Hodges, 576 U.S.___ (2015).

[5] Assuming that the ban fails any relevant standard of review that the Supreme Court sets as part of its decision.

place. (In many non-US constitutional systems, the binding effect of a constitutional court decision on all political actors is express and unquestioned. Given the near-inevitability of a legal challenge to such a measure, it is unclear what practical difference this distinction makes, where it applies). Of course, the Supreme Court may overrule its decision in a subsequent case, but as the only actor that can do so (within the existing constitution), this is part of its supremacy.

This differs from the counterfactual scenario in which the Supreme Court had ruled the other way and held that there is *no* constitutional right to same-sex marriage, in which case the general principle that the Constitution is a floor not a ceiling would permit states and the federal government to supplement constitutional rights through state law or federal statute – if in the case of the latter the measure is otherwise within the scope of federal authority. This latter also covers the situation in which state or federal governments take the view that the Supreme Court's constitutional decisions do not sufficiently protect a constitutional right, as with the well-known Religious Freedom Restoration Act 1993 and the right to free exercise of religion. Whether or not they are motivated by constitutional disagreement with the Court, any such state or federal supplementing measure takes effect as an ordinary, non-constitutional law. Thus, a suitably drafted subsequent statute, reflecting a later Congress's views, would normally trump such a law as an express or implied repeal of it.[6] The 1964 Civil Rights Act is another leading example of a federal statute that supplements the Court's authoritative decision about what the Constitution provides, in this case under the equal protection clause.

Judicial supremacy in the sense just outlined is part and parcel of the standard modern power of judicial review of legislation that now exists in the vast majority of countries around the world. It is precisely the innovation of weak-form judicial review, as recently institutionalized in the various Commonwealth jurisdictions, to show that judicial supremacy in this sense is *not* a necessary or essential part of judicial review. So in New Zealand and the United Kingdom, statutory bills of rights provide that judicial decisions finding legislation in conflict with protected rights are *never* legally authoritative in that such a decision does not affect the validity of the legislation and courts are still required to apply it in the case at hand.[7] In Canada, judicial decisions on most constitutional rights issues[8] can be said to be *conditionally* legally authoritative in that the Charter of Rights and Freedoms empowers federal and provincial legislatures to reinstate statutes invalidated by the courts by ordinary majority vote for a renewable period of 5 years.[9] Hence judicial

[6] So, for example, in the recent Hobby Lobby case in the US (Burwell v. Hobby Lobby Stores, Inc., 573 U.S.___ (2014)) had the Affordable Care Act itself mandated coverage for contraception, this would almost certainly have trumped the earlier Religious Freedom Restoration Act's imposition of the "strict scrutiny" test for laws burdening religion, passed to "supplement" the Supreme Court's interpretation of the scope of this constitutional right. Unfortunately for the Obama administration, the mandate was imposed by administrative regulation and not by statute.

[7] s6 New Zealand Bill of Rights Act 1990; s4 UK Human Rights Act 1998.

[8] Not all because a few specific Charter rights, including voting and minority language rights, are expressly excluded from the operation of section 33.

[9] Canadian Charter, s.33.

review without judicial supremacy. This more limited judicial authority is perfectly possible within a constitutional bill of rights. It is even consistent with constitutional supremacy, where it is understood that the question of whether there is a conflict between the constitution and a statute is authoritatively resolved by the legislature and not the courts. Here, the position of courts and legislatures are reversed as compared with judicial supremacy: the judicial view is relevant and may be taken into account by the legislature, but it is not the legally authoritative one.

Does strong-form judicial review, of which judicial supremacy in the above sense is an intrinsic part, mean or require that a highest court's decision – say, on the same-sex marriage issue – provides the "final word" on the issue for all time? Does the concept of weak-form review implicitly depend on such a strict conception of finality to ground the difference from strong-form? The answer to both is "no." Judicial supremacy addresses the question of whose view on a constitutional issue prevails *for the time being*, and this is sufficient to provide the contrast with weak-form review. Clearly, as noted, the U.S. Supreme Court can change its mind or, more likely, its personnel to overrule the decision – just as under legislative supremacy the one thing a legislature typically cannot do is bind itself for the future. Indeed, the pre-1966 practice of the UK House of Lords binding it to its own previous decisions was, in a sense, more of a limit on judicial supremacy than its current, more usual rule for highest courts – in that later members of the court were bound by their predecessors.

But what about the legal power of the people to enact a constitutional amendment that bans same-sex marriage or declares that nothing in the Constitution shall be interpreted as establishing a right to same-sex marriage? Does this amendment power negate judicial supremacy? Is it, in this sense, equivalent to the legislative override power in Canada? Does the answer depend on how easy or difficult it is to amend the constitution?

I do not think the general power to amend a constitution negates judicial supremacy in the sense outlined above. The reason is that although such a constitutional amendment (where enacted) may practically require a different outcome if and when a new case is brought, it doesn't alter the power of the courts to issue authoritative rulings on whether there is a conflict between the (new) constitution and a statute. To be sure, the raw material over which this power is exercised has changed, and therefore the currency/relevance of its original decision on this issue, but not the power itself. Judicial supremacy does not imply the freedom to ignore constitutional text and only really has bite, as it were, where there are two plausible answers to a constitutional question, which a clear, unambiguous amendment can largely rule out. For example, had Wendell Willkie challenged FDR's run for a third presidential term in 1940 in a court of law rather than of public opinion and lost, I don't believe we would say that the Twenty-Second Amendment overruled the Court or negated its supremacy because it is understood that clear text governs, as a first-order matter. Moreover, if it is only meaningful to talk of judicial supremacy where there is either no power to amend a constitution or the courts are empowered to declare such amendments unconstitutional, then this would be a very narrow usage and we would still need another concept to distinguish the type or degree of judicial authority under a US-style system from a UK-style system (unless ultimately the distinction proves to be meaningless in practice).

For somewhat similar reasons, I do not think that a general power to amend the constitution is fully equivalent – at least conceptually and normatively – to the legislative override power in Canada (or the power of legislatures to retain a statute found incompatible with the bill of rights in the UK and New Zealand), even if both could be achieved by the same percentage of votes: ordinary majority, two-thirds, etc. According to most commentators, the legislative override power is conceptualized and justified as a mechanism to resolve reasonable disagreements about contestable rights issues between courts and legislatures (rather than to enable "rights misgivings"). The point is to reject the legal authoritativeness of the judicial position on the basis that "democracy requires that a reasonable view of the legislative majority trumps the reasonable view of a judicial majority" (Perry 2003, 661). By contrast, the constitutional amendment procedure concedes the authoritativeness of the judicial position and changes the first-order "raw material" on which it was based.

In practice (and internal overriding aside), the staying power of particular judicial decisions, and so the *relative strength* of judicial supremacy in a given legal system, will vary depending on at least three factors relating to constitutional amendment: (1) the ease or difficulty of the constitution's formal amendment rules, (2) the absence or existence of dominant political parties, and (3) whether the decisions are in areas of the constitution that cannot be amended. These three are themselves linked. Thus in India, it was the relative ease of constitutional amendment under a rule requiring a two-thirds vote of both houses of parliament, combined with the relative ease of satisfying it during the period of Congress Party dominance, that led the Supreme Court of India to establish its doctrine that the "basic structure" of the constitution is unamendable.[10] The result is that judicial supremacy with respect to the basic structure is significantly stronger than the rest of the constitution. Here the legal authoritativeness of its decisions is even greater as they cannot legally be rendered redundant through the amendment procedure. By contrast, the decline of the Congress Party and the failure (thus far) of any other party to replace it as a dominant one in terms of two-thirds of parliamentary seats renders judicial supremacy politically stronger while this lasts.

These factors show that judicial supremacy may be stronger or weaker in that the relative difficulty of constitutional amendment and/or the existence of an unconstitutional constitutional amendment doctrine add to the effective legal authority of judicial decisions on constitutional issues by extending their likely duration. Indeed, the issue of judicial review of *constitutional amendments versus legislation* is a fascinating new topic in comparative constitutional law that has obvious implications for, but does not supersede or render redundant, the issue of judicial supremacy within the more traditional and common form of judicial review. A fourth factor is political/legal culture and the "sociological" or political authority/legitimacy of a

[10] Kesavananda Bharati v. State of Kerala (AIR 1973 SC 1461).

constitutional court. Thus, despite a relatively easy formal amendment rule resulting in reasonably frequent textual changes to other parts of the Basic Law, almost never has a constitutional amendment been enacted in Germany to "overrule" a fundamental rights decision of the constitutional court. This example shows that form and practice can of course work in both directions.

Does the judicial supremacy that is part and parcel of strong-form judicial review mean that courts always in fact have the final word for the time being, that they exercise their powers in a maximal way to resolve constitutional issues at every opportunity that arises, that they never defer to the views of other institutions for prudential or principled reasons? I think this question suggests that two different conceptions of judicial supremacy are in use that it would be helpful to distinguish. The first and narrower one is the meaning I have set out above: the normative hierarchy within a legal system that renders judicial decisions authoritative on litigated constitutional issues, as compared with the newer model that denies this authority to exercises of judicial review. It is a conception geared primarily towards institutional allocations of power and constitutional design. The second conception relies on a broader, more all-things-considered sense of which groups, forces, institutions within a society have the greatest overall power or influence over constitutional decision-making and constitutional politics. Whereas strong-form review itself has limited institutional variations (centralized versus decentralized, abstract versus concrete, etc.), judicial supremacy in this broader sense may vary from country to country and from time to time based on a very large number of contextual factors. It is akin to the sociological sense of legitimacy as distinct from the normative one. Or to the observation that in modern parliamentary democracies, legislative supremacy has long given way to executive supremacy. It employs a different, broader sense of supremacy – which institution has greater overall power – than the standard narrower one concerning institutional forms.

Accordingly, the manner in which courts – and other institutions – exercise their powers may vary in ways that make it helpful, and probably essential, to contrast the legal and factual positions. So, for example, where courts with strong-form powers routinely exercise them deferentially, by choosing to accept the legislature's view that there is no conflict between the constitution and a statute, it may be a useful shorthand to contrast them with courts that do not by describing this situation as one of de jure judicial supremacy but de facto legislative supremacy (not in the first-order meaning of the term but in the second, who decides whether there is a conflict sense). The reasons courts may defer are various, ranging from dominant party control of the appointments process and length of term (Japan) to cultural norms, to judicial faith in the legislative review process (Scandinavia), and to the greater expertise of legislatures on the relevant constitutional issue (sometimes under proportionality). Here the court's decision remains the formally authoritative one but its content is largely provided by the legislature.

And the same is perfectly possible in reverse under weak-form judicial review. Thus, even though judicial decisions on rights issues are not (fully) legally authoritative, they may become practically or politically authoritative if legislatures routinely defer to them by (in Canada) refraining from exercising the override power or (in the UK and New Zealand) amending or repealing statutes found by the courts to be incompatible with the bill of rights. Accordingly, in practice strong-form judicial review may be weak and weak-form strong. At this point, determining whether, when and why this is the case undoubtedly constitutes the interesting and important scholarly task, now that the institutional/analytical frameworks are well understood. "Formal" allocation of power or "structural devices" are of course not necessarily, and probably never actually, conclusive as to how a system operates. But this does not mean they have no impact. From a constitutional design perspective, if you were opposed to judicial supremacy, would you likely think that formal powers are formal *only* and place all your bets on de facto legislative supremacy, or vice-versa? At least until the contrary is shown, it seems reasonable to believe that both are outcome-influencing variables.

Note that this same power/practice distinction might apply to other types of supremacy within constitutional discourse. So, for example, where states are well-represented in a federal legislature, in practice it might be said that there is no federal supremacy as things that states oppose do not get enacted. Or because legislatures are heavily constrained by moral, political, and practical factors, legislative supremacy at the ground level looks little different from its alternatives. Even granting these facts, does it follow that federal or legislative supremacy are illusory or useless concepts or that the choice among various institutional allocations of power is practically irrelevant? Variation in practice among models – whether constitutional versus legislative supremacy, presidentialism versus parliamentarism, or judicial supremacy and its alternatives – is to be expected and neither itself renders the model redundant nor negates its status qua model.

In sum, judicial review without judicial supremacy refers to a system in which decisions of courts on constitutional issues are not unconditionally legally authoritative for the time being in the way that they are under strong-form review; they are *not* unreviewable by ordinary legislative majority. In other words, the two types of judicial review differ in their allocation of power between courts and legislatures with respect to the resolution of constitutional issues. Among other factors, how both systems of judicial review do or will likely operate in practice is obviously highly relevant to choosing between them, but not (yet at least) to whether they offer a meaningful choice. The model adopted in the five Commonwealth jurisdictions does not only, however, provide a new form of judicial review; it also provides a new justification of judicial review. For once shorn of judicial supremacy, the task of defending a judicial role in rights protection is a different – and easier – one. A model of constitutionalism that provides for judicial rights review of legislation but grants the legislature the power to authoritatively resolve the rights issue within the existing constitution is normatively, and not only practically, different from one that does not. Let me now turn to the task of elaborating the content of this new and distinctive justification of judicial review.[11]

[11] Section 5.2 of this chapter draws heavily on arguments that I made in chapter 3 of Gardbaum (2013).

5.3 The Case for Judicial Review Without Judicial Supremacy

The essential case for weak-form review is that it is to forms of constitutionalism what the mixed economy is to forms of economic organization: a distinct and appealing third way in between two purer but flawed extremes. Just as the mixed economy is a hybrid economic form combining the core benefits of capitalism and socialism whilst minimizing their well-known costs, so too weak-form review offers an alternative to the old choice of judicial supremacy or traditional parliamentary sovereignty by combining the strengths of each whilst avoiding their major weaknesses. Like the mixed economy's countering of the lop-sided allocation of power under capitalism to markets and under socialism to planning, weak-form review counters legal and political constitutionalism's lopsided allocations of power to courts and legislatures respectively.[12] It recalibrates these two existing choices by effectively protecting rights through a reallocation[13] of power between the judiciary and the political branches (adding to judicial power if starting from parliamentary sovereignty and reducing it if starting from judicial supremacy) that brings them into greater balance and denies too much power to either. As such, it is largely an argument about greater subtlety in constitutional engineering. The result is a more optimal institutional form of constitutionalism within a democratic polity than provided by either traditional model alone, one that provides a better working co-existence of democratic self-governance and the constraints of constitutionalism, the twin concepts underlying constitutional democracy.

5.3.1 The Strengths and Weaknesses of the Two Traditional Models

After the latest round of the debate about judicial review conducted within the conventional bi-polar framework, it seems clearer than ever that there are powerful arguments both for and against legal constitutionalism and that no unanswerable, knock-down case – for one side or the other – that persuades all reasonable people is likely anytime soon. Although political constitutionalists have generally been more comfortable in critical mode, focusing rather more on presenting arguments against legal constitutionalism than on the positive case for their own position,[14]

[12] In the remainder of this chapter, I use the terms legal constitutionalism/judicial supremacy synonymously, as I do also with political constitutionalism/traditional legislative supremacy.

[13] A "reallocation" does not necessarily mean a "transfer" of power from one institution to the other. Thus, in being given the two new powers of declaring an incompatibility and interpreting statutes in a rights-consistent way wherever possible, UK courts are not exercising powers previously held by Parliament. See Kavanagh (2009), at n2, pp. 277–8.

[14] This point is perhaps best represented by the title of Waldron's celebrated article, "The Core of the Case Against Judicial Review" (Waldron 2006). See also, Tomkins (2005) and Bellamy (2007).

these are simply two sides of the same coin within a bi-polar debate so that which one to pick mostly reflects choice of rhetorical strategy. Indeed, one of the benefits of the new three-way debate ushered in by weak-form review is that it becomes necessary to specify what position is being argued for and not only against, as there is no single, dichotomous default option but rather two separate alternatives. The net effect is that the contemporary bi-polar debate has helpfully isolated the two key issues as (1) which model better protects rights and (2) whether judicial review is politically legitimate within a democracy (Waldron 2006; Fallon 2008; Kumm 2007; Sadursky 2002), and also provided an enhanced assessment of the strengths and weaknesses of both traditional models with respect to them.

This enhanced assessment is particularly helpful because in order to explain how weak-form review combines the core strengths of both traditional ones whilst avoiding their major weaknesses, it is of course first necessary to specify what these are. As an institutional form of constitutionalism in a democratic political system, political constitutionalism (or legislative supremacy) has two major strengths or benefits. Firstly, on the issue of legitimacy, by institutionalizing limits on governmental power as political in nature and enforcing them through the twin mechanisms of electoral accountability and structural checks and balances – such as legislative oversight of the executive – political constitutionalism coheres easily and unproblematically with democracy as the basic principle for the organization of the governmental power that it limits. Whether these limits that protect individual rights and liberties remain exclusively in the political sphere as moral or political rights, or are given legal effect as common law or statutory rights, they are ultimately within the scope of the democratic principles of equal participation and electorally-accountable decision-making as determined or changeable by ordinary legislative act.

Secondly, on the issue of outcomes, given the nature of many, if not most, rights issues that arise in contemporary mature democracies – including the existence of reasonable disagreement about how they should be resolved – legislative reasoning about rights may often be superior to legal/judicial reasoning. As powerfully argued by Adam Tomkins and Jeremy Waldron, high quality rights reasoning often calls for direct focus on the moral and policy issues involved free of the legalistic and distorting concerns with text, precedent, fact-particularity and the legitimacy of the enterprise that constrain judicial reasoning about rights.[15] Moreover, electorally-accountable representatives are able to bring a greater diversity of views and perspectives to bear on rights deliberations compared to the numerically smaller, cloistered and elite world of the higher judiciary.

[15] See Tomkins (2005, 27–9); Waldron (2009). Mattias Kumm argues that the sort of legalistic distortions they describe are not a feature of contemporary rights adjudication in Europe under proportionality analysis, see Kumm (2007, 5–13). However, the second-order task of assessing the reasonableness of the government's justification for a law, which Kumm argues is the point of judicial review, arguably replaces one set of distorting filters with another so that courts still do not directly address the merits of the rights issues. Moreover, the absence of such law-like reasoning may heighten the internal concerns about the legitimacy of the enterprise.

At the same time, proponents of judicial review have identified two major weaknesses of political constitutionalism on the key issues. The first is the risk of either understating or under-enforcing constitutionalism's limits on governmental power, especially individual rights, as the result of various "pathologies" or "blind spots" to which electorally-accountable legislatures (and executives) may be prone. These include sensitivity to the rights and rights claims of various electoral minorities – whether criminal defendants, asylum seekers, or minority racial, ethnic or religious groups – given the exigencies and logic of re-election, legislative inertia deriving from tradition or the blocking power of parties or interest groups, and government hyperbole or ideology (Bickel 1962; Dixon 2009; Kumm 2007; Perry 2003; Fallon 2008). Under-enforcement of rights may also result from the circumstance that however high the quality of legislative rights reasoning, it inevitably competes in this forum with other deliberative and decisional frameworks. Undoubtedly, these standard, well-known concerns were primarily responsible for the massive switch away from political constitutionalism towards judicial supremacy around the world during the post-war "rights revolution," as the resources of representative democracy alone were perceived to provide insufficient protection.

Secondly, just as political constitutionalists have attempted to turn the tables on the conventional argument that rights are better protected with judicial review in the way we have just seen, legal constitutionalists have tried to do the same with the standard argument that judicial review is democratically illegitimate. Thus, Richard Fallon has argued that important though democratic legitimacy undoubtedly is, it is not the exclusive source or type of legitimacy in constitutional democracies and that the substantive justice of a society also contributes to is its overall political legitimacy. Accordingly, to the extent that political constitutionalism may undermine substantive justice by under-enforcing rights for the above-stated reasons, it also detracts from the overall political legitimacy of a democratic regime (Fallon 2008, 1718–22). More generally, Mattias Kumm has argued that in addition to electorally-accountable decision-making, a second precondition for the legitimacy of law in constitutional democracies is the requirement of substantively reasonable public justification for all governmental acts, including legislation, burdening individuals' rights. As part of our commitment to constitutionalism, legislation unsupported by a reasonable public justification for the burdens it imposes on individuals is illegitimate regardless of majority support. Political constitutionalism, however, provides no adequate forum for critically scrutinizing the justification for a piece of legislation to determine if it meets the minimum standard of plausibility in terms of public reasons. Given the various potential pathologies noted above, legislative deliberation and political accountability are insufficient to ensure that burdened individuals are provided with the reasonable justification to which they are entitled, as evidenced by many decisions of domestic and international constitutional courts (Kumm 2009).

If these are the most important strengths and weaknesses of political constitutionalism that emerge from the recent academic debate, what are the equivalents for legal constitutionalism? One of its strengths is fostering public recognition and consciousness of rights. A reasonably comprehensive statement of rights and liberties, as found in the typical constitutional bill of rights, renders rights less scattered and more visible or transparent, more part of general public consciousness than either an "unwritten" set of moral and political rights or a regime of residual common law liberties supplemented by certain specific statutory rights.

A second strength of legal constitutionalism – in either its "big-C" or common law variations – is that it may help to protect against the above-mentioned tendency towards the under-enforcement of rights resulting from the potential pathologies and blind spots affecting politically accountable legislatures and executives. Where they are politically independent in the sense of not needing to seek re-election or renewal in office after initial appointment, judges exercising the power of judicial review are in a better institutional position to counter or resist such electorally-induced risk of under-enforcement (Kyritsis 2012; Perry 2003). This is not so much an argument about expertise as about incentives and institutional structure. Courts also decide cases upon concrete facts, some of which may have been unforeseen by legislators (Fallon 2008, 1709), and indeed bring a more context specific or "applied" dimension to rights deliberation that complements the necessarily greater generality of that undertaken by legislatures.

Thirdly, in the positive version of the argument noted above, legal constitutionalists have made the case that judicial review is essential to the overall legitimacy of a constitutional democracy. Thus, Richard Fallon argues that to the extent judicial review promotes substantive justice by helping to protect against under-enforcement of rights, it might "actually enhance the overall political legitimacy of an otherwise reasonably democratic constitutional regime."[16] In this sense, judicial review may result in a trade-off among different sources of legitimacy but not between rights protection and overall political legitimacy. Mattias Kumm has argued that judicial review provides the forum, required for the legitimacy of legislation, in which individual rights claimants can put the government to its burden of providing a reasonable public justification for its acts. As he puts it:

> Human and constitutional rights adjudication, as it has developed in much of Europe, … is a form of legally institutionalized Socratic contestation. When individuals bring claims grounded in human or constitutional rights, they enlist courts to critically engage public authorities in order to assess whether their acts and the burdens they impose on the rights-claimants are susceptible to plausible justification….Legally institutionalized Socratic contestation is desirable, both because it tends to improve outcomes and because it expresses a central liberal commitment about the conditions that must be met, in order for law to be legitimate (Kumm 2007, 4).[17]

Thus, for example, judicial review aims to ensure that an individual burdened by a statutory ban on gays in the military is able to put the government to the task of

[16] *Ibid.*, at 1728.

[17] Harel and Kahana (2010) present a broadly similar justification of judicial review, which they argue is designed to provide individuals with a necessary and intrinsic right to a hearing to challenge decisions that impinge on their rights, although they do not embed their justification in terms of the general legitimacy of law.

providing a reasonable public justification for the enacted law, one not relying on prejudice, tradition, disproportionate means, etc., failing which it is illegitimate.[18]

And what are the weaknesses or costs of legal constitutionalism as an institutional form in a democracy? Starting with the issue of rights protection, one is that just as there may be under-enforcement of rights due to electorally-induced or other legislative pathologies, there may also be under-enforcement resulting from certain judicial pathologies.[19] These include (1) the risk of rights-relevant timidity that comes with responsibility for the final decision and its real world consequences; (2) concerns about lack of policy expertise or legitimacy in the context of assessing justifications for limiting rights – the universal second stage of modern rights analysis; (3) the artificially and legalistically constrained nature of judicial reasoning about rights; and (4) the relative lack of diversity of perspectives among the elite members of the higher judiciary. Now, it might be thought that, even if it exists, the risk of judicial under-enforcement of rights is not much of a concern because it is premised on, simply mirrors, a prior under-enforcement by the legislature. Where it occurs, it is true that the countering force of judicial review does not take place, but we are no worse off in terms of rights-enforcement than before the judicial decision.

This response strikes me as at least partially misguided for two reasons. First, assuming a court has under-enforced the right, it is not true that we are no worse off. The judicial decision formally legitimates the statute and the legislative under-enforcement in a way that would not be the case without; there would simply be a controversial statute on the books which many people reasonably believe violates rights and should be repealed. Moreover, there is now a judicial precedent in place, which may affect the political and/or legal treatment of other or future statutes. It is for these reasons that Justice Jackson famously chided the U.S. Supreme Court for taking the case of *Korematsu* v. United States.[20] It is one thing for the elective branches to under-enforce rights during a perceived national emergency; it is another for the highest court to give its seal of legitimacy to that under-enforcement. Secondly, the response assumes that the existence of judicial review has no effect on the rights deliberations otherwise undertaken by the legislature itself in the course of enacting the statute, that judicial review provides an additional and supplementary layer of rights scrutiny – a safety net – over and above the legislative one. There are plausible reasons to believe, however, that judicial review within a legal constitutionalist framework results in the processes of political rights review being reduced or even bypassed altogether in favour of relying on the courts, which after all have the final word.[21] Why spend precious time on matters you do not

[18] Kumm (2007, 22–4) gives this example, based on the 1981 ECHR case of *Dudgeon v. United Kingdom*.

[19] On judicial under-enforcement of rights generally, see Sager (1978). On the argument that rights have been under-enforced by the judiciary under the HRA, see Ewing (2011).

[20] 323 U.S. 214 (1944).

[21] The classic statement of this argument was made by James Bradley Thayer in his book, *John Marshall* (1901). Thayer considered that the tendency of legislatures within a system of judicial

decide? That is, judicial and political review may well be more substitutes for each other than supplements within legal constitutionalism, so that before opting for the latter one would need to be persuaded that on balance the rights under-enforcement stemming from judicial pathologies is likely to be less than from legislative ones.

A second weakness of legal constitutionalism is that may also lead to the over-statement or over-enforcement of constitutionalist limits on governmental power. There is a term for this weakness and it is "Lochner."[22] So even if, very generally speaking, potential under-enforcement of rights is worse than potential over-enforcement,[23] over-enforcement of the *Lochner* variety is far from harmless error. That is, where courts use their supreme interpretative power to read into a constitutional text certain controversial rights that are the subject of reasonable disagreement, they may be artificially limiting the scope of governmental power in the service of substantive injustice. This type of over-enforcement undermines the overall political legitimacy of an otherwise democratic constitutional regime.

A third weakness of legal constitutionalism is the general weakness and relative ineffectiveness of relying on ex post regulatory mechanisms to the exclusion of ex ante ones.[24] If constitutionalism imposes limits on governmental power, some of which take the form of individual rights, then relying primarily or exclusively on courts to enforce them will often be tantamount to closing the barn door after the horse has bolted. Some laws that raise serious rights issues may never be challenged in court, others may be challenged but under-enforced, and in most cases laws will not be challenged until at least some of the damage they are judicially assessed to impose has already been caused. Abstract judicial review acknowledges, and is designed to deal with, this problem but several systems do not permit this type of review and those that do usually limit standing to elected representatives of a certain number or office, whose political interest in challenging a law may or may not coincide with those likely to be adversely affected by it.[25]

Fourthly, there is a strong tendency within legal constitutionalism for courts to become the primary expositors of rights in society and yet there are serious weaknesses in judicial modes of rights deliberation from the perspective of this important function. Judicial review may be conceptualized and defended (in common law jurisdictions at least) as incidental to the ordinary judicial function of deciding a

---

supremacy to leave consideration of constitutional limits to the courts and to assume that whatever they can constitutionally do they may do, meant that "honor and fair dealing and common honesty were not relevant to their inquiries." Even more famously, he argued that as judicial review involved the correction of legislative mistakes from the outside, it results in the people losing the "political experience, and the moral education and stimulus that come from…correcting their own errors. [The] tendency of a common and easy resort to this great function [is] to dwarf the political capacity of the people, and to deaden its sense of moral responsibility." *Ibid.*, pp. 103–7.

[22] *Lochner* v. *New York*, 198 US 45 (1905).

[23] This argument is made by Fallon (2008, 1709).

[24] For general works on this issue, see Shavell (1987); Kolstad et al. (1990).

[25] For the few exceptions to this standing limitation and for general discussion of the merits and critiques of abstract review, see Ferreres Comella (2009, 66–70).

case,[26] but deciding a specific case is far from all that a highest court typically does when exercising this power in the context of a controversial rights issue. Rather, depending on the scope of its judgment, it resolves not only the case but the rights issue raised in it as far as lower courts in future cases are concerned, and, depending on its accepted or perceived interpretive supremacy within the entire political system, its resolution becomes the authoritative one for all purposes. In this way, the highest court tends to speak for, and in the name of, society as a whole. Here again, the "limitations inherent within judicial forms of decision-making" (Tomkins 2005, 29) discussed by Tomkins and Waldron come to the fore, as does the concern with over-legalization or judicialization of principled public discourse generally, whereby the legal component or conception of rights is over-emphasized at the expense of the moral and political.[27]

These first four weaknesses mostly address the issue of whether or not rights are better protected with judicial review. Last, but by no means least, is the familiar and standard concern with legal constitutionalism from the perspective of legitimacy in a democratically-organized polity, the concern that Fallon and Kumm have attempted to outflank. As this concern is so familiar, I shall be brief. It may perhaps be expressed or captured this way: in the name of attempting to ensure against under-protection of rights, legal constitutionalism gives to an electorally-unaccountable committee of experts unreviewable power to decide many of the most important and weighty normative issues that virtually all contemporary democratic political systems face, even though it turns out that these issues are not ones for which the committee's expertise is especially or uniquely relevant.

The easy, conventional and mostly rhetorical response to this concern is premised on a legal fiction; namely, that a supermajority of citizens has self-consciously, deliberately and clearly pre-committed to a set of higher law solutions to rights issues, and the function of the courts is simply to apply these – in essentially the same way as any other type of law.[28] The legal reality is that many of the most important rights issues as and where they present themselves are inevitably the subject of reasonable disagreement among and between judges, legislators and citizens – as routinely evidenced by closely divided courts, legislatures and referenda on some of the most controversial and difficult topics. Such disagreement – about which rights exist, their meaning, scope and application, as well as permissible limits on them – persists whether or not rights and rights claims are left in the realm of moral and political discourse only, are deemed part of the common law or have been incorporated into the particular textual formulas of a statutory or constitutional bill of rights. As Jeremy Waldron puts it, "the Bill of Rights does not settle the disagreements that exist in the society about individual and minority rights. It bears on

[26] This conceptualization and defence were first presented in *Marbury* v. *Madison*. Harel and Kahana's argument seeks to justify "case-specific judicial review" only and not the broader precedential force of these decisions underlying claims of judicial supremacy, although they believe their argument has "implications" for the latter (Harek and Kahana 2010).

[27] See, for example, Glendon (1991); Waldron (2006); Stone Sweet (2000).

[28] This argument originates with Alexander Hamilton in *Federalist Paper* 78.

them but it does not settle them. At most, the abstract terms of the Bill of Rights are popularly selected sites for disputes about these issues" (Waldron 2006, 1393).

In this context, the case for some of the most fundamental, important and divisive moral and political issues confronting a self-governing society of equal citizens being subject to the rule that the decision of a judicial majority is final and effectively unreviewable, on the legal fiction that they are wholly questions of law akin to the interpretation of a statute or a contract, appears weak – if not duplicitous. So too on the frequently proffered alternative basis that they concern matters of principle (as distinct from policy) best left to, and answered by, courts alone (Dworkin 1977, 81–130).[29] Even were the distinction between principle and policy to be successfully explained and justified, if "constitutional democracy" is taken to require excluding the participation and reasonable judgments of equal citizens and their electorally-accountable legislative representatives on all rights-relevant issues of principle in favour of the reasonable judgments of judicial majorities, then the qualifying adjective has largely swallowed what it qualifies.

5.3.2 A Normatively Appealing Third Way

The persistence of these weaknesses with both traditional models alongside each of their strengths is a major problem because of the structure of the choice between them. In the either-or universe of the bipolar model, we are stuck with one or the other in a "winner-take-all" institutional system that requires the weaknesses of the chosen model to be endured alongside its strengths, whilst the complementary merits of the other model are lost entirely. It is legal constitutionalism versus political constitutionalism, judicial supremacy or no judicial review at all. But this "warts-and-all" structure of institutional design choice is unnecessarily crude and disproportionate with respect to the normative costs and benefits of the two models. By contrast, a major advantage of weak-form review as an intermediate hybrid is that it makes possible a form of "proportional representation" among the strengths of both legal and political constitutionalism, whilst also severing or minimizing the major weaknesses of each.

The core of the case for the new general model is the argument for both weaker-form judicial review and weaker-form legislative supremacy versus either strong-form judicial review or strong-form legislative supremacy. The central problem with strong-form judicial review is not that rights-based judicial review has no value or cannot be justified at all, but that it is too strong. In the familiar language of proportionality, it is not the least restrictive way of achieving this value with respect to others that are also central and essential within a constitutional democracy. Moreover, as already previewed in the previous section, there are good reasons for believing that at least part of this value – protecting against under-enforcement of rights – may not be optimally or best promoted by strong judicial review, even if

[29] In the UK, and drawing on Dworkin, see Jowell (1999).

it were the case that on balance it affords better protection than political constitutionalism.

Similarly, the central problem with traditional strong-form legislative supremacy is also that it is unnecessarily strong. Just as judicial supremacy risks giving not only final but exclusive voice to the highest court, traditional strong-form legislative supremacy needlessly creates a monopoly for elected representatives in terms of whose voice counts or has legal authority on rights issues. If the core concept of parliamentary sovereignty is perfectly consistent with the existence of moral, political and procedural constraints on legislative decision-making, as Jeffery Goldsworthy (2010, 302–3) reminds us, the new model adds two concrete and specific types of such constraint: the procedural requirement of pre-enactment rights review and the very visible political constraint of a formal, but not necessarily legally final, judicial opinion on rights issues raised by enacted laws. By challenging the legislature's institutional monopoly of authoritative voice on rights issues, this second constraint in particular can be said to weaken legislative supremacy compared to the traditional version that remains part and parcel of political constitutionalism.

I have claimed that the general case for the new model, like the arguments for the mixed economy, it that it is combines the strengths of the two purer but flawed extremes whilst avoiding their weaknesses. It is now time to make good on this claim by explaining how this is achieved. As we have seen, to the extent that proponents of legal and political constitutionalism have engaged each others' arguments, it has mostly been in a debate about judicial review in which the common ground is that the two main issues are whether there is reason to suppose that rights are better protected with or without judicial review and whether judicial review is democratically legitimate. Although at times, political constitutionalists almost seem to rue the focus on rights – which they acknowledge has been the trigger for the growth of legal constitutionalism (Bellamy 2007, 15) – as misplaced, it is too late in the rights revolution (at least in the context of mature liberal democracies) to cede this territory to the opposition.

How exactly does the new model accommodate and combine the strengths of both polar positions whilst severing their weaknesses as inessential and dispensable? And what is the argument that the resulting intermediate position better protects rights whilst also maintaining political legitimacy in a democracy? First, on the issue of rights protection, the case for the new model accepts almost everything that critics of legal constitutionalism say as to why legislative reasoning about the sorts of rights issues confronting all modern societies is or may be better/more appropriate than judicial reasoning, with its inherently artificial and constrained nature and relative inability to focus directly on the moral issues involved. This acceptance is institutionalized in pre- and post-enactment political rights review. At the same time, it also accepts and accommodates the legal constitutionalist argument that judicial review may sometimes help to reduce the risk of certain types of under-enforcement of rights, hence the role of courts in between the two stages of political review. Given what has just been said, this is obviously not because courts are better or more expert than legislatures at rights deliberation but because each institution comes to the task from a different perspective, has different strengths and weaknesses that may usefully be brought to bear on rights issues to help improve outcomes and protect against under-enforcement. Again, the relative strengths of legislatures are those expressed by Tomkins and Waldron, as well as the greater diversity of views mentioned above. The relative weaknesses of legislatures are the potential rights-relevant pathologies to which they may be subject. The relative advantage of courts here is independence from these potential electorally-induced pathologies and the dimension of fact-specific, applied rights deliberation versus the more general and abstract approach of legislatures, but the weaknesses are the parallel tendencies towards pathologies of their own and the general problem of relying exclusively on ex post regulation discussed above.

What the argument for the new model rejects as uncompelling, disproportionate and dispensable in the two polar models on this issue is the following. First, in the case for political constitutionalism, it does not accept the consequence of concluding that, on balance, legislative reasoning about rights is superior to (or no worse than) judicial; namely, that rights issues should be left exclusively to the former. This consequence is a function of the either-or universe of the bi-polar framework, in which it is necessary to choose between legislative and judicial modes of reasoning about rights. The appeal of the new model here is that it revises the standard implication of this argument by recognizing the respective strengths and weakness of courts and legislatures and providing a significant and appropriate role for both. Accepting the net superiority of legislative over judicial reasoning about rights may determine which has the power of the final word but it does not entail that no role is served by, or afforded to, the latter.

Secondly, with respect to the legal constitutionalist case for judicial review, the argument for weak-form review rejects the implication that under-enforcement concerns justify not only a judicial role in the protection of rights but also a judicial veto over legislation – what Fallon refers to as one of the "multiple veto points" in the system (Fallon 2008, 1707) – or at least one that is not defeasible by ordinary majority vote of the legislature. Rather, for the new model, under-enforcement concerns mean that courts should be a "checking point" in the system, having an interpretive, alerting and informing function with respect to rights issues, somewhat akin to the delaying power of the House of Lords as the second legislative chamber versus the veto power of the U.S. Senate.[30] This revision, of course, reflects and expresses the difference between weak-form and strong-form judicial review. To the significant extent that the case for legal constitutionalism turns on the incentives and potential rights-relevant pathologies of elected officials, the case for the new model here is that the combined impact of mandatory political rights review and non-final judicial review will sufficiently alter those incentives and counter the pathologies to render the solution of judicial finality unnecessary and disproportionate. This distinct mode of judicial input into rights discourse can be helpful as the legally penultimate word in both informing/spurring rights review by the political branches and raising the costs of legislative disagreement through an alerted citizenry. As with the criminal

[30]The current delaying power of the House of Lords is 1 year under the 1949 Parliament Act.

jury trial to which Fallon analogizes the argument for judicial review as protection against under-enforcement of rights, we may give citizen-members of the jury a veto power in order to minimize erroneous conviction of the innocent, but (and this is the limit of the analogy) we do not give such a power to second-guess their decisions to judges. Accordingly, unlike the two traditional models, the new model recognizes and reaps the respective benefits of both legislative and judicial reasoning in terms of their contributions to rights deliberation and protection against under-enforcement, but within an institutional structure that affords the power of the final word to the former.

Let us now turn to the issue of legitimacy. Once again, the case for the new model is that it is able to combine and accommodate the core insights of both opponents and proponents of judicial review into a package that is more compelling and proportionate than either alone. The democratic legitimacy of collective decision-making procedures (and especially higher lawmaking procedures) is obviously a centrally important value within constitutional democracies. By granting the power of the final word to the legislature, the new model preserves and promotes this value. At the same time, the new model acknowledges and accommodates the broader legitimacy concerns raised by Fallon and Kumm in their defences of judicial review. To the extent that weak-form judicial review helps to protect against under-enforcement of rights by giving courts checking, alerting, informing and decision-making functions that supplement legislative rights deliberations and counter characteristic potential pathologies, it promotes justice and so enhances overall political legitimacy. But it does so, too, when also countering judicial under- and over-enforcement of rights, against which legal constitutionalism is generally powerless.

With respect to Kumm's argument, it is first necessary to distinguish reasonable public justification for general *legislative* acts that burden individuals from administrative and judicial decisions, which are typically subject to forms of judicial review for reasonableness even in systems that do not provide for constitutional review of legislation.[31] These are not at issue and clearly perform the legitimating, rule of law function that Kumm prescribes. As for legislative acts, the new model obviously provides the judicial forum for the required critical assessment of reasons. The question, therefore, is whether strong-form judicial review rather than weak is necessary or essential to fulfil this condition of legitimacy and so is justified as a proportionate departure from the norm of democratically-accountable decision-making.[32] I believe the answer is no. To explain why, let me begin by making explicit what has largely been left implicit in the argument so far: the case for the new model's override power is premised on reasonable disagreement with the

[31] Most famously, "the Wednesbury unreasonableness" test in the UK. *Associated Provincial Picture Houses* v. *Wednesbury Corporation* [1947] 1 KB 223.

[32] Alon Harel and Adam Shinar ask the different, if not unrelated, question of whether strong-form judicial review ("a strong right to a hearing") rather than "constrained judicial review" is necessary to satisfy the right to a hearing that they claim grounds the justification of judicial review. Harel and Shiner (2012).

courts on a rights issue. The basic principle at work here is that democracy requires a reasonable legislative judgment to trump a reasonable judicial one.[33] In one sense, therefore, if courts and legislatures both adhere to their normatively assigned roles and (as in Kumm's theory) courts only invalidate legislation for which there is no reasonable public justification, then legislatures would never exercise their override power – which perhaps becomes redundant. But by the same token, under this scenario it cannot be said that strong-form judicial review is necessary as weak-form review would achieve exactly the same result.

More realistically, however, the risk that both will depart from their normatively circumscribed powers must be taken into account: that courts will invalidate reasonable legislative decisions in favour of the court's view of the correct one and legislatures will exercise their override power in support of unreasonable legislative decisions. In these circumstances, is strong-form judicial review rather than weak justified? In current practice, Kumm's normative standard is not in fact the one that is generally understood to govern judicial review and courts regularly overturn legislative decisions which cannot be said to be unreasonable.[34] But what if it were? Under strong-form review, there is little to counter the risk of judicial overreaching on this issue – as by reason of their very independence, courts face no direct political constraint – and the legislative override power would be a useful institutional check in the absence of others as a form of separation of powers. Moreover, we are by hypothesis here – a court has invalidated a reasonable legislative act – in the situation where the principle of a reasonable legislative judgment trumping a reasonable judicial one applies, so that use of the override would be justified. By contrast, unlike the strong-form judicial power, this legislative power would be subject to a significant institutional or political constraint against the risk of misuse; namely, the fact that a court has issued a formal judgment finding there to be no reasonable public justification for the legislation violating individual rights. Finally, so far we have been discussing the situation in which there have been clear departures from the standard of reasonableness, but as Kumm notes, the limits of reasonable disagreement may also be subject to reasonable disagreement (Kumm 2007, 28 n 43). That is, courts and legislatures may reasonably disagree about whether a legislative act is within the bounds of the reasonable. For the same two reasons just noted – the checking function of the override and the default or tie-breaking nature of legislative power that democracy requires – weak-form review also seems the more justified solution here.

[33] See Perry (2003, 661). Mattias Kumm also appears to accept this principle, which is why for him judicial review is limited to policing the boundaries of the reasonable.

[34] That is, in applying the second and third prongs of the proportionality principle courts tend to ask whether the legislature's justification for limiting a right is in fact necessary (or the least restrictive means) and proportionate in the strict sense, rather than reasonably necessary and proportionate. I, too, have argued that under ordinary (i.e., strong-form) judicial review courts should limit themselves to asking whether the government's justification for limiting a right is reasonable, contrary to the general practice – although for a somewhat different reason than Kumm. See Gardbaum (2007).

In sum, the conventional democratic legitimacy concerns with judicial review are genuine and powerful in the context of pervasive rights indeterminacy. Again, given this context, the argument that democratic legitimacy requires the reasonable view of a legislative majority to trump the reasonable view of a judicial majority seems compelling. Fallon and Kumm are correct that democratic legitimacy is not the only source or type of political legitimacy in constitutional democracies, but it is a critically important and presumptive one. Departures from it carry a strong burden of justification. If protecting against under-enforcement of rights and/or the requirement of reasonable public justification for legislative burdens on individuals are the potential bases for such a justified departure, the means of furthering these components of political legitimacy must be proportionate; in particular, they must promote their objectives in ways that least restrictively depart from the democratic legitimacy of electorally-accountable decision-making. Weak-form judicial review is that least restrictive means; strong-form judicial review is not.

Institutionally, then, the strengths of legal and political constitutionalism that the new model combines in its hybrid status are as follows. From the latter, it employs the benefits of the more unconstrained and all-things-considered legislative style of moral reasoning about rights both before and after the exercise of weak-form judicial review. As part of the "after," of course, the new model also retains the possibility of ultimate reliance on the principles of electorally-accountable decision-making and political equality. From legal constitutionalism, the new model first takes the enhancement of general rights-consciousness that generally comes with a specific and fairly comprehensive statement of legal rights. It then attempts to counter potential legislative under-enforcement of rights in part by empowering politically independent and unaccountable judges to give their considered opinions on the merits of rights claims filed by individuals, thereby providing a forum to critically assess the public justification of laws and bolstering the broader legitimacy of the political system.

At the same time, the new model also avoids or seeks to minimize the major weaknesses of both traditional models. From political constitutionalism, it counters the rights-relevant pathologies or blind spots to which electorally-accountable institutions may be prone by, first, mandating rights consciousness and review in the legislative process itself and, secondly, establishing judicial review. Of the weaknesses of legal constitutionalism, the new model counters certain judicial pathologies that may result in both the under- and over-enforcement of rights by not relying solely on courts for protection of rights but also on rights review and deliberation by the political institutions. This enables the benefits of legislative reasoning about rights to supplement the limitations of judicial rights reasoning. At the pre-enactment stage, this political rights review also introduces the advantages of ex ante regulation in addition to the ex post regulation of judicial review, which may help to prevent rights violations from occurring in the first place. And at the post-enactment stage, it permits the new model to neutralize legal constitutionalism's democratic legitimacy problem.

As part of its hybrid nature, and like the analogous mixed economy, the new model not only selectively incorporates and combines certain existing features (i.e., the strengths) from each of the two polar ones whilst discarding others (the weaknesses), but also revises them and in the process creates at least two wholly novel features that are not part of either traditional model. The normative appeal of these two exclusive features contributes substantially to the overall case for the new model. The first of these is the checking and alerting rights-protective roles of the courts compared to the full veto power of judicial supremacy just discussed in the context of Richard Fallon's arguments. More akin to the delaying power of the UK's second legislative chamber, the House of Lords, than the outright veto of the U.S. Senate – and for similar reasons of democratic legitimacy – one version of these more limited powers is institutionalized in the judicial declaration of incompatibility, a novel judicial power when enacted as part of the HRA.[35] The second exclusive feature is the new model's dispersal of responsibility for rights among all three branches of government rather than its centralization in either the courts (judicial supremacy) or the legislature (legislative supremacy). It is achieved in the three sequenced stages of mandatory pre-enactment political rights review by the executive and legislature, post-enactment judicial rights review, and post-litigation political rights review by the legislature. In this way, the new model not only produces a better, more proportionate general balance of power between courts and legislatures than the two more lopsided models of legislative and judicial supremacy, but also specifically with respect to the recognition and protection of rights.

This dispersal of rights responsibilities has the goal of fostering a stronger and deeper rights consciousness in all institutions exercising public power and is an essential part of the aggregate rights protective features of the new model. Overall, in the three following ways, it creates a different, and arguably more attractive, rights culture than the one produced under judicial supremacy. First, in the context of reasonable disagreement about rights, the dispersal rather than the concentration of responsibility is likely to affect the content of the recognized rights. This is due to both types of "judicial pathologies" about rights discussed above: (1) the artificially and legalistically constrained nature of judicial reasoning about rights that largely excludes direct engagement with the moral issues involved; and (2) the greater diversity of views and perspectives that electorally-accountable representatives can openly bring to rights deliberations compared to the numerically smaller, cloistered and elite world of the higher judiciary. Secondly, in terms of procedure, rights discussions will be far more inclusive and participatory leading to greater rights consciousness among both elected representatives and electorate. In affirming rather than denying Waldron's "right of rights" (Waldron 1998), the new model here institutionalizes a democratically legitimate rights regime. Thirdly, for standard checks and balances reasons the dispersal rather than the concentration of rights responsibilities reduces the risk of under-enforcement that comes with relying exclusively on any one institution – whether courts or legislatures. As noted above, although better known, under-enforcement concerns are hardly limited to the legislature. The key innovation here is the distinctive new model feature of supple-

[35] At the time of its enactment in 1998, no other system of constitutional review of legislation in the world had the same or a similar judicial power.

menting ex post judicial rights review with ex ante political rights review by the executive and legislature. For its goal is to internalize rights consciousness within the processes of policy-making and thereby reduce or minimize rights violations in legislative outputs at the outset.

A final argument for the new model, at least as against legal constitutionalism, relates to judicial appointments. Under judicial supremacy, because of the power that they wield, the claim that constitutional court judges should have whatever partial or indirect democratic accountability they can be given is an irresistible one. As a result, judicial appointments to these courts become political appointments, with several variations in the precise mode of legislative and/or executive selection but in almost all of which political affiliation is taken into account.[36] Yet, for some, observing constitutional court judges deciding important and close cases politically, along predictable ideological lines, is unedifying and problematic, and at least partly in tension with the very independence that the argument for judicial review centrally relies upon. To be clear, this practice does not necessarily affect one aspect or sense of judicial independence – that once in office judges are no longer beholden or answerable to politicians, although it may do where judges sit for renewable terms – but it does in the sense of having impartial, relatively disinterested, non-party political, or at least non-partisan, individuals appointed to judicial office in the first place. For others, the desirability or acceptability of political appointments to the constitutional judiciary is not intrinsic, something that is independently valuable or justified, but rather is instrumentally and essentially tied to the nature of judicial supremacy within a democracy.

Understandably, there have been calls for the new model jurisdictions to follow the same path. As judges now exercise powers of constitutional review, they too should be given whatever indirect democratic accountability is available through the practices of political nomination and public hearings.[37] At the same time, this is anathema to many others within the Commonwealth common law culture in which the new model currently operates, given the longstanding official norms of merit, seniority and peer review for high judicial office and the irrelevance – indeed invisibility– of partisan political views and affiliations. The United Kingdom has recently moved even further in the direction of greater insulation from political factors, and also greater transparency, by instituting the fully independent Judicial Appointments Committee to replace the opaque method of selection by the Lord Chancellor.

Depending on one's point of view on this issue, one advantage of the new model is that, unlike judicial supremacy, it has the resources to resist this call for indirect democratic accountability and political appointments to the highest courts. This, of course, is the direct mode of democratic accountability for rights outcomes resulting from the existence of the legislative power of the final word. Accordingly, there is no necessary requirement for the politically-tinged constitutional decision-

[36] See Stone Sweet (2000, 45–9); Jackson and Tushnet (2006).

[37] Canada held its first ever public hearing for a nominee to the SCC in 2006, albeit brief and non-partisan, but so far this has not been repeated for subsequent appointments.

making everywhere characteristic of judicial supremacy in practice. This can be left to the elected and accountable politicians under the new model. Here, by contrast, the designated task of the courts is to be as independent of political decision-making as possible and in all senses, to provide a complement rather than a supplement to such reasoning by bringing the best of the distinctive judicial technique, including its technical, impartial, disinterested and non-partisan nature, to bear on rights issues. To be sure, these norms are never fully realised in practice and the limitations of this technique speak against its automatically having the final word on contestable rights issues, but it is what justifies a judicial role in the process, if anything does. In short, the new model arguably provides the best of both worlds, and judicial supremacy the worst: more politically independent judicial reasoning and more direct democratic accountability for the ultimate resolution of rights issues versus politically-tinged and, at this point, wholly unaccountable judicial decisions that are final.

5.4 Conclusion

The case just presented depends on certain assumptions about the institutions and rights commitments of a political society that entail it is most centrally and generally applicable to mature democracies. These assumptions are the same as those listed by Jeremy Waldron in presenting his case against judicial review: namely, a reasonably well-functioning legislature and judiciary, broad commitment to individual and minority rights in society, and persistent, good faith disagreement about what specific rights there are and what they amount to (Waldron 2006, 1359–69). Where these conditions obtain, as in many mature democracies, my normative argument, like his, is a general one: that is, the new model is a better institutional form of constitutionalism than the other two. Where they do not, as in many transitional, newer or fragile democracies, the normative case for one of the other models may be stronger – or, indeed, this entire design issue less important than certain others. If either legislatures or courts are not reasonably well-functioning, this should affect their relative allocation of power, so that contextual factors of this sort will be relevant to the issue of which legal regime will likely better protects rights.[38] Other contextual factors, such as the desire for radical regime change and a "new beginning" (Ackerman 1997), may also be highly relevant. So, for example, in the new constitutions of post-Nazi Germany and post-apartheid South Africa, judicial supremacy and strong-form review may have represented the sharper break with the past that was deemed necessary for expressive and practical reasons.

Although the normative case I have presented does not generally apply to transitional, newer or fragile democracies, this does not rule out the possibility that weak-form judicial review might sometimes be preferable to strong-form in this context

[38] As Wojciech Sadurski persuasively argues in the context of central and eastern Europe, although his argument is premised on the two traditional choices only. See Sadursky (2002).

for purely *pragmatic* reasons. This might be so, for example, where robust or aggressive exercise of strong-form review in transitional or fragile democracies risks a wholesale political backlash against the courts that undermines the broader, and arguably more essential principle of judicial independence. Although strong-form review in one sense exhibits the independence of the judiciary to its greatest extent, for that very reason it also poses the greatest practical threat to such independence – as evidenced by recent events in Hungary and Turkey – and in service of a function that is not an essential part of it.[39]

References

Ackerman, Bruce. 1997. The rise of world constitutionalism. *Virginia Law Review* 83: 771–797.

Bellamy, Richard. 2007. *Political constitutionalism: A Republican defence of the constitutionality of democracy*. Cambridge: Cambridge University Press.

Bickel, Alexander. 1962. *The least dangerous branch*. New Haven: Yale University Press.

Carolan, Eoin. 2013. Between supremacy and submission: A model of collaborative constitutionalism? Available at ssrn.com/abstract=1889243.

Dixon, Rosalind. 2009. The Supreme Court of Canada, charter dialogue, and deference. *Osgoode Hall Law Journal* 47: 235–286.

Dworkin, Ronald. 1977. *Taking rights seriously*. Cambridge: Harvard University Press.

Ewing, Keith. 2011. *The bonfire of the liberties*. Oxford: Oxford University Press.

Fallon, Richard. 2008. The core of an uneasy case for judicial review. *Harvard Law Review* 121: 1693–1736.

Ferreres Comella, V. 2009. *Constitutional courts and democratic values*, 66–70. New Haven: Yale University Press.

Gardbaum, Stephen. 2001. The new commonwealth model of constitutionalism. *American Journal of Comparative Law* 49: 759–810.

Gardbaum, Stephen. 2007. Limiting constitutional rights. *UCLA Law Review* 54: 789–851.

Gardbaum, Stephen. 2013. *The new commonwealth model of constitutionalism: Theory and practice*. Cambridge: Cambridge University Press.

Gardbaum, Stephen. 2015. Are strong constitutional courts always a good thing for new democracies? *Columbia Journal of Transnational Law* 53: 51–86.

Glendon, Mary Ann. 1991. *Rights talk: The impoverishment of political discourse*. Cambridge: Harvard University Press.

Goldsworthy, Jeffrey. 2010. *Parliamentary sovereignty: Contemporary debates*. Cambridge: Cambridge University Press.

Harel, Alon Harel, and Tsvi Kahana. 2010. The easy core case for judicial review. *Journal of Legal Analysis* 2: 227–256.

Harel, Alon, and Adam Shiner. 2012. Between legislative and judicial supremacy: A cautious defense of constrained judicial review. *International Journal of Constitutional Law* 10: 950–975.

Jackson, Vicki, and Mark Tushnet. 2006. *Comparative constitutional law*, 2nd ed. New York: Foundation Press.

Jowell, Jeffrey. 1999. Of vires and vacuums: The constitutional context of judicial review. *Public Law* 1999: 448–460.

Kavanagh, Aileen. 2009. *Constitutional review under the UK human rights act*, 417–419. Cambridge: Cambridge University Press.

[39] For an elaboration of this argument, see Gardbaum (2015).

Kolstad, C., T. Ulen, and G. Johnson. 1990. *Ex Post* liability for harm vs. *Ex Ante* safety regulations: Substitutes or complements? *American Economic Review* 80: 888–901.
Kumm, Mathias. 2007. Institutionalizing Socratic contestation. *European Journal of Legal Studies* 1: 1–32.
Kumm, Mathias. 2009. Democracy is not enough: Rights, proportionality and the point of judicial review. *New York University Public Law and Legal Theory Working Papers* Paper 118: 1–38.
Kyritsis, Dimitrios. 2012. Constitutional review in a representative democracy. *Oxford Journal of Legal Studies* 32: 297–324.
Perry, Michael. 2003. Protecting human right in a democracy: What role for courts? *Wake Forest Law Review* 38: 635–694.
Sadursky, Wojiech. 2002. Judicial review and the protection of constitutional rights. *Oxford Journal of Legal Studies* 22: 275–299.
Sager, Lawrence. 1978. Fair measure: The legal status of underenforced constitutional norms. *Harvard Law Review* 91: 1212–1264.
Shavell, Steven. 1987. *Economic analysis of accident law*. Cambridge: Harvard University Press.
Stone Sweet, Alec. 2000. *Governing with judges: Constitutional politics in Europe*. Oxford: Oxford University Press.
Thayer, James Bradley. 1901. *John Marshall*. Boston: Houghton Mifflin.
Tomkins, Adam. 2005. *Our Republican constitution*. Oxford: Hart Publishing.
Tushnet, Mark. 2003. Alternative forms of judicial review. *Michigan Law Review* 101: 2781.
Waldron, Jeremy. 1998. Participation: The rights of rights. *Proceedings of the Aristotelian Society* 98: 307–337.
Waldron, Jeremy. 2006. The core of the case against judicial review. *Yale Law Journal* 115: 1346–1406.
Waldron, Jeremy. 2009. Judges as moral reasoners. *International Journal of Constitutional Law (I-CON)* 7: 2–24.

Chapter 6
Scope and Limits of Dialogic Constitutionalism

Roberto Gargarella

Abstract This chapter takes up the debate that is going on in contemporary legal and political philosophy under the rubric of *dialogic constitutionalism*, *dialogic justice* or *dialogic judicial review*. These issues are studied with special emphasis on historical considerations about the separation of powers and the contemporary context of Latin American Constitutions. In the same spirit of some of my previous writings, including a larger version of this paper, I maintain that, beside the genuine reasons we have to celebrate the coming of dialogic constitutionalism, we also have reasons for concern, particularly if we are not willing to modify the basic structure of the system of checks and balances on which it is usually based.

6.1 The Coming of Dialogic Constitutionalism

Let me introduce the coming of "dialogic constitutionalism" by making reference, first, to the Canadian notwithstanding clause, which can be taken as the starting point of the dialogic approach that will be here under scrutiny.[1] The clause was an integral part of the Charter of Rights that was adopted in Canada, in 1982.[2] It allowed the national or provincial legislature to insist with the application of its legislation for an additional 5-year period, notwithstanding the fact that a Court found it inconsistent with some of the rights contained in the Charter. In principle, this innovation appeared to represent only a modest legal development, but in fact it

[1] Mark Tushnet stated: "I take dialogic judicial review to have been invented in the Canadian Charter of Rights in 1982" (Tushnet 2009, 205).

[2] According to C. Young, "[s]o far, constitutional practice in Canada is the source of the most sustained study of dialogue between courts and legislatures…This style appears apt for…systems that, like Canada (and South Africa) combine a historical commitment to parliamentary sovereignty with a present-day constitutionalism" (Young 2012, 148). Similarly, for Luc Tremblay, the adoption of that clause originated the "theory of institutional dialogue," which – he believes- "may be seen as a Canadian contribution to the debate over the democratic legitimacy of judicial review" (Tremblay 2005, 1).

R. Gargarella (✉)
Facultad de Derecho, Universidad Torcuato di Tella,
Av. Pres. Figueroa Alcorta 7350, 1428 CABA, Argentina
e-mail: robert@utdt.edu

T. Bustamante, B.G. Fernandes (eds.), *Democratizing Constitutional Law*,
Law and Philosophy Library 113, DOI 10.1007/978-3-319-28371-5_6

immediately triggered a fabulous academic debate (Bateup 2007; Hogg and Bushell 1997; Hogg et al. 2007; Langford 2009; Manfredi and Kelly 1999; Petter 2003; Roach 2004; Tushnet 2008).

In fact, I submit, the clause is representative of a series of legal changes that emerged in the last decades, which we may summarize under the rubric of the "new *Commonwealth* model of constitutionalism" (Gardbaum 2013). The *Commonwealth* model refers to a diversity of experiences that followed legal reforms introduced not only in Canada 1982, but also in the United Kingdom (1998), New Zealand (1990), or Australia (2004). In South Africa, we also find numerous decisions by the Constitutional Court, which made use of dialogic strategies and devices, from the famous *Grootboom* case, in 2000,[3] to *Olivia Road* (and the promotion of a "meaningful engagement") in 2008.[4] According to some, this "new model" represents, in the area of constitutional law, what the "mixed economy" does, in economic matters. The new model combines traditional elements of the *common law,* with renewed declarations of rights. As Jeffrey Goldsworthy has put it, the newly introduced mechanisms "offer the possibility of a compromise that combines the best features of both the traditional models, by conferring on courts constitutional responsibility to review the consistency of legislation with protected rights, while preserving the authority of legislatures to have the last word" (Goldsworthy 2003, 484).[5]

In Latin America, the first Court to engage in these kinds of dialogical practices was the Colombian Court (Rodríguez-Garavito 2011), which was shortly after followed by tribunals in many other Latin American countries.[6] Latin American tribunals have demonstrated enormous creativity concerning the design and implementation of dialogic mechanisms. The alternatives that they explored were multiple (I already mentioned some of them in the above examples). We have (i) courts that organized *public audiences* with government officers and members of civil society, trying to obtain extended agreements, gain legitimacy for their decisions and/or obtain better information and arguments in the face of complex cases[7]; (ii) courts that *ordered* the national government to present a coherent plan

[3] 2001 (1) SA 46 (CC).

[4] 2008 (3) SA 208 (CC).

[5] In most cases, the introduction of these changes has implied two main institutional innovations. On the hand, legislative powers have been required to get involved in reviewing the constitutionality of norms, before they get enacted (a "mandatory pre-enactment political rights review"). On the other hand, "weak" forms of judicial review have been introduced, which means that the judicial branch has kept its powers of constitutional review, although the practice of "judicial supremacy" has become diluted. It is not anymore obvious that the decisions of courts are unreviewable by ordinary legislative majority (Tushnet 2008; Gardbaum 2013, 25–27).

[6] For example, in 1997, the Colombian Constitutional Court engaged into an argument related to the importance of having proper legislative debates. It maintained that the voting process required a previous "deliberation", which the tribunal considered an "indispensable" condition for the validity of the law. See Corte Constitucional [C.C.] [Constitutional Court], *Sentencia* C-222, 1997.

[7] See, for example, a decision by the Brazilian Supreme Court, May 29th, 2008, concerning the Biosafety Law.

(i.e., in the face of an environmental or social catastrophe)[8]; (iii) courts that *advised* the government what decision to adopt in order to comply with its constitutional duties[9]; (iv) courts that *exhorted* governments to correct their policies according to prevalent legal standards[10]; (v) courts that launched ambitious *monitoring mechanisms* so as to ensure the enforcement of its ruling over time[11]; or – and this is my favourite example- (vi) courts that challenged the validity of a certain law, because it was passed without a proper *legislative debate*.[12] I should also add that, even though these innovations are not and should not be seen as limited to cases of social rights and structural litigation, it has been in those cases (this is to say cases that involve massive violation of rights and implicate multiple government agencies), where the practice appeared to be more salient and interesting (Courtis 2005; Fabre 2000; Fiss 2003; Gearty and Mantouvalou 2011; Gloppen 2006; Hunt 1996; King 2012; Rodríguez-Garavito 2011).[13]

The novelties introduced through *dialogic constitutionalism* were, and still are, particularly exciting for those working with both *constitutional theory* and *democratic theory.* On the one hand, and concerning *constitutional theory*, these innovations are exciting because they allow us to renovate the unending, fatigued discussions on the justification of judicial review and the counter-majoritarian difficulty. In the face of the seemingly insoluble tensions that exist between constitutionalism and democracy – tensions that no new theory of judicial review has been able to solve- dialogic constitutionalism brings reasons for hope. It suggests a stimulating way for accommodating our commitments to both popular sovereignty and the protection of minority rights.

On the other hand, and in what relates to *democratic theory,* dialogic constitutionalism seems attractive for at least two reasons. First, dialogic theories approach to constitutionalism with an eye placed in democracy: its purpose is to reconcile both values. Second, they do so in a specific way, namely by choosing the perspective of a deliberative democracy, which many of us consider a particularly fruitful approach to democracy.

---

[8] See, for example, a decision by Colombian Constitutional Court in Corte Constitucional, January 22, 2004, *Sentencia* T-025/04.

[9] See, for example, a decisioń by the Argentinean Supreme Court in Corte Suprema de Justicia de la Nación, 8/8/2006. "Badaro, Alfonso Valentín, c/ANSES s/reajustes varios."

[10] Ibid.

[11] See, for example, a decision by the Colombian Constitutional Court in Judgement T-025 of the Colombian Constitutional Court. On the topic, see also Katyal (1998); Mikva (1998); Krotoszynski (1998).

[12] See, for example, a decision by Colombian Constitutional Court in Corte Constitucional, *Sentencia C*- 740/13. Of particular interest, for the purposes of this paper, is the right to "meaningful engagement," in the way it was developed by the South African Constitutional Court. See, for example, Liebenberg 2012, 2014.

[13] Examining the U.S. legal system, Ronald Krotoszynski mentions other innovative initiatives promoted by courts, including the decision to call for an "open dialogue"; to propose "constitutional remands;" to "warn" Congress that failing to consider constitutionally relevant evidence, may transform the statute it is elaborating, invalid one; etc. See Krotoszynski (1998, 4–6).

6.2 Constitutional Dialogue and Deliberative Democracy

In what follows, I will critically evaluate the development of this novel practice. And I want to critically examine this practice precisely because I understand that it can only be defended if it developed in certain particular ways. Now, and in order to proceed with my criticisms, in this section I will first clarify what my normative standpoint shall be, when speaking about dialogic constitutionalism[14]; and in the next one I will say something about the way in which these dialogical devices have helped us re-think our approaches to the issue of judicial review. Let me then start by examining the meaning of dialogic constitutionalism.

Legal theory has already offered many possible definitions for dialogic constitutionalism. For Katharine Young, for example, "dialogue describes a practice in which reason-giving courts are able to adjudicate rights, but elected and accountable legislatures are given the final Word on the shape of the obligations that flow from them" (Young 2012, 147). However, I resist this definition because the way in which it seems to be restricted to inter-branch dialogue (I shall come back to this point below). Another interesting definition is the one provided by Bradley Bakker. For him, "constitutional dialogue encompasses the idea that different governmental branches and people interact in ways that shape the dominant views of constitutional interpretation over time" (Bakker 2008, 216).[15] There are at least three features of this latter definition that I find attractive, namely the fact that it goes beyond inter-branch dialogue; its emphasis in dialogue as an ongoing process; and its focus on constitutional interpretation. In what follows, I shall be thinking about a slightly different version of dialogic constitutionalism, where the idea of "dialogue" aims to preserve the features that make it an appealing notion in our daily language. Summarily speaking, the ideal of dialogic constitutionalism that I will be taking into account refers to a *public and ongoing process of constitutional interpretation where issues of public or intersubjective morality are regularly debated among equals, in an inclusive discussion that embraces the different governmental branches and the people at large.* [16] I must clarify that this definition does not describe but rather tries to refine and build from what I found in actual practice. It will constitute my normative reference in this presentation.

According to this definition, the dialogic procedure would be characterized by different important notes, including those of *equality* (which refers to the equal status of its different participants); *deliberation* (which refers to the process of exchange of reasons); and *inclusiveness* (which stresses the idea of deliberation *by the people*,[17] under the assumption that the entire process gains in impartiality if all

[14] I will do so, even though – I believe- it should also be possible to develop or share most of my criticisms by simply relying on reasons that are internal to the same dialogic practice.

[15] Similarly, G. Dor describes (legal) dialogue as "an open and frank interchange, exchange and discussion of ideas and opinions in the seeking of mutual harmony" (Dor 2000, 17–18).

[16] See also Mauwese and Snel (2013), 125–6.

[17] See also, for example, Fishkin 2011, 242.

the potentially affected intervened in that conversation).[18] In this presentation, I will put a particular stress in this latter point (inclusiveness), and this will not be because I assume that inclusiveness is more important than the other two values, but rather because I think that most reflections on the topic have been merely restricted to "interbranch dialogue" (we shall come back to this point below).[19] In addition, the collective process would refer to an *ongoing conversation* (which would basically mean that courts would not have the authority to pronounce the "last institutional word"); that is developed in *public* and it is *restricted to issues of public morality* (which means that the collective dialogue would not be concerned with issues related to our private moral life)[20]; and that *does not depend on the discretionary will of one of its participants* (in other words, the dialogic process is promoted, rather than discouraged or simply authorized, by the institutional system, which takes the promotion of collective dialogue as one of its distinctive features).

I have said that my definition of constitutional dialogue tried to build from, and at the same time refine, the prevalent practice. I need to make clear, then, that my "refinement" of the practice will be derived from my commitment to a deliberative theory of democracy. This assumption is related to a personal, intellectual conviction, but also to the fact that the dialogical practice seems to constantly appeal to (something along the lines of) a deliberative democracy (Bohman 1996; Bohman and Rehg 1997; Elster 1991, 1998; Gutman and Thompson 2004; Habermas 1992; Nino 1996). Of course, there is also a long discussion about the meaning, scope, implications and virtues of deliberative democracy, but at this point I will not enter into the details of that complex discussion. Here, I will be simply taking a specific version of deliberative democracy as given.[21] According to this view, public decisions gain justification when they are adopted after an ample process of *collective discussion* with *all those potentially affected*. This view of deliberative democracy, it should be clear, emphasizes two main features as definitive of a properly functioning democracy, namely *discussion* and *social inclusion*. These features shall play a crucial role in the critical analysis of dialogic constitutionalism, which I will develop in the following pages.

---

[18] The "inclusive" character of the conversation obviously encompasses the three branches of power (see, for example Young, stating: "In conversational review, all three branches assume a shared interpretive role over the right at issue" Young 2012, 147). However, it must be noted, the idea of "inclusiveness" is supposed to go beyond the three branches: it aims at including the people at large.

[19] On interbranch dialogue see, for example, the discussions generated around Christopher Edley's work (Edley 1991) in *Duke L.J.* or around Dan Coenen's paper (Coenen 2001), in *William and Mary Law Review.*

[20] There are numerous reasons for explaining this restriction. Mainly, the idea is that the "epistemic" virtues associated with collective discussion disappear when we are dealing with issues of personal or private morality: each person is here assumed to be the best judge of his own affairs (Mill 1859; Nino 1991).

[21] My defence of the idea of deliberative democracy is based in the idea of equality, but also in the "epistemic" virtues that I see in it. In this respect see, for example, Cohen 1986; Estlund 1993; Nino 1991, 1992, 1996.

6.3 Constitutional Dialogue and Judicial Review

Among many other interesting developments, the new dialogical practice helps us revise traditional approaches to judicial review. The first thing to say, in this respect, is that through the introduction of the dialogic approach, judges tend to lose the prerogative they hold today to pronounce the "last institutional word" thereby "thwart[ing] the will … of the actual people of the here and now" (Bickel 1962: 17; Kramer 2004, 2005). The dialogic model conceives of the institutional system in ways that significantly differ from the traditional one, where judicial review is reduced to the *binary options* of either upholding or invalidating a statute.[22]

Clearly, this presentation is not restricted to discussions about judicial review. However, it is important to have in mind that what dialogic constitutionalism proposes significantly differs from what many traditional and well-known approaches to judicial review have proposed. Let me illustrate this with two quite opposite cases, among the many that one could choose from. The dialogic approach diverges, for example, from Alexander Bickel's view, which invites judges to step back and exercise their so-called passive virtues, thus allowing private agents to work out, by themselves, solutions for their legal problems (Bickel 1962). Contrary to this view, *dialogic constitutionalism* requires judges to be more active, particularly taking into account their unique institutional position. In effect, judges have direct and permanent access to the complaints of all those who consider themselves to have been improperly treated by the majoritarian decision-making process. This is why dialogic constitutionalism expects judges to enrich the collective conversation with the claims of all those unheard or improperly dismissed voices.[23] As Ronald Krotoszynski has put it, it is not difficult to recognize "the superiority of dialogue to the passive virtues" (Krotoszynski 1998, 57). For him, the dialogic model "better serves the value of interbranch comity than judicial silence followed by invalidation of legislative work product" (ibid.).

The dialogic view also differs from Guido Calabresi's approach, which is quite different from the one that Bickel proposed. Calabresi has once maintained that judges should be authorized to repeal obsolete legislation (Calabresi 1985, 1991, 2012).[24] In his words, courts should be given "the power by legislatures to order the sunset of a statute. If the legislature disagreed with a court's determination, they would of course be empowered to overrule the court and reenact the statute. Whether

[22] Trying to reconcile theories favouring the judicial's "last word" and dialogic theories, see, for instance, Hübner Mendes (2013).

[23] For this reason, judges are assumed to be in an exceptional position to give due weight to the interests of those unjustly excluded from the ordinary democratic political arena (see Liebenberg 2012).

[24] In *United States v. Then* (56 F.3rd 464, 2d Cir. 1995), and acting as a Judge, Calabresi suggested a different relationship between the judiciary and Congress, where judges ("fire a…Constitutional flare"), warn Congress that "if it fails to consider carefully a particular matter in light of evidence [considered to be] constitutionally relevant, the federal courts are likely to enforce constitutionally-mandated constraints on congressional policy-making choices" (Krotoszynski 1998, 7).

and when a law should sunset depends on the law itself. Some become obsolete almost immediately, while others remain relevant for a very long time" (Calabresi 2012). This view would require judges to be very active: judges would thus become profoundly and constantly engaged with the legislative process. However, and for different reasons, Calabresi's views seems also wrong, from a dialogic perspective. Although it is totally fine to have judges deeply engaged in the public decision-making process, it seems erroneous to foster their participation in the way Calabresi does. In fact, Calabresi's suggestion seems to be still too much attached to the traditional system of judicial review, where judges either uphold or invalidate a statute. The methods and procedures of a collective conversation, however, are and should be fundamentally different from the ones that presently characterize our institutional system.[25] The existing instruments appear to be more capable of favouring a confrontation between unequally situated powers, than of facilitating a conversation between equals (we will come back to this point).

6.4 Structural Problems: The System of Checks and Balances as an Exclusive Machinery

Herein, I shall explore some "structural" difficulties faced by the new dialogic practice of constitutionalism.[26] Of course, there are different understandings of what "structure" means, and how to approach to "structural" problems. A Marxist

[25] When I say "our" I am thinking about the constitutional system that prevails in the Americas since the creation of the American Constitution in 1787, although it is probably the case that what I say about these cases also apply beyond the American continent.

[26] Before turning to the study of the structural problems of dialogic constitutionalism, I want to say a few words about one repeated and significant critique to extrajudicial forms of review, like dialogic review, which I do not share, but that became quite popular among legal doctrinaires. I am referring to objections related to the *uncertainty* created by dialogic-type of mechanisms. This critique, which has most famously been advanced by Larry Alexander, goes like this: all these new alternatives to traditional judicial review are finally unattractive because they introduce improper degrees of uncertainty and instability into situations of conflict. By contrast, the traditional system avoids these problems, and ensures that conflicts are settled through the intervention of authoritative bodies (Alexander and Schauer 1997, 2000; Alexander and Solum 2005). Keith Whittington, for example, has presented Alexander's settlement-objection as "the most prominent recent objection to extrajudicial constitutional interpretation" (Whittington 2002, 786). Now, there are numerous things to say about this view, but at this point I will limit myself to simply mention why I do not find it particularly attractive. The practice of dialogic constitutionalism has been developed during more than 30 years already, both in legally advanced countries and in fragile legal communities. It can be subjected to different criticisms – and we just examined some of them – but critiques such as the ones mentioned by Alexander have not acquired particular relevance in actual practice. Rather than legal chaos and uncertainty, the practice of dialogic constitutionalism has generated great expectations in those places where it took place. Moreover, it has insufflated life to unappealing, old-style, eroded and bad-functioning legal systems. As Whittington has put it, Alexander and others' objection "overstates the value of constitutional stability, while simultaneously overestimating the ability of the judiciary to impose constitutional settlements and underes-

approach, for example would recommend us to first focus our attention on the economic or material basis of society; and feminist critiques would suggest us to pay privileged attention to the absence of certain voices or the domination of certain viewpoints in our dialogic experiences, (see, for instance, Phillips 1998; Young 2001; Young 2002; Williams 2000). These kinds of criticisms, I believe, are absolutely relevant for those interested in democratic dialogue, and must be taken in serious consideration. Herein, however, I will only pay attention to a small portion of the different structural problems that merit attention. In what follows, in my references to "structural" problems I will only be thinking about our *institutional* structure; and in my references to the institutional structure I will mainly be referring to the existing system of *checks and balances.*

The reasons of my choice should not be difficult to understand. In part, my choice has to do – simply- with my area of academic expertise. Above all, however, my choice is connected with the fact that the system of checks and balances represents the core of the institutional organization in the Americas, and also one that is gaining growing influence in other parts of the world (even in Europe).[27]

I have two main criticisms related to the system of checks and balances in its relation to dialogic constitutionalism. The first objection says that the system of checks and balances has been designed in order to prevent a civil warfare, rather than *promote a democratic debate*. This fact, I believe, explains why the system is not well prepared and equipped to ensure collective deliberation over time. It can do so, but only as a result of the occasional, informal and discretional will of certain public officers. The second criticism springs from the fact that the system of checks and balances is based on a distrust of majority ruling and a strong preference for internal or inter-branch controls, rather than external or popular controls. This fact, I believe, explains why the system is not well prepared and equipped to *ensure a properly inclusive deliberation*. It is worth noting that these two main criticisms are directly connected to what I consider to be the two main requirements of a deliberative democracy, namely "debate" and "inclusion." In addition, I want to remark that my criticisms will expose the existence of a worrisome tension within our constitutional structures, namely a *tension between an old machinery of power and a renewed system of rights*.

The basic point is this: We are trying to obtain from the system of checks and balances something (an inclusive democratic deliberation) that the system is not (was not) well-prepared to provide. It was created for a different purpose, namely

---

timating the capacity of nonjudicial actors to settle constitutional disputes effectively…Moreover, the question of how constitutional meaning can be resolved most effectively is an empirical one" (Whittington 2002, 788–9). Similarly, Mark Tushnet claimed that critics of dialogic constitutionalism have still to demonstrate that non-judicial constitutional review introduced "more instability than they eliminate.. The empirical case against non-judicial constitutional review remains to be established" (Tushnet 2003, 490, also see Tushnet 1997, 2006).

[27] I explore the influence of the U.S. constitutional model of checks and balances in the drafting of Latin American constitutions in Gargarella 2010 and 2013a. Concerning Europe, I am thinking about the growing importance of judicial review, through a concentrated and "final" jurisdiction by an European Court.

contain social warfare in a situation of social unrest and "oppressive legislation" by state legislatures. This goal helps understand the main characteristics of the system of checks and balances including, for instance, the following two: provide defensive tools to members of the different branches, so as to prevent mutual encroachments; and detach public officers from the people at large, so as to prevent undue social pressures upon the former. Not surprisingly, the created system seems much better equipped to reduce the risk of majority (legislative) oppression than promote any kind of inclusive debate.

In order to support my claims about the tensions between the system of checks and balances and deliberative democracy, in what follows I will pay attention to the *public reasons* offered by the creators of the system in its defence, and also to their *underlying assumptions about democracy*. Later on, I will also suggest that the *actual practice* of the system ratifies my critical claims.

6.5 The System of Checks and Balances and the Promise of an "Armed Truce"

As anticipated, I will here maintain that the system of checks and balances is not prepared to favour collective debate. It does not prevent it and, occasionally, it can coexist with it, but it was designed to serve a different, and rather opposite purpose. Its main object was to channel social warfare, by providing defensive tools to representatives of different sections of society. In other words, its purpose was to prevent social clashes rather than promote any kind of collective conversation. In the end, the idea is that our system offers a bad institutional support for the advancement of a deliberative democracy.[28]

In my view, it is this weakness of our institutional system what accounts for the enormous attention that a (rather minor) institutional reform like the *notwithstanding clause* obtained from the legal academy. In fact, the adoption of the Charter in Canada did not represent a significant progress towards the goal of democratic deliberation, as many authors may assume.[29] If it gained so much attention this was – I submit- because it represented an interesting, unexpected effort aimed at changing the institutional system in the direction of a more deliberative scheme. In other words, I take the academic success of the clause as a first suggestion of the validity of one of my claims, namely that the system of checks and balances has not

[28] On the need to connect discussions about interbranch dialogue and normative democratic theory see, for example, Tushnet (2001).

[29] This is, for example, what Katie Young seems to assume in her excellent book on social and economic rights. For her, the adoption of the Charter would have created in Canada the conditions for a dialogic type of constitutionalism. Compare with Goldsworthy, who states: "the Canadian debate suggests that if Parliament never dared to exercise that power, this arrangement might still be vulnerable to objections based on majoritarian conceptions of democracy" (Goldsworthy 2010, 205).

been even slightly helpful in the promotion of a collective conversation. My assertion, however, is stronger than that. What I am assuming here is that even though the system of checks and balances does not prevent the development of deliberative practices, it neither fosters them, nor fits well with them: the system was aimed to a different goal, namely to prevent social confrontation.

In order to support my claims about the "purpose" and "logic" of the system of checks and balances, I will first resort to legal history and pay attention to the public reasons offered by the ideologues of the system. Those legal arguments, I assume, will make apparent that the system of checks and balances was aimed at responding to a particular type of legal and political conflict – basically, the existence of "hasty", "unjust" and "numerous" laws, passed by "tyrannical" legislatures- rather than favour any kind of collective deliberation. After completing this review of legal history, I will also claim that my argument can also be supported by examining the actual practice of the system. In other words: no matter what the Framers of the system thought or desired concerning the system of checks and balances, I will claim that we have good reasons to assert that the system, in actual practice, does not favour or directly hinders collective deliberation. Let me begin this exploration by focusing on the first, historical analysis.

6.5.1 Containing Social Warfare

Not surprisingly, I will begin this historical investigation with a reference to the *Federalist Papers*, and particularly to the most cited, significant and influential text ever written on the topic, this is to say *Federalist paper No. 51*. The analysis of this line of argument seems particularly important given the decisive influence that it had for the creation and development of the system of checks and balances, first in the United States, and then in other regions of the world, beginning from Latin America.

In *Federalist paper No. 51*, James Madison explained and justified the creation of this system of mutual balances. The core of the paper appears in this crucial paragraph, where Madison stated:

> The great security against a gradual concentration of the several powers in the same department, consists in giving to those who administer each department the necessary constitutional means and personal motives to resist encroachments of the others. The provision for defense must in this, as in all other cases, be made commensurate to the danger of attack. Ambition must be made to counteract ambition. The interest of the man must be connected with the constitutional rights of the place. It may be a reflection on human nature, that such devices should be necessary to control the abuses of government. But what is government itself, but the greatest of all reflections on human nature? If men were angels, no government would be necessary. If angels were to govern men, neither external nor internal controls on government would be necessary. In framing a government which is to be administered by men over men, the great difficulty lies in this: you must first enable the government to control the governed; and in the next place oblige it to control itself.

The passage is extraordinarily rich, and a proper understanding of it would take an entire seminar, so I will limit myself to highlight a few notes about it. First of all, I will claim that, concerning the basic organization of the system of checks and balances, Madison's views were apparent. Madison did not envision a dialogic relationship between the different branches, but rather a scenario of "perpetual war". He assumed that "those who administer[ed] each department" would systematically attempt to violate the limits of their own powers and invade the areas controlled by the other branches. In other words, the ideas of cooperation or mutual collaboration were basically absent from his understanding of the dynamic between the branches. This explains why members of each branch were mainly prepared to "resist encroachments of the others."

The main strategy in order to avoid these mutual encroachments was – and this is probably the main line of *Federalist paper No. 51*- to give "to those who administer each department the necessary constitutional means and personal motives" required for that purpose. For Madison, the representatives' "personal motives" were taken as given: he was mainly thinking about self-interest (and passions). As he put it: "ambition must be made to counteract ambition".[30] In passing, it is interesting to note that this view of human motivations implied the dismissal of other alternative approaches to the topic, and particularly a dismissal of those (then enormously relevant) *republican* views that assumed that *civic virtue* played or could play a central role in politics (Skinner 1983, 1984, 1990, 1998). Madison ridiculed those views, claiming that "[i]f men were angels, no government would be necessary."

Madison assumed that the main motivation of "those who administer each department" was (and was going to be) their uninhibited ambition. So, what to do in the face of this sad fact? His response was to give members of each department "the necessary constitutional means…to resist encroachments of the others." The "necessary constitutional means" were those that still distinguish the system of checks and balances, namely the veto power of the president; the controlling powers of the judiciary; the power of insistence of the legislature; the right of impeachment; etc.

Clearly, these "necessary means" were not dialogical instruments. They were mechanisms that, like arms or guns, were supposed to facilitate the achievement of an "armed truce" between the branches. In other words, it was then assumed that, with these arms at their disposals, members of each department would be able to "resist the encroachment of the others." In other terms – and this was the hope, and at the same time the promise of the system- fearing retaliation, members of the different branches would not be tempted to interfere with the affairs of the other branches. This promise was also a sad recognition of the limitations of the system, which in no way was perceived as favourable to collective dialogue.

The Framers' defense of a system of checks and balances implied the dismissal of an alternative system, which many of their republican and radical adversaries

[30] In this respect, Madison was basically following David Hume's understanding of human motivations (White 1987).

proposed, namely a system of "strict separation" of powers (Vile 1967).[31] According to this alternative scheme, none of the branches enjoyed the right to interfere with the affairs of the others – not even through defensive mechanisms. Radicals inclined toward a system of strict separation of powers because this was an alternative that not only promised to eliminate any confusion regarding which power would be responsible for what tasks, but also one that would preserve the inherent superiority of congress vis-à-vis the other branches of power. By contrast, Madison denounced this model of constitutionalism in his work *Vices of the Political System,* because he considered that it could only produce numerous, changing and unjust laws.

In sum, the Framers promoted an institutional system that was aimed to "economize in virtue" (that, seemingly, their rivals did not want to "economize"), and consequently tried to use the representatives' self-interest ("ambition") in the benefit of all (Ackerman 1991, 198). Their idea was that the mechanisms of checks and balances could ensure an "armed truce" between the then existing social, economic and political interests. Within this picture, the alternative of having a mobilized citizenry and/or an active Congress appeared as fundamentally unattractive.

6.5.2 Thwarting the Ideal of "Government by the People"

In the precedent section I tried to demonstrate that the system of checks and balances responded to the need to contain social warfare, rather than promote collective deliberation. Now, let me say something concerning its deficit in terms of inclusion and popular participation, by making three points, related to the Framers' ideas about *factions*; the *representative system*; and the establishment of a system of *internal rather than external controls.*

The concept of *factions,* which is unquestionably the most important political concept in *Federalist Papers,* represents a good start in order to specify my views on the subject.[32] It seems clear that the entire new structure of government was directed to contain the risks that factions posed to any government. We can put this even stronger: the entire Constitution was primarily justified as a way to contain the evils of factions. Now, a first interesting thing to note is that, in *Federalist Paper N. 10* Madison precisely defined factions as a "number of citizens, whether amounting to a majority or a minority of the whole, who are united and actuated by some common impulse of passion, or of interest, adversed to the rights of other citizens, or to the permanent and aggregate interests of the community." However, a few lines below

[31] For M. Vile, during the era of "radical constitutionalism," all the authors "adhered to the doctrine of the separation of powers, while they rejected, to a greater or lesser degree, the concept of check and balances" (Vile 1967, 133).

[32] Madison defined the concept of factions in *Federalist paper* 10. "By a faction" – he claimed- "I understand a number of citizens, whether amounting to a majority or a minority of the whole, who are united and actuated by some common impulse of passion, or of interest, adversed to the rights of other citizens, or to the permanent and aggregate interests of the community".

he made it clear that "if a faction consists of less than a majority, relief is supplied by the republican principle, which enables the majority to defeat its sinister views by regular vote." As a consequence, the only factions that *really* mattered were majority factions, which allows us to say that the entire Constitution was, in the end, dedicated to restrain the actions of majority groups, given their oppressive tendencies. The risk of minority oppression was not taken seriously at the time (even in the face of slavery).[33]

In the same paper, Madison made reference to the "violence of faction" and the "instability, injustice, and confusion" that factions "introduced into the public councils," which represented "the mortal diseases under which popular governments have everywhere perished." What Madison had in mind was the so-called "paper money crisis" that affected the country during this post-independence (and pre-constitutional) period. This "crisis" had become more threatening and dangerous as a consequence of its legal manifestations than as a result of the armed confrontations that it provoked. In the end, the armed confrontations (symbolized by the famous "Shays rebellion") were generally perceived as illegal actions, and consequently repressed by the troops of the Confederation (Brown 1970, 1983; Feer 1988; Szatmary 1987; Wood 1996). The real problem seemed to be another, which emerged when the same demands that a few had advanced through the use of armed violence (and that were then combated, as illegal actions), began to gain terrain through the use of the law. This is to say, the main threat to a stable and well-ordered government seemed to come from "outside". The suggested solution was then two-fold: restrictions to external pressures, and a system of internal controls.

In other words, a socially explosive situation, which included armed rebellions, unchecked legislatures and the "paper money crisis," explains why most of the Framers came to favor a system of endogenous, rather than exogenous or popular controls.

It was that explosive social situation what moved Madison, in *Federalist No. 10*, to resist direct popular participation in politics and favour, instead, a representative system where representatives of the people would "refine and enlarge the public views by passing them through the medium of a chosen body of citizens".[34] So, for Madison, as for most of the "Founding Fathers," the representative system was not seen as a "second best" or a "necessary evil" (as many of their anti-federalist opponents envisioned it). Representation was, for them, a first and desired option. And this was so because they assumed that the people themselves were still not well-prepared to engage in politics directly. For Madison, the representatives' decisions tended to "better serve justice and the public good than would the views of the people themselves if convened for that purpose". James Fishkin has characterized this Madisonian approach (which he directly relates to the one develop by John Stuart Mill a century later -in his *Considerations on Representative Government*),

[33]This point also in Dahl 1956.

[34]It has also been noted how Madison played with the ambiguous notion of "chosen": "chosen" could refer both to those who had been selected by the people, and/or something more in the line of the "selected few" (Manin 1997).

as one of *elite deliberation* (Fishkin 2011, 243, 246). As we also try to do here, Fishkin distinguishes that elitist system of democracy from deliberative democracy.[35]

The Framers' elitist view derived from some of the assumptions explored in preceding sections, and particularly from the Framers' fear of majoritarian democracy. It was also as a result of those assumptions that they limited popular political participation mainly to periodical suffrage. Of course, the importance of periodical suffrage cannot be denied. For example, in the same *Federalist No.51*, Madison highlighted the relevance of regular elections. He stated: "A dependence on the people is, no doubt, the primary control on the government". Madison's claim was truthful, but only in part.

It is true that periodical elections represent an external control that plays a crucial role in our system of government. However, it is also true that periodical elections constitute only one among the many numerous mechanisms of popular character that could have been then adopted. The fact is that the Framers rejected or choose not to consider numerous other mechanisms of external control, which were very common at their time. These mechanisms included mandatory instructions; the right to recall; mandatory rotation; annual elections; frequent town meetings; etc. Devices of the kind had been advanced by British radicals in Great Britain, during the mid-1700s – from Richard Price, Joseph Priestly and the group of "Radical Dissenters," to James Burgh and John Cartwright- and also in the United States, by the political opposition (the so-called anti-federalists), in the years that preceded the enactment of the national Constitutional (Cone 1968; Hay 1979; Kenyon 1985; Paine 1989; Storing 1981a, b; Wood 1969, 1992, 2002).

Now, the fact that none of these mechanisms found a place in the U.S. Constitution implies at least two things. On the one hand – and we have discussed about this already- the system of endogenous controls became the central feature of the new structure of government. On the other hand, popular suffrage suddenly became the only relevant institutional bridge between the representatives and the represented. In other words, periodical suffrage assumed an extraordinary responsibility: elections became in charge of periodically "revealing" the will of the people, without much additional institutional help. Consequently, the virtual absence of alternative devices make it extremely difficult for the people to control their representatives and make their voice audible, thus undermining the republican character of government.[36] Most early critics of the representative system recognized this risk.

From the perspective of deliberative democracy, this understanding of politics results particularly unattractive. And this is so because the appeal of the new *dialogic system of constitutionalism* entirely depends – or so I shall argue- on its capacity to overcome the democratic deficit that has been affecting our representative

---

[35] By which he means "a theory that attempts to combine deliberation by the people themselves with an equal consideration of the views that result", Fishkin 2011, 247.

[36] As Philipp Pettit stated: "No matter how powerful a system of popular influence, it will not support republican democracy unless it serves to impose a popular direction on government" (Pettit 2012, 306).

system in all these years. Only a wide and inclusive dialogue may become a meaningful dialogue.

6.5.3 Democracy

Having reached this point, I think it is very important to pay attention to the peculiar view of democracy presupposed in the system of checks and balances. The conception of democracy that prevailed among the Framers has already been the object of profound academic analysis (Dahl 1956). We have already some indications about what that conception of democracy looked like: we know about the Framers' distrust of the legislatures or their fear of unchecked majorities. For the Federalists it was clear that "in all very numerous assemblies, of whatever character composed, passion never fails to wrest the scepter of reason" (*Federalist paper* 55).

This fearful approach to politics favored the development of a *negative* understanding of democracy – let us call it *pluralist-* where the main purpose of democracy is not to foster deliberation or promote collective agreements, but rather *avoid mutual oppressions* (Dahl 1956). This goal, together with the assumption that factions had a natural tendency to oppress each other, explains the Framers' overriding concern with the creation of a system of controls and mutual balances. The proposal to balance "ambition with ambition" so as to "control de abuses of government" expresses well the Federalists' assumptions, their fears and their hope. Alexander Hamilton made this point very clear. He stated:

> Give all the power to the many, they will oppress the few. Give all the power to the few, they will oppress the many. Both therefore ought to have power, that each may defend itself agst. the other (Hamilton in Farrand 1937, vol. 1, 288).

James Madison made an identical point. For him, "The landholders ought to have a share in the government, to support the...invaluable interests (of property) and to balance and check the other (group)" (Madison in Farrand 1937, vol. 1, 431).

Now, the object of this view of democracy – avoiding mutual oppressions- was certainly worth of praise, particularly at a time when social divisions implied dire confrontations and even armed clashes between opposing interests.[37] In that context, a negative conception of democracy may appear as a reasonable choice: few things seem more important than preventing extreme social conflict, avoiding the repression of unpopular minorities, etc. However, it seems also clear that this conception of democracy was based on controversial normative grounds – grounds that sub-

[37] The idea, like in the British model of constitutionalism, was based on numerous fundamental assumptions, like the following: (i) society was divided into a few, different sections; (ii) these sections had opposed interests; (iii) that these sections were internally homogeneous; (iv) members of these sections were fundamentally motivated by self-interest; (v) there existed institutional means that were apt to guarantee each of them a certain amount of institutional power (i.e., large districts and indirect elections for the selection of defenders of the interests of the landowners); and that (vi) these powers had to be substantially equal, so as to prevent mutual oppressions.

stantially differ from those that characterize the deliberative approach, and also from our presently shared understandings of democracy.[38] For the moment, it should be enough to say that the institutional system tried to ensure that "the many" and "the few" enjoyed an equivalent institutional power, which seems an odd solution in democratic terms. This sole proposal suggests an idea of democracy that has very little connections with our present approaches to the democratic ideal. Of course, it seems perfectly reasonable to ensure protection to unpopular minorities, but not – I would add- at the cost of so severely undermining the basic majoritarian component of democracy.[39]

6.5.4 Latin America

Given that I take most of my dialogic examples from Latin America, let me add a few lines exploring the existing continuities between Anglo-American legal history and what happened in Latin America during its Founding years.[40] I will limit myself to make two quick points: first, I will claim that there is a clear continuation between the U.S. constitutional history and Latin America's constitutional history; and second, I will show that Latin Americans tended to carry the U.S. institutional model to its extreme, particularly as a result of the influence of conservative/religious groups. These two developments, I should add, make inter-branch and popular dialogue still more difficult to achieve.

Concerning the continuities between the U.S. and Latin America, I would add that, given the importance that liberalism acquired during the Framing Period in Latin America, most countries in the region modeled their Constitutions under the influence of the U.S. Constitution. They organized a system of checks and balances that followed the U.S. model and – accordingly- established a presidentialist system. In addition, they also included a Bill of Rights in their Constitutions, according to the U.S. example. However, I should add that this particular aspect was substantively modified during the twentieth century (and after the 1917 Mexican

[38] Needless to say, this peculiar approach to democracy – and also to judicial review- has also very little in common with a *deliberative conception of democracy.* One early, lucid advocate of deliberative democracy, namely Carlos Nino, criticized the elitist view as a merely "negative" understanding of democracy: democracy would thus have "only a negative value, one that…does not explain the special value of democracy (Nino 1996, 81). He then wondered "whether this view of democracy is nothing more than a legitimization of the crude confrontation of interests constituting the status quo" (ibid., 82).

[39] Presently, it is difficult to think about democracy without making reference, first, to "the rule of the many" (Christiano 1996). Of course, "the rule of the many" may include controls, limits, checks, mutual supervisions, but it cannot simply dismiss the core idea that is that "the many" have to have the crucial say in government. Instead, in the model of the mixed constitution, the different sections of society (no matter the number of people that composes them) had to have a symmetrical power, which implied giving an extraordinary capacity, a day-to-day veto power, to minority interests.

[40] I have explored this comparison with more details in Gargarella 2010, 2013a, b.

Revolution), when most countries began to include social, economic and cultural rights within their Constitutions.

The second point that I want to make is that, given the significant and growing influence of conservative and religious forces in Latin America (particularly during the first half of the nineteenth century), most Constitutions began to at least partially depart from the U.S. example. In particular, the changes that were then incorporated into the new Constitutions implied two things. First, the separation of Church and the State that some Latin countries recognized in their Bill of Rights resulted in one way or another undermined. In cases like the one of Argentina, the Constitution included, at the same time, both a commitment to religious tolerance and a provision ensuring a special status to the Catholic religion. The other change that was introduced in most Constitutions concerned the organization of the system of checks and balances. A majority of Latin American countries modified the U.S. presidentialist system and carried it to its extreme. Consequently, they created hyper-presidentialist systems of government, within the context of already highly centralized countries. This initiative, I should add, put the entire system of equilibriums (which requires the different branches to be relatively equal in power) at risk.[41] Moreover, and more significantly for our purposes, hyper-presidentialist systems tend to be particularly harmful as far as public discussions are concerned. As Carlos Nino has suggested, powerful presidents have very little incentives for engaging in dialogue with the other branches of power (why to do it, when they can simply impose their decisions upon the rest?); and tend to use the strong powers at their disposal so as to foster public acclamation, rather than public debate about their proposals (Nino 1996).

6.5.5 Summing Up

What are the inferences we can derive from of all these initial reflections concerning the system of checks and balances? And what is the connection between those them and our topic of dialogic constitutionalism? The partial conclusion is the following: The system of checks and balances does not represent an appropriate institutional basis for the promotion of deliberative democracy.[42] It was a remedial, institutional response to a situation of extreme social, political and economic conflict.[43] In that

[41] The legal scholar Juan Bautista Alberdi – one of the great constitutional minds of his time-defended this convergence between conservative and liberal ideas, and proposed a peculiar system of checks and balances, which mixed the rather liberal U.S. Constitution with the conservative features that characterized the Chilean Constitution of 1833 (Alberdi 1852, chapter 25).

[42] Jeffrey Tulis has been one of the first authors in highlighting the lack of academic attention to the possible connections between the system of separation of powers and public deliberation (Tulis 2003, 200).

[43] Hübner Mendes maintains that the system (he is actually referring to the system of separation of powers) was created as "an institutional tool for (i) countervailing power with power and for (ii) distributing functions across diverse bodies", and he suggests – acknowledging that the system was

conflictive context, its immediate and fundamental purpose was to contain and channel the existing social crisis, which had begun to manifest itself through the institutional system (i.e., through paper money legislation enacted by seemingly unchecked legislatures). The connection of this partial conclusion with our present topic seems then apparent: taking into account the present characteristics of our institutional system, dialogic constitutionalism faces and (most probably) will continue to face grave problems for becoming a stable and non-discretionary institutional solution.[44] And this is so because the basic structure of our institutional system is not well prepared to favour inter-branch dialogue, and even less to maintain institutional dialogue over time. It can accept it occasionally, but it is clearly not hospitable to it.[45]

The problem we are dealing with seems to be present even in the context of Canada, where the Charter introduced formal mechanisms favouring at least some form of constitutional dialogue. Reviewing the history of dialogic mechanisms in Canada, Kent Roach (who is one of the main academic authorities in the override clause) recognizes these worries. He states: "concerns have been raised that on some issues the Court has had or shaped the last word. Fears have been expressed that whatever its potential, dialogic judicial review can degenerate into judicial monologue and supremacy" (Roach 2004, 75–6; see also Cameron 2001). Clearly, I do not want and I am not able to evaluate the actual working of the Canadian model. At this point, I just want to say that one can perfectly understand existing concerns about the real scope and implications of the Charter reform and judicial review.

The difficulties I mention in relation to the Canadian context are obviously more significant in those countries that have decided to keep their old structure of checks and balances untouched. In Latin America, serious problems emerge as a consequence of the privileged position that judges still enjoy; or as a result of the hyper-

not originally designed for this purpose- a "potential third virtue", which could be to use the system as a "deliberative apparatus, a mechanism for sparking inter-institutional exchange of reasons" (Hübner Mendes 2011, 1). He also admits that "[t]heories about the role of deliberation in democracy do not usually dedicate too much attention to the separation of powers and vice versa. This would be a counter-intuitive relation: branches do not deliberate among themselves, but rather control each other" (ibid., 7).

[44] Exploring the connections that exist between judicial intervention and institutional settings (with a particular focus on the cases of Mexico and Brazil), see Rios-Figueroa and Taylor (2002).

[45] Mark Tushnet announces another, different but still related, stability problem of new dialogic solutions in the context of well-established system of checks and balances. The problem he is thinking about is the difficulty of these (intermediate) weak forms of judicial review not to work either as a system of parliamentary sovereignty, or as a traditional system of judicial supremacy. In his words: "The question of stability is this: Can weak-form review be sustained over a long term, or will it become such a weak institution that the constitutional system is, for all practical purposes, indistinguishable from a system of parliamentary supremacy or such a strong institution that the courts' decisions will be taken as conclusive and effectively coercive on the legislature? Experience with weak-form systems is, as I have indicated, thin, but I think there is some evidence, mostly from Canada but some from New Zealand, that weak-form systems do become strong-form ones. The evidence, such as it is, is that judicial interpretations generally 'stick'" (Tushnet 2004, 17).

centralized and hyper-presidentialist character of the dominant institutional organization. For instance, a recent study by Rodríguez-Garavito (2011) compares the most important dialogic decisions of the noted Colombian Constitutional Court, in cases of structural litigation. These decisions include the famous *Sentencia* T-025, about the rights of displaced people; *Sentencia T*-760, about the right to health[46]; and *Sentencia* T-153, about the rights of prisoners.[47] In one of these cases, namely *Sentencia T*-025, the Court designed a spectacular monitoring process. In Rodríguez-Garavito's words: "Over the course of 7 years, it has engendered 21 follow-up public hearings involving a wide array of governmental and nongovernmental actors, as well as nearly 100 follow-up decisions whereby the CCC has fine-tuned its orders in light of progress reports" (Rodríguez-Garavito 2011, 1694). The situation, however, has been dramatically different in the other two cases, and particularly in *Sentencia T*-153, which did not include any court-sponsored monitoring-mechanisms. The tentative, initial conclusions that may be drawn from this comparison are diverse, but here I want to just insist in one point, related to the informal, discretionary character of our dialogical practices. In he end, and to repeat, the point is that the traditional system of checks and balances (everywhere, and particularly in countries with highly concentrated systems of governments) is not hospitable to dialogic mechanisms: it may accept them occasionally, but only when public authorities want to appeal to them, and insofar they are willing to accept their implications.[48]

6.6 Legal Alienation/"We the People" Outside of the Constitution

I mentioned two structural problems related to the system of checks and balances – one related to its deliberation-deficit, the other related to its deficit in terms of social inclusion. In what follows I will dedicate some additional time to the discussion of the second problem, which I find particularly relevant and also usually neglected by legal theory. More specifically, I want to explore some of the difficulties derived from having institutions that make it so difficult for the people at large to control their representatives and gain a say in the decision-making process – I will call this

---

[46] C.C., July 31th, 2008, *Sentencia T*-760/08 (slip op. at 200–03), *available at* http://www.corteconstitucional.gov.co/relatoria/2008/T-760-08.htm

[47] C.C., April 28th, 1998, *Sentencia T-153/98* (slip op.), *available at* http://www.corteconstitucional.gov.co/relatoria/1998/T-153-98.htm

[48] Similar problems explain also why the interesting public audiences that the Brazilian Supreme Court convened, related to the right to health; or the significant public audiences summoned by the Argentinean Court, concerning the right to freedom of expression, ended up in classic instances of judicial imposition.

a situation of *legal alienation*.[49] At this point I am not able to say much about this problem in general, but I do want to explore some of its implications for dialogic constitutionalism.

The problem of popular exclusion / *legal alienation* that I am thinking about is similar to the one that Roberto Mangabeira Unger once denounced in his often quoted reference to the "dirty little secret of contemporary jurisprudence". For him, that "secret" refers to its "discomfort with democracy", this is to say the "fear of popular action" (Unger 1996).

One possibility, often derived from situations of legal alienation and "fear of majority action" is that instances of inter-branch dialogue, which in principle result appealing and worth-promoting, become for this reason much less interesting. In other words, democratic dialogue loses much of its appeal when it is reduced to a dialogue between elites that are "too far removed" from the people (Madison, *Federalist No. 55*). We would then trivialize deliberative democracy if we were to celebrate the emergence of new instances of inter-branch dialogue as a triumph of democratic dialogue.

This problem, I believe, seems particularly relevant for contemporary constitutional theory. Think for example about the work of Mark Tushnet and Jeremy Waldron, this is to say the work of two legal scholars who have leading the academic discussion against traditional forms of judicial review. As we know, both of them have been harsh critics of judicial review and both of them have favored alternative options that in a certain way "recover" the "last word" for legislative majorities (Tushnet 2004, 2008, 2009; Waldron 1999a, b, 2004, 2009). Now, even though I substantially agree with the purposes and motives of their academic undertaking, I want to call the attention about a risk that may affect it. I am thinking about the risk of assuming a basic identity between legislatures and the people at large, when everything suggests the existence of a profound gap between the elected and their electors.

Let me explore this claim by using Jeremy Waldron's work as an example -particularly, his views as developed in his book *The Dignity of Legislation* (Waldron 1999b). Waldron's book represents a significant (and necessary) effort to defend the role of legislative bodies, within an academic context that has traditionally been

[49] Through this concept, I will be referring to those extreme situations where people can no longer identify with the law, which they neither created nor could reasonably challenge – a situation where they can only be described as victims of the law. This is to say, the notion of legal alienation will refer to those situations where the law begins to serve purposes contrary to those that, in the end, justify its existence. This notion of alienation – a notion of alienation that is objective rather than subjective- is related to the one defended by Karl Marx, for example, in his analysis of work and its products. According to Marx, "the object that labour produces, its product, confronts it as an alien being, as a power independent of the producer…[the] externalization of the worker in his product implies not only that his labour becomes an object, an exterior existence but also that it exists outside him, independent and alien, and becomes a self-sufficient power opposite him, that the life that he has lent to the object affronts him, hostile and alien…the worker becomes a slave to his object" (Marx 1978: 86–7).

contemptuous and disdainful towards Congress and everything related to it.[50] Part of the merit of the book – and of Waldron's project, in general- is that it helps to balance a view that became dominant, particularly in the legal academia. In his words, academics have developed "an idealized picture of judging and…a disreputable picture of legislating" (ibid., 2). This is why he tries to "recover and highlight ways of thinking about legislation that present it as a dignified mode of governance and a respectable source of law" (ibid.). In the end, he wants to develop "a *rosy* picture of legislatures that matched, in its normativity, perhaps in its naivete, certainly in its aspirational quality, the picture of courts –'the forum of principle' etc.- that we present in the more elevated moments of our constitutional jurisprudence" (ibid.).[51]

In my view, the difficulty with this approach is that, even assuming a rosy picture of how legislatures work, the representative system remains profoundly unattractive from a democratic perspective.[52] The problems affecting our legislatures do not merely depend on the bad faith, corruption or greediness of legislators. They derive from a plurality of sources (we have explored some of them), including the virtual absence of popular controls, which tends to alienate the people from ordinary politics. For these and other related reasons -the system has been designed for much simpler societies, composed of few, internally homogeneous groups- I would suggest that our present legislatures are structurally incapable to represent the multiplicity of views and voices existing in contemporary societies.[53] As a consequence, we – meaning those who are convinced about the merits of having an inclusive, deliberative democracy- have not many reasons to celebrate the changes that are seemingly taking place in contemporary constitutionalism. To be more precise: there is nothing particularly exciting in the fact of having contemporary constitutionalism slowly moving away from its traditional picture of pure judicial dominance and towards a different one, where legislatures prevail. Of course, there are democratic reasons that still -and in spite of all the existing institutional difficulties- may make us prefer legislative dominance to judicial dominance. However, the main point remains intact: for those of us who favour deliberative democracy, a system of legislative supremacy may be an improvement, but not a solution. As Karl

[50] This has been particularly so since *public choice theory* began to gain attraction within Law Schools. For public choice theory, see for example Buchanan 1975; Brennan and Lomasky 1997.

[51] For Mark Tushnet through "dialogic judicial review," we "advance the *value of democratic self-governance by leaving the final decision to the legislature*" (Tushnet 2009, 212, emphasis added).

[52] To state this does not mean to say that Waldron or Tushnet refer to legislatures and to the people indistinctly (see, for example, Waldron 2012). But I do think that in part of their work this distinction is not sufficiently stressed, which may create confusions regarding the actual attractiveness of the alternatives they propose.

[53] In Gargarella 2010 I have explored other structural problems, including the fact that the system of checks and balances was designed for a (assumedly) simpler society; composed of few and internally homogeneous groups; which could all become (assumedly) incorporated into the institutional system (i.e., through direct and indirect elections). Modern societies, characterized by the "fact of pluralism" seem to differ substantially from that old picture, which suggests that even a Congress under its best light would be unable to represent the diversity of viewpoints existing in society (Rawls 1991).

Marx would have put it, self-government needs more than legislatures: it requires a different type of constitutional organization.[54] In sum, even in the most promising cases, what we find are processes of elite discussion, mostly promoted by political or economic minorities, in their own benefit.

To illustrate this with an example, think about the problems that followed the judicial decision in the famous *Mendoza* case, in Argentina.[55] *Mendoza*, as we know, represents one of the most remarkable cases of structural litigation and judicial dialogue in Latin America, even though many other examples deserve similar attention.[56]

Initiated in 2004, the case concerned damage stemming from the contamination of the Matanza-Riachuelo River, which passes through Buenos Aires. Several million people live alongside or near the river. The pollution resulted in massive violation of health and environmental rights. Numerous actors with different levels of authority shared responsibility for the problem, including the National Government, the Province of Buenos Aires, the City of Buenos Aires, and 44 private companies that had dumped hazardous waste into the river. In this context, and facing a situation of perennial political paralysis, the Court undertook to intervene, and it did so in an unexpected and original way. The Court convened a series of public audiences, to which all parties involved were invited.

The beginning of the case could not have been more spectacular. The Court recognized the structural nature of the case, refused to limit itself to the binary options of traditional judicial review (either uphold or invalidate a statute), called open public audiences, and engaged in a frank conversation with executive authorities. In considering and revising the proposed clean-up plan, the Court enlisted the help of the public, NGOs, and university experts (rather than abstaining on grounds of lack of technical capacity). It helped to make previously unheard voices audible. However, the entire process has also been subjected to different and serious criticisms. For example, some legal experts described the clean-up process as "clearly top-down, exceedingly centralized" and made the victims feel that "the judicial process" was "closed to them, as it prevented their access to the basin authorities" (Puga 2012, 93).[57] In addition, the dialogic process was also undermined by some significant allegations of corruption. [58]

---

[54] For him, "In democracy, the constitution, the law, the state itself, insofar as it is a political constitution, is only the self-determination of the people, and a particular content of the people" (see Marx 1843, 21 of his "Contribution to the Critique of Hegel's *Philosophy of Right*,").

[55] A well-supported and very pessimist approach to the Brazilian case, in Ferraz 2011.

[56] These include *Verbitsky, Horacio s/ habeas corpus*, decided by Argentina's Supreme Court (2005) (concerning prisoners' rights); and many decisions of the Constitutional Court of Colombia including *Sentencia* T-847 (2000) (prisoners' rights); *Sentencia* T-590 (1998) (concerning state-protection of human rights advocates under threat); and *Sentencia* T-025 (2004) (concerning the situation of internally displaced persons). See Courtis (2005).

[57] A more optimistic approach in Bergallo (2005).

[58] For example, in 2008, the Court designated Judge Armella to monitor the clean-up process. According to an Auditor General's Office report, the judge sought to benefit members of his own family through the project. He contrived to hire by direct recruitment (by-passing competitive bid-

There are many things to say about this process, but here I just want to mention a couple of them, related to what I called situations of legal alienation. My impression is that the process gained attraction because of its attempts to re-connect some of the most disadvantaged groups of society with the decision-making process. However, in the end the entire process turned to be much less attractive than expected, because it began to develop in the contrary direction. More specifically, the people began to realize that the process continued to be managed "from above," and that they had actually few chances to gain control over it. I am not claiming that the process was a failure (it was not), or that the Court coordinated it in bad faith (which is not true). What I am saying, instead, is that, given that the institutional system has not been improved, problems related to its elitist features (i.e., "top-down" directives, difficulties to ensure popular controls; hyper-centralization of power) should not be taken as a surprise.[59]

6.7 Conclusions

The recently adopted and developed dialogical devices promised the people at large to re-gain a central role in the process of constitutional creation and interpretation. Ideally, one could reasonably assume, these dialogic devices would foster democratic deliberation, thus reducing the influence of interest-groups politics.

Now, those initial, optimistic notes, must be balanced with other criteria we have been exploring in the following pages. For instance, I maintained that in most countries -and most notably in Latin American countries- we have significantly renovated and reinvigorated our commitment to rights, while kept the core of our institutional system (this is to say the mechanism of checks and balances), fundamentally unchanged. As a consequence, many of the old vices and elitist features of the system are still in place; while many of the promises of dialogic constitutional-

ding) certain companies to do sanitation work that were owned by his relatives. Those companies are now also under investigation, and the Court removed and replaced Judge Armella.

[59]The situation does not look different if we focus our attention on other crucial cases of dialogic constitutionalism. Think, for example, about the *Badaro* case, in Argentina. *Badaro* concerned retired people in Argentina, whose pensions were not being adjusted in the manner provided in the constitution as a consequence of austerity programs launched by the government at the behest of the economic elite. Resorting to dialogic devices, the Court exhorted the political authorities to correct their policy so as to comport with the demands of the constitution. Thus, the Court forced Congress to act, but allowed Congress to craft its own response. Unfortunately, congress reacted poorly to the Court's demands. So, in a new pronouncement, the Court condemned the "legislative omission" regarding pensions. Unfortunately, after many years from the Court's initial decision (2006), the situation remains fundamentally the same. Again: what is the surprise with this depressing outcome, when the Executive is so extremely powerful, as it is normally the case in Latin America? Why should one be surprised to find that the Executive power acts discretionally? Why should one be surprised to find that the Executive, acting exclusively according to his own will, rather than the people at large decides whether to enforce or not the rights of the most disadvantaged?

ism (particularly in what concerns the enforcement of social rights) appear to be still too dependent on the good will and discretion of those in charge of promoting it.

These unfortunate circumstances mostly affect countries that have not introduced any formal changes in their constitutional organization, so as to facilitate dialogue – affecting Latin American countries in particular, given that most of them still retain a hyper-centralized institutional system. However, I should say that things do not look substantially different if we focus our attention on the *New Commonwealth Model of Constitutionalism,* where attractive and formal institutional changes were actually adopted. And this is so because – everywhere- the representative system seems to have become in control of a political elite and also increasingly subject to the demands and pressures of interest groups. "We the people" still remain outside of the Constitution, fundamentally incapable of managing and controlling our own public affairs.

Now, my worries about the perceived limits of dialogic constitutionalism should not be taken as a defence of the institutional status quo. This prevalent system causes the institutional problems that dialogic constitutionalism has been trying to overcome without much success. We need to replace a system of checks and balances that obstructs rather than promotes public collective dialogue; and we need to transform this institutional system that has become prey of political and economic elites. In the face of these challenges, the modest improvements offered by the new dialogic model of constitutionalism can be celebrated as small steps in the right direction.

Acknowledgment This is a revised and substantively shortened version of my article "We the People Outside of the Constitution," which I published in *Current Legal Problems,* vol. 67, n.1, 1–47.

References

Ackerman, Bruce. 1991. *We the people: Foundations*. Cambridge: Harvard University Press.

Alberdi, J.B. [1852] 1981. *Bases y puntos de partida para la organización política de la República Argentina,* Plus Ultra: Buenos Aires.

Alexander, L., and F. Schauer. 1997. On extrajudicial constitutional interpretation. *Harvard Law Review* 110: 1359–1387.

Alexander, L., and F. Schauer. 2000. Defending judicial supremacy: A reply. *Constitutional Commentary* 17: 455–482.

Alexander, L., and L. Solum. 2005. Popular? Constitutionalism? *Harvard Law Review* 118: 1594–1640.

Bakker, B. 2008. Blogs as constitutional dialogue: Rethinking the dialogic promise. *New York University Annual Survey of American Law* 63: 215–267.

Bateup, C. 2007. Expanding the conversation: American and Canadian experiences of constitutional dialogue in comparative perspective. *Temple International and Comparative Law Journal* 21(2): 1–57.

Bergallo, P. 2005. Justicia y Experimentalismo: La Función Remedial del Poder Judicial en el Litigio de Derecho Público en Argentina. In *Publicación del Seminario*. Buenos Aires:

Editorial del Puerto. There is an English version of the text available in http://digitalcommons.law.yale.edu/yls_sela/44/.
Bickel, A. 1962. *The Least Dangerous Branch*. New Haven: Yale University Press.
Bohman, J. 1996. *Public deliberation: Pluralism, complexity, and democracy*. Cambridge, MA: MIT Press.
Bohman, J., and W. Rehg (eds.). 1997. *Deliberative democracy*. Cambridge, MA: MIT Press.
Brennan, G., and L. Lomasky. 1997. *Democracy & decision*. Cambridge: Cambridge University Press.
Brown, R. 1970. *Revolutionary politics in Massachussets*. Cambridge, MA: Harvard University Press.
Brown, R. 1983. Shays's Rebellion and its Aftermath: A view from Springfield, Massachusetts, 1787. *William and Mary Quarterly* 40: 598–615.
Buchanan, J. 1975. *The limits of liberty*. Indianapolis: Liberty Fund.
Calabresi, G. 1985. *A common law for the Age of Statutes*. Cambridge: Harvard University Press.
Calabresi, G. 1991. The Supreme Court 1990 term. Foreword: Antidiscrimination and constitutional accountability (What the Bork-Brennan debate ignores). *Harvard Law Review* 105: 80–124.
Calabresi, G. 2012. Should the courts be allowed to repeal an obsolete law? Interview in *The Atlantic*, March 20th, http://www.theatlantic.com/national/archive/2012/03/should-the-courts-be-allowed-to-repeal-obsolete-law/254454/.
Cameron, J. 2001. Dialogue and hierarchy in Charter interpretation: A comment on R. v. Mills. *Alberta Law Review* 38: 1051–1068.
Christiano, T. 1996. *The rule of the many: Fundamental issues in democratic theory*. Boulder: Westview Press.
Coenen, D. 2001. A constitution of collaboration: Protecting fundamental values with second-look rules of interbranch dialogue. *William and Mary Law Review* 42: 1575–1870.
Cohen, J. 1986. An epistemic conception of democracy. *Ethics* 97: 26–38.
Cone, C. 1968. *The English Jacobins. Reformers in late 18th century England*. New York: Scribner.
Courtis, C. 2005. El caso 'Verbitsky': Nuevos rumbos en el control judicial de la actividad de los poderes politicos? In *Colapso del sistema carcelario*, 91–120. Buenos Aires: CELS/Siglo XXI.
Dahl, R. 1956. *A preface to democratic theory*. Chicago: The University of Chicago Press.
Dor, G. 2000. Constitutional dialogues in sction: Canadian and Israeli experiences in comparative perspective. *Indiana International & Comparative Law Review* 11: 1–36.
Edley, C. 1991. The Governance crisis, legal theory, and political ideology. *Duke Law Journal* 3: 561–606.
Elster, J. 1991. *Arguing and bargaining in the Federal Convention and the Assemblée Constituante*, Working Paper. University of Chicago, August.
Elster, J. (ed.). 1998. *Deliberative Democracy*. Cambridge: Cambridge University Press.
Estlund, D. 1993. Making truth safe for Democracy. In *The idea of democracy*, ed. D. Copp, J. Hampton, and J. Roemer, 71–100. Cambridge: Cambridge University Press.
Fabre, C. 2000. *Social rights under the constitution. Government and the decent life*. Oxford: Oxford University Press.
Farrand, M. (ed.). 1937. *The records of the federal convention of 1787*. New Haven: Yale University Press.
Feer, R. 1988. *Shays's rebellion*. New York: Garland.
Ferraz, O. 2011. Harming the poor through social rights litigation: Lessons from Brazil. *Texas Law Review* 89: 1643–1668.
Fishkin, J. 2011. Deliberative democracy and constitutions. *Social Philosophy and Policy* 28: 242–260.
Fiss, O. 2003. *The law as it could be*. New York: The NYU Press.
Gardbaum, S. 2013. *The new commonwealth model of constitutionalism*. Cambridge: Cambridge University Press.
Gargarella, R. 2010. *The legal foundations of inequality*. Cambridge: Cambridge University Press.

Gargarella, R. 2013a. *Latin American constitutionalism,* Oxford: Oxford University Press.
Gargarella, R. 2013b. Tres concepciones sobre la libertad de expresión. *Diario Clarín,* September 3th,Availableathttp://www.clarin.com/opinion/concepciones-libertad-expresion_0_986301426.html.
Gearty, C., and V. Mantouvalou. 2011. *Debating social rights.* London: Hart Publishing.
Gloppen, S. 2006. Analyzing the role of courts in social transformation. In *Courts and social transformation in new democracies*, ed. R. Gargarella et al. London: Ashgate.
Goldsworthy, J. 2003. Homogenising constitutions. *Oxford Journal of Legal Studies* 23: 483.
Goldsworthy, J. 2010. *Parliamentary sovereignty.* Cambridge: Cambridge University Press.
Gutman, A., and D. Thompson. 2004. *Why deliberative democracy?* Princeton: Princeton University Press.
Habermas, J. 1992. *Between facts and norms.* Cambridge, MA: MIT Press.
Hay, C. 1979. *James Burgh, Spokesman for reform in Hanoverian England.* New York: University Press of America.
Hogg, P., and A. Bushell. 1997. The Charter dialogue between courts and legislatures. *Osgoode Hall Law Lournal* 35: 75.
Hogg, P., A. Bushell, and W. Wright. 2007. Charter dialogue revisited, or "Much Ado About Metaphors". *Osgoode Hall Law Lournal* 45(1): 1–66.
Hübner Mendes, C. 2011. Neither dialogue nor last word: Deliberative separation of powers III. *Legisprudence* 5: 1–31.
Hübner Mendes, C. 2013. *Constitutional courts and deliberative democracy.* Oxford: Oxford University Press.
Hunt, P. 1996. *Reclaiming social rights.* Sidney: Darmouth.
Katyal, N. 1998. Judges as advicegivers. *Stanford Law Review* 50: 1709–1824.
Kenyon, C. 1985. *The Antifederalists.* Boston: Northeastern University Press.
King, J. 2012. *Judging social rights.* Cambridge: Cambridge University Press.
Kramer, L. 2004. Popular constitutionalism, Circa 2004. *California Law Review* 92: 959–1012.
Kramer, L. 2005. *The people themselves. Popular constitutionalism and judicial review.* Oxford: Oxford University Press.
Krotoszynski, R. 1998. Constitutional flares: On judges, legislatures, and dialogue. *Minnesota Law Review* 83: 1.
Langford, M. 2009. *Social rights jurisprudence: Emerging trends in international and comparative law.* Cambridge: Cambridge University Press.
Liebenberg, S. 2012. Engaging the paradoxes of the universal and particular in human rights adjudication. *African Human Rights Law Journal* 12: 1–29.
Liebenberg, S. 2014. *Deepening democratic transformation in South Africa through participatory constitutional remedies*, manuscript, University of Stellenbosch Law Faculty.
Manfredi, C., and J. Kelly. 1999. Six degrees of dialogue: A response to Hogg and Bushell. *Osgoode Hall Law Lournal* 37: 513.
Manin, B. 1997. *The principles of representative government.* Cambridge: Cambridge University Press.
Marx, K. 1978. Contribution to the critique of Hegel's Philosophy of right. In *The Marx-Engels reader,* ed. R. Tucker. New York: Norton & Co.
Mauwese, A., and M. Snel. 2013. Constitutional dialogue: An overview. *Utrecht Law Review* 9(2): 123–140, March, Available at SSRN: http://ssrn.com/abstract=2244818.
Mikva, A. 1998. Why judges should not be advicegivers. A response to professor Neal Katyal. *Stanford Law Review* 50: 1825.
Mill, J. [1859] 2003. *On liberty,* London: Dover Publications Inc.
Nino, C.S. 1991. *The ethics of human rights.* Oxford: Oxford University Press.
Nino, C.S. 1992. *Fundamentos de Derecho Constitucional.* Buenos Aires: Astrea.
Nino, C.S. 1996. *The constitution of deliberative democracy.* New Haven: Yale University Press.
Paine, T. 1989. *Political writings*, ed. B. Kucklick, Cambridge: Cambridge University Press.

Petter, A. 2003. Twenty years of Charter justification: From liberal legalism to dubious dialogue. *UNB Law Journal* 52: 187–200.
Pettit, P. 2012. *On the people's terms. A Republican theory and model of democracy*. Cambridge: Cambridge University Press.
Phillips, A. 1998. *The politics of presence*. Oxford: Oxford University Press.
Puga, M. 2012. *Litigio y cambio social en Argentina y Colombia*. Buenos Aires: Clacso, Serie Digital.
Rawls, J. 1991. *Political liberalism*. New York: Columbia University Press.
Rios-Figueroa, J., and M. Taylor. 2002. Institutional determinants of the judicialisation of policy in Brazil and Mexico. *Journal of Latin American Studies* 38: 739–766.
Roach, K. 2004. Dialogic judicial review and its critics. *Supreme Court Law Review* 23: 49–104.
Rodríguez-Garavito, C. 2011. Beyond the courtroom: The impact of judicial activism on socioeconomic rights in Latin America. *Texas Law Review* 89: 1669–1698.
Skinner, Q. 1983. Machiavelli on the maintenance of liberty. *Politics* 18: 3–15.
Skinner, Q. 1984. The idea of negative liberty: Philosophical and historical perspectives. In *Philosophy in history*, ed. Richard Rorty, J.B. Schneewind, and Skinner Quentin. Cambridge: Cambridge University Press.
Skinner, Q. 1990. The Republican ideal of political liberty. In *Machiavelli and Republicanism*, ed. G. Bock, Q. Skinner, and M. Viroli. Cambridge: Cambridge University Press.
Skinner, Q. 1998. *Liberty before liberalism*. Cambridge: Cambridge University Press.
Storing, H. 1981a. *The complete anti-Federalist*. Chicago: The University of Chicago Press.
Storing, H. 1981b. *What the anti-Federalists were for*. Chicago: The University of Chicago Press.
Szatmary, D. 1987. Shays' Rebellion in Springfield. In *Shays' Rebellion: Selected essays*, ed. M. Kaufman. Westfield: Westfield State College.
Tremblay, L. 2005. The legitimacy of judicial review: The limits of dialogue between courts and legislatures. *International Journal of Constitutional Law* 3: 617.
Tulis, J. 2003. Deliberation between Institutions. In *Debating deliberative democracy*, ed. P. Laslett and J. Fishkin. London: Blackwell Publishing.
Tushnet, M. 1997. Two versions of judicial supremacy. *William and Mary Law Review* 39: 945.
Tushnet, M. 2001. Subconstitutional constitutional law: Supplement, sham, or substitute? *William and Mary Law Review* 42: 1871.
Tushnet, M. 2003. Non-judicial review. *Harvard Journal on Legislation* 40: 453–492.
Tushnet, M. 2004. Weak-form judicial review: Its implications for legislatures. *Supreme Court Law Review* 23: 213.
Tushnet, M. 2006. Popular constitutionalism as political law. *Chicago-Kent Law Review* 81: 991.
Tushnet, M. 2008. *Weak courts, Strong rights*. Princeton: Princeton University Press.
Tushnet, M. 2009. Dialogic judicial review. *Arkansas Law Review* 61: 205.
Unger, R.M. 1996. *What should legal analysis become?* London: Verso.
Vile, M. 1967. *Constitutionalism and the separation of powers*. Oxford: Clarendon.
Waldron, J. 1999a. *Law and disagreement*. New York: Cambridge University Press.
Waldron, J. 1999b. *The dignity of legislation*. New York: Cambridge University Press.
Waldron, J. 2004. Some models of dialogue between judges and legislators. *Supreme Court Law Review* 23: 7.
Waldron, J. 2009. The core of the case against judicial review. *The Yale Law Journal* 115: 348.
Waldron, J. 2012. *Constitutionalism, a skeptical view*. New York University School of Law, Working Paper 10–87.
White, M. 1987. *Philosophy, The federalist, and the constitution*. Oxford: Oxford University Press.
Whittington, K. 2002. Extrajudicial constitutional interpretation: Three objections and responses. *North Carolina Law Review* 80: 773.
Williams, M. 2000. *Voice, trust and memory*. Princeton: Princeton University Press.
Wood, G. 1969. *The creation of the American Republic*. New York: W.W.Norton & Company.

Wood, G. 1992. *The radicalism of the American revolution*. NewYork: Alfred Knopf.
Wood, G. 1996. *The creation of the American republic*. Chapel Hill: The University of North Carolina Press.
Wood, G. 2002. *The American revolution. A history*. New York: The Modern Library.
Young, I. 2001. Activist challenges to deliberative democracy. *Political Theory* 29: 670–690.
Young, I. 2002. *Inclusion and democracy*. Oxford: Oxford University Press.
Young, K. 2012. *Constituting economic and social rights*. Oxford: Oxford University Press.

Chapter 7
A Defence of a Broader Sense of Constitutional Dialogues Based on Jeremy Waldron's Criticism on Judicial Review

Bernardo Gonçalves Fernandes

Abstract This chapter begins with a discussion of the debate about judicial supremacy *versus* parliamentary supremacy, on the basis of Jeremy Waldron's criticism on *judicial review*; it then takes a critical stand on Waldron's theses, on the basis of the theory of constitutional (institutional) dialogues. The core argument of the text is that the criticism to the *judicial review* developed by Jeremy Waldron can contribute to a defence of the theory of constitutional dialogues. The chapter concludes with a clarification of what this dialogical perspective entails.

7.1 Introduction

Despite of the controversial verdict issued by the North American Supreme Court in the case Bush v. Gore, there were no further reactions from the democrats even though serious questions were raised regarding the political-partisan character that impregnated the ruling that favoured the republican candidate. The candidate defeated in the Supreme Court, Al Gore, as well as the democrat leader Patrick Leahy displayed extremely timid reactions. Leahy stated that as a North American his duty was to accept the decision, recognizing the Supreme Court as the final interpreter of the Constitution regardless of how wrong he believed the decision was. This episode from December 2000 was discussed by Larry Kramer in the work *The People Themselves – popular constitutionalism and judicial review*, to claim that North Americans have increasingly accepted in a passive way the so called judicial supremacy. According to Kramer, the last five decades of the twentieth century have established the competence of the United States Supreme Court to have the final word about the interpretation of the Constitution (Kramer 2004).

Nonetheless, it is fair to say that this phenomenon has been occurring almost on a global scale. The emergence in several countries of a reallocation of power from

B.G. Fernandes (✉)
Universidade Federal de Minas Gerais, Avenida João Pinheiro, 100,
Belo Horizonte, Minas Gerais 30.130-180, Brazil
e-mail: bernardogaf@yahoo.com.br

T. Bustamante, B.G. Fernandes (eds.), *Democratizing Constitutional Law*,
Law and Philosophy Library 113, DOI 10.1007/978-3-319-28371-5_7

the Legislative and the Executive to the Judiciary is and undisputable fact. This, as a matter of fact, does not come as a surprise to any informed participant of contemporary debates about law, politics and democracy in the context of contemporary constitutionalism. An expansion and, even, a reinvention of the jurisdictional activity, especially within the scope of the European and South American Constitutional Courts, has also became evident in the beginning the second half of twentieth century.

In the specific case of Brazil, it has been initially observed that after the Constitution of 1988 a conservative interpretative model that is typically formalist has advanced, connected to a strict separation of law and politics and a self-restraint perspective in the application of the law. However, at the end of the nineties, in the twentieth century, this interpretative model has been gradually "conjugated" with the defence of an "efficacy-oriented constitutionalism" and with a more energetic action by the Judicial Branch through the occupation of a presumed "empty space" left by *omissions* by the other branches (Legislative and Executive). This led to an expansion of the activity of the Judiciary, as well as the Federal Supreme Court, in the pursuit of the more substantial review of constitutional rights, based on the idea of human dignity. This more *proactive* attitude of the courts, *in certain pivotal cases*, lead to a new conception of the role Judiciary (which allows a *judicialization of politics* and social relations), and turned the debate about the limits of the authority of the court, which up to this point was limited to the North American doctrine, into a very relevant theme on Brazilian territory.

As result, the famous "counter majoritarian difficulty" popularized by Alexander Bickel, who questioned how "a small minority of nine justices, that were not elected through a democratic electoral process, could interpret and apply the North American Constitution" (Bickel 1986), has become a recurring subject on debates among constitutional theorists outside the circle of North American jurists.

Accordingly, several issues are raised, such as, for instance: How far the constitutional jurisdiction can go and what are its action boundaries? To what extent the judicial review is democratically legitimate? Can the constitutional review authorize the Judicial Branch to act in a way that invalidates normative acts by the Legislative or even Constitutional Amendments? What is the appropriate relationship between the Judiciary Branch and the Legislative Branch with regards to the interpretation of the Constitution? Who has supremacy over the Constitution? Who should have the "last word" regarding reasonable disagreements in society, regarding the great issues related to *political morality* in societies characterized by *reasonable pluralism*?

Is there an alternative to the question of who should have the "last word" regarding the interpretation of the Constitution, or are we condemned to an either-or alternative between a supremacy of the Judiciary or the Parliament? Do we need a sytem of Strong Constitutional Review? Does it save us? Does it redeem us and protect us against eventual abuses and arbitrariness by an occasional majority (the so called protection against the *tyranny of the majority*)?

The objective of this text is not to comprehensively answer all the questions mentioned above, but rather to point out the inadequacy of the assumption that we should that defend a "supremacy" either of a court or a parliament in order to answer them. To do so, we will defend that the *theory of constitutional (or institutional) dialogues* offers a satisfactory answer to the majority of the problems raised above.

Dialogue theories emerged in academic debates regarding Constitutional Law as an attempt to offer a different viewpoint about controversies regarding the role of Constitutional Courts and other political players within the scope of the interpretation of the Constitution. Accordingly, they endeavour to challenge the assumption that one institution – either the Judiciary or the Legislature – should have the "last word" about the correct interpretation of fundamental rights, on the ground that such assumption overlooks the potential for interaction between or among institutions in a constitutional democracy.

In this sense, the distinctive feature of the theory of dialogues is the pursuit of a broader interlocution among the Courts and other constitutional players (particularly Parliaments), so that the presumed "*judicial monopoly*" in the interpretation of the Constitution is mitigated or even terminated, making the Judiciary and the Legislative *partners* (be it directly or indirectly) in the pursuit of a better settlement of constitutional issues, particularly those related to fundamental rights, in which *reasonable moral disagreements* are typical.

Therefore, the road to be travelled in the text will depart from the debate about judicial supremacy *versus* the supremacy of parliament, having as guiding principle Jeremy Waldron's criticism of the *judicial review*, to, later on, take a critical stand on Waldron's main theses about judicial review on the basis of the theory of constitutional dialogues. The core argument of the text is that the criticism to the *judicial review* developed by Jeremy Waldron can contribute to a defence of the theory of constitutional dialogues. The work concludes making clear what the dialogical perspective defended here entails.

7.2 Judicial Supremacy Versus Parliamentary Sovereignty: Jeremy Waldron's Criticism to Judicial Review

The current debate on *judicial supremacy* versus *parliamentary sovereignty* has evolved a great deal in the last years. Movements such as "popular constitutionalism", by Larry Kramer (2004) and Mark Tushnet (1999), that intends to take the Constitution outside the Tribunals, or "democratic constitutionalism" by Barry Friedman (2009), which questions the centrality of the judicial supremacy based on the influence of the public opinion and the civil society on the decisions by the Tribunals, are only some of the examples of how the dispute involving who should have the *last word* about the interpretation of the Constitution is distant from finding a common ground.

The perspective adopted by the advocates of judicial supremacy in the interpretation of the Constitution defends a settlement function for the Judiciary, as result of several factors Brandão (2012) , endowed by an institutional capacity higher than the Legislative to enunciate *what the Constitution is*. Among the reasons for judicial supremacy, we could enumerate the following: (a) judges would be free from economic, political and partisan interests and would be committed to an impartial application of the law; (b) judges would be instructed to preserve the people's pre-commitments set forth in the Constitution against transitory majorities and their occasional interests; (c) judges would use, according to Dworkin (1985), principled arguments against policy considerations which are characteristic of the legislative; (d) judges would be able to promote a deliberative process guided by reason, and not by political and partisan pressures, a circumstance that would make them, according to Robert Alexy (2005), a type of argumentative representative of the society[1]; (e) the judiciary should be the guardian of the Constitution, which would only be respected and enforced if protected by an agent situated outside the Parliament (the agency charged to produce ordinary norms that could, if unrestrained, disrespect the Constitution); (f) as result of the training and the specialization on judicial matters, judges would be more qualified to interpret the Constitution (which is a political document as well as a judicial one); (g) as a general rule, since judges scrutinize laws after these laws have already been enforced, they have a *privileged position* regarding information as opposed to the legislature, and this would insure to the former a higher interpretive capacity (this refers to the so called "*unpredicted consequences*" by the legislator); (h) the *political isolation* of the judges reassures that they do not suffer direct effects from the political and economic power of lobbying groups; (i) judges would have the duty to ground their decisions on the Constitution; (j) judicial judgment is immune from the strategic behaviour of the legislature, whose activity, as a political actor, has as one of the objectives to broaden his chances to be re-elected and enhance his personal prestige among his voters (or groups that support him), allowing him to give greater relevance to particular political actions to the detriment of the faithfulness to the Constitution and the fundamental rights; (k) parliamentary supremacy could represent a risk in relation to the minorities, and a danger of instituting a *tyranny of the majority* that is impossible to be controlled (which could be empirically demonstrated by historical data).

However, there is a vast number of theorists who criticize the supremacy of the Judicial Branch in the interpretation of the Constitution. Mark Tushnet, for instance, pushing the thesis of *constitutional populism*, postulates the removal of the "*Constitution from the tribunals*", considering that they do not have the right to have the final word when constitutional interpretation is concerned. The fundamental assumption of these critics is that judicial interpretation of the Constitution does not have *a priori* any more weight than the interpretation made by another state

[1]According to Robert Alexy the constitutional courts can be legitimized by a broad conception of representation, which goes beyond the ballots in elections and that refers, above all, to arguments and reasons. Therefore, the courts have *an argumentative representation* to define, by the means of plausible and corrects arguments, legitimate interpretations of constitutional rights (Alexy 2005, 572–581).

department such as Parliament.[2] In the same vein, based on an extensive review of USA history, Larry Kramer enthusiastically defends that there is no basis to support the thesis that the North American Constitution must be definitely interpreted by judges (Kramer 2004).

However, in this chapter, I will discuss in further detail the theorization that I understand as the more sophisticated form of criticism to judicial supremacy, which currently defended by Jeremy Waldron.

According to Waldron in the book "*Law and Disagreement*" (1999), the practice of *judicial review*, that grants to judges the power to invalidate legislative enactments originating from the parliament and to make decisions about basic issues (attributing them the last word about fundamental rights issues) is not in harmony with the pluralist societies where we live in, where there is a recurrent disagreement between the several conceptions of law and its meanings (moral disagreements on the several ways of life and concepts of dignified life). These are, according to him, *reasonable disagreements*, where there shall never exist an argument that is a "*knocks-down*" or, in other words, a final argument. Therefore, it will always be possible to defend a contrary position, for it is possible to imagine good, valid and sincere arguments on both sides or at several sides.

Thus, since people disagree about what justice requires and what are the rights that we have, it is necessary to ask: *who must have the power to make decisions in these cases*? Waldron answer this question in the sense that constitutional theory and the dogma of judicial supremacy have been marginalizing legislative activity. They would present a *dirty, evil, prejudiced and underrated* view of the legislation. The issue would be that, for the large majority of constitutionalists in the twentieth century, judicial review of the laws would constitute the only mechanism capable to remedy parliamentary mistakes and reposition public authorities on the path to a community of principles. Following Mangabeira Unger, Waldron calls this *discomfort* with democracy the "*little dirty secret*" of contemporary jurisprudence.

The major concern, in his argument, is to elevate the legislature to the centrality of the philosophical deliberation regarding the Law. The idea is *to return* to a "*dignity of legislation*" and to *deconstruct* the philosophical justifications for the *judicial review*. He then advocates the legitimacy of the legislator to decide in circumstances where there are reasonable moral disagreements, considering that judges almost always disagree on moral conflicts, along the same lines that citizens

[2] According to Tushnet his theory is populist because it distributes the responsibility about constitutional rights in a broad way. Therefore, he asserts that in populist constitutional rights theory, the constitutional interpretation made by the courts does not have any normative weight resulting from the fact that they were produced by the Courts (Tushnet 1999). According to Roberto Gargarella these are the common features of the popular constitutionalism thesis: they challenge the judicial supremacy, removing the Constitution from the hands of the courts; they recover and recognize the relevance and the institutional weight of popular participation; they defend an extrajudicial interpretation of the Constitution; they promote a critical reinterpretation of the effects of the *judicial review*; they show how society influences, rebuilds, and, sometimes, undermines the value of judicial decisions; and, finally, they propel a large popular participation in political decisions (Gargarella 2006, 1–5).

and their representatives do, and, in addition, also make decisions based on the majority rule (ironically stating: *is it not also the majority that must prevail in the construction of the judicial provision?*). Why, Waldron asks, the political answer to issues about political morality must come from the Courts and not from the parliament?[3]

Therefore, disagreements regarding principles is part of the essence of politics, and excluding the participation of the parliament (the people) from a final deliberation regarding moral disagreements is the same as betraying the spirit of democracy and universal suffrage. To Waldron, the premise of the majoritarian constitutional theory is that judicial review must be affirmed as result of the legislature's alleged lack of respectability and intellectual capacity. He shares this repulse by making the following point: Why has not any contemporary theorist of the Constitution advocated a theoretical interpretation that would dignify the role of the legislator as a super-endowed being (superman) responsible to settle the evils of society under the terms, for instance, of the Judge Hercules de Dworkin's metaphor? Contrary to it, as it has been already said, the mainstream constitutional doctrine states that the courts are the best institutional spheres to determine the adaptation of normative acts in support to the Constitution. This premise is a premise based on a suspicion against the people's representatives and is by definition a mistrust of the people (at the root, once again is the concept that the parliament is a place of negotiation and compromises, that make it incapable of making political decisions based on principles).

It is central for Waldron courts lack the right to take a stand regarding the great moral issues in a political community. Questions of justice, for him, are always political. Accordingly, the majority rule in a parliamentary procedure is guided by the idea of political legitimacy, and based on a theory of authority which requires the recognition that each citizen is equal and as result, has the *right to participate* (and a part in the responsibility to make the law) in the political process to settle controversial matters about political morality. Participation, for him, would be the ***right of rights***. The majority decision would be legitimate for it creates a deliberative *locus* where the voice of each citizen resulting from representation has the same weight. The consent and the feeling of moral affiliation resulting from the submission to the majority decision is what supports the majority principle: as result, each participant can recognize that it is fair to obey a command derived from a procedure which, having treated people as equals and independent, results in a majority deliberation (even the dissident minorities would have this feeling).[4]

---

[3] "When citizens or its representatives disagree about what rights we have or what are the impositions implicit in such rights, it seems almost an insult to affirm that this is not something that allow them reach a conclusion by the means of a majority process, but rather, must be assigned to the final determination by a small group of judges" (Waldron 1999, 15).

[4] It is important to make clear that even though Waldron recognizes in some works that the *majority principle* has an intrinsic moral value, in a recent debate with Dworkin, he admitted that this principle cannot work in an absolute and optimum way under all circumstances. This has taken place in comments about the work *Justice for Hedgehogs* by Dworkin, where Waldron ends up

It becomes clear here that there is an assumption in Waldron's theory that *individuals as moral, autonomous and capable citizens shall promote a responsible debate and yield an impartial and fair political decision*. Therefore, the right to participate is central to all the others and is not even subject to deliberative judgments (there is no factual situation when this right shall not prevail as result of another, considering that the extension of the opposite right and its meaning are defined by the very right to participate). Therefore, in view of the moral disagreement, the most adequate institutional option, according to the logical system of democracy through the self-recognition of a community of free and equal citizens, is the legislative decision.

As it has been pointed out before, Waldron (1999) stresses that individuals have serious disagreements on matters of justice. He points out, based on Rawls, that even after a discursive procedure developed in a satisfactory way, where the participants in the debate raise their claims to validity and reciprocally criticize them, the subjects might continue to disagree in good faith at the end of the dialogue regarding moral issues. The worry here is that we never have a final argument that *knocks down* the opposite arguments regarding the large issues involving political morality.

Waldron states, therefore, that laws are essentially and not only accidentally a product of assemblies (Parliament) with groups that adhere and support distinct conceptions of justice. This fact, in his opinion, must be taken into consideration to interpret them in the broadest context of the law (Waldron 1999, 10).

Based on the foregoing discussion, it can be affirmed that legislation is not necessarily the fruit of a final consensus regarding particular issues, but the result arrived at through a process of vote counting. Since a full consensus is impossible, it is necessary to refute its notion as a deliberative internal logic, and this does not mean that its importance is diminished as an adequate result of the political process (Waldron 1999, 91). Thus, the disagreement needs to be incorporated to the concept of public deliberation, giving attention to its inescapable dissension (Waldron 1999, 95).

Therefore, since the disagreement is unavoidable, the reasons why individuals should obey legislation when it is contrary to their conceptions about fundamental issues of principle must be ascertained. This is, therefore, a pursuit for the foundation of the authority of the former.

Therefore, the issue of the authority of laws is not presented as a matter of absolute deference to them, in order to understand them as something perfect and immutable (Waldron 1999, 100). This law's claim to authority would be associated to a demand for respect and recognition of the legislation, i.e., as something that, at that moment, the community chose as adequate and which, therefore, cannot be ignored based solely on the fact that some of its subjects disagree, with the intention to change them when institutionally possible.

---

recognizing the possibility that in particular situations the *majority principle* does not have the intrinsic moral value that he defended in works such as *Law and Disagreement*. See (Waldron 2010).

In order to handle the problem discussed here, Waldron works the notion of the "circumstances of politics", which comprises the situations where, even though individuals disagree in good faith about the best collective decision to be made, they share a deep commitment that it would be better for them to coordinate their actions by a common solution for the issue, in spite of their disagreement about its content. Thus, the need and the inevitability of a collective decision would create an environment appropriate for the adoption of a morally controversial stand by the collectivity.

Having made this point, he acknowledges that the majoritarian procedure involving decisions, based on the counting of votes, is a procedural technique that allows the adoption of a collective stand in the middle of an existing disagreement (Waldron 1999, 107–108). Hence, according to this understanding, the way to identify a course of action as being collective (as "ours") must be agnostic with regards to its substance (merits), considering that there is the fact of disagreement, making the procedure a neutral way to make a choice among the proposed alternatives.

It just so happens that for Waldron (1999, 108), the majority process is not a mere technique, but also a method that is morally respectable, superior to the other ways to select a stand to be adopted. It can be said here that laws not only deserve respect because they establish a common standard under the circumstances of politics (which is necessary for collective coordination in the face of disagreement), but also because they constitute the product of something accomplished in a legitimate way, considering that, during their elaboration, they respect the individuals that will coordinate their actions.

Therefore it can be said that as far as individuals are concerned the majoritarian process is justified in two ways: (1) it does not ignore different concepts about justice and the common good, inasmuch as it is not necessary that a good-faith opinion of someone be discarded in the search for an alleged consensus; (2) it establishes a principle of respect for each individual, which is intrinsic in the dynamics of this process (Waldron 1999, 109).

Waldron (1999, 111) warns that these considerations are not based on any type of relativism, but rather on an appropriate attitude towards the good-faith disagreement of the participants in the political sphere. He believes that dissent, in most cases, should not be explained as a consequence of a selfish action by individuals or other corrupt actions from the heart of the community, and alludes to the notion of "burdens of judgment", developed by Rawls, to explain the issue. Thus, it consists in the idea that when it comes to the most important judgments regarding themes and conditions of mutual concernt, made by the people, we should not expect that rational individuals, even after a free deliberation process, will arrive at the same conclusion, considering that they will disagree about the relevance and the weight to be ascribed to particular considerations.

Having, therefore, acknowledged the burdens of judgment, Waldron (1999, 304) believes that the common explanation for existing disagreements regarding rights is associated to the complexity of issues upon which a decision is necessary. The reference to our own interests, therefore, would only be part of a special explanation about a particular disagreement.

To summarize the debate on the advantages of a majority decision, Waldron believes that this system would give to the opinion of each individual the maximum possible weight, in the process where political will is forged. Thus, it could be said that it would constitute a fair method to make decisions, respecting the judgments of each participant (Waldron 1999, 114).

It must be pointed out that an equal respect to individuals would not impose, in itself, a majoritarian decision-procedure (Waldron 1999, 115). However, since we disagree (in good-faith) on substantive issues as far as what the appropriate outcomes to equalitarian respect is concerned, we need a decision process that is intrinsically compatible with such. In Waldron's opinion (1999, 116), the majority decision would be the most appropriate candidate to this task.

In short, the author holds that a procedure of this type does not establish, in itself, the authority of the legislation (Waldron 1999, 117). Nonetheless, the majority decision not only would offer a solution for important issues in the sphere of political circumstances, but would do it with respect to the individuals who disagree about the outcome of the procedure (Waldron 1999, 118).

Therefore, the majority process would be grounded on what is regarded as the "right of the rights", that is, the *right to participate in the drafting of laws* (Waldron 1999, 282). The notion defended here is that, if there is a disagreement in society regarding issues where a common decision is necessary, all must have the right to participate in an equal way in the solution to the controversy. By consequence, in his opinion, taking rights seriously means taking each person seriously as he holds opinions regarding rights (Waldron 1999, 311–312).

Thus, Waldron raises against the judicial review an objection based on rights, and more specifically, on the *right to participate* in the political decisions of the polity. Along these lines, since individuals, including magistrates, disagree on matters of principle (major issues regarding political morality), it is better that the decision about its shaping is reached within the scope of a majority decision, such as the legislative process, rather than by a Constitutional Court, since, in the former, unlike the latter, a larger participation is given to the agents, even when dealing with a representative system.

Whittington (2000, 697–698) makes the following remarks about Waldron's criticism to the judicial review:

> Waldron considers essentially two types of justifications for constitutional rights and judicial review: the problem of majority tyranny and the strategy of precommitment. His arguments against each are straightforward and related. Employing an independent judiciary as a check against majority tyranny is only reasonable if we can identify when majorities might be tyrannical, but that judgment requires a substantive theory of rights and justice that we do not have.

Regarding the second argument, that is, precommitment, Waldron (1999, 258) reveals an understating that was later criticized about the constitutional restrictions in which they consubstantiate limits that citizens would impose to themselves while being agents endowed with moral capacities. From this viewpoint, agents would be aware of the possibility that they, at some point in time, could violate individual rights, and this would lead them to adopt certain constitutional limitations as a precaution (Waldron 1999).

In order to prevent the precommitment notion to contradict the autonomy of individuals that have established it, the restraint applied at a given occasion (T_2) must be the fruit of a spontaneous decision taken at an earlier occasion (T_1). Since there is no possibility, in the field of constitutional restraints, for a causal procedure where limits are automatically applied at T_2, after the circumstances set forth in T_1 have been verified, the idea of constitutional precommitments depends on the giving to a social actor, which is not to be confused *per se* with the individuals that have set forth these very restrictions, the power to decide, at T_2, if these constitutional restrictions would apply or not to the occasion (Waldron 1999).

Therefore, it can be noted that for the notion of constitutional precommitments to be adopted, a social agent *A* must grant to another agent (*B*) the power to deliberate (exercise judgment, decision) regarding the applicability or not of the restraints in the cases herein. Nonetheless, Waldron (1999, 262) questions whether, in this case, it is possible to really talk about an *autonomous* precommitment by *A*, considering that, despite of the fact that at T_1 the selection of restrictions has such nature, at T_2 agent *A* is subject to the judgment of another, that is, *B*.

It must be pointed out that the problem verified by Waldron (1999) is aggravated upon the realization that, unavoidably, there is controversy in judgments at T_2: individuals disagree on the material implications of the abstract principles adopted during the time when constitutional restraints are selected. Thus, since there are divergences regarding these judgments, Waldron believes that granting to a third party – such as the Judiciary – the jurisdiction to decide on issues that are the object of disagreements would be the same as refusing the exercise of self-governance (Waldron 1999, 264).

In short, therefore, when a precommitment established by citizens becomes obscure, uncertain or controversial, the idea of precommitment lacks support as a method to defend the judicial review against the democratic objection (Waldron 1999, 266). In practice, what we would be doing would be not to respect precommitments, but rather to recognize the superiority of a view (of agent *B* who makes a decision at T_2) in relation to the others, in an environment permeated by complex and morally controversial considerations. Moreover, the following question needs to be answered: Who is to say that at the time these *very* precommitments were erected, the situation was neutral and not pathological (flawed) from the start? This is, as a matter of fact, another point that is generally forgotten by the defenders of this perspective regarding precommitment.

Therefore, since people reasonably disagree on issues of principles, justice an so on, valuing previous constitutional limitations is the same as *taking a position* among diverging opinions concerning the best interpretation of these themes (Waldron 1999, 269). If the most satisfactory explanation for the existence of a persistent disagreement results from the importance of the objects under dispute, it is necessary to abandon the logic of precommitments and allow that the temporary adoption of a conception as superior to the other ones occur through collective decision procedures during a given period of time (Waldron 1999, 270).

Furthermore, according to Waldron, the force of the notion of precommitment is also weakened by the fact that a change of public opinion concerning a particular issue can be explained more accurately, in most cases, by a change or maturing of the public debate and not as result of a condition of social pathology, that would demand the adoption of previous constitutional restrictions as a precautionary way to such pathological condition. Therefore, it would not be worthy to ponder about such previous limitations (Waldron 1999, 271).

Therefore, for Waldron, the claim made by those who believe that democracy needs a precommitment to some issues for its own existence (such as guaranteeing the rights of the minorities that would assure the possibility of existence of opposition, etc.) would only be valid if two conditions were satisfied: (1) unanimity and constancy regarding an appropriate concept of democracy and the conditions that are necessary for it to exist, and (2) if the minorities had any reason to fear that a legislative change of the rules regarding freedom of expression and thc possibility to oppose was an attempt to silence dissidents. To the mentioned author, none of thesc conditions is met, and for this reason, he rejects the strategy of grounding judicial review on the notion of constitutional precommitments (Waldron 1999, 279).

7.3 Waldron's Deficit: Constitutional Dialogues and Their Different Perspectives

As previously argued, Waldron builds his criticism against judicial review on the fact of reasonable disagreement to, furthermore, value the action of the Legislative Branch. Along these lines, when good-faith individuals disagree on matters of principle, it would be better to reach a collective decision at the discretion of representative institutions such as the Parliaments – where there is a larger number of individuals and the possibility of the participation of the agents is greater – than to the Judiciary Branch.

Nonetheless, Waldron errs in assuming that there is a major difference between Courts and the Parliaments, with regards to the popular participation in these spheres. It can be said that these institutions, in fact, operate in distinct ways, and can provide diverse understandings and viewpoints related to controversial fundamental rights and principles.[5] Therefore, for Waldron, "it is just a matter of whose heads will be counted" (Whittington 2000, 698).

The normative argument supporting dialogue theories is, therefore, connected to the idea that, acting in a different way among themselves, favouring the interaction among the political institutions of the community (such as the Judiciary and the Legislative Branches) may have beneficial impacts in the protection of rights, con-

[5] "I am not assuming that, in relation to rights, courts and parliaments are institutionally equivalent. It seems plausible to verify that both see problems through quite different perspectives, which are not redundant" (Mendes 2011, 206).

sidering that each one of them is capable of providing different perspectives to the debates. Therefore, the existence of the kind of disagreement mentioned by Waldron is not denied; but rather, it is an assumption in accepting that a dialogue contributes for a better identification of the problems and offers possible different solutions. According to Whittington (2000, 697), then,

> Institutions also develop distinct missions, cultures, modes of behavior, norms, and such, which affect both the behavior of individuals within those institutions and their collective output. Not only might a small group reach a different decision than a large group, but a group of judges might reach different decision than a group of legislators (or educators or economists). Even reasonably responsive legislators may behave differently than normal citizens when addressing public issues.

Therefore, the distinct format in the composition, organization, operation and accountability of the Judiciary and Legislative Branches results in a different action related to the way sensitive issues related to principle[6] and "viewpoints" common to each institution are handled. Gardbaum points out (2010, 174), for instance, that, under a model of legislative supremacy, there is always the risk of the development of pathologies that consubstantiate "blind spots" unnoticed by representative political institutions, inclined to political minorities. However, this does not deny that Parliaments have full ability to discuss rights in good-faith and prolifically – as Waldron wishes — , nor does it disregard the political influences that bear upon the Courts, as demonstrated by Friedman (2005), but rather, that the peculiar mechanisms of each institution allows them, in the majority of the cases, a special contribution to the constitutional debate, via a broad perspective, considering the several procedural rounds of an institutional dialogue unfolding in history.

In other words, the argument does not have to assume the best capacity of the Courts to debate matters of principle, nor differentiate some themes selected to be debated only by the Parliament or by the Court: it only assumes that different institutions shall possibly offer distinct observations on the same constitutional issues cherished to both, making the constitutional dialogue productive.

According to Whittington (2000, 699) the Judiciary is largely motivated by a different set of concerns than is the legislature. Although judges might disagree among themselves over matters of political principle just as legislators do, legislators may not bother with such issues at all or give them due regard when they do. Questions such as whether indigent criminal defendants should be entitled to free legal counsel may be of intense interest to those directly involved but are unlikely to rise to the top of a legislative agenda.

In this interaction, the Court can be a deliberative catalyser. In this sense, according to Mendes (2011, 212), it symbolizes an effort to make democracy a regime that not only separates majorities from minorities, structures a frequent political competition and selects the winning and losing elites, but is capable also to discern

[6] Specifically regarding to the Legislative Branch, Whittington (2000, 699) asserts: "legislatures cannot simply be treated as bodies of collective decision making. They are also institutions centrally concerned with political agenda setting, representation, resource redistribution, and government administration, and these additional functions affect their design, behavior, and authority".

between good and bad arguments. This will not exclude competition, but rather qualify it.

Therefore, a model of inter-institutional dialogues makes possible the occurrence of a productive tension. In this sense, the political legitimacy of the Parliaments is no longer an issue of form only (procedural legitimization), as it would be in the sphere of the supremacy of the Legislative, in order to attract the thematic of fundamental principles – notably individual rights – to the sphere of such legitimacy.

This is not, as pointed out before, denying that the debate about rights is present within the scope of the Parliament[7]; we are only refuting the perverse effect that might result of its sovereignty, considering that "the critical and deliberative potential of the separation of powers is anesthetized by a message that the parliament is at the top of the hierarchical scale and that cannot be challenged", where "it is difficult for substantive criticism to legislative decisions to have an institutional expression, except via the parliament" (Mendes 2011, 201).

It can be affirmed, therefore, that the existence of a judicial review might make possible a virtuous tension (Mendes 2011, 202). And, in this interaction among different institutional players within the scope of reasoning and debate on rights, these activities are endowed with a greater insightful capacity (Hiebert 2006, 5).

It is important to point out that, in addition to the possibility of offering distinct views about the same issue involving rights under debate, related to a particular theme, the Courts contribute by the means of the articulation of principles that permeate a declaration of rights (Roach 2001, 485), which favours later discussions within the scope of the society and Parliament. This does not refer, it must be said, to a higher epistemic capacity of judges to prepare this synthesis of arguments as opposed to the legislators, but the peculiarities of their institutional action. On the other side, the Legislative Branch, also as result of its organizational and operational dynamics, offers valuable contributions to solve practical difficulties when implementing constitutional objectives (Roach 2001, 485). Hence,

> By allowing courts and legislatures to add their own distinctive voice, talents and concerns to the conversation, a more enriching and sophisticated dialogue is produced than could be achieved by a judicial or legislative monologue or a dialogue in which courts and legislatures engage in the same task (Roach 2001, 485).

It is then believed that constitutional dialogues create a broader diffusion of the constitutional debate, not restricting it to a specific institution (such as the Judiciary or the Legislative, under the traditional models of judicial supremacy or the sovereignty of the parliament, respectively). It refers, therefore, to a decentralization of discussions on rights, considering not only the number of individuals that participated in the deliberations on issues regarding principles (as Waldron wishes), but also the number of institutional spaces inaugurated as these debates are set in motion and the unfolded.

[7] "It is not necessary to assume that the legislator is more inclined to err and the court is closer to being right, nor that the legitimacy of the legislator is exclusively associated to form and the court's, to substance [...], to defend the contribution of this permanent circularity" (Mendes 2011, 202).

Therefore, the judicial review may serve as a vehicle for expanding the scope of a political conflict beyond the confines of a single institution and introducing additional players and perspectives, especially if we recognize that judicial opinions are often not the "*last word*" in a political dispute (Whittington 2000, 700).[8]

Considering the above, it is seen that the valuing of constitutional dialogues can be grounded[9] on the expansion of the quality of the debate regarding the rights that possibly allows the existence of a system where such issues are not waiting to be resolved by only one institution. This is because each institution, like is the case of the Court and the Parliaments, has different operating dynamics, although in fact discussing the same constitutional themes, which causes the emergence of distinct perspectives at the time of the required interaction.[10] According to Bateup (2005, 76), the following are advantages of a concept of a constitutional dialogue that assumes the referred argument:

> On the normative level, this conception of constitutional dialogue as partnership is indeed worth pursuing as it provides one of the more satisfying accounts of the dialogic judicial role [...]. Recognizing that judges make unique institutional contributions to dialogue in individual cases as a result of the unique features of the adjudicative process, a special and valuable judicial role is thereby proposed. This conception of the judicial role also succeeds in ensuring that the judiciary's contributions are not privilege over the distinct dialogic contributions that legislatures are able to make.

Having disclosed these facts, it is necessary to also discuss the meaning conferred to the expression *dialogue*. This is the objective of the following section.

[8] It should be stressed that the referred normative argument is the basis for the partnership model of dialogue in the typology created by Bateup (2005, 70), as it can be seen in the excerpt collated below: "The partnership model of dialogue centers on the recognition that the differently situated branches of government can make distinct contributions to constitutional dialogue in a way that does not privilege the judicial role. Instead, this account recognizes that each branch of government can learn from the specific dialogic inputs of the other branches in an institutionally diverse constitutional order. Judicial and non-judicial actors are thus conceived as equal participants in constitutional decision making who can both dialogically contribute to the search for better answers as a result of their unique institutional perspectives".

[9] As pointed out before, I do not exclude the possibility that other persuasive normative arguments exist favoring the theories of constitutional dialogue.

[10] "While courts and legislatures thus share responsibility for satisfying themselves that constitutional values are respected, each has a 'distinct relationship' to a constitutional conflict. This is not only because they are differently situated, but also because they each bring distinct and valuable perspectives to constitutional judgment given their different institutional characteristics and responsibilities" (Bateup 2005, 71).

7.4 After All, What Is a Dialogue?

In this chapter, the notion of constitutional dialogues on constitutionalism's sensitive issues has been discussed, like in the case of fundamental rights. However, the nature of these dialogues has not been outlined, in order to explain what is the meaning that this expression would comprehend.

It is believed that the concept of *dialogue* that better falls in line with the exposed normative argument involves a broad meaning, as any manner of interaction (in this case, among different political institutions). Therefore, the purpose is to facilitate the presentation of distinct viewpoints regarding the same constitutional issue, given the several structuring logics and the operation of the referred institutions.

This way, the pursuit of a consensus is not the central object of the dialogue as understood here, even though the normative argument does not condemn it either as something perverse to the broad proposed model. The convergence of comprehension (consensus) would only be harmful, therefore, in case where it occurred on a regular basis and, furthermore, represented a culture of deference of one institution over the other, as the patterns criticized by Gardbaum (2010) when analyzing the practical experience of abstention in using the Canadian *notwithstanding clause*. In this case, the defended normative argument loses all its force, considering that the interchange of distinct comprehensions on the same constitutional issue would not take place.

It is pointed out, therefore, in reference to the consensus issue, that the deference of the Legislative to a judicial decision does not necessarily mean, under this broad perspective, a denial for dialogue. In the understanding of Hogg and Bushell (1997, 82) parliament's silence after a manifestation of Judiciary might, for instance, be configured as a dialogue. As seen before, the preparation of a consensus is not a possibility excluded by the defended argument.

Finally, it is important to point out that a constitutional dialogue is possible, not only when there is the possibility of a reversal, alteration or challenge of the judicial decision by the means of a legislative process through a simple majority quorum, as believed by Hogg and Bushell (1997, 80). In this sense, the meaning of dialogue as something broad – in other words, any possible constitutional interaction among the institutions – does not entail structural restrictions of large dimension to the possible constitutional model type where the dialogue could take place.

Therefore, although structural issues is one of the factors (not the only one) that might impact the capacity of constitutional[11] dialogues, some types of dialogue, in this broader conception, shall always exist in any constitutional framework where there is the separation of powers. For this reason, "in the separation of powers, the interaction is unavoidable"[12] (Mendes 2011, 211).

[11] A dialogue is born from the combination of an institutional blueprint and a political culture. The institutional blueprint creates incentives for different types of interaction. Such incentives do not determine, however, the institutional behavior in an isolated way" (Mendes 2011, 162).

[12] Mendes states in a more emphatic way that: "the interaction is a fact, not a choice or a possibility. It does not result from the manifestation of the will of a power, or from some particular institu-

7.5 Conclusion

Two models of constitutional framework have been traditionally adopted by Western states, namely, the model of parliamentary sovereignty (in the British Commonwealth) and that of judicial supremacy (in the North American tradition). The current academic scenario, however, offers the model of constitutional dialogues as a third way to understand the separation of powers, which intends to overcome the dispute of *Courts versus Parliament* regarding who should hold the power to have the "last word" over sensitive issues such as fundamental rights.

What changes with this third-model is the perspective for the analysis of the discussion. According to the model of constitutional dialogues, the so-called "*final word*" will always be temporary, considering that the theories of dialogue give greater emphasis to the several procedural deliberative rounds regarding these controversies from a historical viewpoint. Looking at the problem in a static manner, as it has been done in the traditional dualism between judicial and legislative supremacy, disregards the potential that constitutional interactions among political institutions might have as far as the protection and development of fundamental rights is concerned.

Thus, it is pointed out that dialogue theories take several shapes, like in the case of internal theories about judicial deliberations and decision-making (*endogenous*) – that focus on the *method* of the decision, where one considers dialogue among judges themselves – , as well as *structural theories (exogenous)* that work with the perspective of devising institutional blueprints that will facilitate the interaction between institutions or, in other words, analyze the dialogue through a perspective that moves beyond the Court (considering the structural relation between the Court and the Parliament).[13]

The fact remains that, in any of the adopted constitutional theory models, the existence of a constitutional review – or at least, of some sort of protection of fundamental rights by the Courts – although possible, is, however, disconnected from the idea of a final nature (*last word*) for its decision.

As pointed out before, any settlement achieved by the Judiciary about a controversial moral or political issue is understood as a single procedural round in a broader inter-institutional debate, to the point of that the action of other institutions is stimulated, even if for the purpose to concur with the referred decision.

Even if the materialization of dialogues, within the sphere of a constitutional framework based on a separation of powers, has been verified, it is necessary a normative argument to demonstrate why this interaction is beneficial for the

tional device, but it is a necessary consequence of the separation of powers. Moreover, there is a 'silent dialogue' among the institutions, leading in a conscious or not, whose responsibility the theorist has to realize and reconstruct" (Mendes 2011, 161).

[13] Among the theories of the judicial method, Bateup (2005) highlights the judicial advice-giving theories, the process-centered rules theories, and the judicial minimalism. As far as the dialogue structural theories are concerned, Bateup asserts the coordinate construction theories, the theories of judicial principle, the equilibrium theories and the partnership theories.

protection of the fundamental rights and, further, to explain the role of the Judiciary in this dialogue in an attractive way.

It must be pointed out the foundation for this model must not be based on questionable notions such as the epistemic superiority of the Judiciary in relation to the Legislative, as well as its immunity against political influences, something that has been even empirically challenged. On the other hand, the Parliament cannot be also characterized as a *locus* where individuals or political factions act in a purely selfish manner, deprived of a deliberative capacity with regards to matters of principle.

Along these lines, Waldron discusses that in fact legislators debate about rights. However, given the fact of the reasonable moral disagreement, individuals continue to differ in good-faith on these sensitive issues, even after a discursive procedure has been developed in a wholesome manner. Therefore, given this irresolvable disagreement, the possibility of violation of the rights by Parliament as result of this uncertainty regarding the conformation of the latter and the limits that entail to the operation of the state is explained.

In this status of divergences among agents, Waldron understands that the matter must be resolved via a majority procedure, which is arbitrary regarding the content of the public decision, since it would be a way to guarantee to all the right of participation in the collective shaping of rights that each one has. This would entail, therefore, a criticism to judicial review, considering that if a disagreement exists, it would be better if a representative institution, such as the Parliament, had the responsibility to resolve it, as opposed to the Courts, that have less individuals.

Having said this, I believe that the normative argument that we need in favour of the model of constitutional dialogue must emerge from Waldron's assumption, which is the fact of the reasonable disagreement. However, it must be noted that distinct political institutions, like the case of the Courts and the Parliaments, are different not only (or mainly) in reference to the number of agents that participate in it – as it seems to be the premise of Waldron's argument –, but also in reference to their structure and different operational dynamics.

As result of this situation, when they interact by the means of a constitutional dialogue, they make the mutual provision of distinct perspectives regarding the same issues possible, exemplified, in kind, by the debate about rights. They can reciprocally clear "blind spots" of the institutions that they interact with.

Therefore, the normative argument favouring dialogue is anchored on the notion that the interaction among the institutions is beneficial to the debate and to the protection of fundamental rights, since, among other issues, it makes an interchange of distinct perspectives in the discussion on the same issues possible, further expanding institutional channels where the theme is breached.

Hence, the model of constitutional dialogues does not assume that an institution is better skilled than other, but only that the distinct logics in the composition, organization and operation of institutions will probably result in offering different perspectives on fundamental controversies, enhancing the debate when as it is viewed through the angle of broad dynamic involving constitutional conversations (several procedural rounds).

To conclude, as a result of the normative argument above, I believe that the best definition for the term *dialogue*, for the purpose of dialogue theories, is a broad understanding, which will embrace any modality of interaction among political institutions regarding the mentioned constitutional issues. It refers to the interaction and reciprocal implications that will take place, to a greater or lesser extent, within the constitutional frameworks where there is the separation of powers.

Acknowledgment I would like to thank Thomas Bustamante for a prolific discussion on this topic and helpful comments on a previous draft of this chapter.

References

Alexy, Robert. 2005. Balancing, constitutional review and representation. *International Journal of Constitutional Law (I-CON)* 3: 527–581.

Bateup, Christine A. 2005. The dialogic promise: Assessing the normative potential of theories of constitutional dialogue. New York: *New York University Public Law and Legal Theory Working Papers*, paper 11: 1–85. Available at: http://lsr.nellco.org/cgi/viewcontent.cgi?article=1010&context=nyu_plltwp. Accessed on 26 June 2015.

Bickel, Alexander. 1986. *The least dangerous branch – The supreme court at the bar of politics*. New Haven: Yale University Press.

Brandão, Rodrigo. 2012. *Supremacia Judicial versus Diálogos Constitucionais: A quem cabe a última palavra sobre o sentido da Constituição?* Rio de Janeiro: Lumen Juris.

Dworkin, Ronald. 1985. *A matter of principle*. Cambridge, MA: Harvard University Press.

Friedman, Barry. 2005. The politics of judicial review. *Texas Law Review* 84(2): 257–337.

Friedman, Barry. 2009. *The will of the people: How public opinion has influenced the Supreme Court and shaped the meaning of the constitution*. New York: Farrar, Strauss and Giroux.

Gardbaum, Stephen. 2010. Reassessing the new commonwealth model of constitutionalism. *International Journal of Constitutional Law (I-CON)* 8(2): 167–206.

Gargarella, Roberto. 2006. El nacimiento del “constitucionalismo popular”. *Revista de Libros* (Derecho, 112). Available at: http://www.revistadelibros.com/articulos/el-nacimiento-del-constitucionalismopopular. Accessed on 25 June 2015.

Hiebert, Janet L. 2006. Parliament and the Human Rights Act: Can the JCHR help facilitate a culture of rights? *International Journal of Constitutional Law (I-CON)* 4(1): 1–38.

Hogg, Peter W., and Allison A. Bushell. 1997. The Charter Dialogue between Courts and Legislatures (or perhaps the Charter of Rights isn’t such a Bad Thing after all). *Osgoode Hall Law Journal* 35(1): 75–124.

Kramer, Larry. 2004. *The people themselves – Popular constitutionalism and judicial review*. Oxford: Oxford University Press.

Mendes, Conrado Hübner. 2011. *Direitos fundamentais, separação de poderes e deliberação*. São Paulo: Saraiva.

Roach, Kent. 2001. Constitutional and Common Law Dialogues between the Supreme Court and Canadian Legislatures. *Canadian Bar Review* 80: 481–533.

Tushnet, Mark. 1999. *Taking the Constitution away from the courts*. Princeton: Princeton University Press.

Waldron, Jeremy. 1999. *Law and disagreement*. New York: Oxford University Press.

Waldron, Jeremy. 2010. A majority in the lifeboat. *Boston University Law Review* 90: 1043–1057.

Whittington, Keith. 2000. In defense of legislatures. *Political Theory* 28(5): 690–702.

Part III
Institutional Alternatives for Constitutional Changes

Chapter 8
New Institutional Mechanisms for Making Constitutional Law

Mark Tushnet

Abstract Traditionally, two general methods have been used to make constitutional law. The first involves creating a constitutional text, and has been done by constituent assemblies convened especially for that purpose or by legislatures either proposing replacement constitutions or more limited constitutional amendments. The second involves interpreting existing constitutional texts, and has been done by specialized constitutional courts or generalist courts. After describing briefly what we know about how constitutional law is made by these traditional methods, this essay turns to some recent innovations in making constitutional law, which I describe generically as involving substantially higher levels of public participation than in the traditional methods: the process of drafting a proposed new constitution for Iceland, and the practice of "public hearings" in the Brazilian Supreme Federal Court. My aim is to identify some features of these newer methods that might be of interest to scholars of comparative constitutional law. For that reason, the essay paints in deliberately broad strokes, isolating features that may point in the direction of a more general understanding of constitution-making processes while ignoring features that may play crucial roles in the two specific processes on which I focus.

8.1 Introduction

Traditionally, two general methods have been used to make constitutional law. The first involves creating a constitutional text, and has been done by constituent assemblies convened especially for that purpose or by legislatures either proposing replacement constitutions or more limited constitutional amendments.[1] The second involves interpreting existing constitutional texts, and has been done by specialized

[1] Sometimes constitutions and amendments take effect upon their announcement by the drafting body, whether constituent assembly or legislature, but more commonly, especially in modern times, replacement constitutions are ratified by some other body, today usually by a national referendum but again occasionally by existing institutions such as the sitting legislatures in the component units of a federation. Amendments sometimes must be ratified as well, and if so similar

M. Tushnet (✉)
Harvard Law School, Areeda 223, Cambridge, MA 02138, USA
e-mail: mtushnet@law.harvard.edu

T. Bustamante, B.G. Fernandes (eds.), *Democratizing Constitutional Law*,
Law and Philosophy Library 113, DOI 10.1007/978-3-319-28371-5_8

constitutional courts or generalist courts. After describing briefly what we know about how constitutional law is made by these traditional methods, I turn to some recent innovations in making constitutional law, which I describe generically as involving substantially higher levels of public participation than in the traditional methods: the process of drafting a proposed new constitution for Iceland, and the practice of "public hearings" in the Brazilian Supreme Federal Court. My aim is to identify some features of these newer methods that might be of interest to scholars of comparative constitutional law. For that reason, this essay paints in deliberately broad strokes, isolating features that may point in the direction of a more general understanding of constitution-making processes while ignoring features that may play crucial roles in the two specific processes on which I focus.

8.2 What We Know

What do we know about how constitutional law is made in constituent assemblies and similar bodies, and in courts? Of course we know a great deal about the details of how specific constituent assemblies created constitutions, and a little about how constitutional courts make constitutional law, with most of our knowledge of the latter derived from studies of the U.S. Supreme Court.[2] My question relates to our knowledge about *general* characteristics of these law-making processes, not about specific details. It therefore locates my inquiry in one of the streams of work in comparative constitutional law, in which we seek to identify common themes rather than to demonstrate how constitutions are specific to the contexts within which they develop.

8.2.1 Constituent Assemblies

Much of what we know – in the general sense – about constituent assemblies comes from Jon Elster's work.[3] Comparing the Philadelphia Constitutional Convention of 1787 and the French Constituent Assembly of 1789–1791, Elster draws a distinction between deliberating and bargaining, and focuses as well on the implications of

methods – ratification by referendum or by some other legislature than the proposing one – are used.

[2]The U.S. Supreme Court has been the focus of study not only because of its prominence, but probably more important, for present purposes, because of the availability of a great deal of information in the personal papers of the justices (including material related to cases), many of which readily available for scholarly study. As I understand it, access to such papers is quite unusual outside the United States. For one study relying on such papers, see Sharpe and Roach (2003). I believe that internal documents from the French Constitutional Council are now available with a multi-year time lag.

[3]Elster (1995).

holding a constituent assembly in public or behind closed doors, and of the existence of a deadline for action, connecting the transparency and deadline issues to bargaining and deliberation. For Elster, bargaining involves appeals to the material interests of different groups, who use their relative political and numerical power to make trades whose sole justification is that the result is acceptable to all. Bargaining ends with agreement on a "deal." In contrast, deliberation is a process of reasoning in which some participants attempt to persuade others that some constitutional provision is more rationally defensible, in terms of goals upon which all agree, than alternatives. Deliberation ends with agreement on principles embodied in specific provisions.

The connection between secrecy versus openness on the one hand, and deliberation and bargaining on the other is this: Bargains are easier to reach out of public view. Participants can state their sincerely held positions, the ones they would must like to see embodied in the constitution. But, when confronted with opposition or alternatives, participants can compromise. They need not defend the compromises as based on principle, but rather can invoke – inside the secret session – the simple need to arrive at a conclusion. Exposed to public view, the process of reaching compromise would open participants to criticism for being "mere" politicians more interested in making a deal than in arriving at the best set of constitutional provisions. Once a bargain is reached in secret, of course the participants can invent principled reasons explaining why the bargain is defensible as more than a bargain.

Unfortunately, openness need not conduce to deliberation. True, participants in open sessions will tend to offer principled reasons for their positions, but they may find it difficult to recede from those positions when other take equally principled but different, sometimes opposing positions: If their positions were correct when announced, departing from them means moving away from the principled position. And, Elster points out, public proceedings may lead participants to posture for the public, appealing to the extremes. They might do so to stake out a position in later bargaining: the compromise reached after moving from an extreme position toward the center might be more favorable to the proponent of that position than the compromise reached after moving from a less extreme position. Yet, the politician who postures in public may find it difficult to explain *any* compromise.

Deadlines force participants to consider whether returning to the status quo – that is, failing to reach agreement before the deadline expires – is better than any result that could be reached near the end of the proceedings.[4] Typically, Elster suggests, deadlines push participants into bargaining for some compromise; deadlines, that is, may reduce deliberation and increase bargaining at the deadline approaches. Sometimes the compromises are reached "under the gun," that is, are rushed because of the imminent deadline. That in turn raises the possibility that the compromises will be flawed, either technically in that the constitution as a whole may have internal inconsistencies or gaps, or substantively in that real differences are papered over

[4]The status quo includes the possibility that another constituent assembly or similar process might be convened after the failure of the initial one.

(deferred for later resolution). Sometimes participants will understand the flaws, accepting them as the cost of reaching agreement before the deadline, but sometimes participants will overlook the deficiencies in the product.

Elster also identifies "upstream" and "downstream" constraints on constitution-making. Upstream constraints determine (or condition) the membership of the constituent assembly. The "round table" form of constitution-making in the course of the collapse of the Soviet empire in 1989–1990, for example, resulted from the "upstream" constraint that the leadership of the local Communist parties would not vacate their positions of power without having some say in the design of the successor constitution; and similarly with the role of white South Africans in the South African constitution-making process. The downstream constraint arises from the fact that the new constitution will have to be accepted through some process. That constraint determines (or conditions) the new constitution's content, because the content plays an important role in eliciting support from the constitution's ratifiers.

In addition to Elster's work, there is some general material on the role of expert advisers, including international advisers, in modern constituent assemblies. Here the evidence suggests that we should distinguish between core and peripheral constitutional issues.[5] Core issues are the ones around which politics revolves, and participants in constituent assemblies know where they stand on those issues. They might bargain or they might deliberate, but whichever path they choose, the participants are rather likely to disregard advice they receive from outside. The reason is that participants know much better than outsiders do the implications of reaching agreement on a particular resolution of a centrally contested issue. Occasionally there may be a "middle" position that participants might have overlooked, drawn perhaps from experience in some other constitutional system, and technical advisers might bring that position to the participants' attention, sometimes with a degree of success. More often, though, participants will have good reason for rejecting a position that outside advisers say is technically better than the one they have settled on. Participants are more likely to accept advice on what they perceive to be peripheral issues, as to which disagreement, if it exists, is relatively narrow. Yet, participants may be mistaken in their classification of issues. Sometimes what they believe at the time of constitution-making to be a peripheral issue will turn out to be extremely important as politics takes hold after a constitution begins operating, and a provision they thought unimportant or merely technical can become central to key political controversies.[6]

---

[5]I develop this distinction in a forthcoming essay, "The Politics of 'Best Practices' in Constitution-Making."

[6]An example might be a provision defining the qualifications for the presidency, which might make it possible for all who are plausibly thought of as potential candidates to qualify, but which might obstruct the candidacy of someone who becomes political prominent shortly after the constitution's adoption. Bulgaria and Egypt both have faced variants of this problem.

8.2.2 Constitutional Courts

Elster's distinction between deliberation and bargaining is relevant as well to constitution-making by constitutional court decision. Most constitutional courts make decisions in secret, which, on Elster's analysis, makes it easier for participants to bargain, making trades that could not be defended as a matter of principle. Yet, at least with respect to the U.S. Supreme Court, studies make it reasonably clear that almost no bargaining of that sort occurs. No one has credibly identified an example in modern times of vote-trading across cases, for example, which would be the paradigmatic example of bargaining.

Some scholars have described strategic interactions among U.S. Supreme Court justices. Those interactions are, in my view, examples of deliberation dominating bargaining. The most significant examples of strategic interactions are ones in which one Justice has a preferred position about a constitutional provision's proper interpretation, but modifies that position to ensure that some other Justice will join his or her opinion. Yet, it seems to me, this phenomenon is one in which deliberation is at least closely intertwined with bargaining and may be one in which only deliberation occurs. The U.S. Supreme Court aspires to operate by issuing judgments expounded in opinions attributed to "the Court" as an entity. An opinion backed by less than a majority has less legal significance than one endorsed by a majority. So, justices drafting opinions with an eye to making them as legally effective as possible will take into account the views of other justices. That, it seems to me, is fairly described either as deliberation as such, or the deliberative form that bargaining takes in an institutional context in which majority decisions are favored.

As the preceding paragraph suggests, U.S. Supreme Court Justices circulate draft opinions to their colleagues, who then can "join" the opinion. Not infrequently, though, another justice will suggest that language in the draft opinion be modified. Sometimes the reason for the suggestion is that the justice disagrees with the language and thinks it unnecessary to the disposition of the case at had. In such cases the objecting justice will explain the reasons for his or her disagreement, and for thinking that the language could be changed without undermining the opinion's rational integrity. Other times, the justice will explain an objection by indicating why the objectionable language might point to the resolution of some future cases, as to which the justice has a different (tentative) view or believes it best to express no view whatever. Although sometimes phrased in terms similar to those used in bargaining, such as "I can join your opinion if you make the following modifications," these comments are examples of deliberation in an almost pristine form. They are based on the author's interpretation of the relevant legal materials, they are backed up by arguments, and they are accepted or rejected based on their cogency, coupled again with the institutional desire to assemble a majority.

Secrecy within the U.S. Supreme Court, then, does not seem to have licensed the unprincipled bargaining that Elster says it licenses in constituent assemblies. One possibility, to which I return below, is that the roles of participants in constituent assemblies and of judges are different enough to generate different norms governing their behavior. To overstate the point: Participants in constituent assemblies typically have been politicians, comfortable with bargaining out of public view, whereas judges adhere to norms favoring deliberation over bargaining. That would explain why, given similar institutional arrangements of secret proceedings, constituent assemblies find it easier to engage in bargaining and judges deliberate and only rarely bargain.

With respect to deadlines, the evidence is almost entirely anecdotal. The U.S. Supreme Court operates with a reasonably strong deadline rule, according to which all cases argued during one "Term" of the Court – running from October through late June or early July – be decided during that Term.[7] There is reason to think that important cases argued late in the Term, in March and especially April, are sometimes rushed, with analytic errors or minor internal inconsistencies that would have been eliminated had the Justices had more time. And, there is similar anecdotal evidence that constitutional courts without deadlines sometimes delay issuing a decision for quite a long time, hoping to identify the strategically best time to announce the decision. These observations are consistent with Elster's analysis of deadlines' effects.

Openness in judicial proceedings with respect to arriving at results is quite rare. Some have suggested that we can observe openness of that sort in the public arguments at the U.S. Supreme Court. Recent reports suggest that deliberation after argument is relatively unusual. That is, justices do not discuss the cases in detail after argument, but announce their positions. After the votes are counted, one justice is assigned the task of writing an opinion, and, apparently, quite often the opinion as drafted garners a majority relatively quickly. That reduces the author's incentive to accommodate principled objections offered by late-comers or potential dissenters. If post-argument deliberation is rare, justices may use the public arguments as the venue for deliberation, in the form of posing questions to the advocates that are actually efforts to persuade their colleagues to see the case in the way the questioner sees it. But, as Elster suggests, the openness of the oral arguments makes it possible for justices to posture rather than attempt to persuade.

Another example that has received reasonably extensive attention is the practice of the Brazilian Supreme Federal Court. My impression is that most scholars who have examined the process find it quite deficient, as is suggested by the title of one study, "Deciding Without Deliberating" (Alfonso da Silva 2013). These critics describe the justices as posturing for the public, a practice exacerbated by the fact that the deliberations are televised live. The critics see justices are hardening their positions when challenged, rather than taking fair rational account of principled objections. To that extent, the critics' arguments are consistent with Elster's analysis. Yet, as my discussion of the U.S. Supreme Court's secret practice suggests, Elster's account does not tell us why secret judicial decision-making would be more deliberate than public decision-making. As I have suggested, perhaps U.S. Supreme Court justices have internalized a set of norms that encourages deliberation even

[7] The Court occasionally sets a case for reargument in the succeeding Term, almost always with the figleaf of a new question the Court asks to be argued.

when bargaining is possible. Then, though, one would wonder whether Brazilian justices, as described by their critics, have not internalized such norms. Perhaps if they posture in public, they would posture in private as well. Norms rather than institutional arrangements might account for the aspects of the Brazilian practice that have drawn criticism.

Summarizing a host of studies, Mark Warren and Jane Mansbridge write, "By now, the empirical evidence on the deliberative benefits of closed-door interactions seems incontrovertible" (Warren and Mansbridge 2013, 108). The studies do not deal with judges, though, and it seems possible that public deliberations *about the law* might be different from negotiations about other matters. The idea is that many of the closed-door negotiations that are the object of empirical study deal with problems in which competing interests are at stake, such as labor negotiations and perhaps, as with Elster's study, constitutional framing, and as to which there is no external standard for evaluating the quality of the outcome. In contrast, at least in principle or, more narrowly, at least in some cases, judges are attempting to determine what "the law" means or requires, and all agree that there is a determinable answer. There might be forms of deliberation in the open in which the participants, all oriented toward reaching the correct result, actually make arguments and consider what each participant is saying, on the merits.

8.3 Recent Innovations in Making Constitutional Law

I turn now to recent innovations in constitution-making processes. The first is a sharp increase in practices of popular participation in constitution-drafting. As the twentieth century waned, popular participation in ratifying constitutions, typically through referenda, increased, though it never completely displaced older modes of ratification through parliamentary approval. This century's innovation is to move high levels of popular participation back to the stage of constitutional drafting. Among other things, that innovation reduces the effects of upstream constraints on the selection of constitution drafters, although, as we will see in connection with Iceland, the weakening of that constraint may have downstream effects.

The second innovation is greater openness in constitution-making by constitutional courts. This openness includes televising hearings in constitutional courts and the use of press offices by such courts, to notify the media of important decisions in advance and to offer court-endorsed summaries and explanations of those decisions. Here I deal with the Brazilian practice of "public hearings," a special form of hearing arguments in cases selected by the Supreme Federal Court for such hearings. Here the secrecy of deliberations is weakened.[8]

[8] In Brazil secrecy's weakening is not as dramatic as it might be in other systems, because of the Brazilian practice of public deliberation by the justices themselves in the course of considering constitutional claims.

The remainder of this Essay presents brief case studies of the recent Icelandic constitutional revision process and the Brazilian public hearing process. I do not claim anything like comprehensiveness, but I hope that my sketches will bring out features of the innovations of which they are examples that deserve closer study, both in connection with Iceland and Brazil and in connection with constitution-making more generally.

8.3.1 Iceland's Failed Exercise in Crowd-Sourced Constitution Making

Iceland's financial crisis in 2008 led to widespread discontent with the nation's political class.[9] The coalition government that melded the Social Democratic Alliance and the Independence Party fell apart. The Social Democratic Alliance formed a minority government, which continued to govern after an election in 2009. That government proposed to initiate a process of constitutional reform; the Independence Party opposed the idea. At first the idea was that an elected constituent assembly would propose a constitution that would become legally effective after approval in a referendum without further parliamentary participation. After being advised that that course would require the adoption of a prior constitutional amendment modifying the permissible methods of constitutional amendment, the proposal was reshaped. In 2010 the parliament adopted an Act stating that a Constitutional Assembly would convene in February 2011 and finish its work by April of that year. To gain the Independence Party's support, the proposal was that a Constitutional Committee appointed by Parliament would do preparatory work for the Constitutional Assembly; the Committee's seven members included academic experts in law, science, and literature. The thought was that this procedure would lead to a set of constitutional amendments channeled through the regular amendment process – simple majority votes with one taken before and the other taken after an election, though by convention more than a majority was required.

The Constitutional Assembly described in the 2010 statute never convened. One difficulty was that the process was elite-dominated and, perhaps more important, was the creature of the very political parties that had been brought into disrepute by the financial crisis. To offset that elitism, the Constitutional Committee convened a National Forum of 950 citizens drawn at random from the census list. The Forum met for one day in November 2010 and discussed basic constitutional principles, such as "one person one vote" – an important issue in a small nation with a population concentrated in the capital city, which in a one-person-one-vote system might disregard the interests of rural voters – and rights to natural resources. As to the latter issue, some Icelanders believed that private control of fishery resources had

[9] An accessible account of the Icelandic process, on which I draw heavily, is Meuwese (2013).

created a network of interest groups that in turn created a culture of financial corruption that led to the crisis (Gylfason 2014).

The Constitutional Committee then organized an election for members of a constitutional assembly. Candidates were basically self-nominated but had to get signatures to place themselves on the ballot. Twenty-five members were to be elected, from a group of 522 candidates, through a single transferable vote system that allowed each voter to vote for up to the full complement of twenty-five. The Independence Party and the Progressive Party, two major political parties in the pre-crisis period, opposed the process as a whole, and did not vigorously participate in supporting candidates.

Iceland's Supreme Court voided the elections for the Constitutional Assembly: it found that the process was flawed because the secrecy of the ballot was threatened by, for example, numbering ballot papers, although there was no evidence that anyone had actually tried to link a voter with his or her ballot after the event. Instead of taking over the constitution-amending process itself or running another set of elections (the latter option was ruled out in part because of the cost of running another election), Parliament designated the twenty-five winners of the election as members of a constituent body – called the Constitutional Council – whose authority derived, at least in theory, from parliament rather than from the people directly.

With an initial deadline two months away, later extended by another two months, the Constitutional Council then got to work. Its members were drawn from a number of professions, and had varying political affiliations, but none were important figures in or seen as representatives of the (discredited) political parties. They broke up into three working groups and, importantly, solicited comments and suggestions from every Icelander by establishing a web-site and social media accounts to which suggestions could be posted. This practice was the basis for describing the drafting process as "crowd-sourced." The Council received about 3600 comments as well as 370 "formal suggestions" – not a trivial number in a nation with a population of under 400,000.[10] Although most of the posts were generic, a fair number suggested substantive provisions for inclusion in the draft constitution. One member of the Constitutional Council stated that the Council members deliberately refrained from setting up special meetings with "representatives of interest organizations."[11]

After public deliberations and by a unanimous vote, the Constitutional Council adopted the draft constitution, anticipating its initial ratification (or disapproval) in a popular referendum. With respect to six specific matters, including "one person one vote," the possibility of national referenda upon citizen demand, a state religion, and ownership of natural resources, the Constitutional Council presented a "yes or no" option.

The referendum, though, would not be the final step even if the voters approved the new constitution. Instead, in light of the Constitutional Council's origins in parliamentary action, parliament would have to approve the constitution *after* the referendum. In November 2012 voters did approve the draft constitution by a mar-

[10] The figure is reported in Meuwese (2013, 484–85).

[11] Quoted in Meuwese (2013, 483).

gin of 67–33 (and chose which of the options they wanted on each separately identified issue), but the 49 % turnout was smaller than many expected or hoped, and the margin of approval was similarly smaller than expected or hoped. After the referendum, parliamentary leaders invited the Venice Commission to provide comments on the draft constitution, nominally to guide the parliament's decision on approving or disapproving the document; the comments found various technical deficiencies in the draft, suggesting that clearer language could have been used on some matters and asserting that some important issues had not been resolved. There is some reason to think that these technical problems resulted from a combination of the strict time limits under which the Constitutional Council worked, with the relative inexperience of the Council's members in politics generally and in constitutional design in particular.[12] The draft was modified to deal with the Venice Commission's comments, without objection from the members of the now-dissolved Constitutional Council.

Parliament never took up the proposed constitution, so it did not go into effect. Throughout, the established political parties held themselves at arms' length from the process, in part because they had been discredited but in larger part because their leaders disagreed with the idea that a totally new constitution had to be adopted, rather than discrete amendments that could have been adopted by the ordinary process of parliamentary vote.

In no particular order, here are some features of the overall Icelandic process.

1. The financial crisis provided the impetus for the constitution-making process. That process took time, with the referendum held three years after the crisis's peak and as Iceland was clearly on a path to recovery. The Supreme Court's intervention required that the process be restructured and seems to have had something of a disruptive psychological effect on the Constitutional Council's members, who nonetheless did complete their work within a four-month period. The passing of time, coupled with a degree of recovery from the financial crisis, reduced the felt urgency of constitutional reform.[13] The default was the existing constitution, which might have seemed "good enough" as reform pressure waned. Elster argues that constitutions are often made in times of crisis, which leads them to be less well-designed than would be the case were the drafting process to be extended over time. But, he observes, when the public does not see the polity as facing a crisis it may lose interest in constitutional design. That seems to have been true in Iceland.
2. The Constitutional Council did not have international advisers as such. The Venice Commission's intervention after the draft constitution's approval in the referndum did bring an outside and purportedly technical perspective to the pre-

[12]The Constitutional Council was open to suggestions, of course, and its work-in-progress was monitored by a "semi-formal collective of individuals sharing an interest in the Constitution process," as quoted in Meuwese, note—above, at p. 483. The collective seems to have brought some degree of focused expertise to the drafting process, but the descriptions I have found do not make clear how much.

[13]Gylfason (2014, 9) refers to "reform fatigue".

referendum discussions. The Venice Commission's views probably reduced enthusiasm for the document. To some degree, in its role as commenter on constitutional amendments and revisions the Venice Commission exists to identify problems. Sometimes doing so leads to improvements in the documents upon which the Commission comments, but only if the domestic process can accommodate the comments by revising drafts and proposals. The document was revised, but the Venice Commission's comments probably cast a modest adverse light on the process that produced the proposal it evaluated.

I think it worth noting that some of the Venice Commission's critical comments identified relatively minor flaws in the draft, such as areas where terminology was unclear or where obvious issues were left unresolved. Crowd-sourcing constitutional drafting, or using a true citizen (nonprofessional) constituent assembly, will almost certainly generate documents with these sorts of flaws, and perhaps outside advisers and commenters should modify their practices when constitutions are drafted with extremely high levels of popular participation.[14]

3. Crowd-sourcing, it might be thought, would be a process in which those who participate in "ordinary" politics at low rates would be enabled to increase their level of participation. Even in a nation as small as Iceland, going to parliament to testify, or even writing a letter to a member of parliament, is likely to be more difficult than going on-line to submit a comment or proposal. Whether crowd-sourcing had that effect in Iceland is as yet unclear. One early study suggests that the constitution-drafting process was *less* demographically representative than the ordinary legislative process (Helgdòttir. 2014). The study examined the relative participation of men and women in the two processes. It found that, relative to the ordinary parliamentary process, men were *over*represented in the social media comments in the crowd-sourcing process. The results are suggestive, but not nearly definitive. For one thing, representation in the ordinary legislative process is mediated through civil society organizations, whereas interventions on social media need not be. That is, it is possible (as the study's authors acknowledge) that *different* subgroups of women and men are represented in the ordinary legislative process and the crowd-sourcing one.
4. The Icelandic process was as open as can be. According to Elster, then, it should not have presented opportunities for bargaining, and that appears to have been the case. Elster's concern that participants in an open process will posture rather than deliberate, though, seems not to have been realized, at least on the accounts currently available in English. Perhaps the reason is that participants were true "one-shotters."[15] That is, not only were they not politicians who might be concerned about appealing to external audiences for future support, but they were complete amateurs (there were eight academics, in fields that included economics, political science, and philosophy, but also mathematics and

[14] Had the constitution gone into effect, I suspect that many of the flaws the Venice Commission identified would have been remedied through interpretation or political practice.

[15] I adopt the terminology of "one-shotters" and, below, "repeat players" from Galanter (1974).

theology – and no legal academics) with no continuing interest in implementing the constitution they drafted.[16]

Relying on the so-called "self-denying ordinance" of the French Constituent Assembly, which barred participants from office under the constitution they were to create, Elster points out that constitutions drafted by one-shotters may be defective because the drafters have no continuing responsibility for the actual operation of the government they are creating. They may adopt provisions that seem in principle desirable, but need not worry about whether the provisions will work well in practice. Because the Icelandic constitution did not go into effect, we cannot know whether Elster's concern would have been realized under it. But, the "one-shotter" concern is related to another, as to which the Icelandic experience is instructive.

5. Continental constitutional theory may have mattered as well. A directly elected Constitutional Assembly could have been seen as a true constituent assembly, speaking for the people as whole without its actions being mediated through preexisting political institutions. As a constituent assembly its actions would be those of the people, and – given modern practices – the referendum endorsing the new constitution would have similarly been a direct act of the constituent power. The theoretical picture changed when the Supreme Court invalidated the election of members to the Constitutional Council. Probably out of a desire to keep the process moving and not for theoretical reasons, parliament appointed the winners to the Constitutional Council. But parliamentary appointment broke the direct connection between the people and the Constitutional Council's members. They became the recipients of authority delegated to them by parliament, and, again as a matter of continental constitutional theory their principal – the Parliament – had to approve of what they did.

   Using Elster's terms, we can say had the Constitutional Council been a constituent assembly, the only downstream constraint would have been the need to obtain popular ratification of the draft constitution. The substitution of the parliament for the people as the source of the Constitutional Council's authority meant that ratification by the parliament, and therefore support by a decent share of the nation's political leadership, became a downstream constraint. But, the parliament's designation of the winners in the voided election as the members of the Constitutional Council meant that satisfying the requirements of the nation's political leaders had not operated as an upstream constraint on the body's composition. Under the circumstances, perhaps, failure was quite predictable.

6. Iceland's political parties did not participate in the drafting process, and indeed the random selection, self-nomination, and other processes for selecting members of the Constitutional Assembly/Council almost guaranteed their exclusion.[17] Then, at the final stage in the process, the parties in parliament defeated the

[16] Except insofar as their participation might have impelled them to greater involvement in political activity in the future than they had done in the past. One member did form a political party to support the constitutional draft, but it did not gather many votes.

[17] Not entirely, because had one or more parties thrown its weight behind candidates in the elections for the Constitutional Assembly, there is a decent chance that those candidates would have won at least some seats.

constitution. Elster's terminology is not exactly apt in this instance, but the intuition behind it, is. Party participation was in fact an upstream constraint on the drafting process, although it was not understood to be such at the outset. The outcome was failure attributable precisely to the fact that this upstream "constraint" was ignored.[18]

Suppose, though, that the parties had been included, to a degree, in the drafting process. Then the problems of posturing (by participants with long-term interests persisting after the constituent assembly ends) and of impediments to bargaining in an open process might have occurred. And, of course, their participation would have tempered those portions of the reform agenda aimed at the features of the pre-crisis political system that were thought (by some) to have produced the crisis. Accommodating the political parties upstream might then have reduced the probability that the resulting proposal would receive downstream endorsement in a referendum.

The general lesson of these observations, it seems to me, is that a program of increasing the level of public participation in constitution-making might have some attractions from a democratic point of view, and might seem achievable with modern technology, and yet implementing that program calls for quite careful thought and attention to the questions of bargaining, deliberation, and constraint to which Elster directs our attention. It probably was not inevitable that Iceland's process would fail, but now that we have seen its failure, we might be able to identify some "red flags" that those who seek to implement similar processes should direct their attention to.

8.3.2 The Brazilian Public Hearings

Brazil's Federal Supreme Court holds its deliberations in public, and there is a television station dedicated to broadcasting its proceedings. In addition, the Court is authorized to hold "public hearings," which are different from ordinary oral arguments in ending cases. When cases arrive at the Court, one justice is assigned responsibility for the dossier. The rapporteur has a discretionary power to call for a public hearing in two circumstances. When the case is a "direct action" on constitutionality – a proceeding filed in the Federal Supreme Court in the first instance, without any lower court proceedings, challenging the constitutionality of a statute – the rapporteur may do so if the record is incomplete with respect to some important facts; when the case is a general claim of unconstitutionality, the rapporteur may do so apparently without restriction. Participants in the public hearing are defined by statute as those with "experience with and authority on" the question at issue.

[18] The term "constraint" is inapt because the parties did not actually constrain choice at the upstream point.

The statute authorizing public hearings was enacted in 1999; the first such hearing was held in 2007, with a total of fifteen through mid-2014.[19] Among other topics, the constitutional challenges dealt with laws on stem-cell research, on the possibility of terminating pregnancies of anencephalic fetuses, on affirmative action in the form of strong quotas, and on banning the importation of used automobile tires. The number of participants has been reasonably large, ranging from 10 to more than 50. The rapporteur generally has divided the participants into two groups, those favoring a finding of constitutionality and those favoring one of unconstitutionality. The participants have been drawn widely from civil society, typically through ordinary civil society organizations.[20]

I begin the analytic portion of this section by distinguishing the public hearings from the U.S. amicus curiae practice. Public hearings do resemble the amicus curiae practice because they allow interested parties to present their views to the court. They differ, though, because in the amicus curiae practice the presentations are almost entirely in writing; rarely the Court will allow one amicus curiae to participate in the oral argument, and never more than one or two. In contrast, the Brazilian public hearings involve in-person presentations by a large number of interested participants.

A study of Brazilian right-to-health-care cases illustrates the public hearing process (Wang 2013, 75). The Supreme Federal Court had considered a large number of such cases prior to 2009, issuing decisions that began to lay out the contours of a constitutionally permissible program for allocating health care. In 2009 it convened a public hearing, which led to a set of decisions in 2010 setting out criteria for allocating health care in a manner consistent with the Constitution. According to Daniel Wang, "These decisions establish a comprehensive set of criteria that present a more refined and realistic interpretation of the right to health than was exhibited in previous BFSC case law" (Wang 2013, 82). The criteria, while sensible, do not establish a fully comprehensive approach to health care because they do not, at least directly, confront questions about rationing that result from mandatory allocations to one population in situations where other populations receive discretionary allocations. Still, the study suggests that there is reason to think that the public hearing improved the quality of the Court's jurisprudence.

Again, some analytic points in no particular order:

1. The public hearings are quasi-legislative in character. The rapporteur who issued the first call for a public hearing relied on parliamentary by-laws dealing with legislative hearings for the procedures to be used in the public hearings (Hennig Leal 2014, 9). They are quasi-legislative in substance as well as procedure. The non-judges who participate present the entire range of arguments bearing on the constitutional question before the court. These include analysis of relevant pol-

[19] The information in this paragraph is drawn from Henning Leal (2014).

[20] In a purely legislative context we would describe the participants as representatives of organized interest groups or non-governmental organization. The point is that the participants are not "ordinary citizens," which seems consistent with the statutory requirement that they have "experience" with the matter.

icy considerations and the relation between sometimes contested facts and constitutional interpretation. One might analogize them to a hearing before a constitutionally responsible legislative committee devoted to legislative consideration of the constitutionality of a specific proposal.

In the United States, legislative hearings are often quite scripted, confirming Elster's sense that public "deliberations" lead to posturing rather than true deliberation; research on whether this is true of the Brazilian public hearings would be valuable. Note, though, that even such hearings are different from the debates in a public constituent assembly. In the constituent assembly all participants are members of the body, and, after the assembly opens, they may quickly stake out positions and become aware of the positions firmly adhered to by others. The "in person" nature of the discussions then might not overcome the scripted posturing. In contrast, legislative hearings and the Brazilian public hearings involve "repeat players" on one side – the legislators or the judges – but, typically, "one-shotters" on the other. It may be that social norms dealing with respect in in-person conversations will induce a somewhat more genuine practice of deliberation in the legislative hearings and the Brazilian public hearings.

2. The quasi-legislative character of the public hearings can be taken to reflect a Kelsenian understanding of constitutional interpretation. I take Kelsen to argue that constitutional interpretation is a complex blend of law and politics. Such an understanding accounts for the structure of the Kelsenian constitutional court in a civil law tradition: those sitting on the constitutional court could not be exclusively drawn from the career judiciary, because career judges, while perhaps talented in doing law, would not have adequate experience in politics. The Kelsenian court is selected outside the ordinary civil-law processes of judicial selection so that some, perhaps all, members will have some facility in blending legal analysis with political sensitivity. That is what happens, at the argument stage, with the Brazilian public hearing as well: participants drawn from civil-society organizations bring something more than a perspective on law alone to the discussions.
3. More recently, scholars have begun to distinguish reasonably sharply between legal (better, "judicial") and political constitutionalism. Legal or judicial constitutionalism lodges final and primary responsibility for constitutional interpretation in the courts; legislators and executive officials may, but need not, take constitutional considerations into account as they act, but the conclusions they reach about constitutional meaning can always be displaced by the judges' contrary conclusions. Political constitutionalism, in contrast, gives legislators and executive officials a large and honored place in constitutional interpretation, and in some versions give them the final word. The Brazilian public hearings can be understood as blending political and judicial constitutionalism. The hearings are before a court, which has the final word on constitutional interpretation. But, the hearings can involve a large number of civil society organizations offering their views on constitutional interpretation, which can be understood as related to the general practice of political constitutionalism. In addition, ministers from the executive government both attend and participate in the public hearings, making

them a locus where the executive government and the judiciary receive simultaneous input from the public on the constitutional issues being examined.

4. An interesting strand in recent U.S. constitutional scholarship examines the ways in which social movements – a subcategory of civil society – affect the development of constitutional law.[21] One mechanism by which they do is straight-forward: Once they gain sufficient force, social movements influence the composition of the courts. Politicians satisfy a movement's supporters by appointing judges sympathetic to the movement's constitutional views to the courts, and then, once on the courts, those judges interpret the constitution as incorporating those views. Sometimes, though, it seems that social movements affect constitutional interpretation *without* having influenced judicial selection. In the United States the most dramatic examples are recent: The Supreme Court adopted constitutional interpretations consistent with the views of the women's rights and gay rights movements at times when those movements were socially significant but well after the justices deciding the cases had been appointed to the Court. The mechanism by which this occurs remains obscure. Public hearings in the Federal Supreme Court are formal mechanisms by which the views of *contemporary* civil society can be brought into the court's deliberations.

Mônica Clarissa Hennig Leal describes the public hearing as a mechanism that advances the "openness and democratization" of the judiciary in a constitutional system that gives the judiciary the final word on constitutionality. The mechanism, for her, is one way in which constitutional interpretation is itself democratized. The finality of judicial interpretations depends in part on the strength of the amendment rules in place. The Brazilian amendment rule relatively lenient: an amendment becomes effective if approved by three-fifths of both houses in two readings. Put another way, the Brazilian Constitution is already a reasonably open and participatory one. Public hearings in the Federal Supreme Court may reflect, but also enhance, that characteristic.

8.4 Conclusion

Because the developments examined here are relatively recent, we cannot draw confident conclusions about how crowd-sourcing and public hearings or similar mechanisms would work if widely adopted. Successful innovations in constitutional technology are rare, and these may turn out to be ventures down paths that end at a blank wall. Yet, both are clearly in a constitutionalist tradition that makes the consent of the public an important part of constitutional foundations. Examining them not only gives us some insights into the processes of constitution-making

[21] The literature is quite large. Some of it is summarized in Balkin (2011).

generally, but also suggests the possibility of institutional innovations to deepen the normative foundation of constitutionalism.

References

Alfonso da Silva, Virgilio. 2013. Deciding without deliberating. *International Journal of Constitutional Law* 11: 557–584.

Balkin, Jack M. 2011. *Living originalism*. Cambridge: Harvard University Press.

Elster, Jon. 1995. Forces and mechanisms in the constitution-making process. *Duke Law Journal* 45: 364–396.

Galanter, Marc. 1974. Why the Haves come out ahead. *Law and Society Review* 9: 95–160.

Gylfason, Thorvaldur. 2014. *Constitution on Ice. CESifo Working Paper No. 5056* (Nov. 2014). http://papers.ssrn.com/sol3/papers.cfm?abstract_id=2529896. Accessed 22 Aug 2015.

Helgdòttir, Ragnhildur. 2014. *Which citizens? – Participation in the drafting of the Icelandic constitutional draft of 2011*. I•CONnect. http://www.iconnectblog.com/2014/10/which-citizens-participation-in-the-drafting-of-the-icelandic-constitutional-draft-of-2011/. Accessed 22 Aug 2015.

Hennig Leal, Mônica Clarissa. 2014. *Public hearings in the Ambit of the Federal Supreme Court: A new form of participation in public affairs?* http://www.jus.uio.no/english/research/news-and-events/events/conferences/2014/wccl-cmdc/wccl/papers/ws16/w16-leal.pdf. Accessed 22 Aug 2015.

Meuwese, Anne. 2013. Popular constitution-making: The case of Iceland. In *Social and political foundations of constitution*, ed. Denis J. Galligan and Mila Versteeg, 469–496. New York: Cambridge University Press.

Sharpe, Robert J., and Kent Roach. 2003. *Brian Dickson: A judge's journey*. Toronto: University of Toronto Press.

Thorarensen, Björg. 2014. *Why the making of a crowd-sourced Constitution in Iceland failed*. Constitutionnet. http://www.constitutionnet.org/news/why-making-crowd-sourced-constitution-iceland-failed. Accessed 22 Aug 2015.

Wang, Daniel W.L. 2013. Courts and health care rationing: The case of the Brazilian Federal Supreme Court. *Health Economics, Policy, and Law* 9: 75–93.

Warren, Mark, and Jane Mansbridge. 2013. Deliberative negotiation. http://www.apsanet.org/portals/54/Files/Task%20Force%20Reports/Chapter5Mansbridge.pdf. Accessed 22 Aug 2015.

Chapter 9
Democratic Constitutional Change: Assessing Institutional Possibilities

Christopher F. Zurn

Abstract This paper develops a normative framework for both conceptualizing and assessing various institutional possibilities for democratic modes of constitutional change, with special attention to the recent ferment of constitutional experimentation. The paper's basic methodological orientation is interdisciplinary, combining research in comparative constitutionalism, political science and normative political philosophy. In particular, it employs a form of normative reconstruction: attempting to glean out of recent institutional innovations the deep political ideals such institutions embody or attempt to realize. Starting from the assumption that contemporary constitutional democracies are attempting to realize the broader ideals of deliberative democratic constitution (ideals outlined briefly in the first section), the paper proposes an evaluative framework, comprised of six criteria, for assessing various mechanisms of constitutional change. It argues that democratic forms of constitutional change embody six distinct ideals—operationalizability, structural independence, democratic co-authorship, political equality, inclusive sensitivity, and reasons-responsiveness—and that these ideals can be used to gauge the normative worth of different mechanisms for carrying out such change. The framework is developed with reference to recent constitutional developments (e.g., in Venezuela, South Africa, Colombia, Bolivia, and Iceland) highlighting distinct criteria and showing how they appear to capture the general direction of institutional innovation. The paper conjectures that the set of six criteria yield the best normative reconstruction of the crucial ideals embodied in the constitutional change mechanisms of contemporary constitutional democracies, and so, ought to be used for purposes of evaluating institutional design proposals.

C.F. Zurn (✉)
Philosophy Department, University of Massachusetts Boston,
100 Morrisey Blvd., Boston, MA 02125-3393, USA
e-mail: christopher.zurn@umb.edu

T. Bustamante, B.G. Fernandes (eds.), *Democratizing Constitutional Law*,
Law and Philosophy Library 113, DOI 10.1007/978-3-319-28371-5_9

9.1 Introduction

This paper aims to develop a normative framework for conceptualizing and assessing various institutional possibilities for democratic modes of constitutional change. Given the ferment of constitutional experimentation witnessed across the globe—especially over the last quarter century—now is a propitious time for developing such a framework. For the purposes of political philosophy and political theory, I hope such a framework can deepen our broad understanding of the meanings of democracy, of constitutionalism, and of constitutional democracy. I am particularly interested in the prospects for a specific conception of constitutional democracy I label 'deliberative democratic constitutionalism' in order to stress two commitments in particular: to *democratic* processes of constitutional development, adoption and ongoing transformation, and, to a *deliberative* interpretation of democratic procedures.[1] For purposes of political practice, I hope the framework elucidated here can provide assessment criteria applicable to proposals for new institutions for constitutional change, as well as provide a bit of 'fire in the belly' to struggles to transform more ossified regimes in the direction of democratic and deliberative constitutionalism—as opposed, say, to juridical or aggregative forms of constitutionalism.

The basic methodological orientation of the project—of which this paper is a part—is interdisciplinary, combining research in comparative constitutionalism, political science and normative political philosophy. In particular, the method is a form of normative reconstruction: attempting to glean out of the diversity of constitutional institutions the deep political ideals such institutions embody or attempt to realize. Rather than starting from pure normative content about abstract ideals, principles or values, reconstruction begins with evidence provided by actual constitutional institutions in democratic systems. Attendant to both historical and more recent institutional innovations, it attempts to reconstruct the normative content such innovations are driven by in such a way that we can get a clearer conception of the specificity of the sub-ideals and principles of constitutional democracy. Finally the normative content reconstructed out of the institutions can be used reflexively for critical evaluation of those very institutions when they don't or can't live up to their normative promise. With such an approach I hope to avoid objections to typical normative theory as presenting merely an abstract utopia, developed out of *a priori* considerations of political philosophy and aiming to dictate reality in light of utopian ideals.[2] The proof is in the pudding however: only if the proposed reconstruction both accurately illuminates the ideals motivating actual institutional

[1] I have developed this conception elsewhere, leaning heavily but not exclusively on Jürgen Habermas's political philosophy (Zurn 2007).

[2] I share the methodological antipathy of both Sen and the critical theory tradition to grand ideal theory developed first out of abstract intuitions and thought experiments and only secondarily applied to an ostensibly fallen reality (Habermas 1996; Honneth 2014; Sen 2009). In the end, political theory must attempt to put the various tensions between facts and norms to productive use.

innovations and provides normatively worthwhile guidance for thought about the institutions of democratic constitutional change will it be worth eating.

Of course, the demands of the reconstructive method are enormous, since one would need to show for each specific conception of an ideal invoked that it is embodied in real political institutions and that it best captures the tendencies of overall institutional history. Because of space and exposition constraints, this paper will not follow the order of presentation—nor present the requisite level of evidence—one would expect from the reconstructive method. The plan is rather to give first, in Sect. 9.2, a thumbnail sketch of the broader ideals of deliberative democratic constitutionalism I believe are at the core of the institutions of modern constitutional democracies. While this paper merely assumes these broad ideals as sufficiently established through reconstruction of actual political reality, I will briefly indicate the general kinds of reasons I take to support them. Then in Sect. 9.3, the paper turns to its main work of articulating an evaluative framework, comprised of six criteria, for assessing various mechanisms of constitutional change. I argue that democratic forms of constitutional change embody six distinct ideals—operationalizability, structural independence, democratic co-authorship, political equality, inclusive sensitivity, and reasons-responsiveness—and that we can use these ideals to gauge the normative worth of different mechanisms for carrying out such change. I put forward this framework in a conjectural mode: as a set of reconstructive hypotheses about the crucial ideals that are embodied in the institutional designs of constitutional democracies. While these hypotheses are developed through a series of case studies which appear to capture the direction of institutional innovation, the full establishment (or disconfirmation) of each would require much more empirical work. The final Sect. 9.4 is less than conclusive, ensuing rather in a set of open questions that a framework such as this would need to address.

9.2 Ideals of Deliberative Democratic Constitutionalism

9.2.1 Basics of the Normative Framework

This paper simply assumes the attractiveness of a particular conception of political normativity labeled 'deliberative democratic constitutionalism.' The basic idea here is that political arrangements are legitimate to the extent to which they approximately realize in and through their institutions that normative conception. For the purposes of this paper, that conception insists on a number of points. First, constitutional democracy is the preferred form of political arrangement. Second, democratic procedures must be constitutionally secured, that is they must be more secured against being changed by current political actors than the first-order policies those actors decide upon through using those procedures. Third, the constitutionalized procedures must themselves, nevertheless, be alterable through democratic means. And fourth, both the ordinary democratic procedures which are constitutionally secured and the procedures for democratic alteration of the constitution must be systematically linked to and dependent upon open, inclusive and diverse public spheres of debate and deliberation that foster wide participation across multiple sites and result in high-quality processes of knowledge and opinion formation.

While I cannot adequately argue for this conception here—let alone provide the reconstructive evidence such arguments would require—it may help to get a sense of some of the reasons behind claims that will be key once we turn to institutional possibilities for constitutional change. Thus I will explicate and briefly indicate arguments in favor of some of the conception's building blocks: co-authorship, proceduralism, democratic constitutionalism, and structured deliberation. With these more abstract and philosophical points in hand, we can turn to the institutions of constitutional change and evaluative criteria arising from them in the next section.

9.2.2 Co-authorship

I assume that political arrangements must be democratic (among other qualities) in order to be legitimate. To be democratic, more specifically, political arrangements must—somehow or other and to a greater rather than a lesser degree—allow those persons subject to a polity's laws to understand themselves simultaneously as the co-authors of those laws. This idea was first most clearly articulated in Rousseau's conception of freedom as autonomy: in order to be both free and under laws, one must in some sense be the author of those laws one is subject to (Rousseau 1997: Book I, chapter 6). But if individuals are to live with others, with the same laws applying to all, then individuals can only be free to the extent to which they can understand themselves as giving themselves their own laws in a collective process of co-legislation. To be sure, this is a demanding ideal and it is not immediately clear which political arrangements could possibly approximate it in reality. But it seems to me that this conception captures the core of the notion of what self-rule could mean in a context of a polity, a context of many selves whose interactions require a common framework of rules. Furthermore, it gives the clearest articulation of the reason why democracies alone put the value of political equality at their center. Individuals must be not only equally subject to the laws—as the rule of law tradition insists—but they also must have equal authority over the creation, modification and extinction of those very laws. Otherwise they are subject to laws they themselves have had no hand in co-authoring: they are rather heteronomous, politically unfree, subject to the will of others.

9.2.3 Proceduralism

One happy solution to the problem of collective co-authorship of common rules would simply be for all subjects to already agree on almost all matters relevant to political decisions before they enter into a process of co-authoring law—in other words, full pre-existing agreement on fundamental values, on the proper priority relations between such values, on the proper policy applications of those values, on the correct ways to understand and assess relevant social facts, and so on. Rousseau himself seemed to endorse this solution but, in consequence, ended up arguing that only a tiny republic could possibly be democratic: where all can be known to one another, where generations of education and civic training have gotten all thinking along the same lines, and, where certain authoritarian policies—a political censor of information, culture and education, a public religious test, and so on—ensured the maintenance of extensive collective agreement on matters of political substance. That distinctly is not the world we live in, nor I think, a world we should hope for. As thinkers from Weber to Berlin to Rawls have stressed, modern complex societies evince a buzzing blooming variety of substantive opinions on political matters, and importantly, since that diversity is the product of well functioning practical reason, we should not expect all of that disagreement to be dispelled over time.

Given then the circumstances of politics as we know them then—the need for collective decisions and persistent reasonable disagreement on matters of political substance—and given our commitment to democratic co-authorship as a key criterion of legitimacy, there is little hope that citizens' substantive agreement with the outcomes of political processes could be a reliable source for the legitimacy of the political arrangements.[3] In short, a substantialist understanding of democratic legitimacy simply does not seem possible, that is, one that gauges the moral worthiness of the outcomes of democratic processes against some determinate substantive ideals that are independent of the procedures used to arrive at the decision. Citizens of contemporary pluralistic societies simply can't be expected to agree on such substantive standards. Hence only a proceduralist understanding of legitimacy seems possible, where the moral worth of the outcome of the political process hangs on the fact that the correct (or worthy or reliable or …) procedures have been followed in producing the decision. In the face of reasonable but persistent disagreement where we nevertheless need to make collective decisions, only suitably democratic procedures could warrant the legitimacy of outcomes, outcomes that will not agree with the substantive views of all citizens. The procedures of democratic co-legislation then hold out the promise for citizens to be able to understand themselves as the co-authors of laws they are simultaneously subject to, and so as both free and in consociation.

9.2.4 *Entailments of Proceduralism*

The next obvious questions are: which procedures are the correct (or worthy or reliable or ...) democratic procedures and why? Eschewing any ambitious attempt to answer those questions through the articulation of a full political philosophy here,

[3] Here I follow Waldron's convincing articulation of the circumstances of politics (Waldron 1999, 100–103).

we can note some clear procedural entailments of what has been said so far. To begin, suitable procedures and their institutional realizations will need to ensure the *political equality* of citizens. This means that all citizens must have some significantly equal opportunities to influence, in some way or another, the lawmaking process.

Furthermore, the scope of democratic lawmaking cannot be restricted only to policy decisions or to matters of who will represent their interests in such policy matters. Rather, the political equality of citizens must extend beyond matters of immediate policy, to *all fundamental matters* of the basic laws themselves. Citizens cannot understand themselves as co-authors of the law if their powers do not extend to all of the law, including the law that structures the basic political arrangements—the constitutional arrangements—within which ordinary lawmaking happens.

The exercise of democratic political equality must be, however, more than a one shot deal. Popular sovereignty cannot be exhausted in one originary, revolutionary moment, allowed only to be exercised by the great men of the past. In part this is due to an essential fallibility built into the idea of democracy—the peristent possibility that the political process may have failed to properly account for essential considerations in making past decisions—and in part due to the political equality of individuals which must extend across generations—political equality is not reserved only for our ancestors. These points entail the essential *revisability* of co-authored law: there are to be no aspects of the current legal regime and the political arrangements it structures that are structurally walled off from future reconsideration.

Finally, however, because the proceduralist conception of democratic legitimacy puts so much normative stress on procedures, basic procedures that structure the political process itself are special. They set the ground rules for collective decision-making itself. Thus there is an in-principle distinction between ordinary lawmaking and fundamental lawmaking, between the workings of constituted powers and the constitutional structuring of those powers, between the operation of political processes and the procedural structuring of those processes themselves. Hence democratic proceduralism requires some kinds of formal and / or institutional separation between those exercises of political co-authorship that are functioning according to extant rules and those that are changing those very rules. In short, it requires some form of *constitutionalization* of democracy. Although I can't argue for it here, I believe this criterion is best met in a formal distinction between fundamental and ordinary law and an institutional securing of that distinction through moderate forms of entrenchment, that is, moderate ways for making that fundamental law more difficult to change than ordinary law. Revisability entails that even constitutional essentials should not be impossible to change in the future.[4]

[4]This conception thus rejects hard, unchangeable entrenchments as evident, for instance, in the German Basic Law's Article 79, section 3 with respect to fundamental individual rights guaranteed in Articles 1 through 20. See further Sect. 9.3.4 below.

9.2.5 Democratic Constitutional Democracy

The conception of legitimacy presented so far insists that political regimes must be, to coin a phrase, democratic constitutional democracies. That is, they must positively structure procedures for realizing democracy, namely the political equality of citizens interpreted as the equality of individuals in a process of co-authoring the laws they are simultaneously subject to—hence *constitutionalized* democracy. But at the same time, those very constitutional structures must themselves be open to democratic change—hence *democratic* constitutionalism. That means, I would suggest, that any institutions or procedures responsible for carrying out processes of constitutional change must be open to and available for the constituent power of citizens in the here and now. And this requirement becomes even more pressing once we see that constitutional systems are not stable clockwork-like mechanisms that continue to run in the same way perpetually. Rather, any constitutional system will itself be subject to modification and elaboration over time as the constitutional principles and institutions go to work on the ordinary problems of government and law.[5] If citizens are to understand themselves as co-authors of the law they are subject to, they must be able to recalibrate the basic law that structures their own practices of self-rule.

9.2.6 Structured Deliberation

I have stressed so far the central importance of well-structured democratic procedures, but have not said much about the actual procedures. One dominant conception of democratic procedures—captured in both Schumpeter's minimalist model of democracy and Dahl's different pluralist model (Dahl 1989; Schumpeter 1943)—has centered on the use of majoritarian voting as an efficient way of aggregating across individual subject's private interests, thereby finding, and serving through government policy, the largest bloc of identical or overlapping individual, pre-political desires. As is well-known, however, majority rule just as majority rule is not particularly attractive.[6] To see this, consider the problem of the loser in such a democracy: why should the fact that my private interests are shared by less than half

[5] I have argued elsewhere that in constitutional systems where there are institutions specifically dedicated to constitutional review—e.g., normal appellate courts or constitutional courts—it is inevitable that constitutional modification will occur through the exercise of constitutional review (Zurn 2007). See further Sect. 9.3.5 below. The scope for constitutional modification through normal political processes is even greater, perhaps, through the interactions of the other centers of power in and outside of government. Consider, for example, the many dynamics through which civilian control of militaries waxes and wanes under different political conditions in different constitutional democracies.

[6] In addition to this normative deficit, majority procedures have real problems of arbitrary cycling and of agenda manipulation. See (Arrow 1963) and (Riker 1982) respectively. Deliberative democracy promises to address these problems as well, but that is beyond the scope of this paper.

of the electorate put me under an obligation to serve the interests of the majority? Pure majoritarian decisions that are intended to merely aggregate private interests provide insufficiently compelling reasons for citizens to trust the outcomes of those procedures.

In contrast to the aggregative conception, a deliberative conception insists that democracy is not exhausted by either voting or majority rule. It conceives of voting, in fact, as a temporary caesura to ongoing deliberation and collective decision-making, a caesura required by the need for binding collective decisions under realistic constraints of time, knowledge and reasonable pluralism. And majority rule is just one threshold for decision making on a continuum between only one person in favor and full consensus. Deliberative conceptions of democracy insist then, to begin with, that good political procedures must encourage deliberation in wide and open public spheres. Of course, this alone doesn't distinguish deliberative from aggregative models, since even the latter insist that majoritarian aggregation is more accurate with the better information provided by open public spheres—consider the traditional epistemic defenses of a free 'marketplace of ideas' and a free and independent press.

The distinctive core of the deliberative conception is, it seems to me, the notion of the reasons-responsiveness of government, rather than its responsiveness to various particular constellations of social, legal or political power. The key is that state action must be responsive to good reasons. Specifically, public reasoning practices among citizens and officials should have some direct or indirect influence over the formation of, decision upon, and execution of governmental policy and action. So deliberative democracy does not just stress reasoned public discussion—it stresses *politically relevant and effective* reasoned discussion. There must be a constitutive link between public reasoning and the use of government power. Why insist on reasons-responsiveness? It should be understood as a demand of politically equal co-authorship. Political equality on this model is not the equal impact of each subject's private desires on government policy, but rather the equal part each has to play in collecting, sifting, sorting and evaluating public reasons for public action. In turn (ideally) reason-responsive government action is equally justifiable to each citizen precisely because it is responsive to reasons rather than arbitrary inequalities of power. Hence the procedures of constitutional democracy will need to institutionally structure both high quality collective deliberations and ensure that those deliberations have a constitutive impact on the outcomes of government decisions.

One more point from deliberative democracy should be stressed here. Quality reasons must draw from a wide and diverse pool. Although this is in part an epistemic consideration about the increasing rationality of opinions and decisions with increasing diversity of contents and reasoners, it is also in part a normative consideration. In particular, to the extent to which individuals are subject to collective decisions those decisions must take into account the actual and potential effects of those decisions, and those affected must therefore be involved in collecting, sifting and evaluating that evidence. In short, deliberation must not only have real political influence, but it also must be widely inclusive and participatory.[7]

[7]This inclusive, participatory position is in some real contrast with more 'expertocratic' strains of some deliberative democratic theory and some republican political theory, strains which assume

9.3 Institutional Possibilities for Democratic Constitutional Change

This section begins to build a framework of evaluative criteria for assessing mechanisms of constitutional change out of the consideration of a few case studies of various institutional experiments. The idea again is that we should reconstruct the key normative ideas by seeing which ideals actually underlie and animate various institutional arrangements and innovations. With the caveats about the need for much more empirical work in mind, I provisionally suggest that there are six crucial normative criteria for assessing constitutional change mechanisms: operationalizability, structural independence, democratic co-authorship, political equality, inclusive sensitivity, and reasons-responsiveness. The order of presentation of the different mechanisms is intended to clarify these criteria, in particular how each case responds to the deficits of the previous case. This overly neat presentation should not, however, be understood as any actual historical sequence, nor even less as some kind of claim about the necessary direction of progress. And again, the normative criteria extracted from these case studies should be seen as reconstructive hypotheses—subject to further research for full support or disconfirmation—rather than reconstructive conclusions.

9.3.1 Direct Democratic Constitutional Change

Let me start by considering an imaginary institutional arrangement: namely, some form of anti-constitutional direct democracy. The idea here involves direct democracy—such as regular periodic assemblies of the entire enfranchised populace—where that assembly has plenary power over all of the law governing the populace. Hence in this scenario, the legislative power is entirely in the hands of the assembled demos. And that legislative power is indistinguishable from a constituent power, since exactly the same procedures apply to passing all forms of law, statutory and regulatory as well as constitutional. Thus the arrangement is anti-constitutional: all laws are equally easy to change; the assembled demos cannot bind future assemblies; every assembly has the ability to overturn any past legal enactments, including any fundamental or constitutive law.[8]

---

that high quality deliberation is best carried out by specialists and experts. Here I side with the upshot of Aristotle's argument for wide deliberation in the *Politics:* "the many, of whom each individual is but an ordinary person, when they meet together may very likely be better than the few good, if regarded not individually but collectively, just as a feast to which many contribute is better than a dinner provided out of a single purse. For each individual among the many has a share of virtue and prudence, and when they meet together, they become in a manner one man, who has many feet, and hands, and senses; that is a figure of their mind and disposition. Hence the many are better judges than a single man of music and poetry; for some understand one part, and some another, and among them they understand the whole" (Aristotle 1943, 1281b1–16).

[8] We could call this a 'Rousseauian' arrangement, but for one feature: Rousseau allows for enactment thresholds to be modified—somewhere between a bare majority and full consensual unanim-

Prima facie such an arrangement satisfies many of the conditions I indicated earlier as central to deliberative democratic constitutionalism. Fundamentally, it is a quite straightforward way of structuring the idea of co-authorship of laws. Citizens are here directly involved in giving themselves the laws, enabling them to understand themselves as simultaneous subjects and authors of the law. Furthermore, suitably designed decision procedures for the assembly should be able to track closely other key conditions. Political equality can be easily secured when all citizens have roughly equal opportunities to influence the lawmaking process. Such political equality is extended to fundamental matters since no law is off limits. And the plenary authority over the entire legal corpus at every assembly means that revisability is likewise ensured. As described so far, these arrangements do not necessarily involve structured deliberation; the assembly could use simple majority rules on secret ballots for both initiating and enacting proposals. More naturally however, we would expect practices of debate and deliberation to arise and it should not be difficult to structure them by procedures sensitive to the other conditions indicated. In particular, with deliberative mechanisms for the exchange of information, opinions and reasons, political equality is enriched beyond a simple equal vote, encompassing real opportunities for equal voice and qualitative input into the law-making process. And because the entire enfranchised citizenry is involved, we should expect the process of opinion formation and decision making to cast as wide an epistemic net as possible: the assembly of all makes it possible for all kinds of different information and opinions from the broadest swath of citizens to be canvassed and included. Decision processes should then be not only responsive to reasons, but quite inclusively sensitive to the broadest diversity of reasons.

Nevertheless, there is one crucial missing condition: namely, some form of constitutionalism, some form of formal or institutional separation of the exercise of ordinary legislative and constitutional legislative powers. This could of course be relatively easily remedied by the adoption of a formal distinction between ordinary legislative and constitutional legislative activity, a distinction reinforced by making the process of constitutional change more difficult and subject to higher standards of opinion formation. Such moves would then constitutionalize the procedures of direct democracy, thereby enabling citizens to understand the outcomes of those procedures as legitimate and binding even when citizens disagree with the substance of those decisions—as many inevitably will under conditions of persistent pluralistic disagreement on matters of substance.

ity—according to the trade-offs needed between alacrity and the seriousness of the issue at stake (Rousseau 1997: Book IV, chapter 2). Even so, however, his arrangement is still anti-constitutional in this sense: no law is put out of reach of a current assembly. In fact, every assembly opens first with this question: "whether it please the Sovereign to retain the present form of Government?" (Rousseau 1997: 120, Book III, chapter 18).

9.3.2 *Legislative Constitutional Change and Operationalizability*

Its no accident that so far I have been referring only to a merely imaginary arrangement. Despite whatever normative attractions some form of direct democracy might have, the fact is that all existing national systems for democratic lawmaking employ elected representative bodies to carry out legislative functions. And the reasons for this are not at all obscure. The costs of operationalizing direct democracy are simply so high as to make it unfeasible for populous, complex and extended nation-states. In particular, the monetary and coordination costs of assembling the entire enfranchised populace regularly, and the time and decision costs of having them deliberate and decide together, are jointly exorbitant.

From a reconstructive perspective it might seem perverse to consider an unrealized arrangement: what does a fantasy have to do with the normative content imminent in historically actualized institutions? I would argue however, that unanimous rejection of the most direct institutional realization of democratic self-rule tells us about a key normative criterion: *operationalizability*. Whatever other values they promise to realize, institutions that cannot be actualized are deficient. It is thus reconstructively clear why all national democratic legislative systems employ indirect modes of democracy.

9.3.3 *Agency Problems and Structural Independence*

With the move from direct to representative systems, however, new normative concerns arise. Most pressingly, there is the general problem of tying officials' actions to the interests, opinions and reasonings of the demos—the central problem of agent-principle relations. It is well beyond the reach of this paper to say anything in general about the problems of agency encountered by representative democracies. But it does seem to me that with agents for law-making, it becomes ever more important to insist on mechanisms for separating the function of ordinary and constitutional legislation. This can be seen most simply by recalling that constitutional procedures are those which structure not only ordinary lawmaking procedures, but also regulate the elections of representatives and structure the workings of government. As Ely among others have made abundantly clear, then, representative democracy is subject to a particular form of procedural distrust: distrust that legislators will manipulate constitutional procedures to freeze the ordinary mechanisms of democratic change and to insulate themselves or status quo arrangements from challenge (Ely 1980). If one thinks that the legitimacy of a system of law making is fully dependent on the integrity of the processes by which those laws are made—as is insisted upon by the proceduralist paradigm urged here—then the processes of constitutional change are of even greater concern than the usual functions of lawmaking and governance.

Agency problems then recommend a real form of *structural independence* between ordinary legislative and constitutional legislative processes. There ought to be a clear institutional demarcation of the difference between the ordinary exercise of government business through established procedures, and, the people's constituent power of changing the procedures—the fundamental institutions and basic rights protections—that are the procedural warrant for the legitimacy of the outcomes of ordinary political processes. Hence whatever mechanisms are available for constitutional change, they ought not to be easily manipulated by current representative majorities in order to lock in future constitutional procedures that systematically favor them or systematically foreclose ongoing possibilities for democratic change.

The need for structural independence is perhaps most easily seen in the recent constitutional history of Venezuela, where the elected officials of one political party (the PSUV forcefully led by the charismatic Hugo Chávez) were able in subsequent rounds of constitutional change to effectively close off avenues of political change and defang opposition candidates and parties. The sequence of changes was inaugurated by the new 1999 Venezuelan constitution, which laid the grounds for collapsing any independence of ordinary and constitutional legislative functions. The 1999 constitution significantly weakened the legislature in relation to the executive, it significantly centralized and strengthened the executive in the direction of strong presidentialism, and importantly, it specified a quite easy threshold for constitutional amendment. Initiatives for constitutional amendments are very easy to propose—either by the president, by 30 % of the legislature, or by 15 % of enfranchised citizens—and ratification of proposed amendments is quite easy—a simple majority in the unicameral national legislature followed quickly (within 30 days) by a simple majority in a national referendum. In effect, this amendment procedure adds only one additional obstacle beyond the requirements for ordinary legislative enactment: namely a bare majoritarian national referendum following legislative action so quickly that there is little time for extended public discussion or debate.

But even that bare recitation of the formal amendment procedures makes it look harder than it is, given the particularly robust and overlapping forms of the centralization of power in the presidency. Consider for instance a major constitutional amendment achieved 10 years after the new constitution: Amendment 1. In that case not only was the majority in the National Assembly effectively voting in lock step with the wishes of president Chávez, but the entire apparatus of the state was brought to bear in a one-sided propaganda campaign to convince voters to ratify the amendment. And the content of 2009's Amendment no. 1? The abolition of term limits for the president, for national and regional legislators, and regional and municipal governors—effectively closing paths of political change and ensuring the long-term single-party dominance of the PSUV.[9]

[9] There is of course much more detail that ought to be added to this story in order to understand it fully. In particular, one would need to account for specific social, economic and cultural conditions, as well as pre-Chávez political history, in Venezuela during this period. Legislation passed in 2004 is also important, which allowed for the destruction of judicial independence through a

It is perhaps not overly dramatic to say that because of a lack of structural independence between ordinary and constitutional mechanisms, Venezuelan constitutionalism has enabled apparently democratic mechanisms to be used strategically in order to foreclose the ongoing possibility of open and competitive democracy for the future.

9.3.4 Entrenchments and Democratic Co-authorship

In the light of such dangers, one might think that constitutional obduracy is a preferred way to ensure the structural independence of constitutional change mechanisms from current regime office holders. Making constitutional provisions very hard to change—even making some impossible to change in the form of hard entrenchments—would seem to protect against future agency problems where office holders attempt to change political procedures in order to capture the political system and remain in power. Constitutional amendment procedures might then be set to require a very high bar to enactment—for instance, as in the United States or Australian constitutions—or even set aside certain portions of the constitution as formally not subject to amendment—as in the hard entrenchments of senatorial representation in the U.S. or of certain fundamental individual rights in the German basic law. Comparative scholarship has established, however, that there are significant perils associated with overly obdurate constitutions. For instance, there is a significant correlation between constitutional flexibility and constitutional longevity (Elkins et al. 2009).[10] Overly rigid constitutions are, to be blunt, more likely to suffer an early death.

More recent constitutions have apparently avoided hard entrenchments.[11] For instance, the exemplary South African constitution of 1996 does make one part more difficult to change than all the other parts: Sect. 2.1 of Chap. 2 concerning the foundational principles of the republic (democracy, human dignity, constitutional supremacy) is harder to change than all other parts of the constitution, subject to 75 % rather than 66 % of the legislature (as well as the normal 6 of 9 regional provinces for amendments affecting regional powers). But even then, these foundational

court packing scheme. And the story would need to mention the failure of a similar attempt at constitutional amendment in 2007 in the face of popular protests. Nevertheless, I believe the rudiments of the story for my purposes—overly easy amendment procedures leading to the collapse of any structural independence between ordinary and constitutional legislation mechanisms—would be unchanged in the main by these and other necessary details.

[10] It should be noted that they also find that constitutions that are too easy to amend suffer diminished longevity. There is then, as they put it, a kind of Goldilocks character to constitutional obduracy, a "just right" balance between two extremes, at least insofar as the long life of constitutions is concerned.

[11] This is a hypothesis that needs further empirical work to support, especially to see whether cases like Brazil's 1988 constitutional entrenchment of certain elements like federalism, the franchise and individual rights are outliers, as I suppose, or more common than that.

principles are not impossible to change, only harder than other constitutional principles. From a normative perspective, it seems clear why hard entrenchments are to be avoided: they violate the criterion of *democratic co-authorship*. In effect, hard entrenchments establish that the people are to be subject to some laws that they themselves cannot alter, or at least cannot alter without a revolutionary replacement of the constitution in its entirety. Thus even the foundational principles of the South African constitutional settlement are in-principle open to democratic renegotiation into the future, even as they are set aside as especially fundamental to the republic—as one would predict from the need for constitutional structuration itself. Democratic co-authorship ought not stop at ordinary legislation, or even at some subset of constitutional law, but must extend to all fundamental matters of law, otherwise subjects can only understand themselves as passive subjects of the lawmaking of others. Apart from hard entrenchments, very difficult procedures for constitutional amendment can also effectively foreclose possibilities for democratic co-authorship of constitutional law, even if they remain in-principle possibilities.

9.3.5 Judicial Interpretation and Political Equality

In light of both pressures for constitutional adaptation to changing conditions and the negative correlation between constitutional obduracy and longevity, it should be no surprise that constitutions with formally rigid change procedures have in fact adopted a number of mechanisms for constitutional change apart from formal amendment procedures. Most prominent here is, of course, constitutional change carried out by judiciaries, usually through the exercise of powers for the judicial review of legislation, regulation, and administrative action. For instance, in his comparative study of 36 democratic nation-states between the end of World War II and the mid 1990s, Lijphart found a statistically significant positive correlation between increasing constitutional rigidity and the likelihood of strong judicial review, that is, assertive forms of judicial policy making with respect to constitutional issues (Lijphart 1999). More recent literature on the judicialization of politics—including constitutional politics—shows that there is a real shift in constitutional legislation away from more democratically accountable actors and towards more politically insulated judiciaries (Ginsburg 2003; Hirschl 2006; Shapiro and Sweet 2002; Stone Sweet 2000; Tate and Vallinder 1995).

It is well beyond the scope of this paper to fully evaluate issues of judicial review; instead I will make just three points concerning the employment of the judiciary as constitutional legislators. The first point is that the criteria of both operationalizability and structural independence speak in favor of constitutional change through judicial interpretation of constitutional law. On the one hand, judiciaries must already specify legal provisions of whatever form in the routine application of those provisions to concrete cases—constitutional provisions no less than any other. It is then an easy mechanism to operationalize. On the other hand, judiciaries are regularly insulated in a number of ways from the vicissitudes of politics and from pressures facing electorally accountable political actors in order to ensure fairness to individual litigants. Judiciaries involved in constitutional change through interpretation are therefore already structurally independent of the ordinary process of legislation carried out by electorally accountable politicians. This structural independence is, of course, the basis for proceduralist justifications for placing the power of constitutional review in the hands of the judiciary: they are to be, in effect, the unelected guardians of the very procedures of democracy, that is, of the constitutional rules which proceduralists take to warrant the legitimacy of democratic outcomes in the first place (Dahl 1989; Ely 1980; Habermas 1996; Zurn 2007).

The second point is that, nevertheless, it will be very difficult, if not impossible, to cabin courts with powers of constitutional review to the pure function of constitutional protection. Because of several different reasons—the abstract and undertheorized character of constitutional norms, judicial responses to informal political changes in a constitutional system and to general social changes, doctrinal development and legal path dependence—court-based constitutional protection will inevitably transmute into positive constitutional elaboration.[12] The clear line between judicial protection of a legal provision and judicial elaboration of the content of law will be constantly undermined: protection will inevitably bleed into elaboration for both ordinary and constitutional law. In the course of enforcing the (constitutional) rules of the political game, then, judiciaries with powers of constitutional review will inevitably become much more than referees: they will become constitutional legislators.

The holders of constituent power however, thirdly, are emphatically supposed to be the entirety of the citizenry in democratic theory (of whatever form). If only a small subset of citizens are the decisive constitutional legislators, and if those legislators are institutionally positioned exactly so that they are not subject to attempts to influence them by the demos, then constitutional change through the judiciary emphatically violates a baseline criterion of *political equality*. Even if that constitutional elaboration is carried out conscientiously and benevolently, it is still a paternalist institutionalization of the power for constitutional change. This worry about judicial paternalism with respect to fundamental constitutional procedures is, I think, the real basis of the democratic complaint against judicial review, and not the extremely misleading idea that judicial review is suspect because it is counter-majoritarian. For there are any number of counter-majoritarian political procedures which are fully consistent with political equality. For instance, counter-majoritarian voting rules requiring either full consensual unanimity or various levels of super-majorities nevertheless afford each voter an opportunity equal with all other voters to influence the outcome of a decision. The democratic problem with constitutional change through judicial interpretation is that every citizen is distinctly not afforded an equal opportunity to influence the law-making occurring—the problem is then one of political equality, not majoritarianism.[13] When judges are empowered as

[12] For more detail, see (Zurn 2007, 256–264).

[13] In terms of debates in the United States, the proper democratic complaint against judicial review is Learned Hand's, not Alexander Bickel's.

constitutional legislators—perhaps out of the necessity for some agents of change in overly obdurate and rigid constitutional systems—enfranchised citizens are effectively shut out of that constitutional law-making process and citizens thereby become mere subjects of laws authored and paternalistically imposed by others.[14]

9.3.6 *Veto Players and Inclusive Sensitivity*

To my knowledge, no democratic constitution formally places the power of constitutional amendment in the hands of courts. Rather, the overwhelming majority provide for amendment through either elected legislatures and executives, or various forms of popular initiative from citizens themselves, or various forms of special constituent assembly of democratically accountable representatives—or frequently

[14]There are also serious normative consequences of employing courts to carry out constitutional change for two of the other six criteria beyond political equality: reasons-responsiveness and inclusive sensitivity. Courts are usually very responsive to reasons in comparison with other political institutions—after all, they often engage in structured reason-giving for their decisions—but they are not particularly responsive to the right kinds of reasons. Especially when constitutional interpretation is carried out concretely—elaborating law through determinate cases and controversies of individual litigants—and where strong traditions of doctrinal development and *stare decisis* have arisen, the reason-giving of courts is excessively *juristic*: focused upon legalistic minutiae incident to the particularities of the case presentation and the finer points of judicially-crafted doctrinal rules, principles and presumptions—rather than on the broad constitutional policy and principle issues at stake in changing fundamental law. Secondly, court-based constitutional change is quite likely to ignore the interests and opinions of wide swaths of the population, and so will perform poorly in the light of the criterion of inclusive sensitivity. The issue here is the available pool of reasons and sensitivity to a diversity of problems felt throughout a society and especially by individuals and groups whose issues and concerns are not felt, noticed nor well represented by political and social elites, nor by those who have the money and political interests to bring strategic lawsuits to change constitutional law. Consider, for example, the ways in which case presentations often systematically ignore the interests of those affected by policy change simply because those interests are not represented by the incident litigants. A recent striking example in U.S. constitutional jurisprudence: a case about health insurance provisions to cover the costs of contraception where the litigants were employers and the government. Hence, before the court, nobody represented those who would actually have to pay or not pay for the contraception, and endure the consequences (Burwell v. Hobby Lobby, 573 U.S. __ (2014))! This insensitivity is standard fare for courts: in part because courts simply do not have the information collection and processing capabilities to gauge the likely effects of various policy regimes, and in part because of basic structural and procedural requirements for the fair application of law to individual cases. (It may be that the recent Latin American development of Amparo proceedings is significantly decreasing the informational deficit of constitutional courts). The general unsuitability of judicial reason-giving and narrow informational basis for purposes of constitutional law making are treated in a lengthy case study of United States jurisprudence at (Zurn 2007: 163–220). My position is developed in reaction against attempts by deliberative democratic theorists of various stripes—Eisgruber, Michelman, and Rawls—to paint judicial review as democratic precisely because it is 'deliberative'.

from some combination of the three.[15] This is not a mere coincidence: the constituent power is always formally recognized as resting directly or indirectly in the hands of the citizenry, at least in democratic systems. These institutional arrangements lend support to the reconstructive hypothesis that they embody the ideals of democratic co-authorship and political equality.

Furthermore almost all democratic constitutions make constitutional legislation more difficult to pass than ordinary law—lending supporting to the hypothesis concerning structural independence. And even the notable exceptions where there is no formal difference between making constitutional and ordinary law—e.g., the United Kingdom and New Zealand—evince robust informal traditions, norms, and customary practices that distinguish between the two, rendering constitutional changes more difficult.[16] There are however several different characteristic mechanisms for increasing the difficulty of enacting constitutional change. For instance, there can simply be higher supermajority thresholds in the legislature for amendment, typically three-fifths or two-thirds, and less frequently three-quarters. Bicameral systems usually require such supermajorities in both houses. Second or third readings of amendment proposals might be required; intervening elections between those readings can further increase difficulty. All of these amendment mechanisms alone, however, in essence employ the same legislative system—and usually the same legislative players—as used for ordinary lawmaking.

By contrast, empirical research has highlighted a different set of mechanisms as important, giving roles to various actors who are differently situated than normal legislators. For instance, amendment proposals might need to be ratified by regional sub-units of the nation, usually the legislatures of federal states, and usually requiring a slight supermajority of such states. Quite characteristic of newer constitutions, especially in Latin America, amendment proposals must be ratified in popular referenda, usually by majorities or slight supermajorities of ballots cast by ordinary citizens. Finally, many newer constitutions—for example, those of Bolivia (1999), Bulgaria (1991), Colombia (1991), Ecuador (2008), and Venezuela (1999)—require

[15] Some constitutions give constitutional courts *ex ante* review powers over amendment bills: either the power to pass on the constitutionality of amendments after they have been proposed but before they have been ratified by democratic bodies—as for instance in Colombia's 1991 constitution and Sri Lanka's 1978 constitution—or to pass on the constitutionality of amendment bills before promulgation—as in Cambodia's 1993 constitution. Interesting questions arise here of the location of the constituent power, especially when, as in the Colombian case, a court uses a limited procedural jurisdiction over amendments to have more expansive review of the substantive content of amendment proposals (Bernal-Pulido 2013; Colón-Ríos 2011).

[16] Witness recent proposals—themselves the latest in a long line of such proposals—in the United Kingdom to fundamentally reform the House of Lords, the second legislative chamber of Parliament, by reducing its size, making it fully elected, and making its basic principle of representation geographic. These clearly count as fundamental constitutional changes. Formally, at least, they could be pushed through Parliament given sufficient party strength, and using the same procedures as those for ordinary lawmaking. But all involved acknowledge that using those simple procedures alone would be an 'unconstitutional' violation of conventional understandings of the gravity of constitutional change. Thus the most recent reform promoters (notably Labour leader Miliband) propose to hold a constitutional convention to process the proposals.

or permit a form of special constituent assembly for constitutional change proposals. While the former arrangements simply make it harder for normal legislative officials to pass amendments, the latter arrangements introduce 'veto players' into the mix. Empirical research suggests that only the introduction of veto players into amendment schemes actually significantly increases the difficulty of amendment. Rasch and Congleton have shown for OECD countries (and others have confirmed in EU countries (Closa 2012)) that just making it harder for legislatures to ratify amendments (e.g., from three-fifths to two-thirds to three quarters) doesn't much change the amendment rate (Rasch and Congleton 2006). What really affects the amendability of constitutions seems to be the presence or absence of veto players in the process.[17] Because currently empowered political parties can frequently muster supermajorities in the legislature in subsequent elections, blocks to constitutional amendment ratification such as moderate legislative supermajorities over a period of time and after subsequent readings are not very different than blocks to enacting ordinary legislation. Hence, "in the absence of powerful external veto players, it seems that political parties' agreements may sail through even the most stringent constitutional reform procedure" (Closa 2012, 309).

Normatively speaking, the difference in amendment mechanisms with veto players is, I want to suggest, significant. In particular, such a difference speaks to the *inclusive sensitivity* of the mechanism: the presence of veto players ensures that amendments are acceptable to a broad diversity of constituencies with distinct interests, ideological positions, opinions, values and perspectives.[18] The arrangements for changing the fundamental procedures of politics and lawmaking ought to structurally incorporate sureties that the full diversity of affected persons and interests will be accounted for. Hence the difficulty-increasing procedures for amendments are not just about increasing difficulty—even as this is important for maintaining structural independence. Many of those procedures are better understood as broadening the usual pool of information available for—and the sphere of influencers of—constitutional legislation beyond the current party regime and beyond the usual way in which representation is structured across the national legislature and the executive branch. Ratification in the federal sub-units, for instance, should enable a different set of political representatives to have their specific concerns taken into account. And ratification by popular referendum—beyond the way it serves the criteria of democratic co-authorship and political equality—promises some greater

[17]The empirical claims in the text are not yet, it seems, fully established. The controversy goes back to a disagreement between (Lutz 1995) and (Ferejohn 1997) about the amendment rate of state constitutions in the United States—on this, see (Dixon 2011).

[18]Empirical research also indicates the importance of broad inclusion. For instance, inclusion—"the involvement of important groups in society in the design and maintenance of the constitution"—is one of only three design features of constitutions that groundbreaking scholarship identifies as strongly correlated with constitutional longevity (Elkins et al. 2009, 208). The other two are the right balance of flexibility and obduracy (noted above in Sect. 9.3.4) and the right balance between constitutional generality and specificity (a factor orthogonal to the concerns of this paper).

sensitivity to the opinions of all those affected by the proposal beyond the normal channels available for citizen influence on elite politicians and political parties.

To be sure, this greater inclusive sensitivity should not be oversold: after all, if the normal legislature is largely responsible for proposing and writing the amendment in the first place, then the role of veto players is largely confined to a simple *ex post* thumbs-up or thumbs-down, rather than direct *ab initio* substantive input into the qualitative content of the initiative. But if the political public sphere is working well and the legislature is at least partly attuned to the likely opinions of veto players, then we can hope at least for some degree of increasing inclusive sensitivity through the use of ratification veto players, even where the original amendment drafting process is driven exclusively by the legislature.

9.3.7 Constituent Assemblies and Reasons-Responsiveness

This last concern about the degree to which a broad spectrum of the citizenry have real effective input into the substantive content of constitutional amendments—as opposed to a simple power of after-the-fact veto or endorsement of that which has already been authored by others—speaks to a central difference between the way political equality is conceived between aggregative and deliberative conceptions of democracy. In particular, while aggregative conceptions emphasize the equal voting power of each in a process of aggregating over the population's simple endorsements or rejections, deliberative conceptions put more emphasis on the equal access all have to the processes of reason collection and evaluation that lead up to and ensue in the design of a particular proposal. Political equality is not then merely a matter of equal impact registered in an equally weighted vote—even as that is quite important to political equality—but must also involve the equal effective part each can play in the processes of deliberation that ensue in policy creation. Voting is then seen as an egalitarian mechanism for temporarily bringing to a halt ongoing processes of collective reasoning when a decision is needed under constraints of time, knowledge, and reasonable pluralism.

Returning to constitutional amendment procedures, the question then is whether we can envision procedures that not only are broadly sensitive to the voting impact of a wide diversity of citizens—as are constitutional ratification mechanisms subject to veto players—but also sensitive to a wide diversity of politically relevant reasons from a broad spectrum of citizens. Is there a way of making amendment procedures specifically reasons-responsive? Clearly one central way in which democracies can be reasons-responsive is by connecting the actual workings and outputs of representative legislatures to robust processes of public opinion formation in free, open and diverse political public spheres (Habermas 1996: especially chapters 7 and 8). However, if we are concerned about two agency problems regularly faced by legislatures—as I think we should be from everyday experience—then we might worry about whether legislatures alone are sufficiently responsive to a wide diversity of relevant reasons, especially when they are taking the lead role in authoring the substantive content of constitutional proposals. First, given that electoral politics as we know it is largely shaped through political parties and party competition, it turns out that legislatures are frequently captured by currently dominant political parties. In these cases, a dominant party will be able to effectively ignore relevant reasons from other parties that are contrary to their preferred policy outcomes. Second, even if representatives do account for the reasons of other like political elites, they may still be wholly insensitive to the reasons of broad swaths of ordinary citizens who are not able to make effective use of the communications media of the public sphere. Most obviously this comparative communicative disability falls along socioeconomic lines, but it also quite frequently falls along indigenous, national, ethnic, religious and/or racial lines. Hence legislative deliberative processes may suffer from both dominant party capture and elite opinion selectivity. Both problems become normatively more serious the more fundamental the matters are for legislative decision, in particular, when they concern matters of basic constitutional law that is to structure ordinary politics.

It seems to me that constituent assemblies—independently elected bodies with a specific mandate to write proposals for constitutional reform either in the form of amendments or a new constitution—promise to improve reasons-responsiveness over constitutional drafting processes that are legislatively driven. Three features in particular would seem to promote reasons-responsiveness. Because constituent assemblies are specifically designed to consider only issues of constitutional change, their deliberative processes are likely to be better focused on constitutionally relevant reasons. Second, because the elected members are not the same as elected legislators and because they do not stand for re-election to the assembly, their deliberations are likely to be less systematically distorted by the incentives of ordinary electoral and party politics. Third, because the assembly is almost always elected through procedures that ensure a wide representation of different segments of the populace, they are likely to be more sensitive to a broader diversity of reasons, interests and opinions than is a legislature controlled by political party elites. For instance Colombia's 1991 constitution has provisions enabling the convocation of a constituent assembly if both one third of the electorate and both houses of the legislature vote in favor of convening one.[19] Members of the assembly are to be directly elected by citizens through a ballot separate from ordinary legislative elections. While the assembly meets, the legislature's powers are suspended. Reform proposals from the assembly are then ratified when agreed to by both a legislative majority and a popular referendum. Such arrangements promise the three deliberative advantages indicated above of an exclusive constitutional focus, of insulation from ordinary electoral politics, and of broader representation of the diversity of available reasons.

[19] Colombia's 1991 constitution was itself written by a constituent assembly, albeit a procedurally irregular one in the sense that the possibility for such an assembly was not cognized in the 1886 constitution previously in force. Nevertheless, after a popular ballot initiative passed in 1990 calling for a constituent assembly to draft a new constitution, such an assembly was held, and a new constitution was drafted and enacted.

That at least is the theory, even if it is not always born out in practice—actual cases are decidedly mixed from the normative point of view of democratic constitutionalism.[20] Brazil's successful transition from military dictatorship to stable constitutional democracy was formally achieved through the adoption in 1988 of a constitution written over 2 years through a national constituent assembly. While the members of the constituent assembly were in fact simply the current members of the legislature meeting in special sessions as an assembly, the procedures adopted in the drafting phase not only required input from a diverse representation of social movements, political interests and ideological positions, they also ensured a great deal of public input through comments, hearings and largely open proceedings.

The successfully democratic Brazilian experience contrasts, however, with Venezuela's 1999 constituent assembly process. While coming into power in 1998, Venezuelan president Chávez promised a referendum to call for a constituent assembly to replace the then-in-force 1961 constitution, even though the latter had no provisions for such an assembly. With very strong support in the referendum (92 % and 86 % on the two questions), an assembly was convened under electoral laws that strongly favored members of the president's party—the party gained 120 of the assembly's 131 seats. The assembly itself wrote the new constitution very quickly, in 2 months. The assembly's debates were well publicized in the drafting phase and, once drafted, the constitutional proposals were subject to inclusive debate with many different opinions sectors of society represented (Landau 2012, 941). The proposal was ratified by a significant majority of voters (over 70 %) in a national referendum. Nevertheless, the new constitution created a government with political power strongly centralized under the authority of a charismatic president, a centralization that has increased as that constitutional settlement has developed—with dramatic results for the loss of structural independence, as discussed above in Sect. 9.3.3. While the Venezuelan case presents a fairly good picture of the way constituent assemblies can heighten broad and inclusive democratic sensitivity, it certainly did not avoid the problem of dominant party capture: indeed, the process made it worse by constitutionalizing capture.

Another even more cautionary tale is provided by Bolivia where an irregular and complicated process between 2006 and 2009 led to the formation of a constituent assembly and the eventual ratification of a new constitution. Simplified, the story begins in 2006 after newly elected president Morales took office in 2005. Employing provisions for constitutional replacement in the 1967 constitution, the legislature approved, by the required two thirds majority, the convocation of a constituent assembly for the total reform of the constitution. After convening in 2007, the assembly was subject to a great deal of disagreement, power struggles and controversy, ensuing in sometimes violent protest. Ominously, after the diverse parties in the assembly failed to come to a agreement, the assembly moved locations twice. After the first move, opposition members refused to participate and, after the second

[20] Again, these recitations of the cases are overly simplified and purged of potentially relevant detail; it is surely an open question whether I have simplified away from factors of crucial importance.

move, opposition members were forcibly prevented from entering the assembly. Nevertheless, by the end of 2007 the remainder of the assembly delivered a draft to the legislature. More political troubles engulfed the process during 2008 until finally a compromise was reached by elites, and in 2009 a popular referendum was finally held that ratified the new constitution with a 61 % majority of the voters. Even without all the necessary detail, it is hard to consider the recent, troublesomely violent and irregular Bolivian process of constitutional change particularly reasons-responsive (not to mention concerns about political equality and inclusive sensitivity).

Perhaps these cautionary tales should not surprise, since constituent assemblies are usually not called in times of political calm and citizen satisfaction with government; they tend rather to be products of crises of governance of one form or another (Negretto 2012). But Iceland's recent experience with a constituent assembly—one born out of the deeply impactful 2008 financial crisis—shows that, when suitably designed and taking advantage of the latest forms of communications technology, such assemblies can evince real improvements in both inclusive sensitivity and reasons-responsiveness. Told briefly, the story is that a collective of grassroots movements organized a kind of proto-constituent assembly called the National Assembly in 2009, three fourths of whose membership was drawn from randomly generated citizens and one fourth from political institutions and associations. The purpose was to brainstorm the key ideals for the future of Iceland through well-designed deliberative small-group discussions combined with larger plenary sessions. In 2010, the legislature established a formal constituent assembly comprised of 25 individuals elected in national elections—the 'Constitutional Council'—in order to revise the 1944 constitution.[21] The legislature also organized a one-day 'Constitutional Gathering' as a participatory event for ordinary citizens before the elections to the assembly. The constituent assembly itself drew heavily on citizen input into its deliberations, particularly through the use of internet communications media. A draft constitution ensued from a full consensus of the assembly and was presented to the legislature in 2011.[22] The draft was endorsed in a non-binding advisory referendum in 2012 (with a 67 % popular majority), but to this date, the proposed constitution is in limbo, as it has not been ratified by the legislature.

[21] I have simplified the story by leaving out the unfortunate intervention of Iceland's supreme court in 2011, attempting to overturn the election of the Constitutional Council's members on questionable grounds. This court ruling was effectively rejected by the legislature by simply appointing the officials actually elected to the Council. There is some legitimate concern about how inclusive the membership of the Council turned out to be. Most of the membership was drawn from established political elites; Reykjavík was over-represented whereas other regions under-represented; and, working and lower classes were under-represented (Landemore 2014).

[22] It seems that many of the institutional innovations were directly modeled on the deliberative democratic opinion polling and decisional forums designed by James Fishkin and allied democratic theorists (Fishkin 2009), including proposals for a national deliberation day (Ackerman and Fishkin 2004), and prominently employing sortition as an alternative mechanism for ensuring broad representation and political equality (at least in the earlier consultative National Assembly)—even if not all procedures met all of Fishkin's preferred criteria (Landemore 2014, 18–20).

This was very much a process of proposed constitutional change that began 'from below' and it maintained throughout a remarkable openness to and constitutive connections with broad and diverse populations, interests and opinions throughout the populace. "The originality and unprecedented nature of the whole process lies clearly in the explicit emphasis on citizen-driven constitutional reform, a form of 'crowd-sourcing' in the form of a civic brain-storming session, and the explicit exclusion of members of political parties to participate in either the National Gathering or to stand for elections for the Constitutional Council. The citizen-driven constitutional revision process is unique in any established democratic society" (Bergsson and Blokker 2014, 161). In short, it seems to me, that the Icelandic constitutional revision process institutionally approximated quite closely the ideal of reasons-responsiveness in manifold ways.[23] It also achieves this responsiveness precisely by institutionally approximating the other ideals I have highlighted of inclusive sensitivity, democratic co-authorship, political equality and structural independence—and its operationalizability is shown by the fact that it has worked.

In considering a few constituent assembly processes, we have then evidence of both successes (Brazil and Iceland) as well as failures (Venezuela and Bolivia). However, when viewed with a bit more discernment and in the light of striking new empirical evidence, the divergence of the cases might be explainable in a way that precisely supports the stress I have been placing on *ab initio* democratic input into the substantive content of constitutional change proposals, as opposed to mere *ex post* democratic ratification. An important recently published paper establishes the crucial causal importance to a polity's future prospects for democratization of the presence or absence of substantive and widely inclusive democratic input *during the drafting stage* of constitution-making processes (Eisenstadt et al. 2015). Comparing the outcomes of 138 constitutions in 118 different countries over the last 40 years, the study focused on two questions. First, does a high level of democratic participation in general in the constitution-making process make any difference to the prospects for democracy in that country after promulgation? Second, does citizen involvement in the earliest drafting stages of constitution-making lead to differences in prospects for democracy, in contrast to citizen involvement during later stages of debate on and ratification of elite drafted proposals? Their evidence is quite striking: the answer to both question is yes, *and* democratic involvement at "the earliest stage, drafting, has a greater impact on democratization than the debate stage or the modalities of ratification" (Eisenstadt et al. 2015, 599). These results seem to confirm a basic hypothesis of deliberative conceptions of democracy, namely that when it comes to constitutional change "direct [*ab initio*] participation through public debate is more important than [*ex post*] voting for deepening democracy" (Eisenstadt et al. 2015, 593). While I certainly do not want to claim that this single causal factor helps explain all of the relevant differences

[23] Apparently influenced by the openness of web-based tools to citizen input, the Irish Constitutional Convention (2013–2014), charged with recommending constitutional changes to government, is another remarkable recent example of combining inclusive sensitivity with reasons-responsiveness.

between constituent assembly successes in Brazil and Iceland and failures in Bolivia and Venezuela, the evidence from my four case studies is largely congruent with the broader trends found through comparative constitutional analysis. The failed processes incorporated inclusive democratic participation only while debating and ratifying proposals that had already been drafted by small groups of elites dominated by a single party; the successful processes, by contrast, incorporated wide, inclusive and diverse participation at the drafting stages as well. It seems a quite plausible hypothesis, then, that institutions of constitutional change that incorporate democratic input into substantive constitutional content as it is being drafted in fact embody the crucial deliberative ideal of reasons-responsiveness, and embody it in a way that effectively contributes to a polity's on-going democratization.

9.4 Objections and Open Questions

In this paper I have sketched a framework of six evaluative criteria—operationalizability, structural independence, democratic co-authorship, political equality, inclusive sensitivity, and reasons-responsiveness—that we can use to assess various ways of institutionalizing processes of constitutional change in contemporary constitutional democracies. My conjecture is that these normative criteria are constitutively built into—and can be reconstructed out of—the actual institutional practices historically witnessed in constitutional democracies. I have not yet provided, however, the full evidential support that would be required to turn these conjectures into robust theoretical hypotheses. In lieu of a simple concluding recapitulation, I would like to indicate how different kinds of objections might be met, before tuning to some areas of future research this framework opens up.

The arguments presented here are then open, first and foremost, to empirical objections: for instance, that the evidence employed here is factually incorrect, that the evidence is not representative of the nature of most democratic systems and their development, or, that the paper has ignored significant counter-examples. But the arguments are also open to reconstructive objections: for instance, that the paper has distilled the wrong conception of relevant ideals out of particular institutions and practices, or that it has ignored other significant ideals or values that those institutions and practices embody. Only attention to a significantly greater number of examples would be able to address such objections and thereby substantiate the empirical and reconstructive conjectures made here.

Of course, the paper's general approach is also open to normative objections: for instance, that democracy should not have the priority assigned to it here, or, that the correct conception of democracy ought to include a thick catalog of substantive legitimacy conditions that must be guaranteed no matter what any contingent demos happens to say. I hope to have provided at least some considerations in response to such concerns in Sect. 9.2 where I reviewed the general kinds of reasons in favor of democracy and proceduralism, even if the full support of deliberative democratic constitutionalism is beyond what can be accomplished here.

Let me further flag three areas where this project opens up intriguing areas for future research. First, there are critical questions about the relationship between the six evaluative criteria I've identified and the contextual specificity of institutional design proposals for amendment mechanisms. Clearly such a framework of normative criteria cannot be translated directly into universally applicable institutional proposals. To begin, there are simply too many other relevant variables differing across contexts that normative content alone cannot address. But even within that normative framework, I think we should fully expect different criteria to have differing weights and relative priorities depending on specific socio-historical and political contexts, including differing constitutional regime types and histories. For instance, ensuring and heightening structural independence is crucial where the constitutional change process can be easily harnessed by the current regime to entrench itself in power, as in strongly presidentialist systems like Venezuela. But structural independence is much less important where—for example, as in Great Britain—there are robust traditions highlighting constitutional change, a diverse, vigorous and independent press and deliberative public spheres including diverse and active civil society organizations specially attuned to proposed constitutional changes. In short, it seems absurd to expect one definitive or universally preferred set of amendment institutions or procedures—the suitability of particular procedures is a matter of complex and sensitive contextual judgment.

Such contextual judgments refer, secondly, to issues concerning the interrelations between the evaluative criteria. Clearly, for instance, operationalizability seems a necessary criterion for any amendment procedure, but beyond that it is not immediately clear whether, say, democratic co-authorship is more or less important than political equality or reasons responsiveness, and so on. And such questions of normative priority and balance across the diverse criteria will become most salient where there are tensions between the criteria. So for instance, we might think that there are typically institutional tradeoffs between reasons responsiveness and democratic co-authorship, on the theory that constitution-writing experts—lawyers, judges, politicians, academics—might have a better grasp on the relevant reasons, while reasonability may suffer in the name of including more of the populous into the process. Even on the optimistic conjecture that experiments like Iceland's demonstrate that the various desiderata might be plausibly met jointly in one overall process of constitutional change, the framework developed here must still conceptually and practically address the priorities, balances and trade-offs involved in attempting to institutionally realize all six normative criteria.

A third area of questions opens up around the disruptiveness of constitutional transitions in general. Processes of constitutional change not only frequently arise from out of societal and political ferment and conflict, but the processes themselves can add significantly to instability and turmoil, with real possibilities of political violence and repression hovering nearby as a specter. Might we perhaps then need to add some criterion of stability to the set of six normative criteria adumbrated here, maybe say, some measure of the degree to which an amendment institution promotes legal continuity, or continuity of governmental authority, or peaceful transitions? While non-violent constitutional change is surely normatively preferable, its unclear how that might be assessed as a differential measure of various institutions. And the other ideas of legal continuity or continuity of authority both seem to overly constrain democratic co-authorship in the kind of constitutional changes citizens might envision and believe warranted. And this in turn raises a fascinating set of questions about the distinction between constitutional amendment and constitutional replacement. While intuitively plausible, and frequently referred to in formal amendment procedures, the distinction is much harder to make in practice than it might seem. This is not only a conceptual problem, but also a problem for empirical research—when is a constitution changed enough to count as a new constitutional regime?—and for law and jurisprudence—when does an official amendment outstrip its authorizing text and constitute a new constitution? This brings us full circle back to the relationship between actual constitutional practices and theory, between fact and ideal. While the framework here has stressed the importance of institutional procedures for embodying various democratic ideals, the fact is that an enormous number of actual constitutional change dynamics are distinctly irregular, not in accord with pre-established procedures. If democratic legitimacy in the face of substantive disagreement hangs on procedural regularity—as the general conception of deliberative democratic constitutionalism insists—what is that conception to make of the fact that many if not most constitutional transitions have significant elements of procedural irregularity? Should we say that facts vitiate ideals here, or might we treat procedural regularity as a regulative ideal of constitutional change processes, a normative lodestar of such processes even if unreachable and only asymptotically approachable in the world? The evaluative framework proposed here thus opens up onto fundamental theoretical questions, from the relationship between theory and practice, to the definition of a constitution, to the nature and justification of constitutional democracy itself. But this is precisely what theory should expect in light of the exciting ferment and experimentation, witnessed today around the globe, attempting to secure increasingly democratic institutions of constitutional change.

Acknowledgments I owe a special debt of gratitude to Tanya Stepasiuk for significant research assistance about existing mechanisms of constitutional change, and I thank Joel Colón Rios for discussions about South American mechanisms; errors about these processes are, of course, my own. Earlier drafts of this paper were presented at the 1st International Congress on Constitutional Law and Political Philosophy; On the Future of Constitutionalism: Perspectives for Democratizing Constitutional Law, organized by Thomas da Rosa de Bustamante at Federal University of Minas Gerais, Belo Horizonte, Brazil, and at XXVII World Congress of the International Association for the Philosophy of Law and Social Philosophy (IVR) in Washington, D.C. I am indebted to many participants of both conferences for insightful discussion, especially to very helpful comments made by Márcio Luís de Oliveira.

References

Ackerman, Bruce, and James S. Fishkin. 2004. *Deliberation day*. New Haven: Yale University Press.

Aristotle. 1943. *Politics*. Trans. Benjamin Jowett. New York: Random House.

Arrow, Kenneth J. 1963. *Social choice and individual values*, 2nd ed. New Haven: Yale University Press.

Bergsson, Baldvin Thor, and Paul Blokker. 2014. The constitutional experiment in Iceland. In *Verfassunggebung in Konsolidierten Demokratien: Neubeginn oder Verfall eines politischen Systems?* ed. Ellen Bos and Kálmán Pócza, 154–174. Baden-Baden: Nomos Verlagsgesellschaft.

Bernal-Pulido, Carlos. 2013. Unconstitutional constitutional amendments in the case study of Colombia: An analysis of the justification and meaning of the constitutional replacement doctrine. *International Journal of Constitutional Law* 11(2): 339–357.

Closa, Carlos. 2012. Constitutional rigidity and procedures for ratifying constitutional reforms in EU member states. In *Changing federal constitutions: Lessons from international comparison*, ed. Arthur Benz and Felix Knüpling, 281–310. Toronto: Barbara Budrich Publishers.

Colón-Ríos, Joel. 2011. Carl Schmitt and constituent power in Latin American courts: The cases of Venezuela and Colombia. *Constellations* 18(3): 365–388.

Dahl, Robert A. 1989. *Democracy and its critics*. New Haven: Yale University Press.

Dixon, Rosalind. 2011. Constitutional amendment rules: A comparative perspective. In *Comparative constitutional law*, ed. Tom Ginsburg and Rosalind Dixon, 96–111. Northampton: Edward Elgar.

Eisenstadt, Todd A., Carl A. LeVan, and Tofigh Maboudi. 2015. When talk trumps text: The democratizing effects of deliberation during constitution-making, 1974–2011. *American Political Science Review* 109(3): 592–612.

Elkins, Zachary, Tom Ginsburg, and James Melton. 2009. *The endurance of national constitutions*. New York: Cambridge University Press.

Ely, John Hart. 1980. *Democracy and distrust: A theory of judicial review*. Cambridge, MA: Harvard University Press.

Ferejohn, John. 1997. The politics of imperfection: The amendment of constitutions. *Law and Social Inquiry* 22(2): 501–530.

Fishkin, James S. 2009. *When the people speak: Deliberative democracy and public consultation*. New York: Oxford University Press.

Ginsburg, Tom. 2003. *Judicial review in new democracies: Constitutional courts in Asian cases*. New York: Cambridge University Press.

Habermas, Jürgen. 1996. *Between Facts and Norms: Contributions to a Discourse Theory of Law and Democracy*. Trans. William Rehg. Cambridge, MA: The MIT Press.

Hirschl, Ran. 2006. The new constitutionalism and the judicialization of pure politics worldwide. *Fordham Law Review* 75(2): 721–754.

Honneth, Axel. 2014. *Freedom's Right: The Social Foundations of Democratic Life*. Trans. Joseph Ganahal. Malden: Polity Press.

Landau, David. 2012. Constitution-making gone wrong. *Alabama Law Review* 64(5): 923–980.

Landemore, Hélène. 2014. Inclusive constitution-making: The Icelandic experiment. *Journal of Political Philosophy*. doi:10.1111/jopp.12032.

Lijphart, Arend. 1999. *Patterns of democracy: Government forms and performance in thirty-six countries*. New Haven: Yale University Press.

Lutz, Donald S. 1995. Toward a theory of constitutional amendment. In *Responding to imperfection: The theory and practice of constitutional amendment*, ed. Sanford Levinson, 237–274. Princeton: Princeton University Press.

Negretto, Gabriel L. 2012. Replacing and amending constitutions: The logic of constitutional change in Latin America. *Law and Society Review* 46(4): 759–779.

Rasch, Bjørn Erik, and Roger D. Congleton. 2006. Stability and constitutional amendment procedures. In *Democratic constitutional design and public policy: Analysis and evidence*, ed. Roger D. Congleton and Birgitta Swedenborg, 319–342. Cambridge, MA: The MIT Press.

Riker, William H. 1982. *Liberalism against populism: A confrontation between the theory of democracy and the theory of social choice*. Prospect Heights: Waveland Press.

Rousseau, Jean-Jacques. 1997. Of the social contract. In *The Social Contract and Other Later Political Writings*, ed. and trans. Victor Gourevitch, 39–152. New York: Cambridge University Press.

Schumpeter, Joseph A. 1943. *Capitalism, socialism, and democracy*. London: George Allen & Unwin.
Sen, Amartya. 2009. *The idea of justice*. Cambridge, MA: Harvard University Press.
Shapiro, Martin, and Alec Stone Sweet. 2002. *On law, politics, and judicialization*. New York: Oxford University Press.
Stone Sweet, Alec. 2000. *Governing with judges: Constitutional politics in Europe*. New York: Oxford University Press.
Tate, C. Neal, and Tornjörn Vallinder. 1995. *The global expansion of judicial power*. New York: New York University Press.
Waldron, Jeremy. 1999. *Law and disagreement*. New York: Oxford University Press.
Zurn, Christopher F. 2007. *Deliberative democracy and the institutions of judicial review*. New York: Cambridge University Press.

Chapter 10
The Unconstitutionality of Constitutional Amendments in Colombia: The Tension Between Majoritarian Democracy and Constitutional Democracy

Gonzalo Andres Ramirez-Cleves

Abstract This chapter analyses the "Constitutional replacement doctrine", developed by the Colombian Constitutional Court in order to enable the judicial review of amendments to the Colombian Constitution of 1991 on substantial grounds. This doctrine is particularly relevant for comparative lawyers because it represents the grounding of a process of judicial review of constitutional amendments in the absence of an express clause granting that competence to the Constitutional Court. The "replacement doctrine", in short, forbids the constituted powers of amendment from changing an "inherent part of the Constitution" or a set of overarching principles the violation of which would undermine the constitutional project as a whole. In spite of some specific dangers that this doctrine might entail, I am generally persuaded that the Court has developed sound arguments for the use of this process to protect the constitutional democracy against a merely majoritarian account of democratic procedures.

10.1 Introduction

The Colombian Constitutional Court in decision C-551 of 2003 introduced the "Constitutional replacement doctrine" or "unconstitutionality for substitution". This doctrine means that the Constitutional Court could review the content of a constitutional amendment and declare them unconstitutional not only due to procedural irregularities in the strict sense, but also for irregularities of competence when such power changes "an inherent part of the Constitution" or the principles and values derived from the international treaties that Colombia had signed, especially related to human rights protection (art. 93 of the Constitution) and Labour protection (The treaties from the International Labour Organization ILO- Art. 53.4 of the Constitution) that it has called "the constitutional block".

G.A. Ramirez-Cleves (✉)
Universidad Externado de Colombia, Cl. 12 #1-17 Este, Bogotá, Colombia
e-mail: gonzalo.ramirez@uexternado.edu.co

T. Bustamante, B.G. Fernandes (eds.), *Democratizing Constitutional Law*, Law and Philosophy Library 113, DOI 10.1007/978-3-319-28371-5_10

The "Constitutional replacement doctrine" is an eminently judicial creation, because the 1991 Constitution does not contain express clauses that prohibit the constitutional amendment such as the "Eternity Clauses" in the German Constitution of 1949 – Basic Law – in Article 79.3, the Italian Constitution of 1947 in Article 139, the French Constitution of 1958 in Article 89.5, the Portuguese Constitution of 1976 in Article 290, and in the Latin American context, among others, the Brazilian Constitution of 1988 in Article 60.4, the Constitution of El Salvador of 1982 in Article 248, the Venezuelan Constitution of 1999 in Article 342, and the 2008 Ecuadorian Constitution in Article 441, where one can find specific prohibitions from changing general aspects related to the concept of Constitution such, fundamental rights and the rule elements of law, the alternation of power, the articles on constitutional amendment and other particular elements that refer to the type of state and political organization of each state, such as the federal character of the state, the social state of law, the republican character, the popular participation in the local government or the prohibition of presidential re-election.

The declaration of unconstitutionality of constitutional amendments in constitutions that lack prohibition clauses of amendment is not common in comparative law. Initially there was the practice in India where the Supreme Court since 1967 in the case **Golaknath vs. State of Punjaba** established that the power of reform could not be confused with the constituent power, a thesis that has led to the doctrine of the "Basic Structure" which was introduced in 1973 in the case **Kesavaranda Bharati vs. Kerala**. In that decision the Supreme Court said that are some structural elements that cannot be modified and that the Court has enabled the power to declare unconstitutional constitutional amendments in that country.

The doctrine of the material limits of constitutional amendment has been adopted as a growing trend in the comparative constitutionalism, as Yazniv Roznai demonstrated in a thesis presented in 2014 at the London School of Economics entitled "*Unconstitutional Constitutional Amendments: A Study of Nature and the Limits of Constitutional Amendment Powers*", where he explains that the Tribunals and Constitutional Courts around the world are increasingly likely to ground judicial review of constitutional reforms on the understanding that there are some structural, inherent, axial, basic or essential elements in the Constitution that cannot be changed through the power of amendment (Roznai 2014).

The same author explains in a shorter article that despite the particularity of judicial review of constitutional reforms in constitutions that have no prohibition clauses, the phenomenon has been expanding in countries such as India, Bangladesh, Colombia, Argentina, Peru, Taiwan and Mexico resulting a form of "*Migration of constitutional Ideas*" (Roznai 2013), using this concept of Sujit Choudry (2006), which means that it has created a constitutional tendency of such practice evidenced, for example, by a recent ruling issued by the Constitutional Court of Turkey in June 2008, which annulled a parliamentary constitutional amendment that removed the ban on wearing headscarves in public universities, because such reform affect the principle of secularism that is a basic principle of the Constitution of that country.

As we said before, Colombia has implemented the doctrine of unconstitutional constitutional amendment since the landmark Judgment C-551 of 2003, that had led to the declaration of unconstitutionality of constitutional amendments on five occasions until now. Those judgments took into account structural principles such as separation of powers (C-1040 of 2005 and C-141 of 2010), the democratic state (C-141 of 2010), checks and balances (C-141 of 2010), equality (C-588 of 2009 and C-249 of 2012), merit (C-588 of 2009 and C-249 of 2012), civil service (C-588 of 2009 and C-249 of 2012), the prevalence of general interest (C-1056 of 2012), the duty of Congress to act at all times with fairness and common good (C-1056 of 2012), the public morality (C-1056 of 2012), the possibility that voters control the actions of the elected (C-1056 of 2012) and a particular configuration of the component assigned to the different mechanisms of judicial review (C-1056 of 2012).

Within the five rulings, special emphasis is deserved by Judgment C-141 of 2010, which reviewed law 1345 of 2009, that called a referendum to amend Article 197 of the Constitution in order to allow the re-election of the President of the Republic for a second time. In this case, the Constitutional Court ruled that the proposed amendment replaced the democratic principles of separation of powers, checks and balances, alternation of the power and equality, and declared it unconstitutional. This historic judgment, perhaps the most important that the Constitutional Court has issued in a political matter in its entire history, has led it to consider as necessary the constitutional replacement doctrine for the protection and maintenance of constitutional democracy in Colombia.

In this paper I will study whether the doctrine of substitution is a good way to resolve the tension that occurs between majoritarian democracy and constitutional democracy, but also but why it is necessary to have in such review elements of rationality and proportionality to avoid the excessive discretion of the Constitutional Court in the application of the constitutional replacement doctrine.

The hypothesis of this chapter is that the "constitutional replacement doctrine" can be a good way of protecting constitutional democracy from the majoritarian conception of democracy, but the doctrine should be applied only in extreme cases where it becomes apparent that some of the structural or axial elements of the Constitution are threatened or jeopardized. To determine this, the Court should use arguments of reasonableness and avoid excessive discretion in applying the doctrine in the judicial review of the constitutional amendments.

Given this premise, the paper will take into account two aspects: firstly (i) constitutional democracy as a way to avoid the risks of majoritarian democracy (or democracy of majorities), and secondly (ii) the constitutional replacement doctrine as a way of protecting constitutional democracy against democracy of majorities, where I will study the potential problems of the adoption of this doctrine in Colombia and the proposals for overcoming them, considering the premise that such doctrine has to avoid extreme judicial discretion.

10.2 Constitutional Democracy as a Way to Overcome the Risks of Majoritarian Democracy

Article XVI of the French Declaration of the Rights of Man and of the Citizen of 1789, the first modern definition of Constitution, provides that "*A society in which the observance of the law is not assured, nor the separation of powers defined, has no Constitution at all*". Taking into account this definition, the Constitution should involve two aspects: firstly the control and the division of powers, and secondly the protection and enforcement of rights that limit those powers.

On the other hand, Emmanuel Sieyès was the first to establish in his book *What Is the Third Estate*? (*Qu'est-ce que le tiers-état?* – 1791) that are two distinct powers: in the first place, a *constituent power* that would be owned by the people directly or the representatives of them in an Assembly whose ultimate aim is to make a constitution, and the *constituted powers* (exercised by those bodies such as the executive, legislative and judicial branch), that are settled and limited by the Constitution itself.

Based on this logic, constituted powers lack the power to change the basic elements proposed by the constituent power, because the constituted powers are regulated by the Constitution and are limited by it. As the French have explained this is a "constituted constitutional power" limited to the structural elements of the Constitution itself. On this point, Sieyès indicates in his *Raisonee Exposition* before the Constitution Committee of the National Assembly of July 20, 1789 that, "*The powers within the public property are subject to all applicable laws, rules and forms that are owners are altering. And as they were unable to build themselves, they cannot change its Constitution*".

This democratic concept of a Constitution that states that the Constitution is the supreme law that limits the powers and protects the fundamental rights is fully in effect and their use is increasingly repeated. Even authors who have been critical of a substantial or material concept of Constitution, like Ricardo Guastini in Italy, have indicated that the despotic states that concentrate power and do not protect the fundamental rights of individuals are not seen nowadays as a "Constitutional State" (Guastini 2007, 16ff).

Nevertheless, the idea of democratic constitution has represented an apparently irresolvable dilemma, that I will call "the democracy paradox" that is expresses thus: because democracy is based on the "majority rule", the rationality of the law will depends on the power of the decision of the greatest number. This paradox is evidenced in a greater magnitude when it comes to the amendment of the Constitution, because it shows the tension between the democratic principle formulated by Rousseau, and the principle of supremacy of the Constitution established by authors such as Montesquieu and Bryce (De Vega 1985).

However, Rousseau's idea that majoritarian democracy could establish unlimited constitutional change and that it was *legibus solutus* regarding the Constitution was changed by Rousseau himself in his text "*Considerations on the Government of Poland*" (1771), where he realized that in most cases the exercise of direct representative democracy is not possible, and for this reason should be limited to the Constitution drafted by the constituents that directly represents the popular will.

On the other hand, the majoritarian conception of democracy proposed by Rousseau contained another problem evidenced by Tocqueville in his "Democracy in America", which is that a "tyranny of the majority over the minority" can occur, and this could jeopardize the principles of pluralism, equality and freedom, when the decision of the majority is arbitrary or unfair.

Moreover the democracy of the majority is in crisis when it is evident that the largest number can not only go against the rights of minorities, but also eliminate the very foundations that enable democracy, turning it into a suicide power. This possibility was in practice in Europe when the majority rule was used to establish governments that ended the pillars of democracy with the emergence of totalitarian and autocratic governments.

I can be argued, furthermore, as highlighted by Norberto Bobbio, that majority rule has no rational justification, "*... as a quantitative criterion trusts a choice or a decision that is essentially qualitative*" (Bobbio 2002, 255), and that even if it could be justified with axiological and teleological arguments it would be in trouble to overcome the "*paradox of self-destruction*" described above.

The arguments for democracy of majorities are divided into pragmatic and evaluative arguments following the division proposed by Weber. On the basis of evaluative arguments one would say that the majority rule is justified because it can, better than any other system of decision, fulfil some fundamental values such as freedom, equality and pluralism, and on the basis of pragmatic arguments it is said that this system is intended to reach a joint decision relatively quickly among people who have different points of views, so democracy of majorities is the best way to form a collective will within an organized social group.

However, as mentioned, the democratic system based on majority rule would have two fundamental problems: (i) the paradox of self-destruction, and (ii) the problem of the protection of minority rights that could be illegitimately restricted by some decisions of the majority. These risks have led to theories of the limits of democracy or to rules stating that there are a number of constitutive elements in a democracy which cannot be eliminated by majority decisions.

Although Kelsen established that there is a *modus vivendi* between the majority and the minority that allows a "*free confrontation between majority and minority*" to create "*...an atmosphere favourable to compromise between the two*" (Kelsen 2008), the coexistence of convenience ignores the necessity of some commitments to refer to the same democratic game and to defend the rights of the minority.

The dilemma of self-destruction and the possibility of elimination of the rights of the minority by the majority rule was raised by Radbruch in his text "Relativism and law", which holds that there comes a moment where one cannot accept or tolerate relativism, and where decisions are made intending to end relativism itself. This is the case when through democratic decisions based on the majority rule it is intended to eliminate the rights of freedom, equality and pluralism that legitimize this system of government.

Therefore, from the theoretical point of view a series of limitations or restrictions on the use of majority rule has started to emerge as the system that best explains democracy. Thus the idea of a democracy has to be different from the idea of democracy of majority, in order to establish rules or minimum standards that limit arbitrary democracy. This order raises the idea of a "Constitutional Democracy" that establishes limits that could not be modified by majoritarian democracy established in parliament and in any case retains both the rights of the minority and the requirements of the democratic system itself, through mechanisms such as judicial review, constitutional actions, constitutional rigidity and intangibility clauses.

This understanding of democracy holds that the supremacy of the Constitution is the best way to limit the power of majoritarian democracy, an idea reinforced after the Second World War in Europe and after the end of dictatorship periods and autocratic systems in the late 1970s, 1980s and 1990s of the last century in countries as Portugal, Spain, Argentina, Brazil and Uruguay.

Nevertheless, when it comes to constitutional reforms, there remains the dilemma of what should prevail if the constitutional provision in its basic structure or the decisions made in a democracy come into conflict, presenting the tension between constitutional democracy and democracy of majorities. This tension has resulted in two clearly defined positions: those who believe that a court should protect the principle of constitutional supremacy to avoid the dangers and risks of democratic majorities and those who consider that democratic decisions under majority rule should prevail over the Constitution.

Among the first would be those who argue that democratic decisions cannot eliminate certain aspects considered as central to the Constitution and to the separation of powers, protection of rights, alternation of power, authority and judicial review, which could be thought of as comprised in the idea of supremacy the Constitution, among other aspects inherent in the idea of constitutionalism. This thesis was developed, within the US doctrine, by William L. Marbury in 1919 in an article entitled "The Limitations upon the Amending Power" where he said, "*the power to amend the Constitution was not intended to include the power to destroy it*" (Marbury 1920, 225).

This same position was held by Justice Robert Jackson in the United States in the case of the "Salute to the Flag" in 1943 stating that these fundamental rights would be not possible to amend, who and stated in the ruling that,

> The very purpose of a Bill of Rights was to withdraw certain subjects from the vicissitudes of political controversy to place them beyond the reach of majorities and officials establish them as legal principles that would be applied by the courts. The right to life, liberty and property, to free speech, a free press, freedom of worship and assembly and other fundamental rights itself should not have a vote: do not depend on the outcome of elections[1]

However, other authors consider that there should be no fears or limits on decisions taken democratically, and that therefore judges should not have the power to make any judicial review of the decisions taken within the rule of majority. Such

[1] West Virginia State Board of Education vs. Barnette, 319, U.S., en: 638.

criticism is based mainly on two aspects: (i) counter-majoritarian criticism, and secondly (ii) criticism regarding the decision-making of plural corporations as the tribunals and constitutional courts that are implemented by majority rule.

The counter majoritarian critic was first raised by Alexander Bickel in his 1962 text "The Least dangerous branch", where it was stated that judicial review in the United States was creating a "government of judges" that can be inconvenient in relation to the possibility that these decisions are more regressive in recognizing rights that the decisions made in the democratically elected parliaments. This criticism has been followed by the so-called "popular constitutionalism", whose most prominente representatives are Larry Kramer on "The People Themselves: Popular Constitutionalism and Judicial Review" (2004) and Mark Tushnet on "Taking the Constitution Away from the Courts" (2000), who use the example of the failures that occurred in the time of Roosevelt's New Deal, and in paradigmatic cases like *Lochner vs. New York* in 1905 where the Supreme Court declared unconstitutional a law establishing maximum working hours for bakers in protection of their labor rights.

The second critique related with the use of rule of the majority by Tribunals and Constitutional Courts, is exposed by Jeremy Waldron in his book "Law and Disagreement" (1999), which emphasizes that the decisions by judges and Courts are taken in most cases using the majority rule, establishing the paradox that the decision of what is amendable and what not is at the end based not in the rationality but in numeric rationality. Kenneth Arrow explains the problems of such method: "neither majority-decision nor any other method of aggregation can guarantee that a coherent group preference can be constructed rationally out of a variety of coherent individual preferences" (Waldron 1999, 89).

From the tension between majoritarian democracy and constitutional democracy arises the idea of building a new concept of Constitution that it will be understood "as the decision of the majority, but without the restriction of the rights of the minority and the elements that makes possible democracy itself".

Against this conception of democracy there emerges the thesis of the "substantive" or "material" limits to constitutional change, which accepts the power to amend the Constitution while not admitting the power to replace it. This thesis is explained by authors such as Jon Elster and Stephen Holmes as a kind of pre-commitment restraint that may be associated with the passage of "Ulysses and the sirens" in Homer's Odyssey, where Ulysses instructs its subordinates to tie him to the mast and fill their ears with wax to avoid falling into the siren's songs that could lead to the sinking of the expedition. According to this metaphor, the Constitution would be the mast where Ulysses is tied to prevent him from falling into the charms of the songs of the sirens of democracy of majorities that could lead to their own destruction.

In conclusion, the "substitution doctrine" in Colombia or the "Basic Structure" thesis in India would be a way of protecting constitutional democracy against the risks of majoritarian democracy in order to protect the basic elements of democracy itself, sucha as the principles of freedom, equality, pluralism, alternation of power, the principle of constitutional supremacy, and the fundamental rights needed to secure the rights of the minority groups.

The following section will discuss how the doctrine of substitution is implemented in Colombia and what were the main problems of the introduction of this thesis in the development of the judicial review, especially with regards to the difficulty to distinguish between substitution and amendment, the indeterminacy of the notion of "irreplaceable elements", and the Court's power to interpret these elements. Finally we face the question of whether the doctrine of substitution in Colombia is a good method to protect constitutional democracy against majoritarian democracy.

10.3 Implementing the "Substitution Doctrine" as a Method for Protecting Constitutional Democracy Against Majoritarian Democracy

As I previously said the "substitution of the Constitution doctrine" was introduced in Colombia in the landmark judgment C-551/2003, where the Court says on paragraph 37 that:

> The derivative Constituent power does not have the power to destroy the Constitution. The constituent act establishes the legal order and therefore any power of the constitutional amendment that the constitutional power recognizes is only limited to a review. The amendment power, which is a constituted power is not, therefore, entitled to the repeal or replacement of the Constitution from which it derives its jurisdiction. The established power in other words does not assume functions of constituent power, and therefore cannot carry out a substitution of the Constitution, not only because it would be erected an original constituent power, but also because it would undermine the foundations of its own jurisdiction.

Similarly, in paragraph 39 of this decision the Constitutional Court stated that, "*the amendment power, as a constituted power, has material limitations, as the power to amend the Constitution does not contain the possibility of repealing, subverting or replacing that constitution in its entirety*". Furthermore, it is also said that, "*the Constitutional Court must consider whether or not the Charter was replaced by another, for which one needs to take into account the principles and values that the Constitution contains, and those arising from the constitutional block* [as we explained before, with special regards to human rights treaties and labour treaties]".

The use of the doctrine of substitution in Colombia, in more than 10 years of existence, is limited and was used only five times, in more than 30 constitutional amendments to the 1991 Constitution. I will explain the decisions briefly:

1. **C – 1040 of 2005**, that undertook judicial review of the proposal of Constitutional Amendment Legislative Act No. 2 of 2004, that amends the paragraphs 2 and 30 of Article 127 of the Constitution, and especially Article 197 of the Constitution, opening the possibility re-election of the President for one period. The same

amendment establishes that if the Congress did not establish a law in a two (2) months term, the State Council, the highest court of administrative jurisdiction, must enact it. The Court ruled in this case that the re-election of the President for one period did not replace the Constitution's separation of powers principle, but declared unconstitutional the possibility that a Court replace the legislative power of the Congress taking into account the principle of separation of the powers.

2. **C- 588 of 2009**, that adjudicated on the Legislative Act Number 01 of 2008, that amended Article 125 of the Constitution, establishing the possibility that provisional and commissioned employees could be named directly without public competition. The Court ruled that the decision replaced the essential principles of merit, civil service and equality, because it limits the possibility that anyone interested in these posts could participate in the same conditions as those provisional and commissioned employees.
3. **C- 141 of 2010**, that reviewed the constitutionality of the project of law 1353 of 2009, which called for a referendum to amend the Article 197 of the CP and permit the re-election of President for a second period, allowing him to stay 12 years in the post. The Court ruled that the amendment was unconstitutional not only because the procedural defects in the passage of the referendum, but also because if the referendum is approved the Constitutional principles of democracy, separation of powers, checks and balances, equality and alternation of power would be replaced.
4. **C – 249 of 2012** that declared unconstitutional the Legislative Act No. 4 of 2011, which, like Judgment C-588 of 2009, established advantages scores for provisional and commissioned employees, because the amendment replaced the essential principles of merit, equity and administrative career.
5. **C – 1056 of 2012**, which declares unconstitutional the Legislative Act No. 1 of 2011, that amended article 183 of the Constitution in order derogate the provision that establishes the loss of investiture for congressmen who violate the regime of inabilities and incompatibilities in deliberations about legislative enactmens. In this case the Court stated that such reform changed axial principles such as the prevalence of general interest, the separation of the powers, the ability of the voters to control the Congressmen, the common good, the public morality, the incompatibility and illegibility regime itself and the rigidity of the amendment process.

Of these five decisions, two had a critical and direct political impact: Decision C-1040 of 2005, which allowed the President to be re-elected for one period, and Decision C-141 of 2010, which prohibited the president from being re-elected a second time. That reform would allow a two term re-election that could redesign the whole structure of the Constitution because a Constitution that was originally designed for a 4 years President's term would accommodate periods of 12 years. Such amendment would produce an imbalance between the powers and affect what Sartori calls the "constitutional engineering".

As we said before this decision is the most important judgement that the Court has taken in political matters, and illustrates the independence and autonomy of the Constitutional Court with regards to the executive and its majorities in Congress. This judgment may be comparable in importance to the cases decided by the Supreme Court of India in the mid-1970s – *Minerva Mills Ltd. vs. Union of India* in 1974 and *Indira Nehru Gandhi vs. Raj Narain* in 1975 – , decisions that had protected the constitutional democracy in that country.

Thus it was evident in this case that the doctrine of the substitution of the Constitution, introduced by the constitutional jurisprudence through the thesis of the lack of competence of the reformer body can become the last resort in the defence of the constitutional democracy and in the prevention from the use of constitutional amendment to remove the pillars of material idea of Constitution.

Although the Colombian Constitutional Court has so far not established a detailed list of principles and values inherent to the Constitution that cannot be replaced, the Court has begun, in the resolution of specific cases, to establish which are such fundamental elements.

Moreover, it should be noted that constitutional case law has been establishing a series of criteria of rationality and weighting – a "replacement" or "substitution test" – to determine when the amendment power is used to change or eliminate the basic structure of the Constitution. Upon the introduction of these criteria highlights the Judgment C-1200 of 2003, C-970 of 2004, C-1040 of 2005, C-588 of 2009 and C – 574 of 2011 as explained below:

1. In the Judgment **C-1200 of 2003**, which reviewed the Legislative Act 03 of 2002, that gave powers to the President in criminal and disciplinary matters, the Court established some parameters for the study of constitutional amendments. In that judgment it was stated that "*constitutional judge can go to the various methods of interpretation based on objective benchmarks, such as the background of the amendment. It can also go to the block of constitutionality, strictly speaking, to delineate the defining profile of the original Constitution and the fundamental constitutional principles and their realization throughout the original Constitution, without authorizing this Court to compare the reform with the content of a specific principle or rule of constitutional law*".
2. In the judgment **C-970 of 2004**, that reviewed transitional Article 4 of Legislative Act No. 3 of 2003, the Court introduced the first elements of the "Test or methodology of substitution". First (i) the Court established that "*the Court is simply stating the general elements that a particular institution has in contemporary constitutionalism, but particularly a defining element as it is configured in the Colombian Constitution and, therefore, it is part of its identity*". Secondly (ii) the Court must examine the act under review to establish, "*... what is its legal effect, in relation to the identified defining elements of the Constitution*". Finally (iii) the Court must make a comparison and synthesis work to verify, "*If reform replaces a defining element that works as an identifier of the Constitution other than fully*".

3. In the ruling **C-1040 of 2005**, which revised Legislative Act No. 2 of 2004, which, as we explained previously, gave the opportunity to the President to be re-elected only once, it was established the "Test of the seven steps", according to which the Constitutional Court must do the following: (i) state very clearly what item is replaced; (ii) draw from multiple legal regulations which are the specificities of such element in the Constitution; (iii) show why that element is essential and defining for the identity of the Constitution fully considered; (iv) verify whether that defining element of the 1991 Constitution is irreducible to a section of the Constitution; (v) verify whether that essential element doesn't constitute an untouchable material limit on the power of reform, in order to prevent the court from adjudication on a something supposedly intangible; (vi) verify that the essential element was replaced by another, and not simply modified, affected, violated or annoyed; and finally (vii) verify if the new defining essential element of the Constitution is fully opposite or different to the point that is incompatible with the defining elements of the identity of the previous Constitution.
4. The Judgment **C-588 of 2009**, that reviewed the Legislative Act 01 of 2008, which stated that provisional employees could remain directly in their positions for a period of time without any other requirement of meritocracy. In this decision the Court introduced the so-called "effectiveness test", according to which it has to check three aspects: (i) that the reform is not apparent, in the sense that the article to be amended does not remain the same, because if it happen to be identical then there has not been any constitutional reform, but merely an appearance of it. Secondly, (ii) that the amendment does not established an *ad hoc* or particular preference that favour or benefit one person or group of people; and thirdly (iii) that it does not allow any tacit constitutional amendment, that allows an article or a part of the Constitution to be replaced indirectly. This doctrine is known as the doctrine of "constitutional fraud".
5. Judgment **C-574 of 2011**, that made the judicial review of Legislative Act No. 2 of 2009, which amended Article 49 of the Constitution on the right to health of "*the size and consumption of narcotic drugs or psychotropic substances*". Despite of the fact that the Court declared itself incompetent to rule on this case, it settled three principles that the Court must continue to carry out this kind of control. First (i) a *major premise* where the inherent element or principle or value of the block of constitutionality is determined irreplaceable; second (ii) a *minor premise* where the principle or new value entered is established and replaced; and thirdly (iii) a *premise of synthesis* in which the Court compares the beginning or irreplaceable value that is introduced to prove they are "opposed or integrally different", in a way that is incompatible with the axial or inherent element.

In the same decision, it is said that in the major premise, the Court must undertake a transversal and comprehensive reading of the Constitution, to determine whether the item being replaced is set as a structural or axial element, and whether this essential element can be reflected or contained in several articles of the

Constitution. Also, it must check if the constitutional element could be determined through historical or systematic interpretation of the Constitution. Finally it ruled that to build this premise it is necessary for the applicant in its action and for the Court in its decision: (i) to state very clearly what that item is; (ii) to draw it from multiple policies regarding their specificities in the context of the enactment of the 1991 Constitution, and (iii) to show why it is essential and defining for the identity of the Constitution as a whole.

Despite the advantages of the substitution of the Constitution doctrine to protect the so-called constitutional democracy against the majoritarian democracy, the introduction of this doctrine in the Colombian constitutional case law has faced some criticisms that can be classified into two types. First, there was (i) a criticism related to the adoption of this thesis itself, and secondly (ii) some criticisms that have to do with the difficulties that can lead to the implementation of the doctrine in constitutional jurisprudence.

With regards to the criticism related of the adoption of the doctrine of substitution, some authors consider that from a formal point of view the Court cannot carry out this type of review because there are no clauses in the 1991 Constitution expressly establishing this competence. This objection has been pointed out for example in the dissenting opinion of Judge Humberto Sierra Porto in the decision C-970 of 2004, who argued that, "*the Constitutional Court has no jurisdiction to review constitutional amendments different from those established in Article 241.1 of the Constitution. This competence is restricted to errors of form or procedure; all others, whether they are material or competence vices are excluded from the review that corresponds to the Court*".

On the other hand, criticisms related to the implementation and development of the substitution doctrine have focused on two aspects: firstly (i), on the difficulty to identify when an amendment to the Constitution can be considered a substitution of the Constitution, and what items or axial values of the Constitution cannot be replaced and to what extent, and, secondly (ii), on the wide discretion granted to the Constitutional Court in the implementation of the substitution doctrine.

Professor Carlos Bernal Pulido in the VII Meeting of the Colombian Constitutional Court held in Bogotá in October 2011, presented an influential paper where he focused on these problems and suggested an alternative test to determine the principles or values that would be irreplaceable (Bernal Pulido 2013).

Bernal, using some ideas related to the proportionality test, established the thesis that a constitutional amendment could only be unconstitutional when it is of such magnitude that it could affect the structural elements of the Constitution. That means that the doctrine would only be used as a last resort, when the "enormity of the abnormality" of the constitutional amendment has been clearly proven. It means that wherever it appears that the amendment power exceeded its faculties and made an intervention in the inherent elements of the Constitution it could be considered an unconstitutional amendment.

Secondly, Bernal proposes two principles that should be considered irreplaceable. First, those elements which relate to the principle of democracy and legality, and those which refer to the fundamental rights catalogue, the principle of rule of law and the principle of separation of powers. Secondly, those elements that are related to the guarantee of a deliberative democracy, which is provided by the effective participation of citizens in decisions that affects them.

Finally, Bernal reviews a dissenting opinion in Judgment C-572 of 2004 by Justice Rodrigo Uprimny. Uprimny noted that the 1991 Colombian Constitution regulates three mechanisms of amendment – reform by the Congress (Article 375), constitutional reform by referendum (Article 378), and reform by a National Constituent Assembly (Article 376) – and thus argued that it should use the rule that a higher degree of popular participation in the mechanism of reform should imply a lesser degree of intensity in the judicial review. Bernal agreed with this statement that *"the more a constitutional amendment is the result of a procedure observing the rules of deliberative democracy, the less intensive should be the judicial review"* (Bernal Pulido 2013, 357).

Although Bernal's proposal is a first attempt to establish a series of conditions of reasonableness for the implementation of the doctrine of substitution in the determination of the constitutional review of the constitutional amendments, the alternative thesis has posed several problems.

One has to do with the scope of what should be understood as the "*democratic and legality principle*" and also the term "*deliberative democracy*". Although there have been some doctrinal and jurisprudential analytic elaborations on how these principles should be understood, the breadth of the definition allows a large degree of discretion in the Court. The experience of comparative law indicates that even express intangible clauses concepts such as "Republic" or "rule of law" have a degree of interpretation that can be extended or restricted, resulting in minimalist or maximalist interpretations in assessing the irreplaceable elements.

For example, in the case of the Constitutions of France and Italy that have an eternity clause related with the concept of "Republic", the doctrine and jurisprudence have offered a maximalist interpretation, so that "Republic" should be understood not only as that regime which differs from the monarchy, but also a regime that establishes and guarantees the separation of powers, protection of rights, the rule of law, the alternation of power, the principle of constitutional supremacy and the possibility of judicial review of laws, among others.

On the other hand, when attempting to perform a detailed list of irreplaceable items such as the case of express clauses of intangibility established in Article 288 of the Constitution of Portugal,[2] many of these maximalist enumerations may become obsolete before changing or informal mutations of the Constitution as has happened in the country after the signing of the Treaty of Maastricht. Authors such as Almeida Santos considered that the clauses of intangibility referring to the principle of collective ownership of the means of production, democratic planning

[2] This article established fourteen intangible clauses related to the democratic principle, but also the guarantee of a Welfare and interventionist Social State, that for example made mandatory the participation of the worker in the profits of the companies, prohibitions that have not been used in the neoliberal constitutional reforms after the fall of communism at the end of the 1980s.

economy and participation of grassroots organizations in the exercise of local power are considered "*unconstitutional by disuse*" (De Almeida Santos 1988, 955).

Given these two experiences we can conclude that the solution to the dilemma of the indeterminacy of the irreplaceable essential elements in the Colombian case cannot be solved through an exhaustive and detailed list of such elements in a maximalist or minimalist way, because it could be the case that the problem of the factual and legal cases exceed the prohibitions listed.

One of these cases in Colombia, not intended as an inherent element, was the amendment that was established for provisional employees in order to avoid the need for competition. This issue lacked any direct relation with the principles of deliberative democracy or legality, but the Constitutional Court, in Judgment C-588 of 2009 and C-249 of 2012, declared the proposed amendments unconstitutional by substitution taking into account principles such as merit, equality, civil service and public competition.

I think the methodology of the Constitutional Court is better. This methodology suggests that the judgement should be open for the idea of a "living Constitution" that constantly changes its interpretation. In effect, the court established that the substitution doctrine "*is not a complete, finished or permanently exhausted concept to identify the total set of hypotheses*". This idea is more practical and allows an effective response of the court while assessing the possible changes of the understanding of the essential elements of the Constitution.

Considering the above, I think the limitations or restrictions of the Constitutional Court in the review of the constitutional amendments must focus on the protection of the constitutional democracy from the democratic majorities held in the Congress. Moreover, I am also persuaded that the precedent settled by the Constitutional Court in the study of a constitutional amendment becomes binding for future decisions related with those principles exposed as structural or axial in a previous judgement.

Finally it should be noted that a new problem begins to appear on the issue of the material limits of the Constitution and the implementation of the of the substitution doctrine in Colombia. This problem refers to the possible collision or tension between principles that are considered essential to the Constitution. This new problem was first evidenced in the recent rulings C-579 of 2013 and C-577 of 2014, that examined the unconstitutionality of Legislative Act No. 1 of 2012, known as the "Legal Framework for Peace", that set the possibility of applying transitional justice rules in the criminalization of the former guerrilla members as well of the political participation or prospective candidates.

In those decisions, the Court decided not to declare unconstitutional this amendment but in the same way introduced modifications of the amendment in topics related with the international treaties related with the rights of the victims of truth, justice, reparation and conditions of non-repetition. In these two cases the Court considered whether the principle of the search for peace and reconciliation, seen as structural, should take precedence over the also essential principle of the rights of victims, and decided to harmonize them through the techniques of balancing (Villa Rosas 2014).

In sum, I believe that the "substitution doctrine of the Constitution" implemented by the Constitutional Court in the judgment C-551 of 2003 has been a good way to safeguard constitutional democracy on the possible excesses of majoritarian democracy. On the other hand I consider that it is better to establish the essential principles in the assessment of each concrete case, since the formulation of a series of maximalist or minimalist principles can represent new problems in the interpretation of the content and meaning of those elements.

10.4 General Conclusions

(i) Majoritarian democracy faces the paradox that its rationality depends on quantitative rather than qualitative criteria. For this reason it has created the idea of a constitutional democracy that attempts to limit majoritarian democracy by an inherent idea of a Constitution related with elements such as human rights, separation of powers and democracy. This idea cannot be the subject of amendment.

(ii) In order to limit majoritarian democracy, constitutionalism has created various instruments such as judicial review, constitutional rigidity and, in some cases, the most growing form, the doctrine of the jurisdictional limits of the power of amendment, which allows the Constitutional Court to declare unconstitutional amendments to the Constitution.

(iii) The doctrine of substitution of the Constitution in Colombia that has been implemented since the Judgment C-551 of 2003, which led to the declaration of unconstitutionality of five amendments to the Constitution, has been a good way to protect constitutional democracy against a majoritarian conception of democracy, for example in cases where the President wants to use the majority in Congress to remain in power – Case of the Re-election of the President, Judgment C-141 of 2010 – or to avoid the effectiveness of constitutional judgments – Judgments C – 588 of 2009 and C-249 of 2012.

(iv) The methods of rationality that the Court have used led the Constitutional Court to rationalize and balance decisions related with the unconstitutionality of constitutional amendments in order to identify the structural element in a particular case.

(v) It does not seem helpful to make either a maximalist or minimalist list of irreplaceable elements of the Constitution. These non-replaceable elements ultimately depend on the interpretation of their content and meaning by Court. However, theoretical tools and rational elements should be implemented to limit the power of the Court in the use of that doctrine. It should be deployed only as a last resort to protect the constitutional democracy from the abuses of the majorities.

(vi) There is evidence that new problems are arising with the replacement doctrine implemented in Colombia, such as the eventual collision of irreplaceable principles with the interpretation or conditioning of the constitutional amendments. This problem requires new theoretical tools that allow a rational decision in such cases.

(vii) Finally, the hypothesis that the doctrine of the substitution of the Constitution has been a way to limit the excesses of majoritarian democracy is well founded, but the Court must set new jurisprudential parameters for the implementation of this doctrine that are reasonable and weighted.

Acknowledgments Thanks to David Landau, Masson Ladd Professor of Law in Florida University, for helping me with the corrections of the translation of the article to english, and Thomas da Rosa Bustamante for the invitation to the I International Congress on Constitutional Law and Political Philosophy in Belo Horizonte.

References

Bernal Pulido, Carlos. 2013. Unconstitutional constitutional amendments in the case study of Colombia: An analysis of the justification and meaning of the constitutional replacement doctrine. *International Journal of Constitutional Law (I-CON)* 11(2): 339–357.

Bobbio, Norberto. 2002. La regla de la mayoría: límites y aporías. In *Teoría General de la Política*. Madrid: Trotta.

Choudry, Sujit. 2006. *The migration of constitutional ideas*. Cambridge: Cambridge University Press.

De Almeida Santos, Antonio. 1988. Los límites materiales de la revisión constitucional a la luz de la doctrina y el sentido común. *Revista de Estudios Políticos* 60–61: 955.

De Vega, Pedro. 1985. *La reforma constitucional y la problemática del poder constituyente*. Madrid: Civitas.

Guastini, Riccardo. 2007. Sobre el concepto de Constitución. In *Teoría del Neoconstitucionalismo: ensayos escogidos*, ed. Miguel Carbonell. Madrid: Trotta.

Kelsen, Hans. 2008. *Teoría General del Estado* (General Theory of Law). México: Coyoacán.

Marbury, William L. 1920. The limitations upon amending power. *Harvard Law Review* 33(223): 225.

Radbruch, Gustav. 1999. *Relativismo y Derecho*. Bogotá: Temis.

Roznai, Yaniv. 2013. Unconstitutional constitutional amendment – The migration and success of a constitutional idea. *The American Journal of Comparative Law* 61(3): 657–720.

Roznai, Yaniv. 2014. *Unconstitutional constitutional amendments: A study of the nature and limits of constitutional amendment powers*. Ph.D. dissertation. London School of Economics, London.

Villa Rosas, Gonzalo. 2014. La Sentencia C-579 de 2013 y la doctrina de la sustitución de la Constitución. In *Justicia de transición y Constitución: análisis de la Sentencia C-579 de 2012 de la Corte Constitucional*, ed. Kai Ambos, 22–101. Bogotá: Temis-Konrad Adenauer Stifung.

Waldron. 1999. *Jeremy, Law and Disagreement*. Oxford: Oxford University Press.

Colombian Constitutional Court Decisions

Sentencia C – 551 de 2003, M.P. Eduardo Montealegre Lynnet.

Sentencia C-1200 de 2003, M.P. Manuel José Cepeda, Rodrigo Escobar Gil.

Sentencia C-572 de 2004, M.P (E) Rodrigo Uprimny.

Sentencia C-970 de 2004, M.P. Rodrigo Escobar Gil.

Sentencia C- 1040 de 2005, M.P. Manuel José Cepeda, Rodrigo Escobar Gil, Marco Gerardo Monroy Cabra, Humberto Sierra Porto, Álvaro Tafur, Clara Inés Vargas.
Sentencia C-588 de 2009, M.P. Gabriel Eduardo Mendoza.
Sentencia C-141 de 2010, M.P. Humberto Sierra Porto.
Sentencia C-574 de 2011, M.P. Juan Carlos Henao.
Sentencia C-249 de 2012, M.P. Juan Carlos Henao.
Sentencia C-1056 de 2012, M.P. Nilson Pinilla.
Sentencia C-579 de 2013, M.P. Jorge Ignacio Pretelt.
Sentencia C-577 de 2014, M.P. (E) Martha Victoria Sáchica.

Part IV
Constitutional Promises and Democratic Participation

Chapter 11
Is There Such Thing as a Radical Constitution?

Vera Karam de Chueiri

Abstract A radical Constitution is at the same time promise and effectiveness. It retains the constituent impulse, which reappears each time it is enforced. As such, the Constitution is a possible mediation to political action. The tension between constituent power and constituted powers or between potentiality and actuality plays a fundamental role for contemporary constitutionalism and democracy. Then, constitutionalism is that which exhibits and reaffirms – instead of annihilating- constituent power, as far as it ensures and renews democratic politics and its commitments. Past events such as protests that happened in Egypt, Turkey, Greece, Portugal, Spain, United States, Brazil, etc. must be understood not as pure political action but as grounded either in the achievements of democracy or in the achievements of constitutionalism, i.e., there is a right to protest (even against the Constitution). A radical Constitution is that which retains the radical impulse of constituent power in the constituted community aiming at a provisory yet necessary agreement between promise and effectiveness; between people's absolute power and its restraints; between political action and the law; between democracy and constitutionalism. Constitution as promise is what makes one act politically, i.e., it is no longer a simple radical impulse but the realization of something, like the enforcement of rights by means of the Constitution. Then, promise soon becomes effectiveness. The recent events I mentioned above are noteworthy as far as they are not an exception to the possibilities of a constitutional democracy but exactly what it is about: potentiality and actuality; promise and effectiveness; stabilization and crisis, not against the Constitution but because of the radicalization of it.

V.K. de Chueiri (✉)
Faculdade de Direito, Universidade Federal do Paraná, Praça Santos Andrade, 50, Curitiba, PR 80020-300, Brazil
e-mail: vkchueiri@gmail.com

T. Bustamante, B.G. Fernandes (eds.), *Democratizing Constitutional Law*, Law and Philosophy Library 113, DOI 10.1007/978-3-319-28371-5_11

11.1 Introduction

This essay concerns the research I have done, since 2010, in the research group on Constitutionalism and Democracy at Federal University of Paraná Law School on the idea (and possibility) of a radical Constitution.

In its first part I discuss, on the one hand, the notion of Constitution as promise and, on the other hand, as the realization of such promise and the bulk of difficulties, precisely, paradoxes, tensions that such approach entails. I take Robert Post's (2000, 187) premise that democratic constitutionalism implies a collective intervention by the people (a shared voice), which assumes the ineradicable tension between collective self-governance and the rule of law in order to establish the ongoing structure of democratic states. In the second part, I discuss the link between constituent power, sovereignty and the Constitution and, in the third part, the relation between constitutionalism and democracy. The discussion on the foundations of such relations is central to this essay as far as it sets the place from where I speak which is either political philosophy or constitutional law. If they were simple relations, of easy connections between categories, it would be irrelevant to face them for the proposal of a radical Constitution.

Contemporary constitutional theory has been generous in arguments, whose disagreements -either in favor of political action or constituted order, of potentiality or actuality, of democracy or constitutionalism, of rights or majorities- have instigated new theoretical positions and new practices. In this essay, I am more focused on theoretical issues concerning the possibility of a radical Constitution. However, I am firmly convinced that another important challenge is the internalization of this idea into social and legal practices in order to deepen the commitment to democracy and constitutionalism. Then, I finally propose the notion of a radical constitution as a possible mediation for political action based on the arguments brought in the first, second and third parts.

This essay is also an effort to deal with constitutional time, which integrates past, present and future as far as it redeems the promises made in the name of constitutionalism and democracy in the *now:* As Balkin and Siegel say, *Constitution is always a work in progress* (2009, 02).

11.2 Brief Excursus: Political Action and Constitution

There are some scholars such as Paulo Arantes[1] for whom political initiative cannot discard mediations without being *demonized.* I do agree with him that every political action without mediation is almost immediately identified with violence, excess, abuse and, then, with the *demon.* I would like, for a while, to stress this metaphor,

[1] I quote Brazilian philosopher Paulo Arantes who gave a conference at UFPR Law School, in November 2013, in the event called *Cidades Rebeldes* (*Rebel Cities*).

having in mind Slavoj Zizek's text *Trouble in Paradise* which I will further talk about.

Pushing Paulo Arantes' argument a little further, I would say that a political action without mediation retains an interesting radicalness, yet not necessarily insurrectional, in the sense he advocates for. For this reason, I would like to explore the idea (and the possibility) of a radical Constitution and therefore of a possible mediation for political action, by means of the Constitution: not exactly the basic norm, nor its text but also them, as far as the Constitution does not let itself to be reduced to the constituted power retaining in it the constituent power. As such, the Constitution radically constitutes us as a political community.

It is noteworthy that in Paulo Arantes's book *Extinção* (2007, 153–154), in the chapter on *Estado de sítio*, he refers to this institution (the State of Siege) as a *exceptional legal regime to which a political community is subjected because of a threat to public order and during which extraordinary powers are given to governmental authorities, at the same time public liberties and constitutional warranties are suspended.* That is, the State of Siege is a situation that takes exception on some basic rights and warrantees, in situations of great political, social and institutional tension but in a constitutional context. It seems to me that despite the author critique about the mediation of the Constitution, at the end he recognizes it, even to stress the paradox in this creature of modern constitutionalism (Arantes 2007, 155): *Exceptional measures authorized by public force must be determined by the law (…).*

The point I first want to make is the link between Constitution and constituent power which is either immanent to a certain notion of Constitution, the radical Constitution or contingent (eventual yet necessary and inevitable). This implies in the following premise: one cannot reduce the constituent moment (promise) and the Constitution (the real thing) to the terms of a dual logic (another world and this world). This premise deconstructs the naïve faith (easily found in Constitutional Law Books) that the Constitution is nothing but a text; or that its norms/rules appease political tensions; finally, that it is enough to constitutionalize political, social, economic, environmental, labor, etc. relations of/in a given society and they will happen in the way prescribed by the Constitution and, therefore, we will live in a community without tensions as if it were paradise.

There is an agonistic sense in politics, which have to be explored in the Constitution. Paraphrasing Chantal Mouffe (2000, p. 99) we need a Constitution able to capture the agonistic nature of the political, i.e., a radical Constitution.

Zizek says (2013, 102), in a essay called *Troubles in Paradise, in the book, Cidades Rebeldes: troubles in Hell seem to be understandable but why are there troubles in Paradise, in prosperous countries or in countries that, at least, are in a period of fast development such as Turkey, Sweden or Brazil?*

Paraphrasing the author, I would say that troubles in States of exception concerning restriction of rights or suspension of rights are understandable (the last Brazilian dictatorship after 1964 *Coup d'État*) however, I inquire why are there troubles of these sort in democratic constitutional States such as Brazil after 1988 Constitution? Raquel Rolnik (2013, 08) talks about the right to have rights, which nourished many contests in the 1970s and the 1980s and has inspired new Constitutions and the emergence of new actors in political scenario. Against the common understanding that in States of exception basic liberties are restricted, there is the difficulty of understanding why in the existence of basic liberties and basic rights one might be in a exceptional State?

Maybe the most problematic question is the following: why are there troubles in constitutional democracies? This essay has in this question its *leitmotiv* or, according to Nimer Sultany (2012, 374), the centrality of the tension between constitutionalism and democracy for political theory and constitutional theory derives from its implications for larger discussions concerning the justification of political regimes.

11.3 Constituent Power and Constituted Power: The Constitution as Promise and the Constitution as Effectiveness

The Constitution as promise refers to an absolute indeterminate (Caputo 1997, 161–162), a structural future, a future to come. The structure of this *to- come, à venir*, of this structural future or of this promise (I am talking about the Constitution) *that in principle cannot come about is the very openendedness of the present that makes it impossible for the present to draw itself into a circle, to close in and gather around itself* (Caputo 1997, 162). The promise from this messianic perspective is the structure of this *to-come* which exposes the contingence and the deconstruction of the present. To that which Derrida calls the very structure of the experience and *where experience means running up against the other, encountering something we could not anticipate, expect, fore-have or fore-see, something that knocks our socks off, that brings us up short and takes our breath away* (Caputo 1997, 162).

According to Derrida (1996, 82) there is no language without the performative dimension of the promise. Then, the language of constitutionalism as well as the language of democracy is in itself promise. To constitutionalism, it is the promise of the Constitution and its realization/effectiveness through the exercise of rights. To democracy, promise means the always-present possibility of reinventing rights.

That which strikes me most is this moment in which the Constitution makes promises, announces and compromises us (with such promises). This moment is very much related to democracy as something to come. The difficulty lies in the impossibility of the full realization of these promises in the present (constituent power and democracy) as far as it would mean the dissolution of their own conditions of possibility. However, this difficulty, contrary to what it seems, opens up an important space of discussion and action for contemporary constitutional theory and political theory such as the relation between constituent power and democracy and between them and constituted power (or the actual Constitution). These relations must not be synthetized in a triumphant constitutionalism.

The Constitution, as the constituent impulse, means promise(s) and then relates itself to democracy. According to Negri (2002, 11), *nell'età moderna i due concetti sono stati spesso coestensivi e comunque inseriti in un processo storico che, avvici-*

nandosi il XX secolo, sempre di più li ha sovrapposti. Such promise, impulse or constituent force prevents the Constitution of being a fixed thing, like a trophy won in a battle by constitutionalism; of being just the source of constitutional norms/rules.

Even considering constitutionalism as a restraint to constituent power and democracy, because of that, it imposes to itself a certain closure that will always be provisory. Then, the Constitution as promise and as a real (effective) thing - likewise constituent power, democracy and constitutionalism - experiences an on-going and unavoidable tension. According to Nimer Sultany (2012, 371) instead of attempting to solve or give a right answer to the difficulties that result from the relation between constitutionalism and democracy, between constituent power and constituted power one should recognize their irreconcilability and, then, one could have a better understanding of the role of law in society.

Democracy as openness, i.e., the democracy to-come it is not the future democracy. According to Derrida (1996, 83) *there is an engagement with regard to democracy, which consists in recognizing the irreducibility of the promise when, in the messianic moment, it can come.* Just like happens with constituent power, the promise of democracy is, at the same time, a suspension, that which is not decidable, as well as an impulse to the real, effective Constitution, to that which is decidable.

In its relation to time constituent power is its suspension as well as its acceleration. Constituent power opposes itself to constitutionalism considered as the limitation of power by the law. Such restraint of power by the law and, by the same token, the control over government does not fit in the constituent impulse, which always happens in the present. Then, it is precisely the opposite, that is, the constituted thing, that which had already happened (in the past). Time in its present continuous constitutes a new time, which not only redeem the past but also changes it. Constitutionalism restrained to an idea of the Constitution as a fixed thing it is always a glance to the past, except if it retains the constituent impulse (the promise).

A radical Constitutions is the one which does not conform itself to liberal tools of mutual negotiation among constituted powers. It dares to be more than that, that is, to be the subject and object of democratic politics. Basic rights are in the Constitution as far as it enables their permanent reinvention through political action. A radical Constitution does not simply synthetizes the tension between constituent power (democracy) and constituted powers (constitutionalism): it is precisely this, the tension. One should interpret Sieyès's (1970, 180–181) statement that the Constitution, before anything else, presupposes a constituent power as the Constitution presupposes itself as constituent power (Agamben 1998, 40–41).

The power of the Constitution, especially a radical Constitution comes from the fact that it imposes itself as the manifestation of constituent power and popular sovereignty binding both. Thus, in order to better face and explore the link between democracy and constitutionalism one has to first face and explore the link between sovereignty and constituent power and between these latter and constituted powers. My task is from now on to discuss the possibilities and difficulties of such relations, as well as the categories to better understand the notion of radical constitution.

11.4 Constituent Power and Sovereignty

In the Sixteenth Century Jean Bodin (1955, 53) says in his book *De la République «(l)a souveraineté est la puissance absolue et perpétuelle d'une République... »*.[2] These two characteristics, absolute and perpetual, were thought as fixed conditions for the exercise of power. It is perpetual as far as "(t)he true sovereign remains always seized of his power. A perpetual authority therefore must be understood to mean one that lasts for the lifetime of him who exercises it."(1955, 54) It is absolute to the extent of its unconditionality. A power is given to a sovereign not in virtue of some office or commission, nor in the form of a revocable grant. If the power given by the people is charged with conditions is neither properly sovereign, nor absolute. So, it is an absolute power in the sense that it does not owe obedience to positive laws passed by whom earlier had the power and, neither to the laws the sovereign himself has made.

One century later, Hobbes (1997, 129) affirms that *"(t)he final cause, end, or design of men, who naturally love liberty, and dominion over others, in the introduction of that restraint upon themselves, in which we see them live in commonwealths, is the foresight of their own preservation, and of a more contented life thereby; that is to say, of getting them out of that miserable condition of war*". This miserable condition of war of everyone against everyone is the consequence of men natural passions, precisely when there is no power to keep them in peace *"and tie them by fear of punishment to the performance of their covenants, and observation of those laws of nature..."* And he adds: *"covenants, without the sword, are but words, and of no strength to secure a man at all."*

For Hobbes (1997, 132), the origin of this coercive power is the will. Initially, the will of every man to concede to one person or to a group of people his or her own will, that is, *"to reduce all their wills, by plurality of voices, unto one will*". The will is a prior condition for constituting the political community and whose structure is paradoxical and without which the State -the great Leviathan or mortal god-would not exist. For this, the sovereign's will becomes the principle of order. For the sovereign must have the monopoly of force. It is in this movement of willing, of monopolizing the force and of establishing the order that remains the very idea of sovereignty.

Hobbes and Bodin identify the sovereign power in its site, which is occupied by the figure of the king. Nevertheless, even Bodin was careful in defining sovereignty abstractly and impersonally. In this sense, one could abstract the figure of the sovereign either form the government or the parliament or still the people.

Late modern thought about sovereignty – I mean, from the end of nineteenth to the twentieth century- has reacted to abstract definitions and formal analysis of sovereignty. That is, the foundation of most part of sovereign States was due to a

---

[2]Bodin "SOVEREIGNTY is that absolute and perpetual power vested in a commonwealth which in Latin is termed majestas ... The term needs careful definition, because although it is the distinguishing mark of a commonwealth, and an understanding of its nature fundamental to any treatment of politics, no jurist or political philosopher has in fact attempted to define it."

situation one might call revolutionary. And even considering that such revolutionary situations are not necessarily spectacular genocides, expulsions or deportations that often go with the foundation of States (Derrida 1990, 991), they are invariably terrible, as far as they are in themselves and in their very violence uninterpretable and indecipherable. This violence is not strange to law; instead it is in the law and suspends the law. It interrupts the established order to found another one.

The force and the Law are the aims of sovereignty. At this point I dare saying that violence and the law do not differentiate them within sovereignty. Sovereignty is, then, a zone of indistinction. This is even more visible when one relates sovereign power to constituent power.

For legal science, the constituent power is traditionally the source from where it springs the new constitutional order. It is the power to make a (new) Constitution from which the remaining (constituted) powers of the State get their structure.

If constituent power does not emanate from any constituted power, if it is not an institution of the constituted power then it is an political act of choice, the radical determination that unfolds a horizon or yet the radical device of something that still does not exist and whose conditions of existence presuppose that the creating act does not loose its characteristics in the creation.

Constituent power opposes constitutionalism as the government constrained by law. The limitation of power by the law and, accordingly, the control over government do not fit in a constituent movement (present time) but is, precisely, the opposite, the constituted thing (past time). We are dealing here with times (in the plural). A time in the present (continuous) that in constituting a new time not just redeems the old time but reverses it. In its relation to time, the constituent power accelerates it, breaking with the past and instituting a new time.

Does the concept of sovereignty work as a criterion of truth to the constituent power? At this point, it is worth recalling the arguments I have just presented on sovereignty and to perceive that once we understand the *locus* of sovereignty as a zone of indistinction, that is, as a zone of an ineradicable tension between that which is outside and inside, one can think it in terms of constituent power without any mutual sacrifice. This interpretation stresses the paradox of sovereignty.

The rule of law as a representation of constituted powers opposes constituent power to sovereignty and it is against this opposition that I claim. My point is that the Constitution – as the result of constituent power – cannot become an obstacle to political action in terms of democratic politics. On the contrary, it must mediate it.

One has to rescue this idea and this practice that sovereign people create and establish its Constitution (constitutes themselves as such) by means of all radical impulse that is in such constituent act and for this very reason they (the people) impose to themselves the norms/rules which will regulate their constituted powers.

In the *Metaphysics*, in the very beginning of book *Theta*, Aristotle (1984, 181) power (δυναμιζ), working (ενεργεια) and fulfillment (ευτελεχεια) belong to the realm of being. Then, power is not a mere category but it is essential to understand being as such what means that a question on power is also a question on being; it is an ontological question. However, power once applied to being is considered as related to change and movement. Accordingly, to understand being implies to understand power as change and movement, that is, as what moves.

Aristotle (1984, 182) affirms that there is a primary kind of power to which genuine powers are really related (1046a9). This primary power "*which is the source of change in another thing or in another aspect of the same thing*" (1046a11-12) is *dynamis*, and cannot be confounded with that which changes -the fixed entity. Then, power is primarily active – power of acting- or passive – power of being acted upon and either one has to be though in relation to the other. For, power is one yet in an active or passive mode. Lack or privation of power is as essential as the (active or passive) presence of power. Then, lack or privation is not a negation of power but essentially constitutes it.

Power and act differ in the sense that "*something may be capable of being without actually being, and capable of not being, yet be*". (1047a21-23)" In the antithesis indicated by this assertion, there is potentiality in one pole and actuality in the other. Yet, Aristotle does not prefer one instead of the other, as both are two modes of primary being.). It would be a mistake to think that potentiality would disappear into actuality.

Dynamis is constitutively also a-dynamis. Both *dynamis* and a-dynamis refer to the same phenomenon: "*...any power in a given object related to a given process has a corresponding incapacity.*" (1046a32-33) Potentiality appears as potentiality to and potentiality not to. The relation between potentiality and actuality can be thought in terms of a suspension, that is, potentiality relates itself to actuality to the extent of its suspension: "*it is capable of the act in not realizing it, it is sovereignly capable of its own im-potentiality.*" (Agamben 1998, 45) Potentiality and actuality are the two faces of the same phenomenon, namely the sovereign self-founding of being.

Aristotle's considerations on being became paradigmatic for modern political philosophy especially for thinking the relation between constituent power and sovereignty. It is possible to associate the Aristotelian structure of potentiality and actuality to the structure of sovereignty and constituent power. To the same extent that potentiality does not pass over actuality, Agamben (1998, 47) advocates that sovereign power does not pass over actuality and then it retains its potentiality or its constituting power in the form of a suspension.

The sovereign power as a constituted order keeps the radical impulse of constituent power. This does not mean that the constituent power is ontologically reducible to the constituted order losing its autonomy and freedom but instead stresses the permanent tension that is present in these two concepts showing that there is no possible *Aufhebung* between the two. There is no dialectics – in the strong Hegelian sense- between constituent power and constituted power.

At a first glance, constituting potentiality seems to be there in the constituted power in the form of its own opposite with which it is identical and whose contradiction is reconciled in the idea of sovereignty that contains within itself the opposition of the other two and yet it contains their unity. However, sovereignty does not appease or resolve the contradiction as it is supposed to do so by the fact that a rational structure cannot rest on what is self-contradictory. On the contrary, constituting potentiality remains there, recalcitrant, as a radical impulse. For, one may think beyond any possible dialectical relation between constituent power and constituted power: first, by agreeing with the fact that sovereignty is not an exclusively political concept or an exclusively legal concept; second, by considering that sovereign power is not opposed to constituent power as they are at a point of indistinction; third, by assuming that there is no possible synthesis between the two and that on this impossibility that one has to remain and fourth because they are somehow incommensurable, therefore, one cannot be the dialectical opposite of the other. Finally, the tension between constituent power and constituted power has to be understood as a vigorous sign towards a radically democratic society.

Thus, I am back to my initial problem concerning the paradoxical relation between democracy and constitutionalism yet from the viewpoint of the relation between constituent power and constituted power(s). My point is that it is possible and desirable to conceive constitutionalism as that which exhibits and reaffirms – instead of annihilating- constituent power as far as it ensures and renews democratic politics and its commitments. This happens when constitutional rights are respected and enforced. If, on the one hand, constitutionalism leads to the past, on the other hand, it can happen in the present not as a mere repetition of the past but as the condition to the exercise of rights. That is, as a condition for political action, constitutionalism makes promises and compromises and then it opens itself to the future. This happens in moments of radial realization of democratic commitments.

Claude Lefort, in a essay written in the eighties talked about democracy as a constant process of reinventing rights (Lefort 1981). According to it, he defends a democratic revolution whose main trait is the daily fight for rights, the conflict, the agonistic perspective, which must not be eradicated form society.

It is necessary to think about conflict in terms of that which, at the same time, supposes the fact of power and search for a consideration for differences at Law (Lefort 1981, 62). Conflicts constitute more and more the specificities of modern democratic societies. So, democracy inaugurates the experience of an elusive and untamable society in which the people are sovereign but do not stop questioning their own identity (Lefort 1981, 118).

For instance, recent manifestations in Brazil and elsewhere put in evidence social, economic, cultural, religious and other kinds of conflicts. Generally speaking, most of the people in the street asked for a more just and equal society- in many aspects- reaffirming, then, the potentiality of constituent power as far as they claimed for the effectiveness of constitutional rights. By doing that they renew constitutionalism.

The tension between constituent power and constituted power or rather between potentiality and actuality plays a fundamental role for contemporary constitutionalism and democracy.

In recent Brazilian constitutional history, constituent power (as potentiality) refers to a series of events carried out by the people, from the beginning of the eighties on, and not exactly to the National Constituent Assembly of 1987–1988. This potentiality reappears every time that someone or something (such as the current demand for a new constituent assembly) intends to hit the Brazilian Constitution.

In this sense, the relation between sovereignty and constituent power, constituent power and constituted powers makes room for (the notion of) a radical Constitution.

Looking from another perspective, this *dynamis* refers to the people's capacity to rule themselves and to impose to themselves a Constitution. In doing so, people constitute themselves as a political community and because of that such Constitution must be respected and experienced. Yet, popular sovereign power has paradoxically to be restrained. This is the whole issue about democracy and constitutionalism.

11.5 Democracy and Constitutionalism

At the very beginning of his book *Brennan and Democracy*, Frank Michelman (1999, 04) asserts that *American constitutional theory is eternally hounded (...)by a search of harmony between (...) two clashing commitments: one the ideal of government as constrained by the law ("constitutionalism"), the other to the ideal of government by act of the people ("democracy").* This is also true for most of constitutional theory and constitutional practices after the terrible experiences of totalitarianism and authoritarianism[3] and the predominance of constitutional democratic States in western societies from the second half of the last century on.

If the settlement of constitutional democracies in most western countries has been a significant achievement in the last 60 years yet the conciliation between constitutionalism and democracy has still been very problematic. Democracy as the sovereign government of the people inevitably implies a tension with constitutionalism as the rule of law. That is, people ruling themselves or the government by the people – majority government - is limited by the Constitution. As Michelman says (1999, 06), *"Constitutionalism" appears to mean something like this: The containment of popular political decision-making by a basic law, the Constitution – a "law of lawmaking,"* Considering that the Constitution for and in democracies is the outcome of a popular constituent power and considering that it is the basic law, then it *must be untouchable by the majoritarian politics it means to contain* (Michelman 1999, 06). This does not mean (and it is not desirable at all) that the constitution shields itself in face of democratic politics but it means that democracy and constitutionalism are, somehow, co-originary. Michelman folds these two principles from the standpoint of that which can be politically decidable. And what is politically decidable? Can the people themselves define it? Yes and no!

Of course the people must decide for themselves those politically decidable issues on moral, political and cultural grounds. But, on the other hand, some decisions taken by the people in constituting their community have to lay beyond the reach of majority, such as the limits of governmental powers, the commitments with human dignity, self-determination, liberty and equality etc.

This paradox between constitutionalism and democracy is somehow unavoidable and necessary and it brings some institutional difficulties. Yet it must be faced if one intends to radicalize the Constitution.

---

[3] I am referring to the event of Nazism in Germany, Stalinism in the former Soviet Union and most south-American dictatorship in the last century.

Constitutionalism means to restraint political power by the law. This notion becomes stronger as far as there is a Constitution, especially a written Constitution, with binding norms/rules to which all other norms/rules are subjected. However, none of this would be enough without a democratic counterpart. It is democracy that does not let constitutionalism to be paralyzed in its achievements. On the contrary, democracy tensions constitutionalism all the time and it renews it by means of the enforcement of the Constitution. As Post and Siegel (2007, 374) proposes democratic constitutionalism *is a model to analyze the understandings and practices by which constitutional rights have historically been established in the context of cultural controversy.* They also take disagreement *as a normal condition to the development of constitutional law.* As matter of fact any attempt to avoid disagreement threats democracy and constitutionalism or rather, politics and the law.

The Constitution is between the political act that established it and the legal act that enforces it. This tension is rather productive than problematic. The challenge for contemporary constitutional theory is then to conciliate a reasonably stable Constitution that assure full protection to people's rights at the same time it restrains power with an intuition in favor of self-government (Gargarella 1996, 128). Besides these aspects it has to take into account the political action to be mediated by the Constitution.

It is worthy to recall Post and Siegel's (2007, 376) considerations about backlash. According to them, it *expresses the desire of a free people to influence the content of their Constitution, yet backlash also threatens the independence of law. Backlash is where the integrity of the rule of law clashes with the need of our constitutional order for democratic legitimacy.* In this sense, people have to act politically expressing their own understanding of the Constitution, which means a certain protagonism by them in enforcing the Constitution.

11.6 Radical Constitution: A Possibility?

A radical Constitution must retain the potentiality of constituent power yet such potentiality becomes actuality by means of the enforcement of rights. In other words, the potentiality of the Constitution (as a radical one) appears when it is enforced, when it gives arguments for decisions that grant rights and when this task is done by the people; it is an individual and collective endeavor of the people who do it by means of political action. In general, it is an institutional task and therefore faces institutional difficulties. To overcome these difficulties institutions of government and the people must be understood as subjects of a radical Constitution and, this latter, must be understood as a dynamic, living thing.

As I have already said, in the past 4 years a sequence of events in different places around the world such as the Arabic Spring, protests in Turkey, Spain, Portugal and Greece, the Occupy movement in Wall Street, New York, June protests in Brazil in 2013, among others, have suggested that political action does not have to be mediated by anything. They are radical in this very sense of not being mediated by anything: no labor unions, no political parties, no traditional mass organizations or any other institution: it is just lots of young people mobilized by social networks acting in the street.

It is as if nowadays none of these young people had the power to decide the most important issues that concern their life in society or rather that concerns their fate. Abandoned by the government they are very skeptical about institutional designs and solutions.

Then, they claim to take their fate on their own hands without mediation. They want to act and they act directly and without a general goal yet with a common feeling of dissatisfaction, which put individual demands together.

Therefore, the argument I am developing in this paper is in the opposite way of that of a political action that renounces the mediation of the Constitution. By saying that, I present and defend the idea that these events happen (and must happen) because they are grounded either on the achievements of democracy or constitutionalism. Put it in other terms: there is a right to protest (even against the Constitution).

One has to consider that not everybody shares the same interpretation and judgment about the Constitution. It seems somehow contradictory that in democratic constitutional States (some of them more or less democratic and more or less constitutional) events such as the ones that happened in Turkey, Egypt, Greece, Spain, Portugal, Brazil and United States were considered as if they were a *state of exception*. At this point my argument takes a step back and goes ahead. It goes ahead in agreeing with Benjamin that the state of exception became paradigm of government or, according to Paulo Arantes, it is the state of exception as the expression of relations between center and periphery in the new global imperial order that makes possible to act politically in the street. It takes a step back in understanding that this state of exception in its pure form as a denunciation or a diagnosis do not activate its own revolutionary dispositive.

Zizek (2013, 101–108) says that problems in the hell seem to be understandable yet problems in paradise should not happen. Do these facts affect the very sense of democracy and constitutionalism? Of course they do, but how do they affect? Or, is there a constitutional democracy without the possibility to put into question its own basis? At this point I recall Michelman's (1999, 06–07) assertion that *by the principle of democracy, the people of a country ought to decide for themselves all of politically decidable matters about which they have good moral and material reason to care.*

The tricky thing is first to define what should be politically decidable by the people (as it is a deliberation and a decision to be taken by the people themselves) and second, how should be? I also recall Post and Siegel's (2007, 375) assertion that *(w)hen citizens speak about their most passionately held commitments in the language of a shared constitutional tradition, they invigorate that tradition. In this way, even resistance to judicial interpretation can enhance the Constitution's democratic legitimacy.*

In spite of the institutional difficulty that the idea of self-government poses to democratic politics, as far as not everybody is able to make the Laws, it (the idea of self-government) can strengthen individual responsibility and, in my opinion, it reveals itself by means of political action. For Post and Siegel (2007, 375) citizens should not acquiesce in judicial decisions that speak in a desinterested voice of law. Such nonacquiescence means to act politically yet without taking into account the constitutional order and the negotiation it allows between the rule of law and self-governance.

A radical Constitution is that which is where popular political action is and it is not dissociated from this. On the contrary, a radical constitution enables popular political action so that democracy and constitutionalism can be renovated reinvented. Then, Constitution is, at the same time, potentiality and actuality, promise and effectiveness, stabilization and crisis (not against the itself but because of it). Radical has to do with that which is at the origin, at the root, as well as, with that which is unstable and provokes chain reactions.

If constituent power is the space and time of making promises then, it is exactly this that the Constitution has to retain from it and by the time of its actualization turn to be effectiveness. By effectiveness I mean the radical character Constitution has retained from constituent power which allows one, in the name of democracy and constitutionalism, to fight for rights, to reinvent them, every time, on the street and from the street. The present time of the Constitution has to be understood in its relation to the past and to the future. Thus, the time of the Constitution is the time of its enforcement by the people and by institutional spheres; the time of the Constitution is the time of the events; it (the time) does not stop; it accelerates, it is the time of life that one lives; it is the now. To radicalize the Constitution means to live it intensively without retreat in face of the dangers of life.

References

Ackerman, Bruce. 2000. *We the people*. Foundations. Cambridge, MA/London: The Belknap Press of Harvard University.

Agamben, Giorgio. 1998. *Homo Sacer: Sovereign Power and Bare Life*. Trans. Daniel Heller-Roazen. Stanford: Stanford University Press.

Arantes, Paulo. 2007. *Extinção*. São Paulo: Boitempo.

Aristotle. 1984. *The complete works*, vol. I & II, ed. Jonathan Barnes. Princeton: Princeton University Press.

Blakin, Jack M., and Reva B. Siegel. 2009. *The constitution in 2020*. Oxford: Oxford University Press.

Bodin, Jean. 1955. *The Six Books on The Commonwealth*. Trans. M.J. Tooley. Oxford: Basil Blackwell Oxford

Braga, Ruy. 2013. Sob a sombra do precariado. In *Cidades Rebeldes: passe livre e as manifestações que tomaram as ruas do Brasil*, ed. Ermínia Maricato et al., 79–82. São Paulo: Boitempo/ Carta maior.

Caputo, John. 1997. *Deconstruction in a nutshell*. New York: Fordham University Press.

Chueiri, Vera Karam de. 2005. *Before the law: Philosophy and literature*. Michigan: Proquest, UMI.

Derrida, Jacques. 1990. Force of law: The mystical foundation of authority. *Cardozo Law Review* 11: 5–6.

Derrida, Jacques. 1996. Remarks on deconstruction and pragmatism. In *Pragmatism and deconstruction*, ed. Chantal Mouffe. New York/London: Routledge.

Dworkin, Ronald. 1982. *Taking rights seriously*. Cambridge, MA: Harvard University Press.
Dworkin, Ronald. 1985. *A matter of principle*. Cambridge, MA: Harvard University Press.
Dworkin, Ronald. 1986. *Law's empire*. Cambridge, MA: Harvard University Press.
Dworkin, Ronald. 1994. *Life's dominion*. New York: Vintage Books.
Ely, John Hart. 1980. *Democracy and distrust. A theory of judicial review*. Cambridge, MA/London: Harvard University Press.
Gargarella, Roberto. 1996. *La justicia frente al gobierno: sobre el carácter contramayoritario del poder judicial*. Barcelona: Ariel.
Gargarella, Roberto. 2007. *El derecho a la protesta*. Buenos Aires: Ad-Hoc.
Gargarella, Roberto. 2008. Una disputa imaginaria sobre el controle judicial de las leyes: El constitucionalismo popular frente la teoría de Carlos Nino. In *Homenaje a Carlos Santiago Nino*, ed. Roberto Gargarella et alli. Buenos Aires: la ley.
Habermas, Jüergen. 1995. *Justification and application. Remarks on discourse ethics*. Cambridge, MA/London: The MIT Press.
Hamilton, Alexander, James Madison, and John Jay. 2003. *The federalist papers*. New York: Signet Classic.
Hobbes, Thomas. 1997. *Leviathan or the matter, form and power of a Commonwealth ecclesisticall and civil*. New York: Touchstone Book.
Kramer, Larry. 2004. *The people themselves. Popular constitutionalism and judicial review*. New York: Oxford University Press.
Lefort, Claude. 1981. *A invenção democrática*. São Paulo: Brasiliense.
Michelman, Frank. 1999. *Brennan and democracy*. Princeton: Princeton University Press.
Mouffe, Chantal. 2000. *The democractic paradox*. London/New York: Verso.
Negri, Antonio. 2002. *Il potere constituent. Saggio sulle alternative del modern*. Roma: Manifestolibri.
Nino, Carlos Santiago. 1996. *La constitución de la democracia deliberativa*. Barcelona: Gedisa editorial.
Occupy: Movimentos de protesto que tomaram as ruas. 2012. Trad. João Alexandre Peschaski. São Paulo: Boitempo, Carta Maior.
Post, Robert C. 2000. Democratic constitutionalism and cultural heterogeinity. *Faculty Scholarship Series*. Paper, 189. http://digitalcommons.law.yale.edu/fss_papers/189
Post, Robert C., and Reva B. Siegel. 2004. Popular constitutionalism, departmentalism and judicial supremacy. *California Law Review* 92: 1029.
Post, Robert C., and Reva B. Siegel. 2007. Roe Rage: Democratic constitutionalism and backlash. *Harvard Civil-Rights Civil-Liberties Law Review* 42: 373–433.
Post, Robert C., and Reva B. Siegel. 2009. Democratic constitutionalism. In *The constitution in 2020*, ed. Jack Balkin and Reva Siegel, 25–34. Oxford: Oxford University Press.
Post, Robert C., and Reva B. Siegel. 2013. *Constitucionalismo democratico: por una reconciliación entre Constitución y pueblo*. Trad. Leonardo García Jaramillo. Buenos Aires: Siglo XXI.
Rolnik, Raquel. 2013. As vozes das ruas. As revoltas de junho e suas interpretações. In: Maricato, Ermínia et al. Cidades Rebeldes, 06–12 São Paulo: Boitempo/Carta Maior.
Rosenfeld, Michel, and Andrew Arato. 1998. *Habermas on law and democracy: Critical exchanges*. Berkley/Los Angeles/London: University of California Press.
Sieyes, Emmanuel. 1970. *Qu'est-ce que le Tiers état?* Genève: Libraire Droz.
Sultany, Nimer. 2012. The state of progressive constitutional theory. *Harvard Civil-Rights Civil-Liberties Law Review* 47: 373–455.
Zizek, Slavoj. 2013. Problemas no paraíso. In *Cidades Rebeldes. Passe livre e as manifestações que tomaram as ruas do Brasil*, ed. Maricato Ermínia et al. São Paulo: Boitempo/Carta Maior.

Chapter 12
Judicial Reference to Community Values – A Pointer Towards Constitutional Juries?

Eric Ghosh

Abstract The practice of justifying judicial decisions by reference to consensual community values, which are distinguished from ordinary public opinion, has occurred in a number of jurisdictions and has been defended by prominent scholars. It provides a response to concern about the democratic legitimacy of judicial decision-making especially in constitutional cases. While it has also been critiqued for exacerbating concern about democratic legitimacy, the community values approach has proved resilient and merits further exploration. This chapter takes seriously its aim of promoting democratic legitimacy in constitutional decisions by connecting those decisions to the community's values. Some of the democratic theorists referred to by adherents of the community values approach are also helpful in understanding how this aim could be achieved. Achieving this aim would depend, for instance, upon understanding community values as informed majority opinion. It is finally argued, drawing on experience with deliberative polling, that this aim might be realised if constitutional juries are introduced.

12.1 Introduction

A central preoccupation of constitutional theory is with the democratic legitimacy of judicial decision-making in constitutional cases. This concern is most acute where judges declare legislation invalid on the ground of inconsistency with rights contained in a bill of rights and those decisions can only be abrogated through constitutional amendment. However, constitutional rights cases can be defined more broadly so that they include cases on rights that are fundamental in the sense that they are understood as a political constraint on government, regardless of whether abrogating judicial decisions on those rights requires constitutional amendment or ordinary legislation.[1] The rights might be contained in an entrenched or statutory bill of rights, or in the common law. Due to the status of these rights, judicial

[1] This draws on a broad understanding of a constitution. See Kramer (2001–2002, 16), but note that Kramer's quote in fn 36 from Bolingbroke (1841, 88) omits Bolingbroke's qualification that con-

E. Ghosh (✉)
School of Law, University of New England, Armidale, NSW 2351, Australia
e-mail: eghosh@une.edu.au

T. Bustamante, B.G. Fernandes (eds.), *Democratizing Constitutional Law*,
Law and Philosophy Library 113, DOI 10.1007/978-3-319-28371-5_12

interpretations of them may be difficult to abrogate.[2] Furthermore, the rights are often of a broad moral or political character, leaving the courts with substantial discretion on controversial matters of public interest.

This chapter examines one response to this concern with democratic legitimacy that is found in decisions of the highest courts in several jurisdictions and which has been defended by some of those countries' most respected scholars. This response is that in hard constitutional cases, judges should base their decisions on shared community values. These community values are distinguished from public opinion, which may be divided and ill-informed. This response will be called the community values approach. It will be argued that some variants of this approach have been, and can be, persuasively critiqued. Judicial speculation about community values, as distinct from public opinion, is likely to exacerbate rather than lessen tension between judicial decision-making and democratic values.

The community values approach has nevertheless proved resilient and merits further exploration. This chapter takes seriously its aim of promoting democratic legitimacy in constitutional decisions by connecting them to the community's values. Some of the democratic theorists referred to by adherents of the community values approach are helpful in understanding how this aim could be achieved. Achieving this aim would depend, for instance, upon understanding community values as informed majority opinion. It is finally argued, drawing on experience with deliberative polling, that this aim might be realised if constitutional juries are introduced.

By connecting the community values approach to constitutional juries, light will be shed on both. While the community values approach is not the dominant judicial response to concern about democratic legitimacy – legal formalism and judicial restraint may be more significant – it has been prominent and is likely to endure.[3] In a democratic culture, connecting reasons offered in constitutional cases to the community's values can appear attractive. However, those concerned about the democratic legitimacy of judicial decision-making in constitutional cases should be concerned about practices and approaches that exacerbate rather than lessen this concern, and should be interested in whether there are feasible, more democratic approaches to decision-making in at least some of these cases.

This chapter proceeds as follows. Section 12.2.1 mentions some examples of the community values approach in the United States and Canada. A US and Canadian

stitutions conform to reason. This natural-law qualification is also excluded from the definition adopted here.

[2]On judicial review relying on bills of rights where abrogation does not require constitutional amendment, see Gardbaum (2013). The common law decisions contemplated include where common law rights are invoked in statutory interpretation or more directly to protect rights. For Australian examples of both, see, respectively, Holloway (2002) and *Mabo v Queensland (No 2)* (1992). In combination with the Commonwealth *Racial Discrimination Act, Mabo* prevented States from extinguishing native title without compensation. For a range of understandings of "common law constitutionalism", see Goldsworthy (2008, 289).

[3]Australia is an example of a jurisdiction where legal formalism has been significant. See Zines (2002).

case will be referred to and the writers discussed are US legal scholar Harry Wellington and Canadian legal philosopher Wil Waluchow. Section 12.2.2 mentions some criticisms of Wellington before critiquing Waluchow. On the other hand, Sect. 12.2.3 suggests that work by US political scientist Robert Dahl, who is referred to by Wellington, supports an understanding of community values as informed public opinion, and this different understanding holds democratic promise. US philosopher Ronald Dworkin's constitutional conception of democracy, endorsed by Waluchow, is also helpful in exploring how deference to informed public opinion could promote legitimacy in constitutional cases.

Section 12.3 considers how the ideal of constitutional review based on informed (or deliberative) public opinion could be supported and realised. Section 12.3.1 suggests that research on deliberative polls supports the distinction found in the community values approach between ordinary and deliberative public opinion. It also indicates how deliberative public opinion can be determined. This leads to consideration of constitutional juries. Section 12.3.2 outlines some proposals for constitutional juries and argues that a proposal I made in 2010 is especially promising in realising how constitutional review based on the community's values could enjoy legitimacy (Ghosh 2010).

12.2 The Community Values Approach

12.2.1 Examples from the United States and Canada

The community values approach is followed when judicial decisions on constitutional rights are at least partly justified on the ground that those decisions accord with a community consensus, or at least with a very substantial majority of the community, when that consensus is nevertheless distinguished from public opinion. This approach was articulated and discussed in the 1970s and 1980s in the US. Perhaps the most recent discussion has occurred in Canada, in the last decade.

Other countries also furnish examples. In the 1980s and 1990s, the Australian High Court employed the community values approach in some of its most important decisions and this approach was also understood as part of a movement from legal formalism. This prompted a provocative understanding and defence of the community values approach by criminologist John Braithwaite, drawing on republicanism and social psychology (Braithwaite 1995). I made the last of three critiques of Braithwaite's approach, and will not reiterate points made there (Ghosh 1998).[4] Instead, this chapter's examples will be from the US and Canada.

[4] See Ghosh (1998, 7, fn 11) for reference to the community values approach in the UK. For an Indian example, where public interest litigation is understood as aiming at a judicial interpretation of the will of the people that would emerge through a properly representative parliament, see Ahmadi (1996). For examples in several jurisdictions where there is reference to public opinion in the context of cases concerned with the death penalty, see Schabas (1996) pp. 79–95.

Beginning with the US, in *Democracy and distrust* John Hart Ely referred to Supreme Court cases and academic writing that followed the community values approach (Ely 1980). One case is *Furman v Georgia* (1972). Ely mentioned that Justices Brennan and Marshall argued that the death penalty was unconstitutional partly because it was out of accord with contemporary community values (Ely 1980, 65). It is worth, however, elaborating more than Ely does on Justice Marshall's judgment. Justice Marshall mentioned that the test in previous case law for whether a penalty constituted "cruel and unusual punishment" was whether it "it shocks the conscience and sense of justice of the people".[5] He said that an opinion poll would be of limited utility, for the question is "whether people who were fully informed as to the purposes of the penalty and its liabilities would find the penalty shocking, unjust, and unacceptable."[6] He claimed that available information against the death penalty was sufficiently strong to suggest that informed opinion would view the death penalty as morally reprehensible.[7]

It is academic writing, though, that articulates more fully the community values approach. Ely mentioned some of the US's most respected legal scholars who followed this approach. They include Alexander Bickel, but Ely regarded Wellington as providing one of the clearest expressions of this approach (Ely 1980, 65).[8] In a 1973 article, Wellington first distinguished legal arguments based on policy, which are instrumental in character, from arguments of principle, which may rely on intrinsic wrongness (Wellington 1973, 222–225).[9] Wellington said that while both arguments are important, legislatures can have an advantage over courts in arguments based on policy (Wellington 1973, 240–241). By contrast, with arguments based on principle, courts' protection from political pressures is a significant advantage (Wellington 1973, 248–249). In explaining the policy–principle distinction, Wellington used the example of the beneficiary of a life insurance policy murdering the insured person in order to collect the payout (Wellington 1973, 222). Denying the benefit of the insurance here may have an instrumental justification: it may deter future killing. However, the main justification would lie in it being intrinsically wrong for the murderer to profit from his own wrong. This justification is found in conventional morality. Turning to constitutional cases, Wellington said: "The Court's task is to ascertain the weight of the principle in conventional morality and to convert the moral principle into a legal one by connecting it with the body of constitutional law" (Wellington 1973, 284). He saw this as a democratic approach: it involves "reference to the people", in contrast to judges drawing on their own values (Wellington 1973, 299). Courts (and especially the Supreme Court) were

[5] *Furman v Georgia* p. 360.

[6] *Furman v Georgia* p. 361.

[7] Justice Brennan, interestingly, referred in *Furman v Georgia* (p. 299) to juries as "expressing the conscience of the people" and voting only rarely for the death penalty.

[8] See also Ely (1980, 65–6) for Bickel (1962) and Ely (1980, 67 fn *) for Perry (1976), which also followed this approach. Cf Perry (1982, 94). For another discussion of Wellington and Perry, see Sadurski (1987, 366–377).

[9] Wellington refers to Dworkin's discussion of the policy–principle distinction at p. 222 fn 1.

well positioned to translate conventional morality into legal principle (Wellington 1973, 266–267). In doing so, Wellington continued, judges should filter out "prejudices and passions of the moment" and instead rely on the moral principles of the community. The latter may be inferred from community views expressed in calmer moments (Wellington 1982, 493).

Turning to Canada, one relevant Supreme Court case is *Rodriguez v British Columbia* (1993). Rodriguez was terminally ill, with amyotrophic lateral sclerosis, and argued that the offence of assisting suicide found in the *Criminal Code* violated section 7 of the Charter. Section 7 states: "Everyone has the right to life, liberty and security of the person and the right not to be deprived thereof except in accordance with the principles of fundamental justice." The majority held that the principles of justice must be "fundamental" in the sense that they would achieve general acceptance among reasonable people.[10] This appears to be the community values approach: there is reference to consensus values of reasonable community members. In this case, though, the majority held that there was an absence of a community consensus in favour of decriminalizing assisted suicide. This suggested that section 7 of the Charter was not violated by the *Criminal Code*.

Of greater interest here, though, is Waluchow's defence of the community values approach. Waluchow mentioned that a popular complaint against judicial review is that it renders the law too dependent on the subjective moral opinions of judges, and this cannot be justified in any society that purports to respect democracy and the rule of law (Waluchow 2008, 65–66).[11] One response to this complaint, Waluchow continued, is that a bill of rights refers to matters of moral truth. However, this is unsatisfactory, for there is so little agreement on moral truth that judges will have a wide discretion. Another response is that a bill of rights refers to norms of positive morality. One difficulty with this response, however, is lack of consensus. A second difficulty is that positive morality may perform poorly in protecting vulnerable minorities against majority prejudices.

Waluchow claimed that judges should instead refer to the community's "true moral commitments". In explaining this, he mentioned that an individual's personal morality may be inconsistent and prejudiced. Here, John Rawls's reflective equilibrium is useful.[12] With reflective equilibrium, individuals reflect on their general principles and their judgments on particular matters in order to achieve a more attractive and consistent set of moral beliefs. This set of beliefs reflects an individual's true moral commitments.

These observations about an individual's morality, Waluchow suggested, are generally overlooked when considering judicial review and the political morality which bills of rights refer to. For example, he said that those who criticise same-sex marriage as being at odds with the received moral views of Canadians are likely to

---

[10] *Rodriguez v British Columbia (Attorney General)* (1993), 607–608. Cf *Carter v Canada (Attorney General)* (2015)

[11] Waluchow's chapter draws closely upon Waluchow (2007, ch 6). Waluchow's exploration of constitutional morality is described as illuminating in Dyzenhaus (2010, 289 fn 285).

[12] Waluchow (2008, 71–72), referring to Rawls (1971).

have in mind mere moral opinions. These opinions, he argued, contradict fundamental principles that enjoy widespread currency within the community. Thus, the principles upon which reasonable Canadians are keen to condemn racial bigotry and sexism equally condemn prejudice against same-sex marriage (Waluchow 2008, 74). He admitted that for many people, recognising that their true commitment to equality requires the recognition of same-sex marriage may be a "long and difficult process" (Waluchow 2008, 74). He suggested, though, that there is no good democratic reason why judges should respect the community's moral opinions rather than the community's true moral commitments or, to put it differently, the community's inauthentic rather than its authentic wishes.[13]

He then distinguished the community's true moral commitments from the community's constitutional morality. The community's constitutional morality consists of those true moral commitments that are tied to its constitutional law and practices (Waluchow 2008, 77). He believes that the Canadian Charter of Rights and Freedoms reflects some of the community's true commitments (Waluchow 2007, 219). Furthermore, judges engaged in judicial review may be in a better position to determine the requirements of a community's true moral commitments than politicians. The reasoning envisaged by reflective equilibrium is similar to the common law reasoning that judges are expert at (Waluchow 2008, 81).

These examples provide a sufficient sense of the community values approach. The existence of community consensus can be employed in justifying a right, as in *Furman*. The absence of consensus can be used to deny a right, as in *Rodriguez*. There are also strong commonalities between Wellington and Waluchow. Indeed, Waluchow referred to Wellington as an example of the approach he favours (Waluchow 2008, 76 fn 16). One common assumption is that progressive decisions by courts at odds with public opinion could gain democratic legitimacy if judges refer to community values. However, there are also some differences. While this is not perhaps evident from the discussion so far, Waluchow relies more clearly than Wellington on general principles rather than attitudes found in the community's morality. There are variants within the community values approach.

12.2.2 Criticisms

This sub-section will mention criticisms of the community values approach, focusing on some of the examples mentioned. It begins, again, with the US and Ely's critique of the community values approach. Ely said that the view that judges, in enforcing the Constitution, should use their own values to measure the judgment of the political branches is seldom endorsed, for it would be difficult to reconcile with democracy (Ely 1980, 44–45). This leads to the search for something "out there"

[13] The authentic–inauthentic distinction is employed in Waluchow (2007, 226) and Waluchow (2008, 73 fn 13).

waiting to be discovered, whether it be natural law or some supposed value consensus (Ely 1980, 48). After critiquing reference to natural law, he turned to value consensus. He said that while consensus may exist in favour of some abstract ideals, that is only because the vagueness of those abstract ideals allows for almost any interpretation (Ely 1980, 64–65).

Ely sought to discredit the claim in *Furman* that contemporary values were against the death penalty by noting that the decision was followed by "a virtual stampede of state re-enactments of the death penalty" (Ely 1980, 65). Ely, however, overlooked the fact that Justice Marshall used what Ely himself had described as a laundering device. A laundering device cleanses public opinion of ill-informed preferences and prejudices so that what remains is community values that judges can safely draw upon (Ely 1980, 67 fn*). Ely mentioned that one laundering device involves favouring the general over the particular (Ely 1980, 64–65). An example would be reference to a consensus in favour of equality rather than to community attitudes on a particular matter implicating equality. Justice Marshall, however, applied a different laundering device: it involved favouring what he perceived as informed over uninformed preferences. In *Gregg v Georgia* (1976), decided a few years after *Furman*, Justice Marshall was in the minority in suggesting that the death penalty itself was unconstitutional.[14] He mentioned that state re-enactments of the death penalty did not provide conclusive evidence about "the opinion of an *informed* citizenry."[15]

Ely was, in any case, scathing about laundering devices. He compared the idea that the genuine values of the people can most reliably be discerned by a nondemocratic elite with the Soviet definition of democracy. This, HB Mayo had written, involves the ancient error of assuming that the "the wishes of the people can be ascertained more accurately by some mysterious methods of intuition open to an elite rather than by allowing people to discuss and vote and decide freely."[16] Finally, Ely said that it made "no sense to employ the value judgments of the majority as the vehicle for protecting minorities from the value judgments of the majority" (Ely 1980, 69).

Ely's critique was extended, and also qualified, some years later by the Polish–Australian philosopher Wojciech Sadurski. The qualification lay in recognising that there are circumstances where it can make sense to invoke the majority's judgments to invalidate legislation that discriminates against a minority (Sadurski 1987, 344–351). For example, the legislation in place may reflect a past majority opinion while judges, in protecting a minority, may be deciding in accordance with contemporary majority opinion.

One extension to Ely's critique lay in Sadurski's discussion of laundering devices that may be more sophisticated than those mentioned by Ely. One is provided by Rawls. Given Waluchow's use of Rawls, it is worth referring to Sadurski's discus-

[14] *Gregg v Georgia* p. 241.

[15] *Gregg v Georgia* p. 232. Interestingly, Justice Marshall also pointed here to some empirical support for his claim about informed public opinion.

[16] Ely (1980, 68) referring to Mayo (1960, 217).

sion (Sadurski 1987, 381). Sadurski mentioned that in post-*A Theory of Justice* articles, Rawls used language similar to the original reflective equilibrium, in that he referred to people's considered convictions and working out a state of harmony between their convictions and principles. Rawls suggested that the political philosopher should seek to bring together the considered convictions of many people with the aim of forming a coherent body of shared notions and principles. While Sadurski found Rawls's original reflective equilibrium helpful in understanding how an individual might engage in critical reflection, he expressed doubts about Rawls's adaptation of this to the community level. While an individual can modify his or her own general principles and judgments on particular matters, how to deal with inconsistencies in general principles and particular judgments when engaging in reflective equilibrium for the community? Sadurski mentioned the risk that the philosopher may eliminate some opinions as unconsidered simply because he or she morally disapproves of them (Sadurski 1987, 383). The appeal to Rawls for shared principles based on the considered judgments of the community does not avoid concern about judges employing their own value judgments in invalidating acts by the popular branches of government.

Turning to Canada, Waluchow did not refer to the critiques discussed here but, instead, to the main concern with the community values approach mentioned in 2005 by the philosopher Andrei Marmor. Marmor, in fact, echoed two of Ely's concerns.[17] One is dissensus, but Marmor's primary concern is how effective majority values can be in securing against majoritarian tyranny. Waluchow's response is that Canadians' true commitments are consistent with minority protection and that reflection on moral questions can engender greater consensus than appears in ordinary public opinion. The next section considers empirical material that throws light on Waluchow's response to Marmor. I will discuss here Waluchow's views about the discretionary character of judgments about the true commitments of the community.

Waluchow admitted that his approach relies on judges' personal views about the community's constitutional morality. The community's constitutional morality, it will be recalled, consists of those true commitments of the community that are recognised in constitutional law. He said that judges' views on constitutional morality may be highly controversial and not amenable to conclusive demonstration (Waluchow 2008, 81). Nevertheless, he continued, the exercise of good-faith judgment in determining the community's constitutional morality is no more disturbing than use of such judgment by, say, judges in ordinary appeal cases.

Waluchow did not, however, address Ely's concern that the exercise of judgment in constitutional cases is more problematic, given their greater finality (Ely 1980, 68). While Waluchow could abandon his claim that there is nothing more problematic about judgment being exercised in constitutional cases, his more fundamental claim is the following: "It is one thing to say that a bill of rights case hinges on the judge's own personal morality, and quite another to say that it hinges on her personal views *about what the community's constitutional morality requires*" (Waluchow

[17] (Marmor 2005, 160–162, referred to in Waluchow 2008, 88).

2008, 81). By the judge's own personality morality, Waluchow meant their values as a private citizen. He mentioned that a judge, for instance, might be a closet racist, but racism may be inconsistent with principles contained in legislation (Waluchow 2007, 220). Waluchow is suggesting here that the judge faces a choice between applying his or her private prejudices or seeking to discover the community's true moral commitments that are consistent with the constitutional material. The assumption is that at least in Canada, those commitments condemn racial discrimination.

Waluchow, however, overlooked alternatives. A positivist might conceptualise decision-making in hard cases as interstitial legislation while an anti-positivist might conceptualise decision-making as an attempt to interpret the legal material in its best light. That last possibility is associated with Dworkin. Dworkin's approach can be confused with the community values approach.[18] Dworkin argued that judges should interpret the legal material so that it expresses a coherent set of principles. In doing so, Dworkin said, judges confirm the principled character of the community (Dworkin 1986, 264). This might suggest that judges aim to express the values that community members are committed to. However, Dworkin said: "...when I speak of the community being faithful to its own principles, I do not mean its conventional or popular morality, the beliefs and convictions of most citizens" (Dworkin 1986, 168). Instead, he meant the commitments of the "community personified", ie, the community imagined as a moral person. The commitments of the community personified are constructed from the legal material; they are not the commitments that most community members necessarily accept. By contrast, Waluchow commenced his discussion of true commitments versus public opinion at the level of the individual community member. His assertion that recognising same-sex marriage is consistent with the "fundamental beliefs, principles, values, and considered judgments that enjoy widespread, if not universal, currency within the community" is a reference to the true commitments of the great majority of Canadians (Waluchow 2008, 73–74).

The positivist, the Dworkinian and the Waluchovian judge will be required to distinguish between values they might hold as a private citizen and those values that appropriately guide public decision-making. It is only Waluchow's approach, though, that is paternalistic, with an elite claiming its decisions are based on what community members truly believe or authentically wish for.[19] This paternalism aggravates rather than diminishes concern about the democratic legitimacy of judicial decision-making, a concern especially acute with constitutional cases. It resonates with a justification for anti-democratic thought that suggests that the state enlarges citizens' liberty when decisions promote citizens' real or authentic wishes, even if those decisions are against the actual wishes of those citizens.[20]

[18] See, eg, Ely (1980, 67 fn *). Cf Sadurski (1987, 370 fn 143).

[19] See also Marmor (2007, 87–90).

[20] See Berlin (1969). A similar point appears in the critique of the community values approach found in Krygier and Glass (1995, 394–395).

12.2.3 Democratic Theory

While the critiques of the community values approach suggest that it aggravates concern with democratic legitimacy, it is helpful to connect that conclusion more closely with democratic theory. The democratic theories referred to or endorsed by Wellington and Waluchow can themselves be employed to shed critical light on the community values approach.

Starting with Wellington, in understanding US democracy, he drew mostly on literature from the late 1950s to the early 1970s. During most of that period, pluralist democratic theory dominated. He referred, for instance, to Robert Dahl's *Democracy in the United States*, where Dahl noted that the legislative and executive branches of government depart from political equality partly by enabling organised minorities to exercise significant power.[21] Wellington referred to this in order to lessen the contrast in democratic credentials between the popular and judicial branches of government. While Wellington's reference to Dahl does not imply endorsement of Dahl's normative democratic theory, Wellington's discussion of US democracy seems broadly consistent with it.

Dahl mentioned that behind the commitment in the US to government by the people lies a belief in political equality and consent (Dahl 1972, 7). One value that justifies this belief is individual freedom. Individual freedom suggests that "…so far as possible no adult human being should ever be governed without his consent" (Dahl 1972, 9).[22] He was not proposing that individuals have a veto over the political system. Instead, the political system must enjoy the "consent of the governed, considered as political equals" (Dahl 1972, 8–9). For Dahl, individual freedom suggested that each citizen should have political power consistent with others enjoying the same power. It is a notion of freedom as individual self-government qualified to make it applicable to collective decision-making. Political equality, he argued, is achieved through majority rule, but the scope for majority decision-making may need to be limited to achieve the protection of minorities (Dahl 1972, 28). Such protection may be necessary in order to achieve their consent. Individual freedom, then, requires political equality and policies that are viewed as sufficiently fair to attract the consent of not just the majority but also minorities.

Dahl associated democracy, though, especially with political equality and majority rule.[23] He also recognised other criteria for authority, such as justice and economy. Economy draws attention, for instance, to the fact that participatory decision-making processes take the time and effort of those participating (Dahl 1970, 40–56). One could say that for Dahl, political equality is the primary criterion

[21] Wellington (1982, 489 fn 420), referring to Dahl (1976, 454). My subsequent references to *Democracy in the United States* will, however, be to Dahl (1972), for it has a suggestive discussion on how presidential authority should be exercised. The third edition's discussion is less abstract, with more detail on the Nixon presidency.

[22] For a broadly consistent but more systematic normative treatment, see Dahl (1989).

[23] See, eg, Dahl (1970, 58). Ch 1 discusses criteria for authority.

of democratic legitimacy. By contrast, general legitimacy takes into account all criteria relevant to legitimate authority.

While that provides some understanding of Dahl's general approach, it is worth noting a few points he made about the authority of the president and courts in the US. In discussing the delegated authority a president enjoys, Dahl said that: "For his authority to be acceptable from a democratic perspective…he would have to exercise it by attempting to satisfy the dominant goals, values, or wills of the citizens, weighting each citizen as the equal of every other" (Dahl 1972, 438). However: "What citizens want, and what they would be likely to want if adequately equipped with technical advice, are… frequently unknown…" (Dahl 1972, 438). Dahl noted, though, that many public officials, elected and non-elected, are in fact able to make decisions in which their own preferences, including their own conception of the public good, carry far more weight than those of ordinary citizens (Dahl 1972, 439).

Turning to judicial review, Dahl claimed that this would lack legitimacy if it permitted judges to impose their own preferences and biases rather than acting to promote through their decisions political equality and fairness for minorities (Dahl 1972, 198). He linked that fairness to the question of minorities being able to freely consent to the political system. He did not, then, suggest that judges should satisfy the dominant values of citizens. Nevertheless, his comments about presidential authority are suggestive when thinking about the community values approach. While he distinguished in his example between what citizens want and what they would want if equipped with technical advice, the more general distinction is between actual and informed preferences, where the latter are achieved through consideration of technical and non-technical information. Dahl's reference to informed preferences can be supported by his conception of individual freedom. It is difficult to see how individuals can freely consent to the exercise of authority unless they possess relevant information on how that authority is and should be exercised.

The distinction between ordinary and informed preferences is also crucial to the community values approach. Wellington distinguished reasonable views from views that are prejudiced or arise from the passion of the moment. Wellington did not elaborate on how to distinguish prejudices and passions, on the one hand, from reasonable community views, on the other hand. In relation to racial discrimination, however, Wellington said that it may take decades before prejudices have weakened. Thus, the correctness of *Brown v Board of Education* (1954) was revealed when, decades later, few could be heard to endorse racial segregation (Wellington 1982, 516). Wellington seemed to assume moral progress over time. Furthermore, Wellington's recommendation that judges decide on the basis of conventional morality is justified on democratic grounds, and it is unclear how decisions based on people's preferences several decades hence, even assuming they can be reliably detected with a crystal ball, can legitimately bind a people today.[24]

Dahl's reference to preferences achieved after the provision of relevant information is less stringent than envisaging preferences that emerge potentially after

[24] See also Ely (1980, 69–70) and Sadurski (1987, 368–369).

several decades. It may indeed be that the racial prejudices that Wellington had in mind are not easily dislodged by the provision of relevant information. Nevertheless, the greater the stringency of the requirement for the expression of informed preferences, the greater the difficulty in imagining any process that could rely on people's expression of their own preferences as a way of validating claims about community values.

Another point of difference is that Dahl's reference to informed preferences involved the application of majority rule, while Wellington said that determining conventional morality requires reasoning from commonly held attitudes (Wellington 1973, 310). Such attitudes, Wellington mentioned in his 1973 article, did not support abortion where the continuance of the pregnancy would gravely impair the physical or mental health of the mother (Wellington 1973, 311). Thus, *Roe v Wade* (1973) went too far (Wellington 1973, 299). Instead, those attitudes would permit abortion to save the life of the mother. Wellington is perhaps partly motivated by concern that the court's legitimacy would be undermined if it made decisions that fell outside what a very substantial majority of people would support if properly informed.[25] The puzzle, though, is that popular responses to court decisions might be better explained by reference to uninformed rather than informed opinion. It is unclear what impact on popular legitimacy there would be if one compares two decisions each of which faces the same degree of opposition from ordinary public opinion, but one of which would enjoy greater support from reflective public opinion. Furthermore, requiring consensus or close-to-consensus would prevent decisions that Wellington favoured, such as *Brown*. It would strongly privilege the status quo.

Apart from providing an alternative understanding of community values, Dahl's discussion is helpful in considering how judicial reference to community values, understood as majority informed opinion, could relate to democratic legitimacy. Dahl's value of individual freedom will be applied to three possibilities: where judges are bound to decide in accordance with majority informed preferences, where judges never bind themselves to decide in accordance with these preferences, and where judges choose on a case-by-case basis whether they will defer to such preferences. Turning to the first possibility, Dahl's value of individual freedom suggests that collective decision-making must accord each citizen political equality, ie, an equal opportunity to exercise decision-making power. With judges being bound to decide in accordance with majority informed preferences, individual freedom would increase, since citizens would actually enjoy some decision-making power on constitutional rights, even if decisions are ultimately made in the name of a judge. Judges would only be able to decide in accordance with majority informed preferences if there were some process that gave citizens an equal opportunity to express such preferences.

Turning to the second possibility, where judges are not at all constrained by informed majority preferences, individual freedom, with its implication of political equality, would not be promoted. Invoking the language of "community values" in

[25] For concern about partisanship in the context of policy decisions, see Wellington (1973, 241).

this context would not promote democratic legitimacy. It might instead provide empty symbolism.

The third possibility mentioned is where judges can choose on a case-by-case basis whether to defer to such preferences and they sometimes chose to do so. The extent to which individual freedom is promoted in this circumstance would depend partly on whether a probabilistic or a power-centred approach to individual freedom is applied. I have previously used these terms to describe how the philosopher Philip Pettit understands a liberal versus a republican approach to freedom, where those conceptions of freedom are negative, or have affinities with negative liberty.[26] These terms can be applied here, however, to freedom as self-government.

With a probabilistic approach, individual freedom depends on the probability that the power of self-government is available. Thus, if there is a 50 % chance that judges will defer to majority informed opinion, there is half the degree of self-government as when judges always defer to such opinion. Of course, qualitative criteria are also relevant. Thus, if deference only occurs in less significant cases or cases about which judges are indifferent, that would diminish self-government. Also, if judges only defer when they expect or see that informed opinion accords with their personal views, there is only slight or sham deference.

With a power-centred approach, individual freedom is absent when the opportunity to exercise it depends upon the discretion of another. Pettit suggests that a slave lacks republican freedom even if the slave has a master who is extremely unlikely to interfere; the slave remains a slave, for the slave is vulnerable to the arbitrary power of a master (Pettit 1999, 31). This idea can be applied to individual freedom as self-government that in the collective context requires political equality. One could say that where the possibility of majority informed opinion being reflected in constitutional decisions is dependent upon the discretion of judges, the people suffer an absence of freedom on those constitutional issues.

Nevertheless, if judges defer on occasions to majority informed preferences, that would support considerations that are relevant to individual freedom even under this power-centred approach. One can distinguish outcome- from process-related considerations. The outcome consideration focuses on the quality of decisions produced by a process, while process-related considerations focus upon values promoted by the process itself, not taking into account the quality of the decisions it produces. A commitment to political equality may be supported by the claim that it achieves more attractive outcomes and promotes process considerations such as demonstrating appropriate respect for the autonomy of citizens. From the perspective of a commitment to political equality, an official who sometimes defers to the citizens' informed preferences is preferable to an official who never does. The former is likely to reach more attractive outcomes and also demonstrates greater respect for citizens' autonomy.

It is not necessary to decide here, however, between probabilistic and power-centred approaches. Under either approach, there are significant differences in the

[26] Ghosh (2008, 154–155), referring to Pettit (1999).

extent to which self-government or its supporting considerations are promoted depending on whether judges are bound to defer to majority informed opinion or where such deference is discretionary or such deference never occurs.

In summary, this sub-section started with Wellington and his reference to Dahl. Dahl was then used to critique Wellington. First, Dahl provides an understanding of community values as informed majority opinion and this is more democracy-friendly than reliance on a consensus of future preferences. Secondly, where judges retain a discretion on when to constrain themselves to informed majority preferences, individual freedom (and consequently democratic legitimacy) may be promoted minimally or not at all.

Turning now to Waluchow, criticisms just made of Wellington are also applicable here. Like Wellington, Waluchow suggested that for some individuals, reflective opinions on certain issues may take a long time to achieve. Waluchow used the example of favouring same-sex marriage. To adapt my earlier response to Wellington, one might wonder how enforcing the values that would perhaps be endorsed by the community decades later is consistent with democratic values. Again, envisaging short-term reflection is necessary to render reference to community values democracy-friendly. Only in this way is it imaginable that there could be a process which relies on citizens' expression of their own preferences. Also like Wellington, Waluchow is committed to consensus (Waluchow 2008, 77–78). However, decisions such as favouring same-sex marriage as a constitutional right may be justifiable on the basis of current community values when majority rule is applied instead of consensus.

It is worthwhile, though, considering the democratic theory that Waluchow endorses, for that articulates what objections need to be overcome if decisions on rights conforming to informed majority opinion are to be legitimate. In *A Common law theory of judicial review* Waluchow rejected a procedural conception of democracy. This conception equates democracy with majority rule (Waluchow 2007, 106–107). He instead endorsed Dworkin's constitutional conception of democracy. Quoting *Freedom's Law*, Waluchow said:

> [This constitutional conception]...denies that it is a defining goal of democracy that collective decisions always or normally be those that a majority or plurality of citizens would favour [even] if fully informed and rational. It takes the defining aim of democracy to be a different one: that collective decisions be made by political institutions whose structure, composition, and practices treat all members of the community, as individuals, with equal concern and respect..." (Waluchow 2007, 108, quoting Dworkin 1996, 17).[27]

Dworkin believed that in the US, judicial review is justified where judges employ arguments of principle rather than policy, for judges have an advantage here over parliamentarians. Dworkin's understanding of principle and policy is similar to Wellington's (Wellington 1973, 222–225). Dworkin also argued that judges should justify their decisions as an interpretation of the legal material. As mentioned in Sect. 12.2.2, for Dworkin, the morality of the community personified would be

[27]At (1996, 16), Dworkin referred to what a majority favours "if it had adequate information and enough time for reflection."

determined by reference to, for instance, judicial and legislative decisions. A Dworkinian judge considering constitutional recognition of a right to same-sex marriage would interpret the legal material in its best light.

Let us suppose that a Dworkinian judge was dealing with same-sex marriage quite some decades ago, and assume further that reflective public opinion would not have yielded a clear majority in favour of same-sex marriage being a constitutional right. If the judge were able, through the interpretive approach, to reach an understanding of what constitutional rights require in this case that is superior to what reflective public opinion would endorse, the judge should decide in accordance with his or her own understanding. Dworkin would have justified this as the approach most likely to promote his ultimate democratic values of equal concern and respect. Exploring how this approach would achieve this requires addressing again outcome- and process-related considerations. The focus on the outcomes of judicial decisions in constitutional cases that is found in Dworkin (and also Wellington, Dahl, and Waluchow) might suggest that process-related considerations are overlooked. However, the focus on outcomes should instead be understood as reflecting the view that any compromising of process values resulting from the more elitist form of decision-making constituted by judicial decision-making is unlikely to be substantial, given the divergence from political equality that occurs with electoral democracy (Waluchow 2007, 17; Dworkin 2000, ch 4). Thus, significant gains in outcomes produced by judicial decisions are likely to outweigh any loss captured by process considerations.

However, even in this case, the judge might have reason to defer to majority informed opinion if general deference to such opinion would, overall, lead to better outcomes. The best process for obtaining sound decisions on moral questions may be one which relies on what a majority of diverse individuals in the community would decide after reflection rather than what a judge, or a small group of judges, would decide. With the individual not being able to reliably determine when their individual judgment is superior to informed majority opinion, general deference may be the best strategy. On process considerations, one mentioned by Dworkin in *Sovereign Virtue* is symbolic: it is concerned with what message the process conveys relating to citizens' status as free and equal (Dworkin 2000, 187). Deference to majority informed opinion could convey the message that citizens have the autonomy to reach sound decisions on questions of justice. This is an attractive message to convey, at least if citizens do in fact enjoy this autonomy.

With certain assumptions, Dworkin's constitutional conception of democracy might be promoted by deference to informed majority opinion. It is also important to note, though, that Dworkin's constitutional conception of democracy is helpful in indicating that judicial deference to informed public opinion may not necessarily promote democracy legitimacy. Of course, Dworkin had a broad conception of democracy. Dahl, on the other hand, identified democracy with popular control or, more specifically a substantial degree of political equality. This narrower, procedural conception of democracy involves a conception of democratic legitimacy that is distinct from general legitimacy. As mentioned earlier, general legitimacy would take into account justice. Thus, if judges are bound to defer to community values, democratic legitimacy may be enhanced even if this deference leads to more unjust outcomes assuming, at least, that the unjust outcomes do not impact on political equality within the popular branches of government. General legitimacy, though, may not be promoted. It would be to general legitimacy that Dahl would have referred in explaining why he did not suggest that judges should follow the majority's informed preferences.

12.3 Deliberative Polls and Constitutional Juries

12.3.1 Deliberative Polls and the Community Values Approach

The previous sub-section explored some theoretical considerations pertaining to whether judicial deference to informed majority opinion could promote democratic or general legitimacy. Neither Dahl nor Dworkin endorsed such deference, but it was explained how conformity to informed public opinion could be justified using the values they recommend. Whether such conformity would be justified is illuminated by this sub-section's consideration of some empirical research on informed public opinion. Some of the most useful findings derive from US political scientist James Fishkin's deliberative polls.

Fishkin noted that George Gallup touted polling as an instrument of democratic reform, calling it the "sampling referendum" (Fishkin 2005, 286–287). However, Fishkin mentioned that the "typical respondent answering the typical political attitude item has barely ever thought about the question before being interviewed and can call on precious little information in answering it" (Fishkin 2005, 287). The deliberative poll seeks to elicit, by contrast, deliberative public opinion. Fishkin's work fits within the dominant contemporary democratic theory of deliberative democracy (Fishkin and Luskin 2000; Lafont 2015, 44). This has involved close examination of the ideal of deliberation. Fishkin's deliberative public opinion is substantially similar, though, to the informed preferences that were mentioned in discussing Dahl (1991, 229–230).

Deliberative polls commence with a pre-deliberation survey of a statistically representative sample of the population (Luskin et al. 2002, 463). The sample is then invited to participate in a weekend discussion a few weeks later concerned with the same issues as those raised in the survey. Inducements offered include free accommodation, meals and travel, and an honorarium. On the weekend, there is small-group discussion assisted by a moderator and plenary sessions in which questions can be put to experts and policy-makers reflecting opposed positions. At the end of the weekend, the participants are surveyed again.

Typically, participants in the weekend discussions have attitudes to the issues in question which are similar to the attitudes of those initially surveyed. They also have sociodemographic attributes similar to the population as a whole. They are generally a bit older, better educated and more interested and knowledgeable about those issues than non-participants, but not by much.[28] The polls typically result in significant shifts in opinion. Two examples will suffice. In a poll concerned with which party to vote for in the 1997 British election, support for the Conservatives and for Labour decreased by 7 and 8 percent respectively, and increased for the Liberal Democrats by 22 percent.[29] In a 2001 poll concerned with reconciliation between indigenous and non-indigenous Australians, there was over a 20 % increase in support for certain positions sympathetic to indigenous Australians, including an apology to the "stolen generation", ie, an apology to indigenous people affected by the policy of forcibly removing children from their families and placing them in institutions or with non-indigenous families.[30] The polls also typically produce gains in knowledge (Fishkin 2005, 290). Indeed, the changes in opinion seem information-driven: those who gain the most knowledge are most likely to change their opinions (Fishkin 2005, 291).

These polls demonstrate that empirical evidence of deliberative public opinion is obtainable. That evidence is not, of course, conclusive. Deliberative polls involve compromises. Their voluntary character affects their representativeness, but may well enhance their deliberative quality. Sampling error must be recognised, as with any poll, and also contingencies specific to deliberative polls, such as the selection of experts and the persuasiveness of particular experts in plenary sessions. Nevertheless, the deliberative polls indicate that people are prepared to deliberate on issues, acquire information, and change their views in the light of that information. The occurrence of significant shifts in opinion in polls concerned with whom to vote for suggests that the public opinion that can determine election results may be different from reflective opinion. This, together with the fact that public opinion can influence what legislation is passed or proposed, suggests that legislation could be quite different from what would be endorsed by deliberative public opinion.

Furthermore, deliberative polls on issues relating to minority protection have tended to elicit opinions more sympathetic to these groups. The poll on indigenous Australians is one of several examples (Fishkin 2010, 69).[31] The number of polls dealing with minority protection has, admittedly, been small, but it nevertheless provides some support for Waluchow's assumption that reflective opinion may be more sympathetic to minority groups than the public opinion that influences legislation.

On the other hand, Waluchow's hope that deliberative opinion will involve greater consensus than non-deliberative opinion is not supported. Significant minorities continued to oppose the majority positions in many polls. More significantly,

[28] Fishkin (2005, 290). This provides a summary of general experience with the polls and also the first poll.

[29] Fishkin (2009, 137–8).

[30] Center for Deliberative Democracy. In relation to an apology, support increased from 46 to 70 percent. See also Issues Deliberation Australia et al. (2001, 55).

[31] For evidence of a slight tendency of attitudinal change towards egalitarianism, see Gastil et al. (2010, 15).

the existence of an empirical approach to determining reflective public opinion throws into sharp relief the inadequacy of relying on assertions by judges as to what such opinion would endorse. It raises the question of whether this empirical method could assist in constitutional cases. If it can, the idea of grounding constitutional review in deliberative public opinion, which is found within the community values approach, could perhaps be vindicated.

12.3.2 Constitutional Juries

This sub-section mentions some proposals for employing deliberative public opinion in constitutional review. US scholar Ethan Leib recommended in 2002 that if judges wish to make claims about the community's deliberative values, they could be obliged to consult a deliberative poll (Leib 2002, 369, 409). However, even if Leib's recommendation were adopted, it is unlikely that there would be much, if any, recourse to deliberative polls. Given their expense, judges are unlikely to call a deliberative poll and will instead base their decisions on other justifications. Furthermore, Sect. 12.2.3 indicated that vesting in judges a discretion to consult a deliberative poll, rather than obliging such consultation, involves less promotion of Dahl's liberty as self-government under a probabilistic approach, or no direct promotion of this value under a power-centred approach.

By contrast, Argentinian scholar Horacio Spector recommends vesting a discretion in complainants rather than judges. He proposed in 2009 that complainants in constitutional cases might choose between a judge or jury trial (Spector 2009, 117–118).[32] Vesting the discretion in complainants rather than judges removes the possibility of the slight or sham deference referred to in Sect. 12.2.3, where judges, for instance, only defer to informed public opinion on matters about which they are indifferent. Nevertheless, from a probabilistic perspective, it promotes less liberty as self-government than when such trials always involve juries. From a power-centred perspective, the fact that the arbitrary discretion not to employ juries is dispersed amongst complainants, rather than concentrated in judges, alleviates some of the evils of arbitrary power, such as the deference it can engender towards those who enjoy power. Nevertheless, it leaves such jury trials at the arbitrary discretion of others and it thereby fails to directly promote liberty as self-government. Cases can involve trade-offs between rights. A complainant successfully asserting a right before a judge can lead, say, to the diminution of a different right, a diminution that may not be endorsed by majority informed opinion. Rights cases implicate matters of collective concern.

Spector envisaged juries of around 36–72 members "to ensure the jurors represent a great diversity of viewpoints in the whole community" (Spector 2009, 118).

[32] See also Spector (2015, 36–37), where support for complainants enjoying a choice between judge and jury trials is maintained and greater restrictions on the types of constitutional matters that could be heard by a jury are articulated.

With a jury of 36–72, Spector points to an alternative that involves greater political equality and greater representativeness than current benches, and which can give reasoned responses. However, the size of these juries indicates a different ambition from Leib's. Leib hopes to inject into judges' recourse to community values an empirically grounded understanding of deliberative public opinion. A deliberative poll with around 200 members is large enough to permit a plausible claim of representativeness. A random sample of several hundred is very unlikely to differ radically from the population (Fishkin and Luskin 2000, 20).

In an article published in 2010, and without awareness of Spector's article, I sketched and defended a proposal for an Australian court, called a Citizens' Court, which employs constitutional juries (Ghosh 2010).[33] I suggested that bill of rights matters be only decided by constitutional juries modelled on some features of deliberative polls. The juries would be large, say, 200. Voluntary participation, with the assistance of inducements, could also be followed partly because this should enhance deliberation. Constitutional juries would, of course, be expensive. They should only be employed where it is fairly clear that legislation or an executive act may well be at odds with deliberative opinion about matters of principle and that the issue would be viewed as significant by deliberative public opinion. Juries should also play a role in determining matters that go to a hearing. With this proposal, the calling of constitutional juries would not lie in the discretion of a judge or a complainant, in the sense that they can chose between a judge- or jury-trial, and the juries would be large enough to enable a plausible claim of representativeness.

That article provided further details of the proposal, which will not be repeated. It suffices to mention here that if the Citizens' Court could achieve the popular legitimacy that confers significant authority on its decisions, it could provide a check upon the other branches of government that is broadly consistent with deliberative public opinion. It would further Dahl's conception of democratic legitimacy, which is tied especially to political equality. The article appealed, though, to a broader notion of legitimacy, which can be equated with Dahl's notion of general legitimacy, or Dworkin's expansive conception of democratic legitimacy. Outcome- and process-related considerations were explored in comparing constitutional juries with judicial review.

This was also attempted in the 2010 article, and that appraisal is summed-up here (Ghosh 2010, 348–352). On the process-related consideration of popular legitimacy, I suggested that constitutional juries may eventually obtain greater popular legitimacy than courts. Being representative of the people is a strong source of legitimacy. On the outcome consideration, factors relevant to sound decision-making include diversity, analytical skills, deliberation, empathy, and capacity and willingness to act on understanding of justice reached. On diversity, the juries would do significantly better. Australian judges are appointed from an elite group

[33] This argued in favour of constitutional juries against a backdrop of, first, Waldron's concerns about the democratic legitimacy of judicial review and, second, the way in which some constitutional scholarship, such as that seeking to revive republicanism, drew on Athenian practice but not its use of sortition.

within the legal profession. Furthermore, governments can sometimes decisively shape the ideological complexion of benches especially after a lengthy period in office. On analytical skills, judges would be superior, but this advantage can be reduced if juries are presented with accessible information. Furthermore, part of the complexity associated with judicial decisions is due to a formalist style of reasoning, a consequence of which is discussion of precedent that goes beyond what is necessary to reach sound outcomes. It is true that judges can be expected to deliberate more than jurors, but much of the time expended by Australian judges is devoted to demonstrating that their decisions are authorised by previous cases rather than demonstrating that they are justified through substantial and open discussion of the competing policy considerations. On willingness of decision-makers to decide in accordance with conceptions of justice, concern about democratic legitimacy can lead judges to be deferential towards the elected branches of government. That is less likely to affect jurors. I suggested that juries could well make better decisions than judges. In that case, an additional process consideration is promoted. The juries provide a symbolic affirmation of citizens' capacity to reach sound conclusions about justice when provided with appropriate deliberative opportunities.

The most detailed critique of my proposal (and indeed Spector's) was provided by US philosopher Christopher Zurn (2011). Zurn has himself used the model of deliberative polls in recommending the democratisation of the constitutional amendment process. He has suggested juries could determine what constitutional amendment proposals would go to a referendum (2006, 336).[34] To elaborate, the first step would be a citizen initiative, involving the collection of signatures in favour of a proposal, or a referral from a legislature. The second step would be certification of a proposal, requiring agreement by three separate deliberative and representative forums spaced over a significant time span. The third step would be a deliberation day concerned with the certified proposal, involving as much of the population as possible in deliberative forums. The fourth step would be a popular referendum on the certified proposal.

Zurn's critique of constitutional juries is launched from a stance that is supportive of using representative samples of the population to enhance the deliberative democratic character of decision-making relating to constitutional matters. Zurn's critique merits a full response, but I will only make four observations here. First, some of Zurn's criticisms are based on the assumption that the Citizens' Court would only examine the legality of actions by the executive. He suggested, for instance, that the Citizens' Court would lack effectiveness due to its inability to review legislation and that ordinary courts would step into this vacuum (Zurn (2011, 81, 83, 85–86). In fact, I envisaged constitutional juries as primarily concerned with the validity of legislation (Ghosh 2010, 349).

The second observation is that his support for representative groups of citizens being involved in democratising constitutionalism sits awkwardly with his worry that the juries would be relatively if not entirely unconstrained by an interest in

[34] An alternative approach to democratising constitutional amendment is suggested in Ghosh (2012, 112–113).

achieving coherence with past juries' decisions or to follow judicially developed substantive or methodological doctrine (Zurn 2011, 83–84). With respect to precedent, the extent to which consistency should be favoured even where a decision-maker believes that some previous decisions are wrong can be a difficult value-choice. It is unclear why Zurn's faith in the rationality of deliberative polls does not extend to this choice. With respect to judicially developed doctrines, Zurn mentioned principles of statutory interpretation (Zurn 2011, 83). However, I envisaged trials with a panel of judges presiding over their conduct and the parties enjoying legal representation. It should not be assumed that juries would ignore the advice they receive. Perhaps the most important question here is not whether juries may be less constrained by precedent or legal methodology but whether juries may be in a better position to reach attractive understandings of how strong those constraints should be in particular cases.

However, Zurn could reply that even if juries give appropriate weight to values such as predictability, which might be furthered by following precedent, they will nevertheless be engaged in what he describes as constitutional legislation, which properly belongs to the people (Zurn 2011, 85). The distinction between constitutional legislation and the application of constitutional norms in a particular case is a distinction between the application of constitutional norms in a way that involves significant, as opposed to modest, development of those norms. Zurn recognises that judges engage in some constitutional legislation, but says that juries would engage in much more.[35]

While Zurn has perhaps overstated the contrast between juries and judges by assuming that juries would be entirely unconstrained by precedent, juries may well be bolder than judges not only because the former may be less inhibited by concerns about their own democratic legitimacy but also because, as Zurn indicates, I propose a fairly open-ended bill of rights. This leads to my third observation. Zurn's concern about the Citizens' Court engaging in constitutional legislation sits oddly with his disapproval of my suggestion that parliament with a 60 % majority should be able to abrogate Citizens' Court decisions or pre-empt review (Zurn 2011, 80). The possibility of pre-empting review could easily be dropped from my proposal, but a power of abrogation is appropriate for reasons including the fallibility and novelty of constitutional juries. Zurn, however, fails to acknowledge that the possibility of parliamentary abrogation denies to Citizens' Court determinations the fundamental status that amendments through a referendum process enjoy. Constitutional legislation that is unalterable by parliament will require a process that has a stronger claim to legitimacy than constitutional legislation that is alterable by parliament through a fairly weak supermajoritarian requirement.

My final observation is that one might wonder if Zurn has identified an appropriate process for the most fundamental of constitutional legislation. Zurn sets a gold standard for legitimate amendments, but in a broader sense it risks legitimacy by privileging the status quo to an extent that goes beyond the desirability of constitutions enjoying some stability. Zurn has not challenged my argument in 2010 that

[35] On judges inevitably being engaged in some constitutional legislation, see Zurn (2011, 74).

very few amendments might make it through his proposed process (Ghosh 2010, 344). The sheer expense of the process, with its use of deliberation days, might be a factor that juries consider in determining whether to certify a proposal. And that is, of course, assuming that a party is able to clear the hurdle of the initiative process, with the substantial resources that involves. Constitutional legislation is likely to remain largely with judges. By contrast, my proposal enables constitutional legislation at admittedly a less fundamental level by a body that is deliberative and inclusive.

As indicated, my intention is not to provide here a full response to Zurn's critique. Instead, the principal aim of this chapter is to link my proposal to the community values approach in order to illuminate both. Light on constitutional juries is thrown by recognising that there is a strand of justification found in judicial reasoning and scholarly defences of judicial review which suggests that judicial decisions would be more legitimate if they were based on reasonable community values. It was argued that these values should be understood as informed majority opinion, and a consideration of how this can promote the democratic legitimacy of constitutional review leads to consideration of constitutional juries.

Understanding of the community values approach is also enhanced. First, attempting to connect the community values approach to constitutional juries involves a sympathetic look at the approach's aim of promoting democratic legitimacy by connecting constitutional review to community values. The previous critiques of this approach do not examine this ideal and how it fits with the democratic theories referred to by its scholarly followers. They fail, therefore, to explore this provocative aspect of the community values approach. Secondly, the critiques do not consider if the community values that the approach refers to can be understood in an empirical way that is consistent with democracy.

Of course, the discussion also sheds critical light on the community values approach. Pointing to the existence of an empirical approach to deliberative public opinion more starkly reveals the inadequacy of relying on judicial intuition. An additional and final point is that it also renders more problematic a narrow focus on the outcomes of judicial review when assessing its legitimacy. I have mentioned that the deviation from political equality found in the popular branches of government can be used by defenders of judicial review to suggest that the latter does not significantly undermine political equality. However, if constitutional juries are feasible, the existence of judicial review instead indicates a lost opportunity for significantly greater political equality. Rather than judges interpreting fundamental rights, a representative group of citizens could themselves decide cases that another representative group views as raising the greatest concern.

12.4 Conclusion

The community values approach, where judges justify decisions in hard cases by referring to the community's own values, has enjoyed judicial and academic support in several jurisdictions. It has continued to be asserted despite critiques that have argued that it aggravates rather than lessens anxiety about the democratic legitimacy of judicial decision-making.

However, rather than simply dismissing this approach as offering a false path to democratic legitimacy, this paper has explored the underlying aim of promoting the democratic legitimacy of constitutional review by connecting decisions with community values. This partly involved discussion of democratic theorists referred to by two adherents of the community values approach, Wellington and Waluchow. Wellington referred to Dahl, and Dahl's democratic theory is helpful, for instance, in understanding community values as informed majority opinion. Waluchow, on the other hand, refers to Dworkin's constitutional conception of democracy. This is helpful in providing a fairly stringent approach to the conditions that have to be satisfied before judicial deference to informed majority opinion would be justified.

The paper then employed findings from deliberative polls to support, for instance, a distinction between informed and ordinary public opinion. Deliberative polls provide a feasible methodology for determining informed public opinion. This methodology was adapted in my proposal for constitutional juries. Constitutional juries promise a way to achieve democratic legitimacy in constitutional review. Their feasibility would support the attractiveness of the aim in the community values approach of connecting constitutional review to the community's values.

An analogy can be made between the community values approach and community values, on the one hand, and the community values approach and constitutional juries, on the other hand. Just as it would be wrong to use broad values the community agrees with to suggest that the community truly supports, or would support a particular decision if it adopted a rational perspective, it would be wrong to suggest that the community values approach contains a deeper commitment to constitutional juries, assuming the latter can be attractively implemented. However, just as one could argue that if the community agrees with a certain general value, it should also be committed to a certain position on a particular issue, one could argue that the ambition of the community values approach to link community values to constitutional review should lead to consideration of constitutional juries.

Acknowledgments I thank Thomas Bustamante for inviting this contribution and for his questions of the oral paper delivered at the University of Minas Gerais in Belo Horizonte in November 2014. That presentation also prompted helpful discussions with Wil Waluchow and Chris Zurn. I also thank the insightful commentators on my paper, Marcelo Maciel Ramos and Marcelo Kokke. Finally, I am grateful for the opportunity to present the paper at the law schools at the Indian Institute of Technology, Kharagpur, and Jindal Global University, Delhi, and to Madhumita Mitra for a helpful discussion.

References

Ahmadi, A.M. 1996. On the problems and prospects of Indian democracy: An evaluation of its working for designing the processes of change for peaceful transformation. *Supreme Court Cases (Journal)* 2: 1.

Berlin, Isaiah. 1969. Two concepts of liberty. In *Four essays on liberty*. Oxford: Oxford University Press.
Bickel, Alexander. 1962. *The least dangerous branch: The supreme court at the bar of politics*. Indianapolis: Bobbs-Merrill.
Bolingbroke, Henry St John, Viscount. 1841 [1733–4]. A dissertation upon parties: Letter X. In *The works of Lord Bolingbroke*, 88–96. Philadelphia: Carey & Hunt.
Braithwaite, John. 1995. Community values and Australian jurisprudence. *Sydney Law Review* 17: 351–372.
Brown v Board of Education 347 US 483 (1954).
Carter v Canada (Attorney General) 2015 SCC 5.
Dahl, Robert. 1970. *After the revolution? Authority in a good society*. New Haven: Yale University Press.
Dahl, Robert. 1972. *Democracy in the United States: Promise and performance*, 2nd ed. Chicago: Rand McNally.
Dahl, Robert. 1976. *Democracy in the United States: Promise and performance*, 3rd ed. Chicago: Rand McNally.
Dahl, Robert. 1989. *Democracy and its critics*. New Haven: Yale University Press.
Dahl, Robert. 1991. A rejoinder. *Journal of Politics* 53: 226–231.
Dworkin, Ronald. 1986. *Law's empire*. Cambridge, MA: Belknap.
Dworkin, Ronald. 1996. *Freedom's law: The moral reading of the American constitution*. Cambridge, MA: Harvard University Press.
Dworkin, Ronald. 2000. *Sovereign virtue: The theory and practice of equality*. Cambridge, MA: Harvard University Press.
Dyzenhaus, David. 2010. *Hard cases in wicked legal systems: Pathologies of legality*, 2nd ed. New York: Oxford University Press.
Ely, John Hart. 1980. *Democracy and distrust: A theory of judicial review*. Cambridge, Mass: Harvard University Press.
Fishkin, James. 2005. Experimenting with a democratic ideal: Deliberative polling and public opinion. *Acta Politica* 40: 284–298.
Fishkin, James. 2009. *When the people speak: Deliberative democracy and public consultation*. New York: Oxford University Press.
Fishkin, James. 2010. Response to critics of *When the People Speak*: The deliberative deficit and what to do about it. *The Good Society* 19: 68–76.
Fishkin, James, and Robert Luskin. 2000. The quest for deliberative democracy. In *Democratic innovation: Deliberation, representation and association*, 17–28. London: Routledge.
Furman v Georgia 408 US 238 (1972).
Gardbaum, Stephen. 2013. *The new commonwealth model of constitutionalism: Theory and practice*. Cambridge: Cambridge University Press.
Gastil, John, Chiara Bacci, and Michael Dollinger. 2010. Is deliberation neutral? Patterns of attitude change during 'The deliberative polls'. *Journal of public deliberation* 6(2): Article 3.
Ghosh, Eric. 1998. Republicanism, community values and social psychology: A response to Braithwaite's model of judicial deliberation. *Sydney Law Review* 20: 5–41.
Ghosh, Eric. 2008. From republican to liberal liberty. *History of Political Thought* 29: 132–167.
Ghosh, Eric. 2010. Deliberative democracy and the countermajoritarian difficulty: Considering constitutional juries. *Oxford Journal of Legal Studies* 30: 327–359.
Ghosh, Eric. 2012. The Australian Constitution and expressive reform. *Giornale di Storia Costituzionale (Journal of Constitutional History)* 24(2): 95–116.
Goldsworthy, Jeffrey. 2008. Unwritten constitutional principles. In *Expounding the constitution: Essays in constitutional theory*, ed. Grant Huscroft, 277–312. Cambridge: Cambridge University Press.
Gregg v Georgia 428 US 153 (1976).
Holloway, Ian. 2002. *Natural Justice and the High Court of Australia: A study in common law constitutionalism*. Aldershot: Ashgate.

Issues Deliberation Australia et al. 2001. *Australia deliberates: Reconciliation – Where from here?* http://www.ida.org.au/deliberative.php. Accessed 4 Sept 2015.
Kramer, Larry. 2001–2002. The Supreme Court 2000 term foreword: We the Court. *Harvard Law Review* 115: 5–169.
Krygier, Martin, and Arthur Glass. 1995. Shaky premises: Values, attitudes and the law. *Sydney Law Review* 17: 385–396.
Lafont, Cristina. 2015. Deliberation, participation, and democratic legitimacy: Should deliberative mini-publics shape public policy? *Journal of Political Philosophy* 23: 40–63.
Leib, Ethan. 2002. Towards a practice of deliberative democracy: A proposal for a popular branch. *Rutgers Law Journal* 33: 359–456.
Luskin, Robert, James Fishkin, and Roger Jowell. 2002. Considered opinions: Deliberative polling in Britain. *British Journal of Political Science* 32: 455–487.
Mabo v Queensland (No 2) (1992) 175 CLR 1.
Marmor, Andrei. 2005. *Interpretation and legal theory*, 2nd ed. Portland: Hart.
Marmor, Andrei. 2007. Are constitutions legitimate? *Canadian Journal of Law and Jurisprudence* 20: 69–94.
Mayo, Henry. 1960. *Introduction to democratic theory*. New York: Oxford University Press.
Perry, Michael. 1976. Substantive due process revisited: Reflections on (and beyond) recent cases. *Northwestern University Law Review* 71: 417–469.
Perry, Michael. 1982. *The Constitution, the courts, and human rights: An inquiry into the legitimacy of constitutional policymaking by the judiciary*. New Haven: Yale University Press.
Pettit, Philip. 1999. *Republicanism: A theory of freedom and government*, paperbackth ed. Oxford: Clarendon.
Rawls, John. 1971. *A theory of justice*. Cambridge, MA: Belknap Press of Harvard University Press.
Rodriguez v British Columbia (Attorney General) [1993] 3 SCR 519.
Roe v Wade 410 US 113 (1973).
Sadurski, Wojciech. 1987. Conventional morality and judicial standards. *Virginia Law Review* 73: 339–397.
Schabas, William. 1996. *The death penalty as cruel treatment and torture: Capital punishment challenged in the world's courts*. Boston: Northeastern University Press.
Spector, Horacio. 2009. The right to a constitutional jury. *Legisprudence* III: 111–123.
Spector, Horacio. 2015. The theory of constitutional review. In *Constitutional review and democracy*, ed. Miodrag Jovanović, 17–37. The Hague: Eleven International Publishing.
Waluchow, W.J. 2007. *A common law theory of judicial review: The living tree*. Cambridge: Cambridge University Press.
Waluchow, W.J. 2008. Constitutional morality and bills of rights. In *Expounding the constitution: Essays in constitutional theory*, ed. Grant Huscroft, 65–92. Cambridge: Cambridge University Press.
Wellington, Harry. 1973. Common law rules and constitutional double-standards: Some notes on adjudication. *Yale Law Journal* 83: 221–311.
Wellington, Harry. 1982. The nature of judicial review. *Yale Law Journal* 91: 486–520.
Zines, Leslie. 2002. Legalism, realism and judicial rhetoric in constitutional law. *Constitutional law and policy review* 5: 21–30.
Zurn, Christopher. 2006. *Deliberative democracy and the institutions of judicial review*. New York: Cambridge University Press.
Zurn, Christopher. 2011. Judicial review, constitutional juries and civic constitutional fora: Rights, democracy and law. *Theoria* 58: 63–94.

Part V
Legal Theory and Constitutional Interpretation

Chapter 13
Common Law Constitutionalism and the Written Constitution

Wil J. Waluchow and Katharina Stevens

Abstract This paper is a contribution to the development of a common-law approach to constitutional interpretation. It provides an answer to the objection that drawing on common-law principles in the interpretation of a constitutional text makes the meaning of its normative terms dependent on the subjective moral views of judges. To this end, it uses David Strauss' notion that any interpretation of constitutional law should be compatible with the current meaning of the words of which a constitutional text is composed. It argues that the current meaning of words referring to a constitutional text's normative concepts is tied to the current moral and political commitments of the community. As a result, judges who employ the common-law approach to constitutional interpretation are able to ensure that their decisions are in harmony with developments in the community's own moral and political commitments.

13.1 Introduction

This paper is intended as a contribution to the development of the common law approach to constitutional interpretation as it is advanced by David Strauss and W.J. Waluchow (Strauss 2010; Waluchow 2007, 2008, 2015). Our aim is to explore the role a written constitution is capable of playing within a legal system that utilizes common law methodology for purposes of interpreting the abstract civil rights provisions of its charter or bill of rights. More specifically, we aim to show how common law development of constitutional meaning can be tied both to the relevant constitutional text as well as to moral developments within the relevant community. To that end, we supplement Strauss' theory with Waluchow's notion of a community's constitutional morality (CCM), the set of moral norms to which the community has committed itself by way of its legal practices and decisions (e.g. through the enactment of laws with moral implications). A key tenet of the resultant theory is that, by interpreting a written constitution according to the current, everyday

W.J. Waluchow (✉) • K. Stevens
Department of Philosophy, McMaster University,
1280 Main St W, Hamilton, ON L8S 4L8, Canada
e-mail: walucho@mcmaster.ca; radziewsky@web.de

T. Bustamante, B.G. Fernandes (eds.), *Democratizing Constitutional Law*,
Law and Philosophy Library 113, DOI 10.1007/978-3-319-28371-5_13

meaning of its words within the relevant community, judges are able to take steps toward ensuring that their decisions accord with their community's constitutional morality, thus avoiding one potentially fatal objection: that the common law approach renders the development of constitutional meaning – and hence constitutional rights and freedoms – completely unsettled and utterly dependent on the variable and subjective moral views of individual judges.

Even though Strauss's portion of the combined theory is centered on his account of US constitutional practice, the theory we defend here can be applied to any legal system with a written constitution similar to the American one. By this we mean it can apply to any system with a written constitution containing abstract clauses, some of which make reference to basic civil rights (e.g. the rights to free expression and due process) against which government actions of various sorts are to be measured. Our aim is to show that a written constitution can, despite its seemingly underdetermined nature and apparent propensity to unsettle constitutional practice, serve as a stabilizing factor. It can do so by linking development of the constitution to moral and social developments within the relevant community.[1]

In *The Living Constitution*, Strauss suggests that the US constitution both should be and has been treated as an inherently adaptable part of US law. The US constitution has developed in an evolutionary way according to the same methodological principles that guide development of common law more generally.[2] Just as familiar common law notions like *negligent* and *inherently dangerous* continue to be developed as new circumstances arise, new tort cases are decided and precedents distinguished, abstract notions like *due process* and *the equal protection of the law* continue to develop as new circumstances arise and judges decide the many constitutional cases in which they figure. As Strauss demonstrates, such a common law approach to constitutional law renders it capable of being both flexible enough to stay relevant for an ever-changing society and yet stable enough to constitute a reliable constitutional framework within which everyday law and politics can play out. If constitutional law evolves in line with standard principles of common law methodology, then change will always be possible, but (usually) in a controlled, incremental manner.[3]

In Chap. 6 of his book, Strauss undertakes the task of integrating the written US constitution into his overall approach to constitutional practice. He argues that the written US constitution serves a vital role by providing a kind of *common ground* to which those involved in the evolution of the common law constitution can refer when deciding how to proceed with its interpretation and implementation. A key element in Strauss' argument is the common assumption in moral and legal theory

[1] Henceforth, the term 'common law constitution' should be taken to refer to that part of constitutional law that develops through the process of common law reasoning. The term 'written constitution' should be taken to refer to the text that was written and presented as the text of the constitution. The more general term 'constitution' will be used to refer to a complex entity consisting both of the written constitution and the common law constitution so understood. It is not completely clear how Strauss uses these terms, but for the sake of the clarity we simply stipulate these usages.

[2] As noted, Strauss argues that the US constitution both should be and is characteristically treated this way. Our focus will be on the normative aspect of his argument.

[3] For a similar line of argument, see Waluchow (2007, 2011).

that sometimes it is more important that a decision be made and (within reason) strictly adhered to than that an ongoing search for the ideally right decision take place. This applies as much to constitutional practice as it does to the making of decisions in more familiar, every-day contexts. Suppose there is a restaurant somewhere in town that would, as a matter of fact, maximally satisfy everyone's preferences for a good meal. If we need to agree quickly on a time and place to meet, it may be more important that we make a (reasonable) choice than that we continue searching for this ideally best option. Likewise, on some matters falling within the scope of constitutional law, it may be more important, when faced with the seemingly intractable differences of opinion that appear to be an indelible part of modern, pluralist societies, that we settle on answers than that we continue to search for ideally best solutions. According to Strauss, a written constitution is capable of providing the desired answers in many such instances and in so doing establishes a kind of common ground for constitutional argument and development. And even in those instances where it fails to provide a singular answer, it can nevertheless restrict the range of available answers, thereby serving to focus discussion and encourage the necessary compromises and agreements. If development of the common law constitution is in these ways limited by the text of the written constitution, then we increase our chances of reaching the compromises and agreements essential to manageable governance in modern, pluralistic societies.

But if the written constitution is to serve as a common ground, there must be some basis for agreement on its meaning. Otherwise, the intractable disputes it was intended to settle or minimize will continue unabated. If Americans cannot agree on the meaning of phrases like *equal protection* or *due process*, then the 14th Amendment cannot serve its role of eliminating or reducing disputes over whether, how and to what extent these notions serve as benchmarks against which to measure government actions. According to Strauss, if the written constitution is to play its stabilizing role, it should be read as meaning, not what its words meant when the constitution was first established (or amended) but what they currently mean within the relevant society. But this renders his theory vulnerable to the objection that the written constitution cannot really function as a stabilizing, common ground because the meanings of words routinely change over time. This is certainly true of those abstract and deeply evaluative terms one typically finds in modern constitutions – that is, all those abstract clauses that make reference to basic civil rights. If so, then it appears as though the meanings of written constitutions that include such terms – i.e. virtually all modern constitutions – are continually open to change, thus threatening, if not completely undermining, the stabilizing, common-ground role constitutions are supposed to serve.[4]

[4]The theory is, of course, open to other objections as well, many of which Strauss admirably deals with in his book. For instance, one might question the extent to which there is any agreement at all as to what 'equal protection' or 'freedom of speech' mean within contemporary American society. Our focus, however, will be on this one particular objection: that meanings change over time, thus robbing the written constitution of any capacity to serve as a stabilizing, common ground.

Our principal objective in this paper is to answer this potentially fatal objection to what, following Strauss, we will call *the common ground theory of the written constitution*. We begin by sketching the common law approach to constitutionalism as Strauss presents it. We then move on to a summary of his conception of the written constitution. Finally, we attempt to show how a written constitution can provide the desired common ground. That is, we attempt to demonstrate how a written constitution can fulfil its purported stabilizing function *despite* the acknowledged fact that the meanings of many of its words are perpetually open to the possibility of change. And finally, we will attempt to show how a written constitution, understood as we suggest, can not only serve as a stable, common ground for political and legal deliberation, it can do so without becoming estranged from the people whose constitution it is. It does so because, and insofar as, its development is tied to underlying developments within the wider community, including developments within the community's constitutional morality, that is, its CCM.

One final word of caution. This paper is intended as a contribution to the development of the common-law approach to constitutional interpretation, not as a defense of this particular method against rival theories of constitutional interpretation, such as Dworkinian interpretivism or the various originalist theories defended by writers such as Keith Wittington, Larry Solum and Antonin Scalia.[5] As such, it will not engage with these rival theories. Nor will it attempt to assess their respective merits and disadvantages in relation to the common law theory. We assume here only that the common-law theory is at least plausible enough to justify developing it further so as to ward off at least one potentially serious objection to it. That is the extent of our ambition.

13.2 Strauss' Common Law Constitutionalism and the Place of the Written Constitution

13.2.1 The Common Law Approach

Strauss claims that a good constitution must meet two sets of requirements that appear difficult to reconcile. On the one hand a constitution needs to be flexible and adaptable. An unchanging constitution would serve its constituency badly. Societies, their common views and practices, as well as their technological possibilities, are

[5] For Wittington's approach see, e.g. *Constitutional Construction* (Whittington 1999a, b) & *Constitutional Interpretation: Textual Meaning, Original Intent, and Judicial Review* (Whittington 1999a). Larry Solum's views can be found in, e.g, "What is Originalism? The Evolution of Contemporary Originalist Theory" (Solum 2011). For Justice Scalia's views, see "Originalism: The Lesser Evil" (Scalia 1989) & *A Matter of Interpretation: Federal Courts and the Law* (Scalia 1997). Dworkin's theory of interpretation is developed and defended in a number of places, most notably *Freedom's Law: The Moral Reading of the American Constitution* (Dworkin 1996) & Law's Empire (Dworkin 1988).

all subject to continual change. In order that they might stay relevant, constitutions must therefore also be capable of change. An unchanging constitution would be at risk of either being ignored or being a serious hindrance to progress (Strauss 2010, 1–2). On the other hand, a constitution is meant to fix a set of rules, fundamental principles and values that can serve as a stable basis in terms of which a society is able to define itself morally and politically and conduct its most important affairs. If these rules, principles and values are continually subject to change and manipulation according to fleeting opinion and social changes, then it is far from clear how the constitution can serve its purported stabilizing and defining function (Strauss 2010, 1–2). A constitution therefore has to be 'both living, adapting, and changing and, simultaneously, invincibly stable and impervious to human manipulation' (Strauss 2010, 1–2).

Strauss claims that the US Constitution has been able to accomplish an adequate blend of fixity and adaptability because it has been permitted to develop along the lines of well-established principles of common law methodology (Strauss 2010, p. 33, 34). According to the common law approach, law develops over time as the evolutionary product of a great number of decisions in specific cases (Strauss 2010, p. 37). The common law principle of *stare decisis*, ('let the decision stand') requires that every new legal decision be consistent with precedents established in earlier cases. An implication of this doctrine is the following: once a court has answered a question, then unless certain special conditions obtain, the same question in new cases must meet with the same response from that particular court or level of court, or from courts lower in the judicial hierarchy. This is not to say, of course, that precedent must be followed in all cases. In some instances, a court is able to depart from an otherwise binding precedent by *distinguishing* the facts of the case before it from those that obtained in the precedent-setting case – that is, by citing at least one legally relevant difference between the two cases in light of which a different decision is warranted. That it cannot only be negligently manufactured but is also *inherently dangerous* might serve to distinguish a lethal weapon from a washing machine. This difference might serve to relieve a court of its duty to follow a precedent involving the latter in deciding whether to hold a weapons manufacturer liable for injuries caused by his negligent manufacturing practices. In rarer cases, a court is also capable of overturning an earlier precedent entirely, thus enabling it to depart significantly, if not dramatically, from a former line of thinking. This is arguably what occurs in so-called "landmark" decisions like *Brown v Board of Education*, where the US Supreme Court repudiated the *separate but equal* doctrine it established in *Plessy v Ferguson*. The Court declined to follow precedent, thus rejecting a long-standing decision that had been used to legitimize racial segregation for well over 50 years.[6]

According to Straus, common law methodology is especially well suited to constitutional law. On the one hand it facilitates change and adaptation in the face of pressing social needs, changing circumstances and new views about justice. It does so insofar as it embraces the possibility of distinguishing cases or overturning prec-

[6] For his analysis of *Brown* and *Plessy*, see Strauss (2010, chapter 4).

edents established under its terms. On the other hand, it also allows for a degree of stability insofar as it requires judges normally to respect and follow earlier decisions involving similar facts. Normally, no adequate basis for distinguishing cases and/or overruling relevant constitutional precedents will be available to the judge and so she will be bound to follow the prior ruling even if she might have preferred a different course of action. And even when the relevant precedents leave open the possibility of deciding differently, they can narrow the range of available options considerably (Strauss 2010, 40). This most evidently occurs in cases of distinguishing, where judges are barred from disturbing the decisions made in earlier cases. Suppose the relevant precedent establishes the following *ratio decidendi*: Whenever A, B, & C, then X (e.g. the defendant is liable in negligence).[7] The instant case features A, B, and C as well, but for some relevant reason it seems wrong – unjust, manifestly contrary to reason, etc. – to hold the defendant, D2, liable. Perhaps he, unlike the earlier defendant, D1, took all reasonable steps to avoid the harm. The judge will be able to absolve D2 of responsibility by distinguishing the two cases and adding a new condition to the *ratio*. It now reads: Whenever A, B, C & *not-R*, then X, where *R* stands for "the defendant took all reasonable steps to avoid the harm." What is crucial here is that had the modified *ratio* been applied in the earlier case, the result would have been the same: i.e., D1 would still have been liable since he, unlike D2, did not take all reasonable steps. In this way the law can be developed, but not in a way that seriously threatens its capacity to serve the cause of stability, as would be the case were judges free in all cases to substitute a wholly new *ratio* for the one relied on in earlier cases. Of course, sometimes cases arise in which no relevant precedent seems available. In such cases, Strauss suggests, judges must make decisions according to their own views of what is just or unjust (Strauss 2010, 38). The judge's decision will enter the law as a precedent, its weight and influence being determined by further developments within the common law, the place of the judge within the judicial hierarchy, and so on. The important point to stress is that the influence that such a novel decision has on the common law will be determined, not by a single judge, but by the slow and cautious working out of the principle for which the precedent is later taken to stand. Even seemingly radical decisions that overrule weighty precedent are often not as radical and productive of instability as is often portrayed. Such decisions, e.g., *Brown* and *MacPherson v Buick Motor Co*., are usually preceded by a lengthy development within the common law system that justifies such breaks with tradition (Strauss 2010, 80 ff.).

[7] Theories of precedent are varied and somewhat controversial. For our purposes here we rely on one of the most widely used theories according to which, in citing her reasons for judgment, a judge establishes a rule that serves as the *ratio decidendi* of the case. Those reasons are whatever facts the judge cites as sufficient to justify the judicial action taken. In citing facts A, B and C, as her reasons for holding the defendant liable, X, the judge establishes a rule to the effect that whenever these facts obtain, X must be the result, i.e., the defendant must likewise be held liable. For further discussion of distinguishing and overruling precedents, see Joseph Raz (1977, 183–192). See also A.W.B. Simpson (1963). For a very helpful survey of rival theories of precedent see Lamond (2014).

13.2.2 The Written Constitution

After having introduced and defended his common law approach to constitutionalism, Strauss sets out to integrate the written US Constitution into the theory. He sees the primary role of the written constitution as the establishment of a *common ground* for the community, making it possible for its members to settle disputes by appealing to a written and stable text that is respected by all of them (Strauss 2010, p. 101). In most cases, the text of the US constitution either settles the relevant question completely, or it considerably limits the number of available answers (Strauss 2010, p. 104). Furthermore, the text is precise or vague in exactly the right places. It is precise enough to settle questions regarding matters like the President's length of office, a matter about which it is more important to have a clear, firm, reasonable answer known and agreed upon in advance, than it is to have a solution that allows for further assessment of all the relevant factors as they arise in different cases (see Sect. 1). On the other hand, when it comes to certain other questions the text is vague enough to guide, but not completely settle the relevant issues – e.g., when and where we should be permitted to express ourselves freely. Here the quality of the answer provided in any given case is likely to be much more important than that a clear, firm, agreed-upon solution be available beforehand. When these latter sorts of questions are in play, room must be made for further argument and development, which the underdetermined, vague provisions of the written constitution make possible (Strauss 2010, 111). As Strauss puts it,

> It takes a certain kind of genius to construct a document that uses language specific enough to resolve some potential controversies entirely and to narrow the range of disagreement on others – but that also uses language general enough not to force on a society outcomes that are so unacceptable that they discredit the document. The genius of the U.S. Constitution is precisely that it is specific where specificity is valuable and general where generality is valuable – and it does not put us in unacceptable situations that we can't plausibly interpret our way out of (Strauss 2010, 112).

So according to Strauss, the written US constitution is able to serve, to varying degrees, a stabilizing, settlement function and hence serve as a common ground for settling disputes. It allows disputes to be decided in the right ways at the right times, and in ways that even those who might otherwise not have agreed in advance can nevertheless accept as legitimate. However, in order for the constitution to be able to serve its role of establishing a common ground, its meaning must be accessible to all those over whom it is supposed to hold sway, not just that small number of individuals who happen to be educated in the history of its interpretation and development. It is for this reason that Strauss suggests that, in interpreting the written constitution, judges should attribute to it the meaning its words bear in current, common English (Strauss 2010, 106).[8] It makes sense to adhere to the text so

[8] Since Strauss utilizes the US Constitution to illustrate the role of a common law, written constitution, his focus is on the English language in which it is expressed. We will follow his lead here with the understanding, of course, that the relevant language is whatever native language is used in writing a constitution.

understood even if it does not thereby provide the best possible solution for the case at hand. The main reason is that the function of a written constitution as a common ground would be seriously endangered if it were not interpreted this way. The "words of the Constitution should be given their ordinary, current meaning – even in preference to the meaning the framers understood. The idea is to find common ground on which people can agree today. The current meaning of words will be obvious and a natural point of agreement. The original meaning might be obscure and controversial" (Strauss 2010, 106). So the common ground function of the written constitution has implications for the plausibility of originalism, the main competitor to Strauss's common law constitutional theory. It provides strong reason to adhere to the text's current, common meaning rather than to any meanings and intentions ascribable to the framers. The former is much more accessible and therefore capable of serving as a common ground (Strauss 2010, p. 108).

13.3 The Stabilizing Function of a Written Constitution

At first glance, it might seem strange to suggest that a written constitution, interpreted in terms of contemporary common meanings, could possibly have a stabilizing function. And the reason is not hard to fathom. The meanings of words are constantly subject to change over time in various ways. From this it seems to follow that the meaning of a constitution is likewise constantly susceptible to change. Not only do we seem to have a *common law constitution* that changes according to case-by-case reasoning guided by the principle of *stare decisis*, we also seem to have a *written constitution* whose meaning and import constantly change according to developments in the English language and the ever-changing ways we understand the words and sentences of which it is constructed. Nowhere, it seems, do we find a stable instrument whose meaning remains constant and which citizens and legal officials can use as a common ground on which to orient themselves.

But this appearance is illusory. An unacceptable level of instability will be seen to arise only if we assume that the only stability achievable is one guaranteed by a completely rigid and determined foundation. In his analysis of common law constitutions, Strauss has already demonstrated that there are other possibilities: His common law approach provides stability through the flexible but restraining force of the principle of *stare decisis*. In the following sections, we will show how the written constitution, despite and even *because* its meaning can change along with corresponding changes in the language in which it is expressed, is capable of providing a suitable degree of stability. The success of our explanation will depend strongly on the notion of a *speech community*. Because of this, it would be prudent to take a short detour in order to explain that notion and its connection to the written constitution's capacity to serve its common ground function.

13.3.1 Speech Communities

The term 'speech-community' describes "any human aggregate characterized by regular and frequent interaction by means of a shared body of verbal signs and set off from similar aggregates by significant differences in language usage." (Gumperz 2001) A speech-community can consist of all the people of a nation, all the people that share one language, or the group of people who are members of a small neighbourhood-gang with a special kind of slang. Obviously, all people who speak the English language, or all US-Americans, or all Canadians, form a speech-community.[9] Interestingly enough, though, the community of legal officials within a country also forms a speech-community: It is a superposed speech-community, one that is formed within a larger community for the purpose of a certain activity (Gumperz 2001, 69–70). The language used by those people who belong to a country's legal community is in many respects different from, and might develop differently than, the language used by the wider community of which it forms a subset. The concepts they use, for example, might be understood as applying to different objects, activities or situations, and certain sentences might mean different things within the two overlapping communities. Take, for example, the concept of *assault*. Under common law, an assault is the threat of bodily injury, not its infliction. Within the common law legal community, the term *battery* is, strictly speaking, understood to apply only to the actual infliction of harm. Hence the phrase *assault and battery*. However, within the wider communities in which common law legal communities

[9] We are aware that countries like Canada and the US present complicated cases when it comes to speech communities. Even though the US has one official language, many different languages are spoken in it. Arguably, Spanish is so prevalent that it might be considered America's second unofficial language. Canada, of course, has two official languages, French and English, and the written constitution is expressed in both languages. It may be a problem that so many citizens cannot speak English (or speak it only poorly) in the US, where all official legal matters are dealt with in English. Such individuals may end up being more or less excluded from the discourse that shapes the concepts invoked in the constitution. However, that linguistic minorities do not participate (at least fully) in influencing the meaning of the constitution is only one of many problems they face. The exclusion of linguistic minorities in all kinds of ways is a serious political and social problem. Canada, on the other hand, introduces a somewhat different complication. Here it seems that two speech communities can influence the meaning of a written constitution that is expressed in two different languages. Given that many Canadians speak both languages at some level of competence, that all laws are written and applied in both languages, and that Canadians have the right to express themselves in all matters involving the state – including matters that impinge on the application and development of constitutional law – in either official language, perhaps the two communities can actually be thought of as one. Or perhaps the fact that there are two official versions of the written constitution, one in English the other in French, means that there are, in actual fact, two separate, written constitutions each of whose meaning is a complicated function of a range of factors. Among these might be social and moral developments within the two speech communities, and legal decisions concerning how a development in the meaning of the one constitution influences the meaning of the other. These questions are both puzzling and fascinating but, fortunately, there is no need for us to answer them here. The point remains that, whatever speech community is in play, developments within it can influence developments in the meaning of the relevant written constitution.

operate, the term *assault* is widely understood as also extending to the actual infliction of physical harm. Similar things can be said about the notion of *speech*, which in American constitutional practice is taken to include things like flag burning and exotic dancing. Most Americans, however, would be inclined to think that the word *speech* refers only (or almost only) to spoken or written communication.

13.3.2 Constitutional Law and Speech Communities

As noted above, not all speech-communities exist at a national level. Within any nation or country one will inevitably find various sub-communities. The fact that a country's professional legal community constitutes a superposed speech-community that uses a language relevantly different from that of a country's larger speech-community is crucial when it comes to understanding constitutions and their role in helping to frame legal, political and moral debates.[10] This is especially true when what is at play is a constitution interpreted and applied as recommended by common law constitutionalism. If we assume, as many philosophers of language do, that the meaning of a word, phrase or sentence is determined (at least to a significant extent) by its use in the language, then it follows that the meaning of a word, phrase or sentence will change along with any change in its use.[11] Suppose that words like *humans* and *equal* find their way into a constitutional provision that declares that *All humans are to be considered equal.* What do these words mean in this particular circumstance? The answer will depend on the particular speech community one has in mind and how those terms are used at that particular time and within that particular context. In times of slavery, for example, they will have meant something very different from what they mean now, when discrimination based on the colour of one's skin or on one's sex is considered both immoral and illegal. It is at this point that it becomes crucial to bear in mind that legal officials constitute a superposed speech community. If the meanings of the words in a written constitution are significantly determined by their use, and therefore change if that usage changes, then it is possible that the words of a written constitution will come to mean very different things within the speech community of legal officials as opposed to the wider

[10] Of course, not all constitutions exist at a national level. Many federal states include provinces or states each of which has its own constitution. Again, this can introduce complications worthy of exploration on another occasion. Fortunately, it is one that, once again, we needn't address here since it does not disturb the force of our overall argument that a written constitution, interpreted in light of contemporary meanings within a relevant speech community, can play the stabilizing role that Strauss attributes to them. All references to *nations*, *countries* and *national speech-communities* should be read with this caveat in mind.

[11] See, e.g., Wittgenstein, who believed that the meaning of a word is its use (Wittgenstein 2009). Other philosophers who developed usage theories of meaning include, e.g. Michael Dummett and J.L. Austin. However, one does not have to agree with these authors that meaning just is its use to accept the much more modest idea that linguistic usage has some significant *influence* on meaning. It is only on this more modest idea that we draw in what follows.

speech community constituted by that country's citizens. This will happen whenever legal officials come to use those words in ways that are relevantly different from the ways in which they are used within the wider community. Consider the following two characteristic differences between these two speech-communities that might lead to such differences in meaning.

First, legal officials constitute a relatively small group when compared with the citizens of a country like Canada or the United States. The class of legal officials is obviously a much smaller group than the class of citizens if only because members of the former are drawn from members of the latter, but only a very small number of the latter are also members of the former. Furthermore, the class of legal officials tends to be much more homogenous than the overall citizenry, owing to the fact that it consists only (or almost only) of people with a certain level of education and experience who are skilled and educated in the interpretation and application of law. This difference is relevant if only because, all else being equal, it is plausible to think that changes in meaning occur much more quickly in small, homogenous groups than in big, heterogeneous ones. Also relevant is the fact that those changes can occur as the result of a singular decision made by the even smaller group of individuals charged with the task of settling a particular question of legal interpretation. Flag burning can come to be accepted as a form of speech on the basis of one authoritative decision by nine members of a Supreme Court. Changes in meaning at the broader social level are often much more gradual, and causally responsive to a much broader range of different social factors.

Second, legal officials –if they function more or less according to the principles of common law reasoning – follow certain rules governing meaning-change by which citizens, for the most part, remain unencumbered. These are the rules, mentioned above, that determine how precedents are to be handled. It is safe to assume that within the relevant legal context, e.g. the adjudication of civil disputes or the prosecution of criminal defendants, the development of the meaning of a sentence that forms part of the relevant law will largely be determined by decisions in particular cases. This is because law, in the common law systems upon which we are here focussing, is developed through an evolutionary process according to the principle of *stare decisis*. This means that every case decision has some effect (either a reinforcing or a changing one) on the meaning of the words that appear in that part of the law the particular decision in question is about. That effect might be very small or very great, but it is always there, because every *intra vires* case decision enters the common law as precedent that must in some way be considered when the next, relevantly similar case is decided.

To illustrate this with an especially obvious example, take the celebrated Canadian case of *Edwards v. Attorney-General of Canada*, commonly known as *The Persons Case*. The question that was ultimately answered in *Edwards* was whether women are eligible to be appointed to the Canadian Senate. And of course the decision was that they are. What interests us here, however, is the very obvious effect this monumental ruling had on the speech community constituted by Canadian legal officials. The law at issue in *Edwards* was section 24 of the *BNA Act*, according to which the Governor General was empowered to summon qualified *persons* to the senate.[12] Prior to *Edwards*, the word *persons*, in this context, had a meaning that extended to men only. Following the decision, *persons* meant women as much as men.[13] The meaning of the word *persons* (whenever it appeared in the context of laws about legislative appointment) had, with the decision in *Edwards*, changed within the speech community of legal officials. Because this case entered Canadian constitutional law as an important precedent, and because the principle of *stare decisis* makes it obligatory to pay respect to binding precedents, the legal meaning of the word *person* was now to include women. Its use, and hence its legal meaning, was determined, in a profoundly significant way, by the decision in *Edwards*.

Unlike legal officials who are bound by the rule of *stare decisis*, ordinary citizens usually do not observe binding rules (at least ones of which they are aware) that govern changes in the meanings of the words they use. The development of meaning within this particular speech community is influenced by a host of largely, if not exclusively, informal factors. It is very difficult work to find rules or principles that might be thought to govern this process of meaning-change. But this much at least seems clear. While the rule of *stare decisis* that regulates meaning-changes within legal officialdom is normative and followed intentionally by the members of that particular speech community, the same cannot be said for any rules and principles that might conceivably be at play within the wider speech-community of citizens. Changes in the meaning of words in this community reflect a host of developments in, e.g., moral views, social circumstances and scientific worldviews.

They may also, it is worth stressing, reflect developments in the law. As Waluchow argues elsewhere, a community's morality is, to some extent, shaped by its laws. Laws and landmark case decisions can solve moral indeterminacies and thereby close gaps in the morality ascribable to the community and its members (see Waluchow 2008, p. 83). And if what we say above is true, such decisions will shape the ways in which citizens reason about how they are to behave. Certain options that might earlier have been permissible (or at least seemed so) will now be rejected as outside the boundaries of both morality and/or law. And this will in turn shape, in largely subtle and unpredictable ways, the very meanings of the terms in which their reasoning takes place. The informal, unpredictable nature of these influences entails that it will be hard to predict whether and how a certain decision will have such an effect. It might, for example, be that the decision is perceived to be so out of bounds, morally speaking, that instead of bringing about a change in the meaning(s) of the relevant words, the decision has precisely the opposite effect. It might, that is, serve to entrench established meaning(s) within the wider community.

[12] "The Governor General shall from Time to Time, in the Queen's Name, by Instrument under the Great Seal of Canada, summon qualified Persons to the Senate; and, subject to the provisions of this Act, every person so summoned shall become and be a member of the Senate and a senator." (British North America Act 1867, 30–31 Vict., c. 3 (UK)).

[13] For a detailed description see e.g. Waluchow (2011).

13.3.3 Problems

The scenario described in the last section suggests a potential difficulty with respect to the development of constitutional meaning. Put simply, the legal community's understanding of a constitution's key terms and provisions might develop much more quickly, or in significantly different directions, than the understandings of these same terms within the larger speech-community. This is especially problematic because the constitution with a bill or charter or rights is a kind of law that is very much concerned with entrenching a foundational set of moral norms to which a community commits itself and in terms of which it is able to orient its activities. If authoritative decisions made by the judiciary develop the meaning of key terms or provisions of a community's constitution in ways that diverge significantly from the understandings of citizens, then the legal community's understanding of the moral foundations their constitution is supposed to provide might be very different from the ones that citizens either do or could accept. And this can have serious consequences, ranging from a loss of perceived judicial credibility and authority, on the one hand, to constitutional crisis and perhaps even revolution, on the other.

So one consequence of divergent meanings is that citizens might well become estranged from their own constitution, the same constitution that was supposed to give them a moral foundation to which they can relate – i.e., a common ground. And this can have even more serious consequences for democratic legitimacy. In healthy constitutional democracies, judicial decisions about the meanings of the key terms and provisions of a constitution have a tendency to impact the behaviour of citizens significantly. In other words, in healthy constitutional democracies, where judicial decisions are generally accepted as legitimate and authoritative, citizens tend to alter their behaviour and moral thinking in line with judicially generated constitutional meaning. Yet this same tendency also has the potential to lead to a situation that raises serious questions of democratic legitimacy. The judiciary, in making its decisions about what citizens can and cannot do, will significantly influence the latter's behaviour, beliefs and perhaps even language, but no corresponding effects will be seen to flow in the opposite direction. That is, citizens will not – as they should in a healthy constitutional democracy – exert much if any influence on the development of constitutional meaning within the legal community. The result is that judges themselves will end up establishing the fundamental law of their society, not the citizens or their democratically chosen representatives. Waluchow describes this kind of potential problem as follows:

> Over time, judicial decision, not the community's own morality, sets the appropriate standards for decision in bill of rights cases. (…) It no longer is the community's (…) morality that is being enforced in bill of rights cases; it is the (…) morality of the judiciary, particularly those members of the legal profession who happen to occupy the nation's supreme court (Waluchow 2008, 82).

Waluchow's general defence of judicial review suggests a potential solution to this serious problem of democratic legitimacy. Judicial decisions about the meaning of the relevant terms and provisions of a constitution should, he argues, be reflective of the democratic community's own fundamental moral beliefs and commitments. Were judges to attempt, faithfully, to interpret the constitution in this manner, the effect will be to eliminate the above threat to democratic legitimacy. This is because it will ultimately be the morality of the democratic community that influences the way the meanings of the constitution's key terms and provisions develop within the judiciary, not the other way round.[14] Waluchow argues that judges both can and should identify the morality of the democratic community by exploring the implications of the moral commitments previously established by the community in its democratically generated laws and precedent-setting interpretations of these laws by the judiciary (Waluchow 2008, 77). To the extent that they succeed in doing so, democratic legitimacy is preserved.

Our aim in the present paper is to extend this analysis and to argue that, in the case of decisions about constitutional meaning, the written constitution functions as a vital connection between the development of citizens' considered moral views, on the one hand, and corresponding developments within constitutional law and practice, on the other. If judicial decisions resulting in the development of the common law constitution must always be reconciled with the written constitution, and if the meaning of the latter is to a very large extent reflective of what the relevant words mean within the broader speech community, then the common law constitution will be capable of serving the role Waluchow's theory assigns it: constitutional decisions will reflect the considered moral views of the democratic community. And to that extent at least, those decisions will enjoy democratic legitimacy.

13.3.4 The Written Constitution: A Link Between Speech-Communities

Let us assume, for the sake of argument, that the written Constitution is constructed and understood in the way Strauss suggests (see Sect. 2.1). Its meaning is significantly fixed in just the right places, while it is suitably vague or abstract enough in other places. The result will be a blend of flexibility and stability that is almost always more valuable than the much greater degree of stability arguably achieved were the written constitution as a whole is taken to establish an absolutely fixed, unchanging foundation. The hazards of the latter option are well established.[15] But

[14] One must be careful here. In instances where the community's morality is underdetermined on some issue, the judiciary can provide a valuable service by *specifying* or *determining* the relevant moral notions for the community. But to the extent that such specifications are consistent with the community's other fundamental moral beliefs and commitments, its democratic legitimacy can be preserved. On this see, e.g., Waluchow (2007 232–236; 2015).

[15] The most pressing hazard, of course, is that our choices today end up being severely constrained by the *dead hand of the past*. This is said to be undesirable in at least two ways. First, the Constitution is rendered incapable of dealing sensibly with radically changed social and technological circumstances. Constitutional norms capable of dealing sensibly and responsibly with blunderbusses are unable to do the same in a world populated by drones, heat-seeking missiles and

what about flexibility? Do we not face a potential hazard here too, specifically one tied to democratic legitimacy? If the constitution is flexible, then will it not end up meaning whatever the judiciary currently say it means? And will not this too represent a serious violation of democratic principle? Not if, as Strauss recommends, the basic meaning of the written constitution is taken to be whatever its words currently mean in common English. And not if, as Strauss also recommends, judicial decisions regarding the common law constitution are made in such a way as to be reconcilable with the written constitution so understood (Strauss 2010, 104–111). In discerning or developing the meaning of the written constitution, judges will be ultimately bound to honour developments in meaning (and corresponding beliefs, moral and otherwise) within the speech community of citizens. Owing to the requirement that they reconcile their constitutional decisions with the written constitution, the judiciary will thereby be required to gear their decisions regarding the meanings of the latter (i.e. words like *equality* and *freedom of expression*) to the well-considered, contemporary moral views of the speech community of citizens. Not only will this prevent the judiciary from developing a meaning for the written constitution that is radically at odds with the meaning that would be ascribed to it by competent speakers of the language, it compels the judiciary to respect, in their constitutional decisions, any *developments* in the meanings of the words employed by members of that wider community. The meaning of the constitution, as it is developed through the common law approach, is therefore not only prevented from becoming estranged from the community and their beliefs and practices, it also tracks developments in their language. Now, as we have already observed, these developments in language – especially with respect to the meaning of words that belong to the normative realm (like *equality*, *freedom*, and the like) – will mirror developments of moral views and practices within the relevant community. It follows that the written constitution can serve as a link between the judiciary and citizens, one that provides a significant means by which the latter's developing moral views can significantly influence the moral and legal commitments made through the development of constitutional law. This is further facilitated by the fact that the judiciary is composed of individual who are, in addition to being part of the judiciary, also part of the much larger speech community and will likely be well-versed in whatever developments in meanings and views occur therein. Indeed, as members of that democratic community, judges will *participate* in the development of language within that wider community. The result is this: that they have to reconcile all decisions regarding the common law constitution with the written constitution will establish an obligation on the judiciary to reconcile their decisions regarding the common law constitution with the state of moral and social development found within the broader democratic community. So while the common law approach to constitutionalism, with its inherent flexibility, protects us from being governed by

automatic weapons. Second, contemporary citizens are arguably disenfranchised if their choices today are severely constrained by constitutional choices made decades or centuries ago. Democratic legitimacy demands *ongoing* self-government, not a form of self-government that empowers past selves to encumber the choices of later selves.

the dead hand of the past, the presence of a written constitution helps ensure that we will not be governed by the whims of democratically unanswerable judges. The written constitution, interpreted and applied as we have suggested, will help ensure that social and moral developments within the democratic community play a key role in the controlled development of constitutional law. Furthermore, it will facilitate understanding, on the part of members of the democratic community, of the principles by which they are governed. The fact that the meaning of the written constitution reflects the moral views of her community means that any knowledge a citizen has of the latter will guide her understanding of the former whenever she reads it and seeks its guidance. Furthermore, it will allow her to see the constitution as reflecting moral choices she and her fellow members of the democratic community have made. The stability that the written constitution provides is not that provided by a never-changing foundation that inevitably loses touch with contemporary social and moral reality, but that of a common law constitution that is responsive and reflective of the needs and convictions of the community for which it has been created.

13.4 Conclusion

In this paper we have argued that a written constitution is capable of providing a stabilizing effect within a common law approach to constitutionalism, a stabilizing effect that robs the constitution of neither its adaptive nature nor its democratic legitimacy. It does this not by having one unchanging meaning fixed for all time, but by having a meaning that develops in certain controlled but responsive ways that are reflective of developments (especially of a moral nature) within the community of citizens it is intended to govern. The written constitution stabilizes development of the common law constitution not by tying it to a rigid meaning designed to prevent departures from age-old moral commitments. Instead, it ties the meaning of the constitution to linguistic and moral developments within the community it governs. And it militates against its diverging from the task it is ultimately meant to fulfil: of supplying the democratic community with a foundation, a common ground, in terms of which it is able to orientate itself.

References

Dworkin, R. 1988. *Law's empire*. Cambridge: Harvard University Press.

Dworkin, R. 1996. *Freedom's law: The moral reading of the American constitution*. Cambridge, MA: Harvard University Press.

Gumperz, John. 2001. The speech-community. In *Linguistic anthropology: A reader*, ed. A. Duranti. Malden: Blackwell Publishers.

Lamond, Grant. 2014. Precedent and analogy in legal reasoning. In *The stanford encyclopedia of philosophy*, ed. Edward N Zalta. http://plato.stanford.edu/archives/spr2014/entries/legal-reas-prec.

Raz, J. 1977. *The authority of law*. Oxford: Clarendon.
Scalia, A.G. 1989. Originalism: The lesser evil. *University of Cincinnati Law Review* 57: 849–865.
Scalia, A.G. 1997. *A matter of interpretation: Federal courts and the law*. Princeton: Princeton University Press.
Simpson, A.W.B. 1963. The ratio decidendi of a case and the doctrine of binding precedent. In *Oxford essays in jurisprudence*, vol. 1, ed. A.G. Guest. Oxford: Clarendon.
Solum, L.B. 2011. *What is originalism? The evolution of contemporary originalist theory*. Available via: Social Science Research Network. http://papers.ssrn.com/sol3/papers.cfm?abstract_id=1825543.
Strauss, D.A. 2010. *The living constitution*. New York: Oxford University Press.
Waluchow, W.J. 2007. *A common law theory of judicial review: The living tree*. Cambridge/New York: Cambridge University Press.
Waluchow, W.J. 2008. Constitutional morality and bills of rights. In *Expounding the constitution*, ed. G. Huscroft, 65–92. Cambridge: Cambridge University Press.
Waluchow, W.J. 2011. Democracy and the living tree constitution. *Drake Law Review* 59: 1001–1046.
Waluchow, W.J. 2015. Constitutional rights and the possibility of detached constructive interpretation. *Problema* 9: 23–52.
Whittington, K.E. 1999a. *Constitutional construction: Divided powers and constitutional meaning*. Cambridge, MA: Harvard University Press.
Whittington, K.E. 1999b. *Constitutional interpretation: Textual meaning, original intent, and judicial review*. Lawrence: Kansas University Press.
Wittgenstein, Ludwig. 2009. *Philosophical investigations*. West Sussex: Wiley Blackwell.

Cases Cited

Donald C. MacPherson v. Buick Motor Company 111 N.E. 1050, 217 NY 382 (1916).
Henrietta Muir Edwards et. al. v. Attorney General of Canada et. al. A.C. 124, 1929 UKPC 86 [1930] A.C. 124.
Homer A. Plessy v. John H. Ferguson 163 U.S. 537, 16 S. Ct. 1138, 41 L. Ed. 256 (1896).
Oliver Brown, et. al. v. Board of Education of Topeka et. al. 347 U.S. 483, 74 S. Ct. 686, 98 L. Ed. 873 (1954).

Chapter 14
On How Law Is Not Like Chess – Dworkin and the Theory of Conceptual Types

Ronaldo Porto Macedo Jr.

Abstract The present article aims to show how the contemporary legal philosophy became centred on a methodological debate and how Ronald Dworkin's thinking holds a central position in this debate. Dworkin argues that law is an interpretive concept, ie., that it requires an interpretive attitude towards its object. Thereafter, the analogy between chess and law is misleading and inappropriate, precisely for its inability to capture the interpretive dimension of law. As an alternative, Dworkin offers a different analogy, with the interpretive practice of courtesy. With a few changes from how Dworkin presents it, the author describes an argument to help illustrate how interpretive activity for "interpretive concepts" takes place. The development of the interpretive theory of law, as formulated by Dworkin, leads to a refutation of countless conventionalist theories of meaning and introduces a theory of controversy. He understands that conventionalism and the semantic sting are two core elements of the methodological failure that legal positivism represents. Law is an argumentative practice, its meaning as a normative practice depends on the conditions of truth of the argumentative practices that constitute it. Hence. it is impossible to engage in such a practice with archimedean viewpoints external to the interpretation itself. External skepticism towards interpretation is unrealistic in face of the inevitability of the interpretive engagement. The interpretive practice is established through three stages of interpretation: the pre-interpretive, the interpretive and finally the post interpretive or reforming stage. All of them share the purpose of unveiling the meaning of the point of law's interpretive practice. Dworkin answer his critics masterfully while incorporating central questions of contemporary philosophy in his theory and thereby, sets a paradigm for and illustrates the theoretical-philosophical problems that have been center-stage in recent years.

R.P. Macedo Jr. (✉)
Faculdade de Direito, Universidade de São Paulo, Largo São Francisco, 95 – Centro, São Paulo, SP, 01005-010, Brazil

Fundação Getúlio Vargas – Escola de Direito, R. Rocha, 233 – Bela Vista, São Paulo, SP, 01330-000, Brazil
e-mail: ronaldo.macedo@terra.com.br

T. Bustamante, B.G. Fernandes (eds.), *Democratizing Constitutional Law*, Law and Philosophy Library 113, DOI 10.1007/978-3-319-28371-5_14

14.1 The Contemporary Methodological Debate

It has become commonplace to acknowledge that the contemporary agenda of debate on legal theory has taken on a markedly methodological nature in recent decades, particularly in the Anglo-Saxon legal intellectual arena. Although this methodological trait fed by post-linguistic turn philosophy of language was already present in the works of H. L. A. Hart, I believe it gained new momentum and direction with the publication of the studies of Ronald Dworkin. Dworkin radicalized and deepened some of these methodological topics and took on a leading role in the creation of the legal theoretical agenda of recent decades. The centrality of his work is due not only to its pioneering and the strengh of his criticism, but also to the fact that it can be seen as a response to almost every new viewpoint and to many of the methodological subjects that have gained preeminence, even though it is not limited to this. In this sense, Dworkin's work not only makes a significant contribution to the construction of today's legal-theoretical agenda and casts the author as one of the most original thinkers therein, but also sets a paradigm for and illustrates the theoretical-philosophical problems that have been center-stage in recent years.

The Dworkinian argument that *law is an interpretive concept* amounts to one of the great and innovative contributions the American philosopher has introduced into the legal-methodological debate. The view of interpretation that he develops, however, is not to be confused with the hermeneutical approach of Max Weber and Herbert Hart.

One of the hermeneutical approach's distinctive traits is the importance it assigns to the issue of the meaning of action. Weber, for example, analyzes this issue by using chess as a preferred illustration. In fact, the analogy between law and chess has fascinated many legal theorists, and methodological positivists in particular. Despite the similarities between Weber's analysis and Hart's criticism of his predecessors, there are some differences between them that justify the comparison made in this paper. They concern how both define the meanings of the *internal and external meaning of rules-regulated action* and of *intentionality*. The Hartian theory of law is based on an innovative analysis of the concept of *rule* and provides new methodological foundations for legal positivism. Notwithstanding, it retains from classic positivism a commitment to some of its basic arguments, particularly its concern with the thesis of the separability of law and morality, and with the descriptive nature of the theory of law. Ronald Dworkin harshly criticizes Hart's methodological commitments.

Several dimensions of the methodological debate in Dworkin's writings are dispersed across the various stages of the famed Hart–Dworkin debate, which has occupied countless legal theorists in recent decades. I believe that the central themes of the debate are still poorly understood. I believe that the debate established by theses authors, as well as its connection with the contemporary legal theorethical agenda is central for understanding the classic questions concerning the conection between law and morals, the descriptive or normative nature of legal theory and the role of intentionality in interpretative practices of interpretive concepts. Dworkin argues that the analogy between chess and law is misleading and inappropriate, precisely for its inability to capture the interpretive dimension of law. For this reason, he proposes the social practice of courtesy as a better model for understanding law. This shift, which I refer to as "From chess to courtesy," lies on a deep conceptual and methodological change that separates Dworkin from Hart and many of his predecessors.

Ronald Dworkin builds an interpretive theory of law. To this end, he deepens a conception of interpretation other than Hart's hermeneutical understanding, although the latter may be seen as a starting point for the former. The distinctive trait of the Dworkin's concept of *interpretation* is how, on analyzing interpretive practices such as "courtesy", the theorist poses new and mighty challenges for his contemporaries. For Dworkin, interpretation, as a creative and reconstructive endeavor, rather than "conversational" interpretation, or one intended to merely identify the agents' subjective intent, is the best means to understanding the nature of law.

For Dworkin, the correct understanding or grammar in our use of language is a vital endeavor to both prevent philosophical misunderstandings and to view the genealogy of such misunderstandings. On the other hand, distinctions are relevant in practice insofar as they affect how we practice law – in particular, how we interpret it in our everyday practices.

14.2 Dworkin and the Theory of Interpretation

> A main cause of philosophical disease – a one-sided diet: one nourishes one's thinking with only one kind of example (Wittgenstein 1953, §593).

Dworkin understands that conventionalism and the semantic sting are two core elements of the methodological failure legal positivism represents. In his opinion, the presence of theoretical disagreements in legal reasoning and interpretation undermined the assumption of the purely descriptive, non-evaluative, intent of positivist theory of law, even in its Hartian-inspired hermeneutical version.

This central point in his criticism does not, however, completely deplete his methodological objection to positivism (Coleman 2002, 316). Dworkin offers a broader methodological challenge for several contemporary legal theories, besides legal positivism (such as realism, naturalism, pragmatism and some versions of moral and political skepticism), calling their approaches "Archimedean". As Stephen Guest notes, "you are an Archimedean skeptic if you believe that propositions cannot be true because nothing in the world – a fulcrum – arises due to the fact that the propositions can be shown to be true." (Guest 2010, 162). It is based on this concept that Dworkin challenges all unengaged forms of non-evaluative and methodologically detached aspirations found in countless variants of these approaches. For him, it is a methodological error to intend to stand above the substantive and evaluative battlefield, above judgments of moral correctness.

Dworkin's criticism of Archimedeanism is grounded on two interconnected observations. The first states that certain social practices, including law, are argumentative social practices. This is, for Dworkin, the distinctive trait of law relative to other social practices (it is, for Dworkin, "the central and pervasive aspect of legal practice") (Dworkin 1986, 419). The second observation concerts the dual – internal and external – dimension through which law can be seen. For him:

> Of course, law is a social phenomenon. But its complexity, function, and consequence all depend on one special feature of its structure. *Legal practice, unlike many other social phenomena, is argumentative.* Every actor in the practice understands that what it permits or requires depends on the truth of certain propositions that are given sense only by and within the practice; the practice consists in large part in deploying and arguing about these propositions. People who have law make and debate claims about what law permits or forbids that would be impossible—because senseless—without law and a good part of what their law reveals about them cannot be discovered except by noticing how they ground and defend these claims. This crucial argumentative aspect of legal practice can be studied in two ways or from two points of view. *One is the external point of view of the sociologist or historian*, who asks why certain patterns of legal argument develop in some periods or circumstances rather than others, for example. *The other is the internal point of view of those who make the claims.* (Dworkin 1986, 13).

This internal view of those who make the claims in a complex and argumentative practice (as opposed to other non-argumentative social practices, such as a game of chess) demands a new standard for analog comparison. This is our next topic.

14.2.1 From Chess to Courtesy: A new Model for Law

At this point, it is worthwhile to return to two non-legal examples to clarify the dimension and meaning of Dworkin's statement. One example concerns chess. The game, as seen by Ross, Kelsen, Weber and Hart, involves a normative dimension. This means that, in order to understand the behavior of a chess player, we must understand that his actions are driven by the rules of the game of chess. For the very same reason, we may only say that an individual makes a chess play, or "plays chess", if the individual takes the rules of the game into account. Clearly, the player may be right or wrong, he may or may not correctly follow the game rules. To make a mistake in the game, however, does not mean not playing chess, unless, of course, the mistake itself is evidence that the game rules are not being taken into consideration at all. Let us now say that a cat walking on a chessboard should move a pawn from e2 to e4. It would be incorrect to say that the cat is playing chess. The animal's involuntary move is not regarded as a chess play, even if the move ("by chance") happens to be in accordance with the game's rules. The reason for this lies precisely in the fact that the animal does not take the normativity of the social practice in to consideration. After all, cats do not *play* chess.

Still on the same case, we might say that one is playing chess when one has mastered the technique of making moves according to the rules of the game as one has learned them (from lessons, observation, repetition, etc.). Knowing how to play is crucial to recognizing the social practice of the game. It is worth pointing out that a player may *know how to play* without ever having read a book on chess theory or even *knowing the theory* of the game at hand.

Unlike authors such as Kelsen, Hart, Weber and Ross,[1] Dworkin never argued that the analogy between law and chess was particularly useful or enlightening for the theory of law. This relates in part to the fact that, even in his earliest criticism of the positivist model, Dworkin rejected the description of "law as a model of rules". The main reason, however, lies in the fact that although chess is a social practice, it does not usually, at least in its pivotal cases, involve dispute on the interpretive concepts. Quite the opposite, in fact: it is almost natural and intuitive to consider the game based exclusively on its conventionally accepted rules or even rules set by and act of will from the agents.

In a 1965 paper on the thinking of Lon Fuller, Dworkin provides clues to the limitations involved in the analogy between chess and law by stating that:

> An important qualification is now in order. So far I have been assuming that the *standards* locked in the concept of law are crisp, precise rules, the limits of their authority clear-cut and evident, and I have discussed their logic and their force on that assumption. But, of course, this is a false picture: these *standards* are matters of degree over some range of their application, are to some extent controversial, and are continually redefined in small and imprecise ways by the operations of institution and language which they regulate. *In this way they are quite unlike the relatively precise and unmalleable rules of ordinary games.* This qualification makes it more difficult, but also more important, *to appreciate their special role in legal argument and reasoning. If the concept of law were as clear and uncontroversial as, for example, the concept of a move in chess or a play in bridge, we would not expect by analyzing it to improve our understanding of, or influence on, legal argument, because anything in the concept pertinent to that process would already be obvious to all its participants.* There would then be point to the criticism that analysis of legal concepts cannot yield legal arguments, for appeals to the concept of law would be too obvious or too trivial to count as such. *Controversies over the meaning of law are significant only because*

[1]Another exclusivist positivist might be added to the group: (Marmor 2006). In this intriguing essay, Marmor – after defending a complex conventionalist theory of the rules of the legal game that involves deep conventions and surface conventions – writes: "*As Hart himself seems to have suggested, the rules of recognition are very much like the rules of chess: they constitute ways of creating law and recognizing it as such. Once again, it is not my purpose to deny that the rules of recognition solve various coordination problems*. They do that as well. It would be a serious distortion, however, to miss their constitutive function. The rules that determine how law is created, modified, and recognized as law, also partly constitute what the law in the relevant community is. They define the rules of the game, thus constituting what the game is. […] Let me sum up: the conventional foundation of law consists of two layers. There are deep conventions that determine what law is, and those deep conventions are instantiated by the surface conventions of recognition that are specific to particular legal systems. The concept of law is constituted by both layers of conventions. *Our concept of law partly depends on the deep conventions that determine what we take law and legal institutions to consist in, and partly on the specific institutions we have, those that are determined by the rules of recognition. Basically, this is just like chess. Without the rules of chess, we would not have a concept of chess. But we can only have such a concept, because we already possess the deeper concept of playing competitive games, of which chess is just one instance. Both are profoundly conventional, and in this general insight, I think that Hart was quite right.*", my italics.

the strands making up the concept of law are difficult to isolate and require judgment to apply.(Dworkin 1965, 682, highlighted by me).

In reality, unlike other practices such as law, chess does not involve an interpretive question in association with evaluative judgments (not understood from a conventional evaluative angle[2]). For this reason, Dworkin's analogy involves an interpretive social practice: courtesy (Dworkin 1986, 46–49). The analogy with chess reveals a different logical grammar than the one used in the *game* of courtesy. For this reason, it must give way to a new analogy. Dworkin abandons chess[3] (Guest 2010, 67).

---

[2] Dworkin, in his essay on Lon Fuller, makes clear the difference, not always recognized by theorists of law, between the conventional moral dimension and the proper moral dimension. Commenting on the text of Lon Fuller on the inner morality of law, he notes that: "*the canons of morality, of course, are criterial standards*; they are addressed to those who make moral judgments or arguments and govern their success or failure. Like the canons of law, they may also be pertinent to the question of whether someone has behaved morally or immorally. If I harm you in some way, claiming myself justified because you broke some alleged moral rule which I invoke, then the fact that this 'rule' is self-contradictory or impossible to observe might count as a step in showing that what *I* had done was morally improper. *But a failure to comply with the canons of morality is not, as such and for that reason, a moral fault* [...]". By not using this distinction and using a merely criterial concept of morality, Fuller was falling to a categorial mistake that in later texts Dworkin (notably, Dworkin 2006a, b) would emphasize: : "If so, he is guilty of two confusions. First, and less important, he confuses related but not identical legal and moral standards. *Second, and more important, he confuses criterial standards directed at determining whether some act has succeeded in producing a moral criticism, or a moral argument, with standards stipulating whether some act is moral or immoral, praiseworthy or blameworthy in character.* If he is to establish his claim that compliance with the canons constitutes moral behavior, he must show his canons of law to be moral standards of the latter sort, instead of or as well as the former sort." (Dworkin 1965, 685–686, highlighted by me).

[3] Guest also observes a similar point when he asserts: "The fastest way to the interpretive concepts is through the idea of something 'having an intentionality' (point). Note that we can describe a practice without making any statement about the meaning or purpose of the practice. Thus, a purely descriptive report of chess game can take various forms, for example, in its simplest form, "pushing pieces on a board of wood" or, in a more refined one, 'move pieces of wood in accordance with a set specific rules'. A description like this tells us that this is chess, instead of saying that is, let's say, checkers, but fails to describe what many of us might consider some of the vital features of the game. Were we short of a 'true' description here? Is anything else necessary? What additional ingredients would be required to make the description of the 'chess game' an adequate or 'true' description? What would make people happy? If I provide the details of the rules and then say that the sense of the game was to win, many people would agree. But I could, as many people do, go ahead and say that it is an intellectual game, which requires only intellectual strategies, no strategy how to make an opponent lose by disturbing him with the use of a false board, for example. Or I could say that point of chess is the development of intellectual skills of the players and that victory was only incidental to that purpose. I could, in other words, offer many descriptions of the 'real' point of chess. Dworkin does not analyze the idea of in-depth description. For him, I think, it refers to a level of description that incurs relatively little controversy. He provides an example of a social practice of courtesy, to bow before a superior." (Guest 2010 31–32, highlighted by me).

It is noteworthy, however, that the assignment of an evaluative "point" to chess game somehow removes this practice of our clearest mental picture about it, since we usually imagine this game as an agreement between players without associating an evaluative "point". Andrei Marmor seeks to

One of Dworkin's favorite language games to use as an analogy for law involves courtesy practices. With a few changes from how Dworkin himself presents it,[4] the argument might be described as follows. Let us imagine a social normative practice involving an *interpretive concept.* Say that Francisco, a handsome young man, tells his friend Roberto that he invited a young lady to dinner the previous night and that each paid for his or her half of the bill. Roberto then criticizes Francisco, saying that he was extremely *discourteous* towards the young lady, since men are expected to pay the bill when they invite women out to dinner. Francisco disagrees with Roberto and says he was not discourteous at all, as his income is not greater than the young lady's and that he saw no reason for uneven treatment simply because she is a woman. He even argues that, in the past, he willingly paid a friend's bill because the friend in question was in financial trouble. However, he says, that was not the case in the dinner with the young lady.

Let us assume that the disagreement between the two is sincere and authentic and that, therefore, they were not just "shooting the breeze", or taunting one another for fun or to pass the time. They really had a disagreement "on the level of ideas" or concepts about the courteous or discourteous nature of Francisco's behavior the previous evening. We can imagine that the arguments provided by the young men could multiply and become more sophisticated. Let us imagine that Roberto counters by presenting a concept of "courtesy towards women" as follows: "being courteous towards a young lady means prioritizing her and offering her presents or favors." As paradigmatic examples to support the concept, he mentions the easily observed practice of men allowing women to step out first from, holding the car door open for them, not allowing them to carry suitcases and heavy parcels, offering them flowers and candy before a date, etc. With these examples, Roberto attempts to show that his view is appropriate and well suited to the social facts that he used as reference. Without denying the paradigms, Francisco replies that courtesy towards women involves expressing consideration of and respect to their dignity, a concept that also implies respect for the value of equality. He offers new paradigms in support of his ideas, listing situations where unbounded prioritization could seem offensive and undignified, as it might be symbolically construed as a representation of female inferiority. To illustrate, he mentions professional women who are offended by and deem it discourteous that they are never allowed or asked to carry heavy luggage, or to fully return acts of kindness when in the presence of men. Finally, he argues that his rival conception of "courtesy towards women" is superior to Roberto's, as it is more comprehensive and consistent (or coherent). The paradigm cases the two suggest are a proper fit for their respective conceptions. Roberto's

identify deep conventions presupposed in this practice. However, even if he is correct they only report the values (playing a good game) as conventional criteria of moral evaluation and not as moral evaluations per se (Marmor 2006).

[4](Dworkin 1986, 46–49, 68 et seq.) In Dworkin (1986), the author examines another situation (language game) involving a debate about the objectivity of an aesthetic judgment on a novel by Agatha Christie. I explored a similar example concerning a dispute between friends about the aesthetic qualities of "action movies" Rambo IV and Clockwork Orange in (Macedo Jr. 2010).

conception, however, does not fit the paradigms Francisco lists. In fact, it challenges them, as *unbounded prioritization* and *non-reciprocity* would be recognized, at least in many paradigm cases, as examples not of courtesy, but rather of the lack thereof.

What is the meaning of this *argumentative practice*? Roberto argues that Francisco breached a rule of *courtesy*. Francisco understands the meaning of his friend's argument and chastisement, but disagrees. The suggested example is not a false dispute where two people disagree because they are speaking of different things. Quite the opposite, the dispute is sincere because each completely understands what the other means to say. However, they disagree as to the best way to understand the *concept of courtesy*.

Analysis of this example reveals the argumentative dimension of this practice. The central question that drives the two friends' argumentative social practice assumes the following question: what truth-condition would cause Roberto's proposition – "Francisco was discourteous" – to be true or false? Admitting the absence of a condition of truth, that is, that there is no criterion capable of assigning a truth value to the proposition, it would be difficult to understand even the behavior of the two. Of course, they might hypothetically be simply "simulating disagreement" as a means to pass time, to play at insincere taunts, or just to annoy one another. However, as I noted earlier, *this is not the case at hand*, this is not the hypothetical case we are building. In the suggested example, Roberto and Francisco argue about the best *conception* of the *concept* of courtesy.[5]

In this case, what correctness criterion might signal that one conception is superior to the other? What might make Roberto's proposition true or false? Another point must be stressed here. Of course the two friends are not arguing over the best conception of the concept of *courtesy* based on a merely stipulative definition. Had it been stipulated that being courteous towards women always implies paying their bills, then there would be no dispute to settle. Roberto would be right by definition or by stipulation. In this context, the concept at hand is not criterial, but interpretive, as we will see ahead. In the case at hand, the dispute emerges precisely because the rule that determines the concept of *courtesy* is a social rule, that is, a rule that is intersubjectively constituted.

Their dispute is about the *concept of courtesy* as socially and normatively understood. In this case, the best *conception of courtesy* is the one that best interprets a real social normative practice, that maintains a certain fit with a set of socially shared practices serving as a metric or paradigm. But how to determine which concept of courtesy best meets the (socially admitted) requirements of what amounts to the "best conception"? The important thing now is not to go to greater depths into Dworkin's answer to the question. Certainly, this is not a conventional compromise, as the very criteria for what amounts to "the best interpretation" also involve an interpretive question. What is important is to realize that the criterion is

[5] The distinction between concepts and conceptions became common in contemporary philosophical discourse, especially in moral debates. It is widely used by authors such as Hart (1994a), and (Dworkin 1972) and was originally highlighted by (Gallie 1956b).

argumentatively built, by means of reflection and methodologically regulated construction (assuming, for example, consistency, non-contradiction among arguments, clarity, leanness, simplicity, etc.) of the best arguments.[6] The arguments of Roberto and Francisco, therefore, will be better the more they meet the requirements of what makes a good argument, that is, the dimensions of fit and of the acknowledgement of the criterion's evaluative appeal. After all, "[...] a plausible interpretation of practice [...] must also undergo a test on two dimensions: it must fit the practice and prove its value or its purpose." (Dworkin 1986, 239). Simply put, in the arrangement proposed earlier, Francisco would have offered a more satisfactory conception of "courtesy towards women," as it was more comprehensive and consistent with its paradigmatic practices.

The trait that sets the social practice or courtesy apart from the social practice of chess is that the former includes an *evaluative-reflective practice on a certain value* from the part of the agents (that is, the *courtesy value*), which is absent in the case of chess. In chess, the rules are made up of shared public standards, or social rules, to use the terminology of H. L. A. Hart. In the case of courtesy, the shared behavior standards are relevant, necessary, conditions, but not sufficient to correctly describe the grammar of the activity. For the Hartian understanding of chess, it would be sufficient to record what the players understood by the rules to which they were subject to be. The example of chess is perfectly appropriate to the understanding of how a *criterial concept* works, but is inappropriate to describe the functioning of an *interpretive concept*. Gerald Postema points out that Hart does not in fact explicitly exclude the reflective dimension. However, he does not assign to it any relevant meaning in his hermeneutical understanding of social practice (Postema 2011, 422). This one of the reasons why he does not believe that comparing law with a game of chess is in any way inappropriate, as the comparison does not miss anything essential, contrary to what Dworkin claims. It is symptomatic that, in *The Concept of Law*, Hart always uses *criterial concepts* for examples, such as baldness, the summit of a mountain, and the *concept of the Paris meter standard*[7] (Hart 1994b), instead of examples involving interpretive concepts.

---

[6](Dworkin 1986, 53): "But we should notice in passing how the constructive account might be elaborated to fit the other two contexts of interpretation I mentioned, and thus show a deep connection among all forms of interpretation. Understanding another person's conversation requires using devices and presumptions, like the so-called principle of charity, that have the effect in normal circumstances of making of what he says the best performance of communication it can be. And the interpretation of data in science makes heavy use of standards of theory construction like simplicity and elegance and verifiability that reflect contestable and changing assumptions about paradigms of explanation, that is, about what features make one form of explanation superior to another. The constructive account of creative interpretation, therefore, could perhaps provide a more general account of interpretation in all its forms. We would then say that all interpretation strives to make an object the best it can be, as an instance of some assumed enterprise, and that interpretation takes different forms in different contexts only because different enterprises engage different standards of value or success." The theoretical framework used by Dworkin are the works of Thomas Kuhn, specially (Kuhn 1962).

[7](Hart 1994b), esp..p. 10, 18–19, 29, 64 (concept of *bald*), p. 20 (foot of a montain), p. 120 (Paris' subway). See p. 18–19 about the analysis of criterial concepts produced by social practices. Both examples extracted from (Wittgenstein 2009, § 66–67).

In an argumentative practice such as the one illustrated by Francisco and Roberto's discussion of courtesy, the propositions of the arguing agents depend on the truth of propositions that only have meaning within that same practice[8] (Dworkin 1986, 13). An argumentative practice's distinctive trait is precisely the fact that it assumes the presence of *arguments about* the practices themselves. However, it is not simply the act of being courteous (in that case, to pay the young lady's bill or not) and the paradigmatic cases of courtesy – from which come the rules that give the participants reasons to act – that must be considered in an argumentative practice. Even the very action of arguing and challenging arguments about and evaluations of courtesy itself is part of the "courtesy game". An argumentative self-reflection exists here. The *argumentation practices* involved in the *practices of courtesy* only gain sense within the argumentative practices themselves, justifying and challenging meaning and conceptions of courtesy. Finally, the arguments about courtesy themselves are also parameters to determine what the best conception of courtesy is.

Gerald Postema accurately points out that

> [...] No theoretical account of this kind of social practice can hope to be adequate to the phenomena unless it addresses fundamental questions that arise *within* this discursive activity of offering and assessing reasons. Such a theory cannot stand outside this practice without losing a grip on what is essential to the practice. An external theory of the practice would be a theory of a quite different object, just as a purely physical theory of football articulated in terms of velocity, mass, etc. would have a different object than an account of its strategies would have. In particular, no theory that contented itself with reporting what participants took its rules to mean would be adequate (Postema 2011, 423, highlighted by me).

Therefore, for Dworkin, understanding an argumentative practice about an interpretive concept involves understanding the meaning that agents lend to the values and arguments involved in these practices and, as a result, understanding the "internal" (pre-practice) interpretation done by the agents. When Francisco and Roberto discuss whether the behavior of the former did or did not breach a rule of courtesy, they do not report to *the meaning they, personally, want to lend to courtesy*, but to the meaning of courtesy in a certain shared social context in which they hold the discussion, which, finally, is embedded and referred to in a certain shared *form of life*.[9]

Finally, for Dworkin, a philosophical theory of an argumentative practice will have many central aspects in common with that of a concrete practice. It will, however, *be more abstract*, as it includes an act of interpretation and theorization of the practice itself. It is worth noting that the practice will be normative (because it is governed by rules) and so will the theoretical activity itself. This is because, on the one hand, the construction of the best argument, the best justification and the best

[8](Dworkin 1986, 13): "Every actor in the practice understands that what it permits or requires depends on the truth of certain propositions that are given sense only by and within the practice".

[9]The approach of the thinking of Ronald Dworkin to a Wittgensteinian reading has already been proposed by other authors. In this sense, see (Patterson 1992); (Wolcher 1997); (Patterson 1988); (Bix 1993a, b); (Arulanantham 1998); (Patterson 1994); (Sebok 1999); (Morawetz 1992).

conception are also governed by rules (concerning what amounts to the best argument). On the other hand, it is also normative because it acts on the practices' normative criteria and, therefore, to a certain extent, regulates these criteria as well. In this sense, it involves a certain degree of self-reference or *circularity*.[10] The circularity, however, is not tautological, but interpretive.

14.2.2 Law as an Interpretive Practice

For Dworkin, law is an interpretive practice because its meaning as a normative social practice depends on the conditions of truth of the argumentative practices that constitute it. It is not a system of rules *tout court*. It involves a complex web of practical articulations of authority, legitimization and argumentation. Argumentative practices, which are so typical of the daily working lives of lawyers, illustrate how the concept of law is controversial and subject to dispute, as is "the concept of *courtesy* towards women." Furthermore, the concept only makes sense if one can assume a value of truth for the sentences that enunciate it; otherwise, they would be no more than empty rhetoric. Roberto and Francisco disagree because each one believes himself to be right. Otherwise, they would not be actually disagreeing, but playing

[10]There is an inevitable hermeneutic circularity on Dworkin's thought, insofar as in an interpretative activity about an interpretative concept, we cannot lie completely outside the hermeneutic game. There isn't an exterior to the interpretation, an outsider's look, an Archimedean's point of view that allows us to describe from the outside of and interpretive enterprise carried on in these situations. That does not exclude, however, the possibility of a hermeneutics' sense of action that is exterior to the practice, as it was conducted by Weber. This path, however, does not lend itself to the interpretation of interpretative concepts, governed by a distinct "logical grammar". Cfr. (Dworkin 2011, 123 et seq.); (Dworkin 1986, 53 et seq.); (Guest 2010 29 et seq.) On hermeneutic circularity, compare : "In any case, we can enquire the consequences that sciences" of the spirit's hermeneutics will suffer from the fact that Heidegger derives fundamentally the circular structure of comprehension from the temporality of pre-sence. Those consequences do not need to be such, as if it applies a new theory to praxis and this last one is exerted in the end, in a different manner, in accordance with its art. They could also consist that the self comprehension constantly exerted has been corrected and depurated art of comprehension. That is why we will turn ourselves back into Heidegger's description about the hermeneutical circle, with the purpose of turning our own purpose into something fecundated the new and fundamental meaning that the circular structure gains here. Heidegger writes: "The circle must not be degraded to a vicious circle, even if it is a tolerated one. Inside of it veils a positive possibility from a more original knowledge that, obviously, will only be comprehended from an adequate manner, when the interpretation comprehends that its first, constant and last task remains being not receiving beforehand, by one 'happy idea' or by popular concepts, nor the previous position, nor the previous vision, nor the previous conception (Vorhabe, Vorsicht, Vorbegriff), but to assure a scientific theme in the elaboration of these concepts from the thing, itself (Heidegger 1989)." (Gadamer 2002. v. 1, 400). On the theoretical-juridical field this vision holds certain resemblance with the thoughts of Ernest Weinrib, who also recognizes certain circularity in the hermeneutical thought that goes "[…] from the law's content to the juridical immediate comprehension of this content, to an implied form in this comprehension, to the explicit elucidation of that form, to the test of the content's adequation to its form now explicit." (Weinrib 1988, 974).

at disagreement. Likewise, in most cases (and certainly in their focal meaning), court arguments are arguments that must be taken seriously. This means that lawyers, the "players of the argumentative-legal game," acknowledge the meaning and possibility of a truth value for their arguments before the courts. The attitude is more typically and ideally perceived in the judge, as he or she, due to institutional neutrality and assumed absence of a material interest in the claim, more clearly acts according to his or her legal conviction.[11] Therefore, if some legal cynicism may be more commonplace in the "results-oriented" or "mercenary" practice of attorneys, the attitude is probably less frequent among judges. But even among results-oriented attorneys, moral cynicism, the offer of arguments without conviction, is recognized as normatively disputable, or "degenerate", indicating that the ideal of argumentative correctness for such professionals must also abide by a criterion of moral correctness.

It is worth emphasizing that this final point articulates with a second characteristic of the argumentative practice that, according to Dworkin, eludes the Archimedean views of rival theories. For him, legal practices occur within and impact a context. This contextual impact is measured and evaluated in moral terms. For this reason, the concept of *law* is a *political concept* (Dworkin 2006a, 162). It is important to stress that what makes it political is the presence of a point in reference to a claim for moral legitimacy. This is not about acknowledgment of its political nature simply because it involves an influence from the interests articulated in the form of power[12] or because they report to a public differentiation between friends and enemies,[13] but rather a demand for moral legitimacy of the exercise of power itself. In Dworkin's words, "law is a political endeavor whose general point, if indeed it has a point, is to coordinate social and individual effort, or to resolve social and individual disputes, or to ensure justice between citizens and between them and their government, or any combination of the above."[14]

According to Dworkin, "The concept of law works in our legal culture as a *contested concept*[15], [...] because it provides a focus for disagreement on a certain range of issues, not a repository for what has already been agreed" (Dworkin 1983a, b, 255). Furthermore, "[...] it is a political concept because of the manner according to which it is contested. It acquires meaning from the use that is made of

[11] Stephen Guest enlights the conviction's concept rol in Dworkin's interpretativist model: "If you cannot believe in something, repeatedly and fully, you must believe in it. Not [...] because your beliefs argument on its own truth, but because you cannot find any other argument that is a decisive refutation of a creed that it isn't even capable of harming. In the beginning and in the end, there is the conviction." (Guest 1997, 27, 169). See also (Dworkin 2011, 68–70; 153–154).

[12] See, among others, the work of the Weber (1968, 54–56); Schmitt (1992, 43–50; 52–53); (Schmitt 2006). On the contrary, to Dworkin the political sense is normative political or political philosophical since ir reports itself to justice's value.

[13] For example, Carl Schmitt. I have developed this subject in (Macedo Jr. 2011).

[14] See "How law is like literature", in (Dworkin 1985, 160).

[15] See Dworkin's "Reply by Ronald Dworkin", in (Cohen 1983). Dworkin uses the "refuted concept" terminology, which is from (Gallie 1956a) and (Gallie 1956b), republished in (Gallie 1964). Dworkin directly discusses it in (Dworkin 1958, 70 et seq.).

it: from the contexts of the debates on what law is and *from what turns on which view is accepted*" (Dworkin 1983a, b, 256). The argumentative and discursive nature of law, together with the fact that disputes and controversies are created within it about the best way to conceptualize concepts, lends law an essentially interpretive nature. In other words, the logical grammar of the legal game, in addition to involving a normative social practice, also implies that it is interpretive and not merely conventional.

One of the criticisms leveled against Dworkin's theory of controversy (based on the notion of contested concepts) was articulated by theorists like Leslie Green (1987), who understood that the point of law was not moral in nature and merely involved eliminating controversy to ensure peace. This school of thought, which dates back to Thomas Hobbes, Hume and Bentham, understood that the purpose of law was to ensure peace by means of the certainty law provides.[16] For Dworkin, the explanation is not satisfactory because it is unable to explicitly explain legal practices and their assumed points. For him, law is the forum of principle (Dworkin 1985, 33–71), that is, the space for moral-political debate about the topics a community holds relevant. The point of the exercise of political power is driven by the objective of political justice. Note that this is not simply desirable, an ideal and abstract *should be*, but an intentional characteristic embedded in real legal practices. Clearly, this may mean to some that, being a *contested concept*, legal and political action is not intentionally driven by the concept of *justice* or by a specific concept of justice. This clearly may occur and frequently does. However, even if disagreement does arise between conceptions of justice that provide the *telos*, or purpose, of legal practices, this is not to say that the point does not exist. The common situation in contested legal practices is similar to the debate between Francisco and Roberto, where both agree that courtesy is essential at friendly dinners and represents an important aspect of social practice, but disagree as to what conception of courtesy provides the best interpretation of the concept of *courtesy*.

14.2.3 Interpretation According to Dworkin: The Point of Practices and the Grammars of Concepts

As we attempted to show, Dworkin's methodological criticism of legal thinking in the final decades of the 20th century revolved around the Archimedeanism assumed in the descriptivist approach, an approach conceived "from nowhere" that he assigns to his rival theorists and to positivists in particular. The semantic sting was one of his expressions and the emphasis given to his theory of controversy was one of Dworkin's main arguments in criticizing his rivals. The frame of "Dworkinian agenda" would not be complete, however, without presenting the positive theory he proposed on how to overcome the problems Dworkin sees in the theories he

---

[16] On David Hume's formulation, law's function is "[…] cut off all occasions of discord and contention." (Hume 2000, 322). For Hobbes, see Hobbes (1651, § XIV, 79–88).

criticizes. His response to the *defects* present in semantic theories was crystallized in his interpretive theory of law.

As pointed out earlier, Dworkin starts to build his interpretive theory of law in essays published in-between the books *Taking Rights Seriously* (1977) and *Law's Empire* (1986) and later collected in *A Matter of Principle* (1985). In *Law's Empire*, Dworkin recaps his arguments on objectivity and interpretation and develops them more systematically in a positive formulation of *law as integrity*. For the purposes of this chapter, I am interested in more directly showing the discussion of the assumptions of his theoretical construction, his methodological response, rather than his specific, substantive, answers to topics of a moral, legal and political nature.[17] Despite their enormous relevance and the interest they attract, I will focus mainly on the methodological agenda they raise.

Ronald Dworkin says in *How Law is Like Literature* (Dworkin 1985, 146–166) (one of the short texts that, in my opinion, best describe his theoretical project) that legal interpretation can be understood as a particular case of the interpretive endeavor in general. It is very similar to literary interpretation, since in both cases the interpreter drives his or her actions in search of a point contained in the endeavor to be interpreted, be it literature or law. Dworkin writes in his essay that "[...] constructive interpretation is a matter of imposing purpose on an object or practice in order to make of it the best possible example of the form or genre to which it is taken to belong. [...] A participant interpreting a social practice [...] proposes value for the practice by describing some scheme of interests or goals or principles the practice can be taken to serve or express or exemplify" (Dworkin 1986, 52).

The excerpt enables realizing that, for Dworkin, legal (and literary) interpretation requires the establishment of an *interpretive attitude* (Dworkin 1986, 46–47), which, as he rather emphatically notes, is *a matter of imposing a purpose on an object or practice*, a notion admittedly borrowed from Hans-Georg Gadamer (Dworkin 1986 55, 419–420; reporting to [Gadamer 2002]). This is obviously not about arbitrarily and subjectively selecting and imposing a purpose foreign to the nature of the practice being interpreted. Dworkin is referring to the required engagement of the interpreter with the constructive job of discovering (Dworkin 1986, 66), finding, describing and assigning a point to practice.

There is a second important aspect to this engagement that concerns the fact that interpreters "[...] characteristically understand that their practice must serve a constituent value of practice that each one assigns to the standard this value establishes (and not merely their understanding thereof)."[18] This engagement is therefore based

---

[17]Dworkin is a public intellectual and he develops moral and juridical analysis on several themes that occupy the Americans' debate agenda, such as abortion, euthanasia (dominion), affirmative actions, pornography, freedom of speech (Dworkin 1985, 1996a, 2000); yonder general political philosophy themes, such as iguality, freedom, individual responsability (Dworkin 2011), over and above several articles directed to a more ample public, published in New York Review of Books. A complete bibliography of Dworkin's work until 2005 can be found in (Burley 2005).

[18]According to Stavropoulos, "'The first is the assumption that the practice of courtesy does not merely exist but has value, that it serves some interest or purpose or enforces some principle—in short, that it has some point—that can be stated independently of just describing the rules that

on two assumptions. "[…] The first is the assumption that the practice of courtesy does not simply exist but has value, that it serves some interest or purpose or enforces some principle—in short, that it has some point that can be stated independently of just describing the rules that make up the practice." (Dworkin 1986, 47).

Secondly, the requirements of the practice being interpreted (for example, the practice of courtesy towards women, as mentioned earlier), the behavior it demands or the judgment it supports, "[…] are not necessarily or exclusively what they have always been taken to be but are instead sensitive to its point, so that the strict rules must be understood or applied or extended or modified or qualified or limited by that point" (Dworkin 1986, 47). The remark can be made more concrete by returning to the previous example of courtesy towards women.[19] Firstly, it is easy to see that for both Roberto and Francisco courtesy is a value, a positive value. The statement that Francisco was discourteous therefore takes on the nature of chastisement in the imaginary dialogue. Furthermore, there is a point to courtesy. This point is essential to its correct conceptualization. Mere observation of the conventional rules of courtesy is a useful and important descriptive effort, but not sufficient to properly understand what courtesy is. The more controversial the case, the truer this is. The very non-existence of such a specific rule about *Francisco's courtesy-related obligation of always paying the bill when he goes out with a young lady* are evidence of a point that provides the parameters for the proper determination of the meaning and extent of the rule.

Secondly, the example shows that the meaning of *courtesy towards women* does not purely and simply mean what it has meant in the past. The limits and meaning of courtesy towards women are importantly changed in a world grown morally less sexist and more egalitarian from the angle of gender relations. The point of courtesy therefore plays a crucial role in determining its current normative meaning (Dworkin 1986, 47). This is the means by which one can understand the meaning of *courtesy* in its best light. This second element adds a critical and reflective dimension to meaning itself. The history of the practice constitutes the practice; but its criticism, which now becomes part of its history as well, transcends the past reference. The conceptual reconstruction of practice integrates the very metric used to evaluate and identify the practice (Shapiro 2011, 8–10).

---

make up the practice. The second is the further assumption that the requirements of courtesy—the behavior it calls for or the judgments it warrants—are not necessarily or exclusively what they have always been taken to be but are instead sensitive to its point, so that the strict rules must be understood or applied or modified or qualified or limited by that point'. Dworkin's two components capture two independent conditions, both of which must be satisfied. It is not enough that the practice be thought to serve some value (which would satisfy the first condition); further, the value must be taken to be constitutive of the practice, which is what the second condition amounts to. Together, the conditions have important consequences in respect of the practice's character." (Stavropoulos 2003). The quote within the quotation are from Dworkin (1986, 47).

[19] Dworkin himself refers to cortesy as na example of interpretative practice. I've rather qualify this example in the form of men's cortesy to women by understanding that it would gain more "didatical strength".

Dworkin emphasizes that these two aspects of interpretation are independent and that not every social practice is interpretive in the strict sense he assigns to the concept. For him,

> The two components of the interpretive attitude are independent of one another; we can take up the first component of the attitude toward some institution without also taking up the second. We do that in the case of games and contests. We appeal to the *point* of these practices in arguing about how their rules should be changed, but not (except in very limited cases) about what their rules now are; that is fixed by history and convention. Interpretation therefore plays only an external role in games and contests. It is crucial to my story about courtesy, however, that the citizens of courtesy adopt the second component of the attitude as well as the first; for them interpretation decides not only why courtesy exists but also what, properly understood, it now requires. Value and content have become entangled (Dworkin 1986, 47–48).

This excerpt clearly indicates *the strict meaning of interpretation* (which Dworkin will thereafter refer to as "*interpretive*" instead of "*interpretative*") that he finds in some practices – but not in others such as games and contests – that are similar to legal practices. The grammar of legal practices is not well described, as I noted earlier, by its mere comparison with the grammar of games like chess. In its grammatical structure, the game of law looks a lot more like the game of courtesy than chess. As Wittgenstein warned, to prevent the philosophical disease, we must avoid a one-sided diet whereby we nourish thinking with a single kind of example.[20] Dworkin proposes a dietary change.

In the interpretive-reflective game of law and courtesy, the value of the practice at hand becomes somewhat independent from conventionally accepted rules. Rules become conditioned on and sensitive to values themselves and their evaluative interpretation. In this way, interpreters may recognize that certain conventional and widely accepted practices may be wrong from the angle of the values that provide their basic point. Recognizing the criterion by means of which a practice must be evaluated is not o be confused with conventional practices pure and simple, nor do they merely translate dominant practices. Such shared practices provide a reference. However, understanding their point and identifying the best coherence[21] for certain practices and conceptualizations will depend on a more complex and reconstructive analysis. As Postema puts it:

> The practice does not always make perfect and to assume that a practice serves a worthy value is not to assume that all currently accepted or historically enshrined aspects of the practice do so. A deeper understanding of the complex value or point served by the practice may lead participants to revise their understandings of what that practice requires or

[20] See (Wittgenstein 2009, § 593): "A main cause of philosophical disease—a one-sided diet: one nourishes one's thinking with only one kind of example".

[21] An analysis on the concept of *coherence* and its relationship with the concepts of *truth* and *law* in Dworkin and Maccormick is presented by (Schiavello 2001, 233–243). Ernest Weinrib also shares a coherentist conception of truth. For him, "the reason coherence functions as the criterion of truth is that legal form is concerned with immanent intelligibility. Such an intelligibility cannot be validated by anything outside itself, for then it would no longer be immanent. Formalism thus denies that juridical coherence can properly be compromised for the sake of some extrinsic end, however desirable" (Weinrib 1988).

authorizes. And since interpretation is an integral part of the practice, this deeper understanding of the practice will alter their actions and potentially the practice itself (Postema 2011, 426).

According to Dworkin, "[…] interpretation folds back into the practice, altering its shape, and the new shape encourages further reinterpretation, so the practice changes dramatically, though each step in the progress is interpretive of what the last achieved" (Dworkin 1986, 48). At this point, a return to the example of courtesy might lead to new conclusions. We could argue, for example, that even if Roberto were able to find repeated practices (and even a majority of them, in the context of the discussion) based on an etiquette of courtesy driven by traditional courteous behavior (such as listing the restaurants where men usually pay the bill, counting the number of times men yield to women at the elevator door, etc.), Francisco might still be correct in his interpretation of courtesy that would forever release him from paying the entire bill when he went out to dinner with a young lady. This might be case, for example, were he able to find arguments applicable to a significant portion of paradigmatic courteous behaviors that, consistently with the point of the practice, *provided the best interpretation for it.*

I earlier proposed that Francisco might argue that courteous treatment assumes treating women with *dignity and equality* and, that, as a result, automatic preferred treatment is often *discourteous*. This might be the case were he to invite a militant feminist to dinner who might understand the act of sharing the tab as symbolically offensive. Even if Roberto never accepted this argument and the dispute never saw a consensus, it would be accurate to state, under the circumstances, that Francisco was right and his critic was wrong. The criterion for correctness, from this angle, does not depend on consensus or certainty, but on the presence of better supporting arguments.[22]

Obviously, the criterion for the correctness and truth of his arguments would itself depend on other interpretive assumptions and unavoidably open to challenge. According to Francisco's argument, his justification would depend on the equally challengeable concepts of *equality* and *dignity*. In this sense, an interpretation's evaluation criterion has no outer aspect. The interpretation's challengeability or defeasibility, however, implies neither the absence of a correctness criterion, nor

[22]This point is important because it usually causes a lot of confusion. One thing is to affirm that there is no right answer to some question. Another one, distinct, is to affirm that we are not sure what the right answer is. Therefore, for example, we cannot be *sure* whether the 'Big Bang' occurred over eight billion years ago. However, even if it is slightly likely that we come to the certainty about such fact, we do not doubt the existence of a right answer to that matter. There are cases, nevertheless, in which we doubt the very existence of a correct answer, and not only about our certainty about what it consists in. Hart believed he had indicated, with his renowned example about not parking a vehicle in the park, such a situation. For Hart there is not a correct answer on considering or not a toy scooter a vehicle, since the rule that enunciates the prohibition is formulated through a language that possesses an open texture and, therefore, undetermined. In such case what we have is not the uncertainty or the doubt about the right answer, but the conviction that it does not exist. It is oblivious that a theory on truth that understands that correction is a synonym of certainty would not make such a distinction. However, our use of the language in general and in moral language suggests that this is a relevant distinction. About this point see Wittgenstein (1972).

preference for one interpretation over others. Reconstructive interpretation must address any skeptic objections. Challengeability always leaves room for a consensual or even hegemonic interpretation to be challenged. The form of the challenge, however, as Dworkin will point out, must come from an interpretive viewpoint. Only a new (interpretive) *interpretation* may effectively challenge another interpretation. There is no room for an external challenge, one from without the interpretive-argumentative game itself. The interpretive game does not admit Archimedean viewpoints external to the interpretation itself. One interpretation will only be superior to or better than another if, and only if, according to the rules of interpretive reconstruction, it better meets the requirements for what the best argument is. Note that the "concept of *best argument*" is also interpretive. The search for an evaluation criterion outside the interpretive game would be remindful of the imaginary hypothesis Wittgenstein described, where the reader of a newspaper doubted what he had just read and bought a second copy to verify the information.[23] In this sense, if an interpretation lacks an outer side, an external point of view capable of evaluating it,

[23]This episode is remembered by Dworkin himself in Dworkin (2011, 37–38), where he explores again the question about the possibility of an external justification for a moral interpretation. "When are we justified in supposing a moral judgment true? My answer: when we are justified in thinking that our arguments for holding it true are adequate arguments. That is, we have exactly the reasons for thinking we are right in our convictions that we have for thinking our convictions right. This may seem unhelpful, because it supplies no in de pen dent verification. You might be reminded of Wittgenstein's newspaper reader who doubted what he read and so bought another copy to check. However, he did not act responsibly, and we can. We can ask whether we have thought about the moral issues in the right way. What way is that? I offer an answer in Chap. 6. But I emphasize there, again, that a theory of moral responsibility is itself a moral theory: it is part of the same overall moral theory as the opinions whose responsibility it is meant to check. *Is it reasoning in a circle to answer the question of reasons in that way? Yes, but no more circular than the reliance we place on part of our science to compose a theory of scientific method to check our science.* These answers to the two ancient questions will strike many readers as disappointing. I believe there are two reasons for this attitude, one a mistake and the other an encouragement. First the mistake: my answers disappoint because the ancient questions seem to expect a different kind of answer. They expect answers that step outside morality to find a nonmoral account of moral truth and moral responsibility. But that expectation is confused: it rests on a failure to grasp the in dependence of morality and other dimensions of value. Any theory about what makes a moral conviction true or what are good reasons for accepting it must be itself a moral theory and therefore must include a moral premise or presupposition. Philosophers have long demanded a moral theory that is not a moral theory. But if we want a genuine moral ontology or epistemology, we must construct it from within morality. Do you want something more? I hope to show you that you do not even know what more you could want. I hope you will come to find these initial answers not disappointing but illuminating. The second, more encouraging, explanation for your dissatisfaction is that my answers are too abstract and compressed: they point to but do not provide the further moral theory we need. The suggestion that a scientific proposition is true if it matches reality is actually as circular and opaque as my two answers. It seems more helpful because we offer it against the background of a huge and impressive science that gives the idea of matching reality substantial content: we think we know how to decide whether a piece of chemistry does that trick. We need the same structure and complexity for a moral ontology or a moral epistemology: we need much more than the bare claim that morality is made true by adequate argument. We need a further theory about the structure of adequate arguments. We need not just the idea of moral responsibility but some account of what that is."

then its (interpretive) rejection will lack it as well. For Dworkin, external skepticism towards interpretations is impossible. The only viable and possible form of skepticism is the one represented by internal skepticism, that is, by the kind of skepticism that argumentatively attempts to show the inexistence of a better argument of criterion for the interpretive correctness of a certain practice (Dworkin 1986, 64; 78–85; 237).[24]

Back once again to the dialogue on courtesy, we might argue that the only way for Roberto to show that Francisco's interpretation of courtesy is wrong would be by argumentatively deconstructing it. It would not be possible to argue, *ex-ante*, that a correct or superior interpretation does not exist. Such an endeavor, then, would be inevitably interpretive in and of itself. What would be impossible is to argue *ex ante*, from without, without engaging in the interpretive task, that no criteria exist to determine that a better interpretation exists. Insofar as interpretation assumes identifying the point and value of the principle or interest involved in the practice, interpretation becomes an unavoidable path. When we think about interpretive concepts such as courtesy, law, or the arts, we are bound to play the interpretive game. The Archimedean game is impossible. Trying to play the Archimedean game with interpretive objects means to play a different game and not to talk about the same thing or interpret the same object. It is comparable to providing a sociological description when asked about the morality of a behavior. It would be similar to translating the question "was slavery considered morally correct in Greece in the 5th century b. C.?" as "was slavery morally correct in the 5th century b. C.?" The former question concerns the conventional morality (a fact) of the times. The latter concerns a value or non-value assigned to the practice of enslavement. It would be like saying that we were obligated to do something when we mean that we had an obligation to do something.

A new clarification may avoid confusion surrounding this argument. Clearly, up to a certain point, there may be an "external" sociological interpretation. Max Weber's comprehensive sociology, based on the assumption that values are irrational preferences and, therefore, mere rationally irreducible positive expressions of will (Kronman 2009, chapters 2–3), may yield an enlightening and useful analysis of many social practices. In general, much of the theoretical production of anthropologists and sociologists shares this dimension. It is also important to clarify that not all practices regulated by social rules have the strict interpretive dimension we find in courtesy, as they do not involve interpretive concepts. In these cases, in the absence of the dimension of value and principle, the kind of interpretation involved might dispense with the "circular" inner dimension I have described earlier. A hermeneutical sociological analysis (such as Weber's) might involve considering the "inner" meaning of the action in a detached manner not committed to the described "interpretive game".

[24] See also (Dworkin 1996b). The subject is retaken in (Dworkin 2011, 23–98).

In this sense, the Dworkian interpretation is not properly a rival of the classic sociological interpretation, as many critics – and Frederick Schauer[25] (Schauer 2009, 35–44) in particular – appear to suggest, but rather a philosophical approach to certain interpretive practices of a reflective, normative and evaluative nature, such as law. Classic sociological analyses may be highly relevant to the determination of the interpretive materials involved in legal practices. Their approach, however, is incomplete and limited to a part, or a moment, of the interpretive activity needed for an appropriate *description* of what law is. Dworkin does not intend – contrary to what Hart argues in the postscript to *The Concept of Law*[26] – to engage in a project separate from the Hartian law description project. He understands, however, that the appropriate description of law, given its unique characteristics compared to other, normative, social practices such as chess, demands a philosophical and reconstructive approach to the concepts and values that make up its *evaluative point*.[27] Games like chess form a subset of social normative practices that do not involve a reflective interpretive activity of and within the practice. As Postema summarizes:

> It follows that the case for the appropriateness of constructive interpretation for understanding a given practice must follow a precise protocol. It must be shown that an apparent regularity is not merely a matter of habitual behavior, but normative, and not merely normative, but reflective, and not merely reflective but internally critical in a way that supports the interpretive attitude. Clearly, to show that constructive interpretation is indicated for a given social practice is already to engage in interpretation – and that interpretation may be contested. Dworkin would surely not deny this (Postema 2011, 428).

[25] See also Dworkin's answer to Schauer in (Dworkin 2006a). The critical dialogue has began with the publication of (Schauer 2006). Neil Maccormick presents an objection less radical, but similar, in MacCormick (2007, 296–297).

[26] See (Hart 1994b, 301–302): "The legal theory conceived this way as if it is at the same time descriptive and general, constitutes an enterprise radically different from Dworkin's concept of juridical theory (or 'General Theory of Law', how he often designs it), conceived, partly, as an evaluation and justification's theory and as 'directed to a concrete juridical culture', which is usually the theorist's own culture and, in Dworkin's case, Anglo-American's law. The central task of juridical theory this way conceived is designed by Dworkin as 'interpretative' and it is, partly, evaluative, since it consists in the identification of principles that simultaneously 'adjust' better to the law established and to the juridical practices of a juridical system, or that show themselves in coherence whit them and also give the best moral justification to the same, showing, this way, the law 'in its best enlightment'. Footnotes were suppressed, highlighted by me. See the passage already quoted in this chapter" (Dworkin 1986, 47–48).

[27] See (Dworkin 1986, 47–48): "Everyone develops a complex 'interpretive' attitude toward the rules of courtesy, an attitude that has two components. The first is the assumption that the practice of courtesy does not simply exist but has value, that it serves some interest or purpose or enforces some principle—in short, that it has some point that can be stated independently of just describing the rules that make up the practice. The second is the further assumption that the requirements of courtesy—the behavior it calls for or judgments it warrants—are not necessarily or exclusively what they have always been taken to be but are instead sensitive to its point, so that the strict rules must be understood or applied or extended or modified or qualified or limited by that point. Once this interpretive attitude takes hold, the institution of courtesy ceases to be mechanical; it is no longer unstudied deference to a runic order. People now try to impose meaning on the institution—to see it in its best light—and then to restructure it in the light of that meaning".

According to some critics, the negative consequence of this interpretive conception of law is that it disregards the institutional dimension. For positivists in general, law is a social practice based on the institution of an authority, be it as the sovereign power constituted by regular obedience (Austin), be it as the recognition of exclusionary reasons to obey (Raz). For them, this essentially institutional dimension of law made the analogy with chess far more convincing. For positivists, although the normativity of law is partially reflective, normative interpretation and arguments are deemed external to the practices that constitute law. They are, at the most, "[…] investigations that explore the grounds to support or amend the rules, but do not offer considerations in favor of conclusions about that the rules of the practice currently are" (Postema 2011, 428). As a result, some positivists have accused Dworkin of offering an unacceptable argument, since its explanation would require them to accept something they deny, that is, that internal normative reflections exist in the game of law. Andrei Marmor represents this kind of criticism when he argues that Dworkin, on formulating his criticism of positivists, relies on an interpretive assumption they do not accept. In this sense, the Dworkian critique is question begging, as it does not offer an argument opposite the positivist perspective, but assumes the thesis it aims to prove (Marmor 2005, 27–46).

This might lead to the conclusion that the struggle between positivists and non-positivists, such as Dworkin, would not be appropriately comparable, insofar as they emerge from different starting points. The two offer different constructions that are, to a certain extent, irreconcilable, as their starting points cannot be directly confronted or challenged. The Dworkinian response to this is surprising and ingenious. Although it may appear purely rhetorical at first glance, it does not seem to counter even the dominant attitude between the contemporary advocates of positivism and Dworkin himself. The central issue to be answered, Dworkin says, is this: which of the two interpretive approaches (external or internal) is more illuminating for legal practice? The answer to this question, again, can only be interpretive. On the one hand, it depends on the existence of better interpretive criteria capable of showing its fit with the reality one wants explained. Ultimately, the existence of a best-fitting approach depends on the integrity and fit of *the theory as a whole*, that is, of its ability to answer a series of philosophical challenges in an articulate, coherent and integrated manner. In a very particular way, the best approach should be judged based on its ability to provide satisfactory answers to central questions of contemporary philosophy, such as the possibility of objectivity in morals, the normative criteria for the construction of a theory of justice, etc.

Dworkin offers a more concrete answer in his rejection of the analogy of chess to explain law. In *Law's Empire* he argues that a more comprehensive observation of law allows identifying court decision patterns over a longer period of time (Dworkin 1986, 136–138). Such an observation would allow spotting changes in legal rationality patterns that cannot be explained based on a conventionalist assumption. The best understanding we can achieve of those implies identifying the internal criticism movement that affected them.[28] A correct interpretation of the his-

[28] In a very similar sence, at least in this aspect, are the thoughts of (Ewald 1986) in his reconstruction archeological-genealogical of law's rationality of civil responsability law in french law and the formation of social law.

tory of law itself and the changes its rationality underwent showcases the internal nature of the normative criticism of law. In other words, the conventionalist explanation fails because it does not fit well with a correct interpretation of the history itself of legal practices. An appropriate interpretation of legal interpretive materials over a longer period of time would show this inadequacy. This is an important dimension of Dworkin's interpretive theory for the history of law.

Postema summarizes this point for Dworkin as follows:

> Lawyers, judges, and legal academics did not merely challenge the conventional, accepted ground-rules; they challenged the underlying "orthodoxies of common conviction" in which the more superficial agreement on the rules was rooted. However, these arguments "would have been powerless, even silly," Dworkin maintained, "if everyone thought that the practices they challenged needed no support beyond convention or that these practices constituted the game of law in the way the rules of chess constitute that game" (Law's Empire, p. 137). Over its history, the substance of the practice of American law, for example, has changed in profound ways, but much of this was driven by internal argument, challenge, and adjustments to them. Over its history, judges in the American legal system, for example, treated the techniques they use for interpreting statutes and measuring precedents—even those no one challenges—not simply as tools handed down by the traditions of their ancient craft but as principles they assume can be justified in some deeper political theory, and when they come to doubt this, for whatever reason, they construct theories that seem to them better. (Ibid., p. 139) Dworkin, then, rested his case for the strongly interpretive approach to legal practice on an interpretation of its history (Postema 2011, 430).[29]

14.2.4 Stages of Interpretation

Finally, it is important to point out that Dworkin attempts to show how the stages of constructive interpretation are established. Although their purpose is chiefly heuristic ad didactic, they help understand the structure of the interpretive process. Each stage has a distinctive requirement for the level of consensus needed for interpretation. As shown earlier, during the analysis of a given social practice, such as courtesy, law or art, there must be a *pre-interpretive stage* that identifies the rules and standards or paradigms deemed to provide the experiential content of the practice (Dworkin 1986, 65 et seq.). In the case of courtesy, this stage involves gathering the *interpretive material* made up of common practices, paradigms, examples, illustrations of courtesy as portrayed in literature, film, etc. In the case of the determination of a film's aesthetic qualities, the stage involves identifying a consensually recognized repertoire as exemplary cases of "film", "action film", "good action film," etc. These materials allow identification of the paradigms of the practices at hand – for example, the film "2001: a space odyssey" as a paradigm for a "good science fiction film."

It is worth stressing that, in a sense, this *"pre-interpretive" stage* already involves some degree of interpretation. Dworkin clarifies: "I write 'pre-interpretive' in quotes because, even at this stage, some kind of interpretation is needed. Social

[29] Here Postema is summarizing Dworkin (1986, 65–67).

rules lack identifying labels" (Dworkin 1986, 66). This early phase involves a more intense sharing of the materials. As Dworkin writes, "*But there must be a high degree of consensus – perhaps an interpretive community may be usefully defined as needing consensus at this stage* – if one expects the interpretive attitude to be fruitful and one can, therefore, abstract from this stage in ones analysis, assuming that the classifications it offers are treated as a given in everyday reflection and argumentation" (Dworkin 1986, 66).

After this early stage comes an "*interpretive stage*" in which the interpreter relies on a general justification for the main elements of the practice identified in the "*pre-interpretive*" stage. This will amount to an argument about the reasons why, if at all, it is worth searching for a practice with this general form (Dworkin 1986, 66). This interpretive moment now takes on an argumentative dimension. In this sense, "[...] The justification need not fit every aspect or feature of the standing practice, but it must fit enough for the interpreter to be able to see himself as interpreting that practice, not inventing a new one." The important point to emphasize is, as noted earlier, that at this stage judgments are made about the fit and justification (or evaluative appeals) that form the heart of the interpretive conception.

Finally, Dworkin indicates a post-interpretive, or *reforming*, stage at which the interpreter "[...] adjusts his sense of what the practice "really" requires so as better to serve the justification he accepts at the interpretive stage" (Dworkin 1986, 66). He offers an example: "An interpreter of courtesy, for example, may come to think that a consistent enforcement of the best justification of that practice would require people to lip their caps to soldiers returning from a crucial war as well as to nobles" (Dworkin 1986, 66). At this point, however, some challengeable possibilities can be found: "Or that it calls for a new exception to an established pattern of deference: making returning soldiers exempt from displays of courtesy, for example. Or perhaps even that an entire rule stipulating deference to an entire group or class or persons must be seen as a mistake in the light of that justification" (Dworkin 1986, 66).

Of course, in a real society, the stages would be less evident and stark. Notwithstanding, one might establish a similar analysis of its practices. How might we recognize these criteria for a given society's rules? Dworkin's response is clearly Wittgensteinian[30]: "People's interpretive judgments would be more a matter of

[30] Let's compare it with the meaning by which this rule is recognized. (Wittgenstein 2009, § 197): "'It's as if we could grasp the whole use of a word in a flash.'— And that is just what we say we do. That is to say: we sometimes describe what we do in these words. But there is nothing astonishing, nothing queer, about what happens. It becomes queer when we are led to think that the future development must in some way already be present in the act of grasping the use and yet isn't present.—For we say that there isn't any doubt that we understand the word, and on the other hand its meaning lies in its use. There is no doubt that I now want to play chess, but chess is the game it is in virtue of all its rules (and so on). Don't I know, then, which game I want to play until I have played it? or are all the rules contained in my act of intending? Is it experience that tells me that this sort of game is the usual consequence of such an act of intending? so is it impossible for me to be certain what I am intending to do? And if that is nonsense—what kind of super-strong connexion exists between the act of intending and the thing intended?——Where is the connexion effected between the sense of the expression 'Let's play a game of chess' and all the rules of the

seeing at once the dimensions of their practice a purpose or aim in that practice, and the post-interpretive consequence of that purpose." (Dworkin 1986, 67). This is how agents "pick up the rule". "And this seeing would ordinarily be no more insightful than just falling in with an interpretation then popular in some group whose point of view the interpreter takes up more or less automatically" (Dworkin 1986, 67). In other words, there are no "ultimate grounds" for this recognition. It is the sharing itself of a form of life that will enable the members of a community of meaning to "see" how the criterion exists and works.

This, however, will not avoid controversy. After all, people may not see exactly the same things, or may interpret things in different ways. Disagreement, therefore, may arise either in the recognition of the paradigmatic practice and the rule or, even more so, when arguing about the best justification of the latter. What then, is the level of sharing or consensus needed to enable such an interpretation? Dworkin's answer is once again inspired in the Wittgensteinian concept of *form of life*. The excerpt below sums up his thinking rather well:

> We can now look back through our analytical account to compose an inventory of the kind of convictions or beliefs or assumptions someone needs to interpret something. *He needs assumptions or convictions about what counts as part of the practice in order to define the raw data of his interpretation at the pre-interpretive stage; the interpretive attitude cannot survive unless members of the same interpretive community share at least roughly the same assumptions about this.* He also needs convictions; about how far the justification he proposes at the interpretive stage must fit the standing features of the practice to count as an interpretation of it rather than the invention of something new (Dworkin 1986, 67).

In this excerpt, Dworkin clearly shows how and why convictions are part of the interpretive attitude. They are constituents of the inevitable human and intersubjective point of view such an attitude involves and assumes. There is no room for a "view from nowhere." As Dworkin likes to insist: "The interpretive situation is not an Archimedean point, nor is that suggested in the idea that interpretation aims to make what is interpreted the best it can seem. Once again *I appeal to Gadamer, whose account of interpretation as recognizing, while struggling against, the constraints of history strikes the right note*" (Dworkin 1986, 62).

In order to survive, an interpretation must fit the form of life of the community in which it is presented. It would be appropriate, however, to ask how to measure the fit of an interpretation. How to tell when a good interpretation better fits the reality it attempts to describe? Dworkin once again explains using the example of courtesy: "Can the best justification of the practices of courtesy, which almost everyone else takes to be mainly about showing deference to social superiors, really be one that would require, at the reforming stage, no distinctions of social rank?". He pro-

game?—Well, in the list of rules of the game, in the teaching of it, in the day-to-day practice of playing.". Ver também, da mesma obra, § 138: "But can't the meaning of a word that I understand fit the sense of a sentence that I understand? Or the meaning of one word fit the meaning of another?—Of course, if the meaning is the *use* we make of the word, it makes no sense to speak of such 'fitting.' But we *understand* the meaning of a word when we hear or say it; we grasp it in a flash, and what we grasp in this way is surely something different from the 'use' which is extended in time!"

ceeds: "Would this be too radical a reform, too ill-filling a justification to count as an interpretation at all? Once again, there cannot be too great a disparity in different peoples convictions about fit; but only history can teach us how much difference is too much" (Dworkin 1986, 67).

The excerpt clearly shows that there is an external, transcendental criterion from without the social practice that may serve as a metric for fit. But how and why will history teach us? Through the confrontation of interpretive practices and the production of "interpretive materials" that will enable us to justify the best interpretation possible of them. In other words, there is no outer side of the interpretive process.[31]

Finally, it is important to once more emphasize the active role of convictions on the values that govern the social actions being interpreted. Therefore, insisting on the previous example:

> He will need more substantive convictions about which kinds of justification really would show the practice in the best light, judgments about whether social ranks are desirable or deplorable, for example. These substantive convictions must be independent of the convictions about fit just described, otherwise the latter could not constrain the former, and he could not, after all, distinguish interpretation from invention. But they need not be so much shared within his community, for the interpretive attitude to flourish, as his sense of pre interpretive boundaries or even his convictions about the required degree of fit (Dworkin 1986, 67–68).

Substantive convictions, therefore, establish a requirement of sharing (or consensus) other than that required in the "pre-interpretive" phase. This is because the field of controversy on the various conceptions of a single concept is vast and unavoidable. Many will claim that the meaning of practice is the one lent by the agent's personal intent. One might, therefore, ask: if the courteous meaning of an action is given by the conviction of the agents, how to avoid subjective interpretation? If Francisco's courtesy depends on his own conviction as much as Roberto's depends on his, how to assign a value of truth to the proposition that the former was discourteous? In order to answer this question one must first clarify the relationship between the *point* of social practices and how it connects with the forms of life in the community in which they acquire sense.

14.2.5 Practical Intent and **Forms of Life**

One of the recurring questions in interpretive discussions concerns the meaning of the *point*. In the domain of artistic interpretation, a consolidated debate exists on the topic. We might ask, as Dworkin himself did, whether artistic interpretation inevitably consists in uncovering an author's intentions. We might also ask whether uncovering an author's intentions is a factual process independent from the values of the interpreter himself.

[31] Dworkin retakes this point in (Dworkin 2011, 123–156).

Dworkin answers that artistic interpretation is not simply about recovering an author's intention: "[...] if by "intention" we mean a conscious state of mind and do not lend the statement the meaning that artistic interpretation always attempts to identify a specific conscious thought that coordinated the entire orchestration in the author's mind when he said, wrote, or created his work" (Dworkin 1986, 57). Artistic intention is far more complex. This is due to the fact that, in artistic interpretation, the notion of the author's intention, when it becomes a method or style of interpretation, itself implies the interpreter's artistic convictions[32] (Dworkin 1986, 57). Furthermore, even within the tradition of artistic interpretation, the theory according to which the best way to interpret art is through the artist's personal intentions is subject to challenge (Dworkin 1986, 57). Besides, this would prevent artistic interpretation from being neutral and objective, as the interpreter would have to explore someone else's motives and purposes. Finally, this does not appear to be the way in which we use language when we speak of artistic interpretations. After all, "[...] it is characteristic of such practices that an interpretive statement is *not* just a statement about what other interpreters think" (Dworkin 1986, 55). The question stands, therefore.

How could this form of interpretation ever hope to uncover something like an author's intention, be it in the arts or in any other form of social activity, without implying either the impossibility of objective interpretation or pure subjectivism? Dworkin counters the challenge as follows: "Two possibilities exist. One might say that interpreting a social practice means to uncover the purposes or intentions of the other participants in the practice, such as the citizens of the hypothetical community, for example" (Dworkin 1986, 55). In this case, the intention would refer to each intention taken individually. But another possibility exists: "Or that it means to uncover the purposes of the society that houses this practice, conceived as having some mental form of life or group awareness" (Dworkin 1986, 55). The former alternative seems more appealing, as it does not involve somewhat mysterious concepts like "mental form of life or group awareness". But the alternative is not viable for the reasons provided in the foregoing paragraph. The latter alternative, then, must be chosen. A preliminary distinction must be made, however. "A social prac-

[32] For Dworkin understands "Works of art present themselves to us as having, or at least as claiming, value of the particular kind we call aesthetic: that mode of presentation is part of the very idea of an artistic tradition" (Dworkin 1986, 59–60). The way of seeing the debate among critics explains why some periods of literary activity are more associated than others with the artistic intention: its intellectual culture entails art's value more firmly to the process of artistic creation. Cavell observes that "[...] in modern art, the problem of author's intention [...] has taken a more visible role, in our acceptance of their work, than in previous periods [...]"and that "[...] the poetry practice is transformed in the XIX and XX century in such a way that the questioning the intention [...] are imposed to the reader by the poem." (Cavell 1969, 228–229). Therefore, our dominant style of interpretation has settled down in the author's intention, and the discussions, inside that style, about what it is, more precisely, the artistic intention reveal doubts and divergences more refined about the nature of the creative genius, about the conscientious and unconscientious and about what is instinctive in its composition and expression. In the artistic interpretation, the interpret must "[...] firstly remember a crucial observation of Gadamer, that the interpretation must put in practice an intention." (Dworkin 1986, 56).

tice creates and assumes a *crucial distinction* between *interpreting the acts and thoughts of individual participants*, in that sense, and *interpreting the practice itself, that is, interpreting what they do collectively*." (Dworkin 1986, 63). In this respect, Dworkin resumes the social meaning of the rules that create patterns for the evaluation of behaviors and values. As Wittgenstein, Winch and Hart argued before him, rules are social.

Dworkin ponders that "[…] this distinction would be of no practical importance if the participants in a practice always agreed on how to best interpret it. But they do not, at least on details, when the interpretive attitude is lively" (Dworkin 1986, 63). At this point we return to the different levels of consensus that must be found at the various stages of the interpretive process as seen in the previous topic. This, however, is far from meaning that a basic, background, consensus need not be present among the participants, who

> […] must, to be sure, agree about a great deal in order to share a social practice. *They must share a vocabulary*: they must have in mind much the same thing when they mention hats or requirements *They must understand the world in sufficiently similar ways and have interests and convictions sufficiently similar to recognize the sense in each other's claims, to treat these as claims* rather than just noises. That means not just using the same dictionary, *but sharing what Wittgenstein called a form of life sufficiently concrete* so in at the one can recognize sense and purpose to what the other say a and does see what sort of beliefs and motives would make sense of his diction, gesture, tone, and so forth. *They must all speak the same language" in both senses of that phrase*. But this similarity of interests and convictions need hold only to a point: *it must be sufficiently dense to permit genuine disagreement, but not so dense that disagreement cannot break out* (Dworkin 1986, 63).

In short, for the interpretation process to occur and in order recognize "intentions" that do not merely translate subjective purposes, the interpreters must share a single form of life. This sharing is at the same time, and almost paradoxically, what enables and ensures disagreement.[33] Returning to the argument of the previous item, one may claim, as Dworkin did:

> So each of the participants in a social practice must distinguish between trying to decide what other members of his community think the practice requires and trying to decide, for himself, what it really requires. Since these are different questions, the interpretive methods he uses to answer the latter question cannot be the methods of conversational interpretation, addressed to individuals one by one, that he would use to answer the former. A social scientist who offers to interpret the practice must make the same distinction (Dworkin 1986, 63).

Finally, it is worth pointing out another contrast between Dworkin's position and Max Weber's hermeneutics. For the former, merely reporting the opinions and values of a community and how these beliefs affect their behavior might amount to a kind of hermeneutical sociological "explanation",

> But that would not constitute an interpretation of the practice itself; if he undertakes that different project he must give up methodological individualism and use the methods his subjects use in forming their own opinions about what courtesy really requires. He must, *join* the practice he proposes to understand; his conclusions are then not neutral reports

[33] This subject has been exemplarly brought out in (Dworkin 2007).

about what the citizens of courtesy think but claims about courtesy competitive with theirs. (Dworkin 1986, 64).

In other words, sociology does not perform the same kind of interpretation required in the contexts of creative, artistic or social interpretation. This also means that because sociological interpretation lies seated on a conversational interpretation model, is inappropriate to interpret law from the angle of the theory of law. For Dworkin,

> [...]*Conversational interpretation* is inappropriate because the practice being interpreted sets the conditions of interpretation: courtesy insists that interpreting courtesy is not just a matter of discovering what any particular person thinks about it. So even if we assume that the community is a distinct person with opinions and convictions of its own, a group consciousness of some sort that assumption only adds to the story a further person whose opinions an interpreter must judge and contest, not simply discover and report. He must still distinguish, that is, between the opinion the group consciousness has about what courtesy requires, which he thinks he can discover by reflecting on its distinct motives and purposes, and what he, the interpreter, thinks courtesy really requires. He still needs a kind of interpretive method he can use to test that entity's judgment once discovered, and this method cannot be a matter of conversation with that entity or anything else. (Dworkin 1986, 665).[34]

Starting in the 1990s, Dworkin attempts to clarify the scopes and domains of these different ways of interpreting law, by introducing new conceptual distinctions to help explain the meaning of a sociological, jurisprudential and doctrinal understanding of law (that is, relative to the truth value of legal propositions). Analyzing it, however, would excessively expand this paper's scope and ambition.

[34] Dworkin plunges into this quention in a long footnote (number 14) enlightening how he reaches to such conclusions. "Habermas observes that social science differs from natural science for just that reason. He argues that even when we discard the Newtonian view of natural science as the explanation of the theory-neutral phenomena, in favor of the modern view that a scientist's theory will determine what he takes the data to be, an important difference nevertheless remains between natural and social science. Social scientists find their data already pre interpreted. They must understand behavior the way it is already understood by the people whose behavior it is; a social scientist must be at least a 'virtual' participant in the practices he means to describe, lie must, that is, stand ready to judge an well as report the claims his subjects make, because unless he can judge them he cannot understand them, (See Habermas 1984, 102–11). *I argue, in the text, that a social scientist attempting to understand an argumentative social practice like the practice of courtesy (or, as I shall claim, law) must therefore participate in the spirit of its ordinary participants, even when his participation is only 'virtual'. Since they do not mean to be interpreting each other in the conversational way when they offer their views of what courtesy really requires, neither can he when he offers his views. His interpretation of courtesy must contest theirs and must therefore be constructive interpretation rather than conversational interpretation.*" (Dworkin 1986, 422). Dworkin atributes this same orientation in the direction of a constructive interpretation of history per se, in opposition to the conversional interpretation also to Habermas. Against Dilthey's historical Archimedianism, "Habermas makes makes the crucial observation (which points in the direction of constructive rather than conversational interpretation) that interpretation supposes that the author could learn from the interpreter" (Dworkin 1986, 420).

14.3 Conclusion

Chess is a game that develops the chess-playing intelligence (Fernandes 1996, 499).

This paper attempts to show how the contemporary theoretical legal debate became a "methodological debate" and how Ronald Dworkin's thinking holds a central or noteworthy position in this debate. The methodological nature is expressed in several ways. It manifests itself by means of the incorporation of a series of contemporary philosophical questions regarding the concepts of *objectiveness*, *certainty* and *truth*.

The 1986 publication of Dworkin's *Law's Empire* was a new milestone for this agenda. In the book, Dworkin develops some of the ideas introduced in several previous essays, the principal among which were republished in the book *A Matter of Principle*. In it, Dworkin introduces his interpretive theory of law. To do so, he develops a detailed analysis of the concept of *interpretation* that is its cornerstone.

For Dworkin, there are many kinds of social action. Some social actions are driven by conventional interests or objectives. Others, however, are driven by values and demand interpretation from agents. The interpretation of values requires interpreters to recognize a distinctive kind of point. Dworkin's favorite example to illustrate the idea resorts to the analysis of literary interpretation. In this kind of interpretive practice, which is commonplace among literary critics, interpreters oppose interpretations that assume some kind of aesthetic hypothesis. Similarly, Dworkin argues that law requires a evaluative interpretive type of practice and this, in turn, requires interpreters to formulate, even if provisionally, a political and justice hypothesis. This is why Dworkin abandons the chess metaphor. Chess is a social practice that does not involve the existence of a evaluative point. Law has grammatical characteristics that are essentially different from those of chess, and to insist in the comparisons would involve insisting in a philosophical mistake.

An important corollary of the development of the interpretive theory of law as formulated by Dworkin, as well as of the concept of *interpretation* he uses, consists of the refutation of countless conventionalist theories of meaning and the introduction of a theory of controversy, which appears to be essential to an accurate and appropriate understanding of the legal phenomenon. For Dworkin, when two interpreters become involved in an interpretive dispute about evaluative concepts (later renamed interpretive concepts), they must share some identification practices and paradigms to enable identification of the values involved. This sharing, however, is frequently not enough to establish a convention to eliminate dispute about the best way to interpret the meaning of a certain value. The interpretive endeavor therefore involves a second moment at which rivaling conceptions of a single concept may compete in an effort to provide the best interpretation. That one that shows the best fit and that best recognizes the evaluative appeal in question must be recognized as the best (correct) conception of the concept. Clearly, the best interpretation does not depend solely on the existence of a social convention that recognizes it as such, even if it does require some manner of shared practices and a common "form of life". What it demands is the existence of better supporting arguments or justifications (better fit and attention to the evaluative appeal) and that they may be reconstructed by means of the shared practices that provided their reference at an initial interpretive moment. The analysis of the concept of *courtesy* attempted to illustrate how the interpretive activity for "interpretive concepts" takes place.

References

Arulanantham, Ahilan T. 1998. Breaking the rules? Wittgenstein and legal realism. *Yale Law Journal* 107: 1853–1884.

Bix, Brian. 1993a. *Law, language and legal determinacy*. Oxford: Clarendon.

Bix, Brian. 1993b. The application (and mis-application) of Wittgenstein's rule-following considerations to legal theory. In *Law, language and legal determinacy*, ed. Brian Bix, 36–62. Oxford: Clarendon.

Burley, Justine (ed.). 2005. *Dworkin and his critics: With replies by Dworkin*. Malden: Blackwell.

Cavell, Stanley. 1969. *Must we mean what we say?* Nova York: Scribner.

Cohen, Marshall (ed.). 1983. *Ronald Dworkin and contemporary jurisprudence*. Totowa: Rowman and Allanheld.

Coleman, Jules, and Scott Shapiro (eds.). 2002. *The Oxford handbook of jurisprudence and philosophy of law*. Oxford: Oxford University Press.

Dworkin, Ronald. 1965. Philosophy, morality and law: Observations prompted by professor Fuller's novel claim. *University of Pennsylvania Law Review* 113: 668–690.

Dworkin, Ronald. 1977. *Taking rights seriously*. Cambridge, MA: Harvard University Press.

Dworkin, Ronald. 1983a. My reply to Stanley Fish (and Walter Benn Michaels): Please don't talk about objectivity any more. In *The politics of interpretation*, ed. Thomas W.J. Mitchell, 287–313. Chicago: University of Chicago Press.

Dworkin, Ronald. 1983b. Reply by Ronald Dworkin. In *Ronald Dworkin and contemporary jurisprudence*, ed. Marshall Cohen, 247–300. Totowa: Rowman and Allanheld.

Dworkin, Ronald. 1985. *A matter of principle*. Cambridge, MA: Harvard University Press.

Dworkin, Ronald. 1986. *Law's empire*. Cambridge, MA: Harvard University Press.

Dworkin, Ronald. 1996a. *Freedom's law: The moral reading of the American Constitution*. Cambridge, MA: Harvard University Press.

Dworkin, Ronald. 1996b. Objectivity and truth: You'd better believe it. *Philosophy and Public Affairs* 25: 87–139.

Dworkin, Ronald. 2000. *Sovereign virtue: The theory and practice of equality*. Cambridge, MA: Harvard University Press.

Dworkin, Ronald. 2006a. *Justice in robes*. Cambridge, MA: Harvard University Press.

Dworkin, Ronald. 2006b. Hart and the concepts of law. *Harvard Law Review* 119: 95–104.

Dworkin, Ronald. 2011. *Justice for hedgehogs*. Cambridge, MA: Harvard University Press.

Dworkin, Ronald. 1972. A special supplement: The Jurisprudence of Richard Nixon. *The New York Review of Books*, May 4.

Dworkin, Ronald. 2007. *Can we disagree about law or morals?* Conference by Dworkin at the New York Institute of Philosophy (NYU). Available at http://www.thirteen.org/forum/topics/can-we-disagree-about-law-or-morals/14/. Accessed in 20 Aug 2012.

Ewald, François. 1986. *L'Etat providence*. Paris: Grasset.

Fernandes, Millôr. 1996. *Millôr definitivo*, 8th ed. Porto Alegre: L&PM.

Gadamer, Hans-Georg. 2002. *Verdade e método: traços fundamentais de uma hermenêutica filosófica*. Trans. Flávio Paulo Meurer, vol. 1 & 2, 4th ed. Petrópolis: Vozes.

Gallie, W.B. 1956a. Art as an essentially contested concept. *The Philosophical Quarterly* 6(23): 97–114.

Gallie, W.B. 1956b. Essentially contested concepts. *Proceedings of the Aristotelian Society* 56: 167–198.

Gallie, W.B. 1964. *Philosophy and the historical understanding*. London: Chatto & Windus.

Green, Leslie. 1987. The political content of legal theory. *Philosophy of Social Sciences* 17: 1–20.

Guest, Stephen. 1997. *Ronald Dworkin*, 2nd ed. Edinburgh: Edinburgh University.

Guest, Stephen. 2010. *Ronald Dworkin*. Trans. Luís Carlos Borges. Rio de Janeiro: Elsevier.

Habermas, Jürgen. 1984. *The theory of communicative action*. Boston: Beacon.

Hart, H.L.A. 1994a. *The concept of law*. 2nd ed. Oxford: Oxford University Press.

Hart, H.L.A. 1994b. *O conceito de direito*, 3rd ed. Trans. de A. Ribeiro Mendes. Lisboa: Calouste Gulbenkian.

Heidegger, Martin. 1989. *Ser e Tempo*, vol. I. Petrópolis: Vozes.

Hobbes, Thomas. 1651. *Leviathan or the Matter, the Form, & Power of a Commonwealth Ecclesiastical and Civil*. London: Adam Crooke. Reprinted for the McMaster University Archive of the History of Economic Thouht. Available at http://socserv2.socsci.mcmaster.ca/econ/ugcm/3ll3/hobbes/Leviathan.pdf.

Hume, David. 2000. *A treatise on human nature*, ed. David Fate Norton and Mary J. Norton. Oxford: Oxford University Press.

Kronman, Anthony. 1983. *Max Weber*. Stanford: Stanford University Press. (Kronman, Anthony. 1983. *Max Weber*. Tradução de John Milton. Rio de Janeiro: Elsevier, 2009. (Coleção Teoria e Filosofia do Direito))

Kuhn, T. 1962. *The structure of scientific revolutions*. Chicago: The University of Chicago Press.

MacCormick, Neil. 2007. *Institutions of law*. Oxford: Oxford University Press.

Macedo Jr., Ronaldo Porto. 2010. Como levar Ronald Dworkin a sério ou como fotografar um porco-espinho em movimento. In *Ronald Dworkin*, ed. Stephen Guest, VII–XVIII. Trans. Carlos Borges. Rio de Janeiro: Elsevier.

Macedo Jr., Ronaldo Porto. 2011. *Carl Schmitt e a fundamentação do direito*, 2nd ed. São Paulo: Saraiva.

Marmor, Andrei. 2005. *Interpretation and legal theory*, 2nd ed. Oxford: Hart Publishing.

Marmor, Andrei. 2006. How law is like chess. *Legal Theory* 12: 347–371.

Morawetz, Thomas. 1992. Understanding disagreement: the root issue of jurisprudence: Applying Wittgenstein to positivism, critical theory, and judging. *University of Pennsylvania Law Review* 141: 371–456.

Patterson, Dennis. 1988. Wittgenstein and the code: A theory of good faith performance and enforcement under article nine. *University of Pennsylvania Law Review* 137: 335–430.

Patterson, Dennis (ed.). 1992. *Wittgenstein and legal theory*. Boulder: Westview Press.

Patterson, Dennis. 1994. Wittgenstein and constitutional theory. *Texas Law Review* 72: 1837–1856.

Postema, Gerald J. 2011. *A treatise of legal philosophy and general jurisprudence*, vol. 11. New York: Springer.

Schauer, Frederick. 2006. (Re)Taking Hart. *Harvard Law Review* 119: 852–883.

Schauer, Frederick. 2009. Institutions and the concept of law: A reply to Ronald Dworkin (with some help from Neil Maccormick). In *Law as institutional normative order: Essays in honour of Sir Neil Maccormick*, ed. Zenon Bancowsky and Maksymilian del Mar, 35–44. Burlington: Ashgate. Also available at http://ssrn.com/abstract=1403311. Accessed in 07 Sept 2012.

Schiavello, Aldo. 2001. On "coherence" and "law": An analysis of different models. *Ratio Juris* 14(2): 233–243.

Schmitt, Carl. 1992. *O conceito do político*. Trans. Álvaro Valls. Petrópolis: Vozes.

Schmitt, Carl. 2006. *Teologia política*: *quatro ensaios sobre a soberania*. Trans. Elisete Antoniuk. Belo Horizonte: Del Rey.

Sebok, Anthony J. 1999. Finding Wittgenstein at the core of the rule of recognition. *Southern Methodist University Law Review* 52: 75–110.

Shapiro, Scott. 2011. *Legality*. Cambridge, MA: Harvard University Press.

Stavropoulos, Nicos. 2003. Interpretivist theories of law. In *Stanford encyclopedia of philosophy* (2010 edition). Avalibale at http://stanford.library.usyd.edu.au/archives/sum2010/entries/law-interpretivist/.

Weber, Max. 1968. *Economy and society*, vol. 1. Berkeley: University of California Press.

Weinrib, Ernest. 1988. Legal formalism: On the immanent rationality of law. *Yale Law Journal* 97: 949–1016.

Wittgenstein, Ludwig. 1953. *Philosophical investigations*. Trans. G.E.M. Anscombe. New York: Macmillan.

Wittgenstein, Ludwig. 1972. *On certainty (Uber Gewissheit)*, ed. G.E.M. Anscombe, and G.H. von Wright. Trans. Denis Paul, and G.E.M. Anscombe. New York: Harper Torchbooks.

Wittgenstein, Ludwig. 2009. *Philosophical investigations*, ed. P.M.S. Hacker, and Joachim Schulte. 4th ed. Oxford: Wiley-Blackwell.

Wolcher, Louis E. 1997. Ronald Dworkin's right answers thesis through the lens of Wittgenstein. *Rutgers Law Journal* 29: 43–66.

Index

T. Bustamante, B.G. Fernandes (eds.), *Democratizing Constitutional Law*, Law and Philosophy Library 113, DOI 10.1007/978-3-319-28371-5

D

E

F

G

I

J

K

CPSIA information can be obtained at www.ICGtesting.com
Printed in the USA
BVOW06*1100240416

445415BV00008B/42/P

9 783319 283692